Winter Food in Provence

Other titles by the same author:

Novels:
Entertaining Angels
Childish Things
Breathing Space
Travelling Light
There is a Season
Just Dessert Dear
Time Out

Non-fiction:
Where the Heart Is
Summer Food in Provence

Short stories:
Short Circuits

Children's and youth books:
Rhinocephants on the Roof
Mia's Mom
The Hidden Life of Hanna Why

First published in 2014 by Tafelberg,
an imprint of NB Publishers, a division of Media24 Books (Pty) Ltd,
40 Heerengracht, Cape Town 8001

Copyright © published edition: Tafelberg (2014)
Copyright © text: Marita van der Vyver (2014)

All rights reserved.
No part of this publication may be reproduced, stored in a retrieval system,
or transmitted in any form or by any means, electronic,
mechanical, photocopying, recording or otherwise,
without the prior written permission of the copyright owners.

Publisher: Ansie Kamffer
Project manager: Lindy Samery
Editor: Natasja Lochner
Translator: Vanessa Vineall
Cover and design: Anton Sassenberg
Typography: Jean van der Meulen
Photographer, food: Myburgh du Plessis
Photographer, lifestyle: Lien Botha
Food stylist: Sonja Jordt

Reproduction by Resolution Colour (Pty) Ltd, Cape Town
Printed and bound through Craft Print, Singapore

ISBN: 978-0-624-05777-2

Winter Food in Provence

Marita van der Vyver

in association with Alain Claisse

Tafelberg

CONTENTS

Before we sit down 9

For the love of an olive tree 13

Wild about mushrooms 19

Through the grapevine 23

Rice rules! 29

Salt of the earth 33

The brilliance that is beetroot 39

The quirky quince 43

The pleasures of pumpkin 49

Say "prunes"! 53

The big cheese 59

Hidden treasures 63

Game on 69

Proud of potatoes 73

Cod by any other name 79

Of cabbages and kings 85

Oh shucks, it's shellfish! 89

Festive fare 93

Just desserts, dear 99

The stuff of legends 103

In the soup 109

Traditional tarts and pretty pies 115

Ah, anchovies 119

In praise of pulses 125

Bulls and beef   129

Plenty of pancakes   133

Duck for cover   139

In a nutshell   143

Here's looking at you, kidney   147

When life hands you lemons …   153

Our daily bread   157

You can't make an omelette without breaking eggs   163

Succulent spring lamb   167

Chocolate season …   173

Indispensable   177

Acknowledgements   180

Index   181

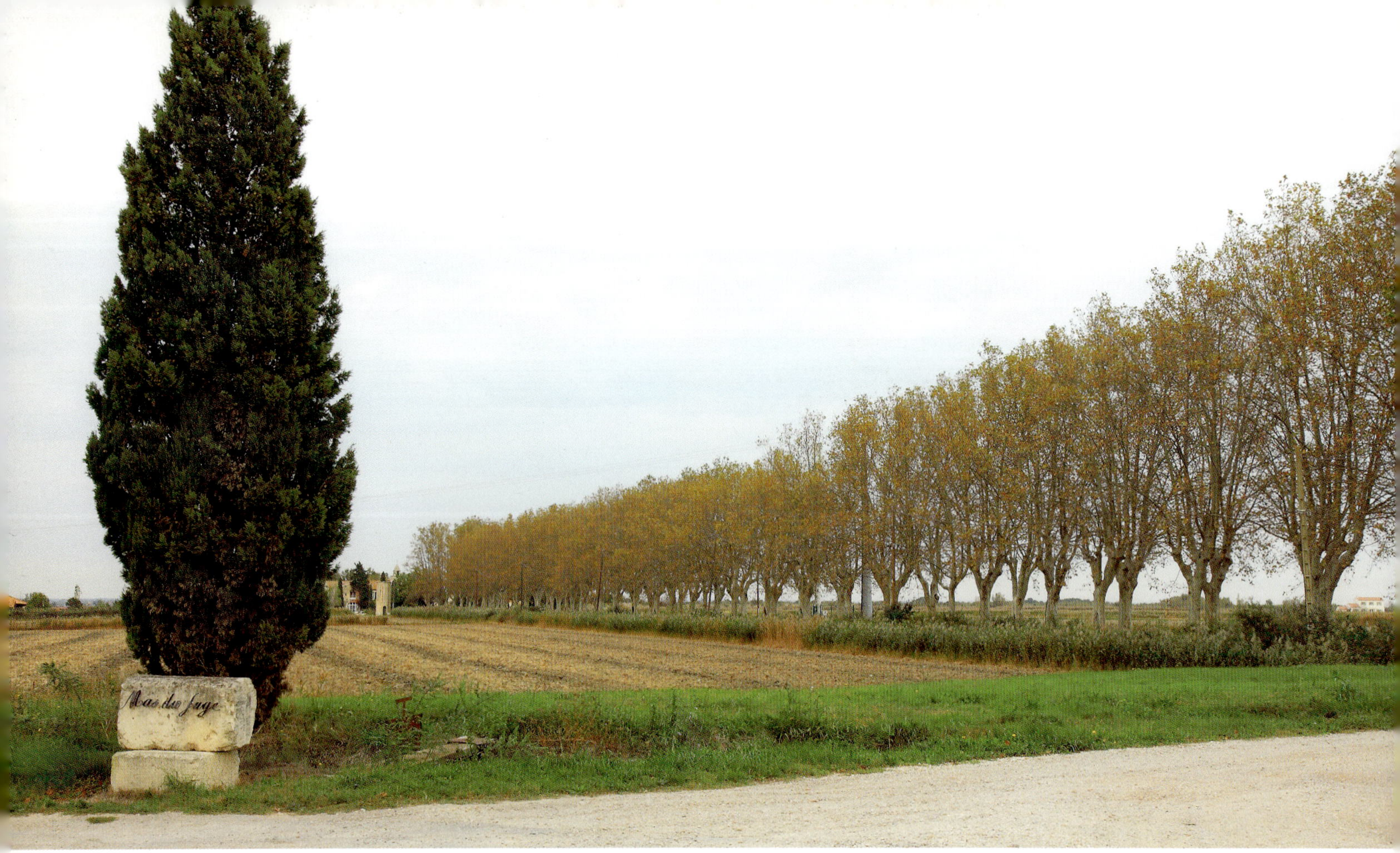
Mas du Juge

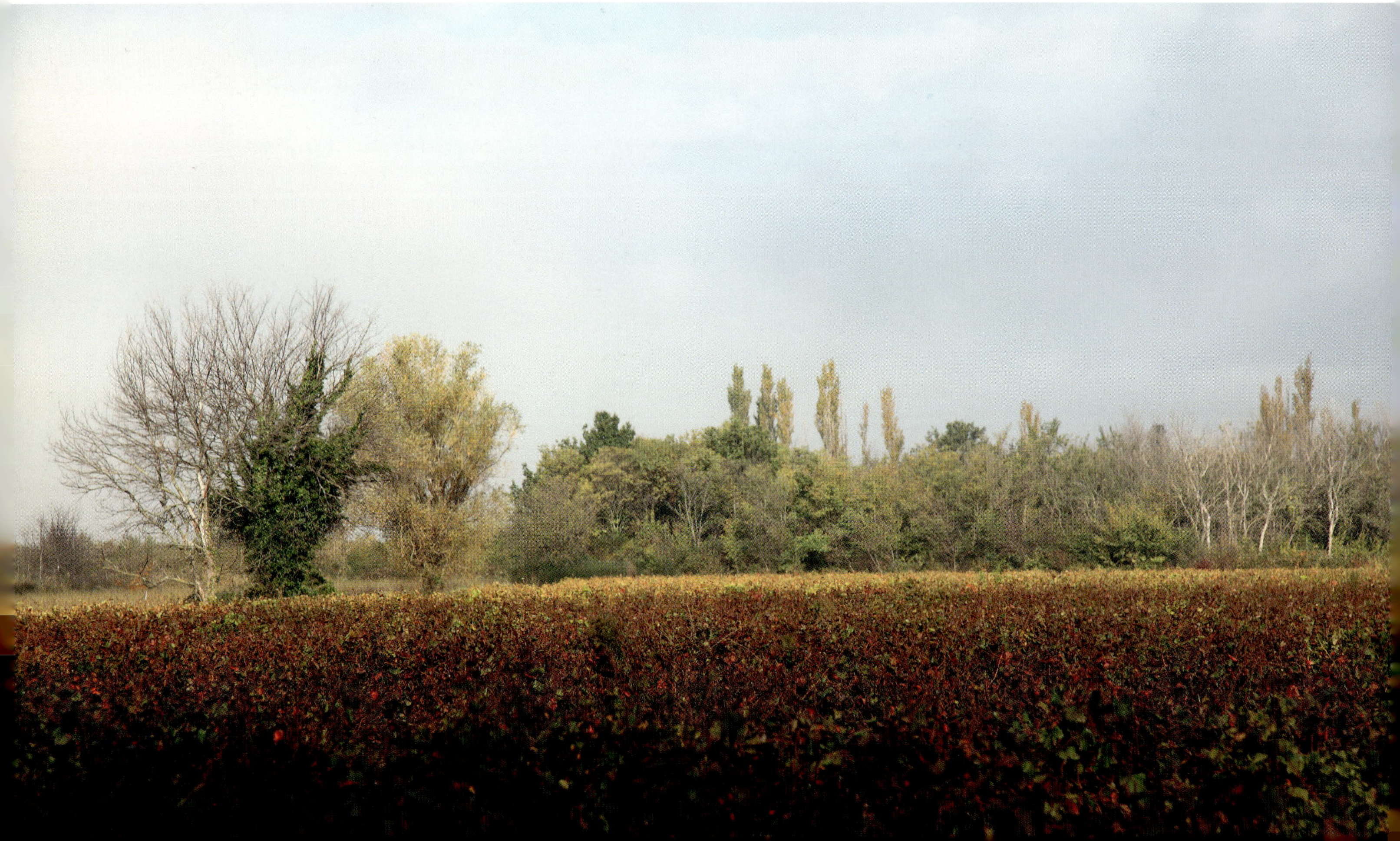

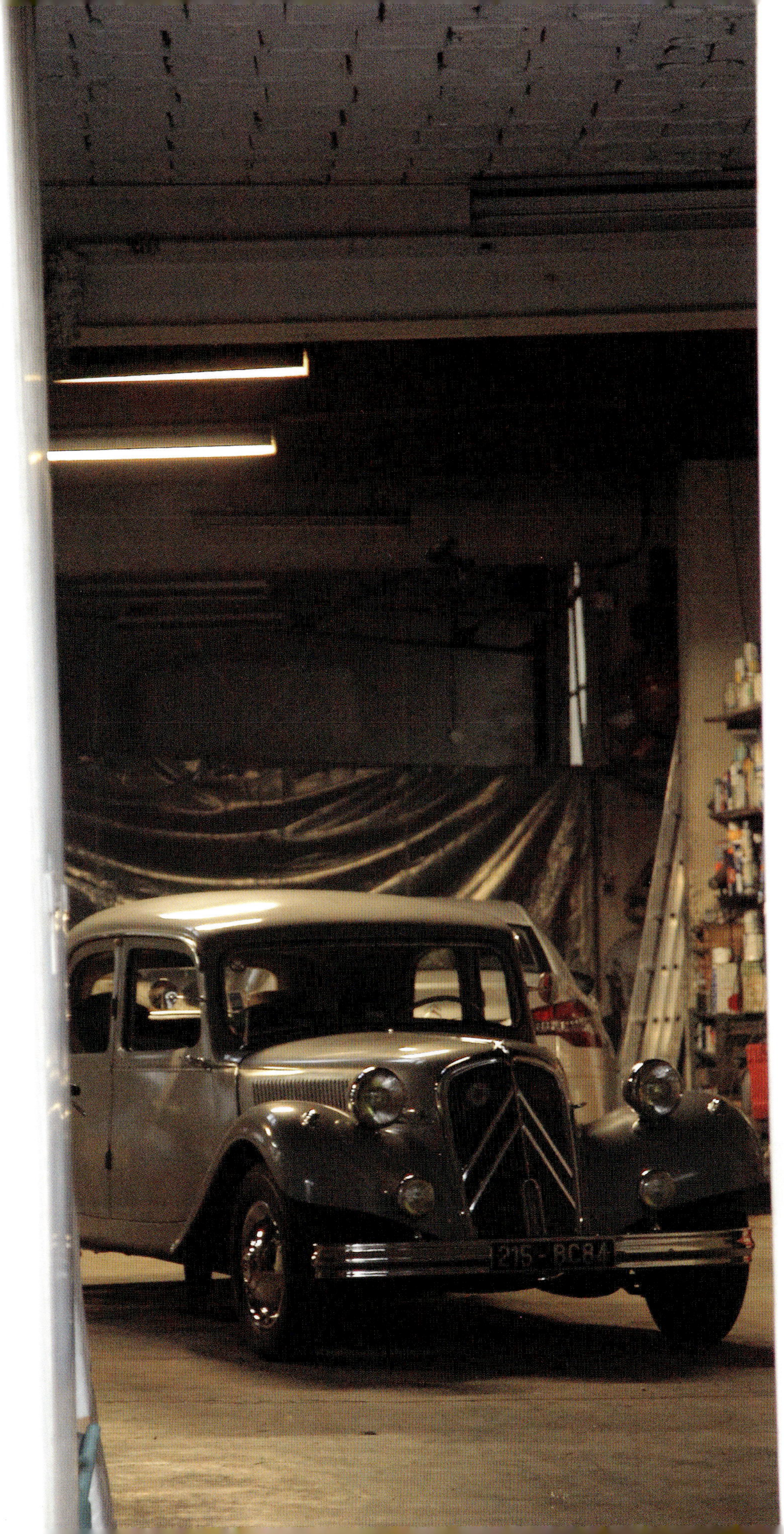
215 - BC84

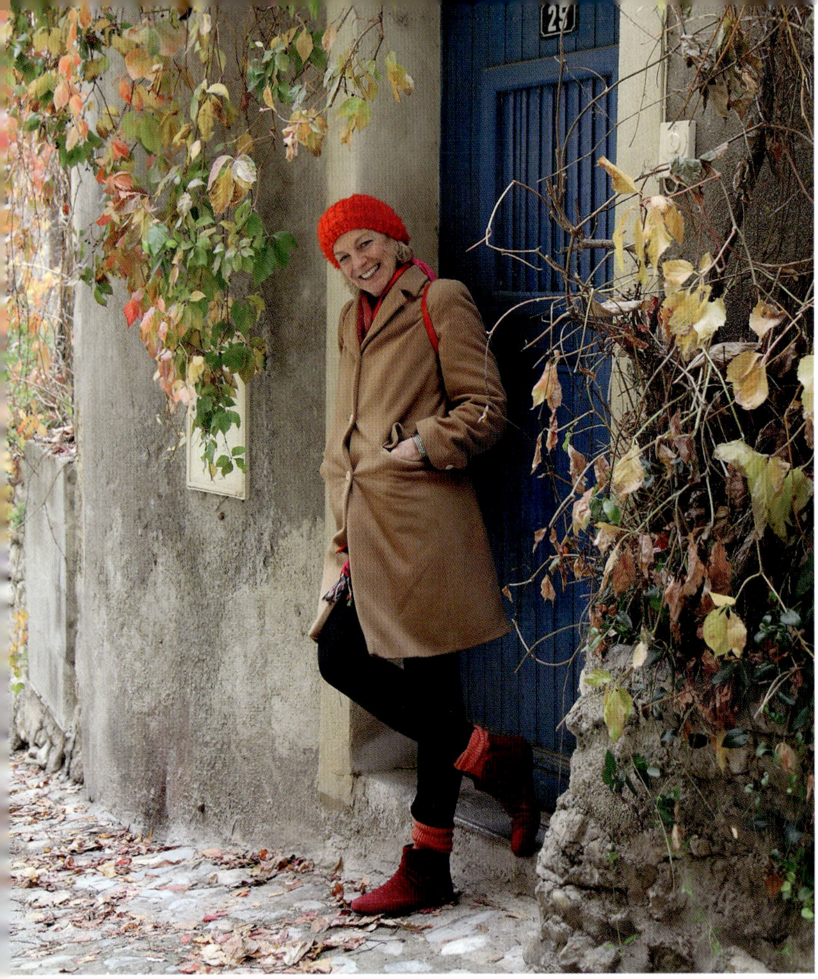

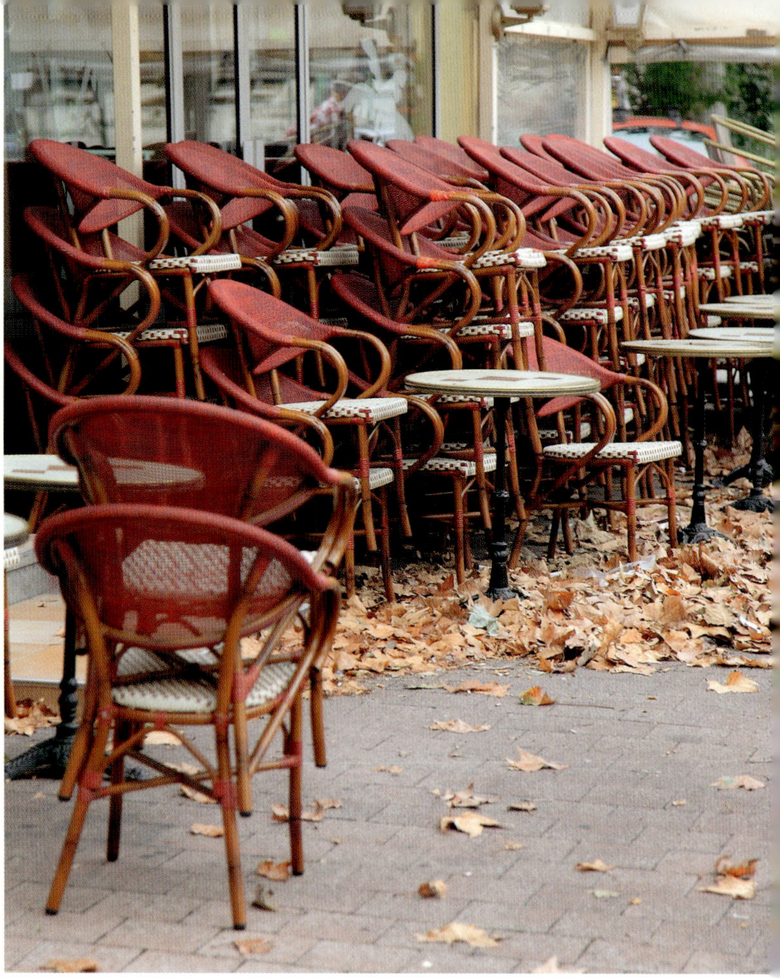

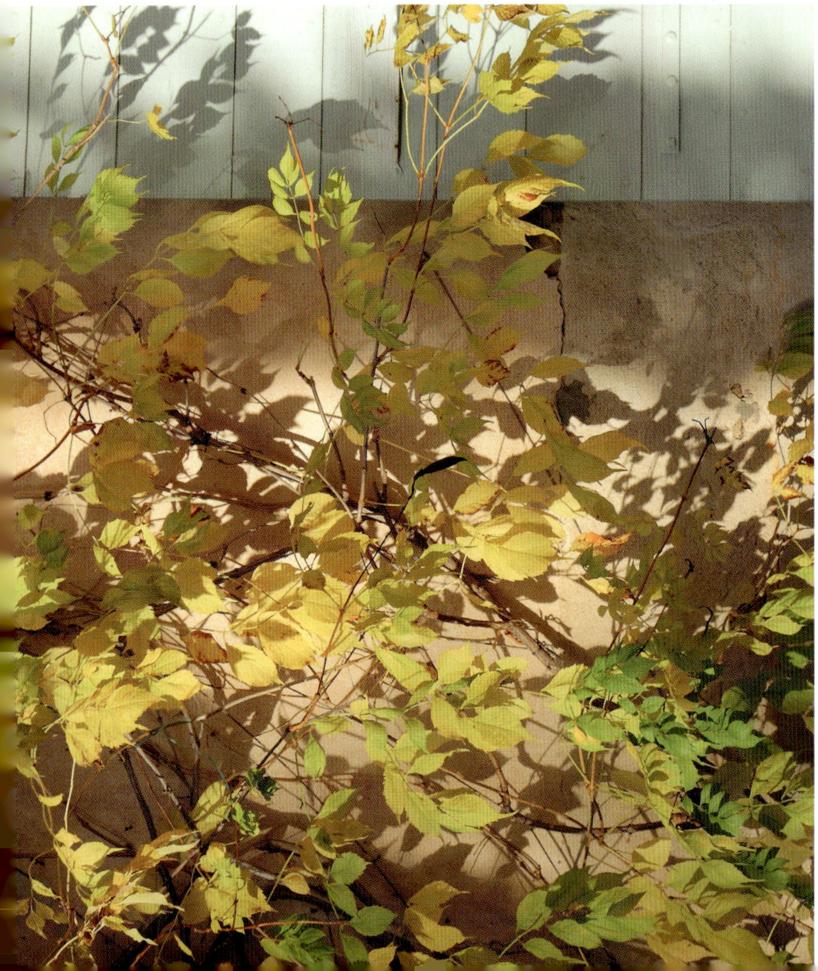

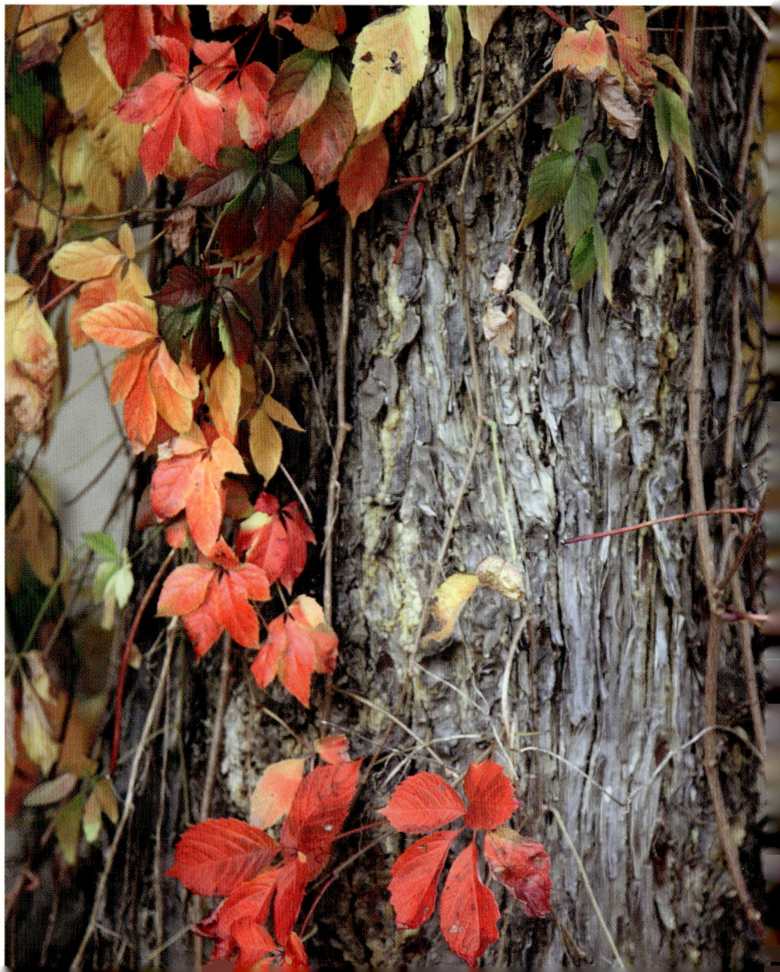

BEFORE WE SIT DOWN

"WINTER IS THE TIME FOR COMFORT, FOR GOOD FOOD AND WARMTH, FOR THE TOUCH OF A FRIENDLY HAND AND FOR A TALK BESIDE THE FIRE: IT IS THE TIME FOR HOME."

EDITH SITWELL, BRITISH POET (1887-1964)

For most people, Provence conjures up images of summer: fields of sunflowers and lavender, the hum of cicadas and the clink of *pétanque* balls, the colours, aroma and tastes of fresh fruit at open-air markets, a glass of cloudy pastis, a town square with a babbling fountain … This is the picture-postcard vision of Provence that attracts tourists in their droves every year.

But there is another Provence. Mysterious, quieter, more interesting. And for those adventurous tourists and travellers who have already experienced the postcard version, I have no hesitation in suggesting that they get to know the region in winter.

In one of my previous books, *Where the Heart Is*, I praised the colourless, bare landscape thus: "Things you cannot see in summer take your breath away in winter. Like the pale trunks of the plane trees that are literally and figuratively put to shade by their lush green crowns in summer. The same way the antique stone walls are often hidden by climbing plants in summer. In winter you can admire every bare stone in every bare wall.

"More than anything else, Provence seems to me a place of stone. The simple stone walls of the houses; the impressive stone towers of the churches; the dilapidated packed-stone walls, without cement or any other binding material, that wind along the edges of fields and orchards; the uncomfortable stone seats in Roman amphitheatres; the stony ruins of castles and village gates. To really appreciate the stone, you have to be here in winter."

Well, okay, so perhaps you would consider a winter visit to this part of the world. But what about the food, you say? Because that is what this book is all about, isn't it? Absolutely! Winter is in fact when many of the region's most famous food products are harvested, picked, dug up or gathered. You only have to think of the traditional *vendange* or grape harvest in September, the region's famous olives whose time comes later in the year, and the even more famous truffles that come into their own during winter. Some of the most glorious food traditions are winter traditions, such as the oysters and foie gras knocked back with such gusto at Christmas, the *Treize Desserts* or Thirteen Desserts that conclude any respectable Provençal Christmas meal, the King's Cake with lucky charms hidden in the marzipan filling to celebrate the feast of Epiphany in early January, the stacks of Chandeleur pancakes in February …

So, although I will grant you that there is a smaller choice of fresh fruit, vegetables and herbs available at the markets, what there is remains a feast for all five senses. And what is more, the French have always been experts at pickling, drying and preserving all types of food. You only have to think of the anchovies and the huge variety of dried sausage and smoked hams, salt cod – known locally as *morue* – which is served with a tasty garlic mayonnaise as the main ingredient of the Provençal *grand aïoli*, duck preserved with snow-white duck fat and displayed in shiny glass jars, not to mention all the delicious pâtés and jams. Oh yes, I will admit that we eat differently in winter, but we certainly do not eat less well than in summer.

In *Summer Food in Provence* I explained our family's "food philosophy" as follows: To eat seasonally and as well and as sensibly as possible for as little money, time and effort as possible. Nothing has changed. In winter we simply have to buy and

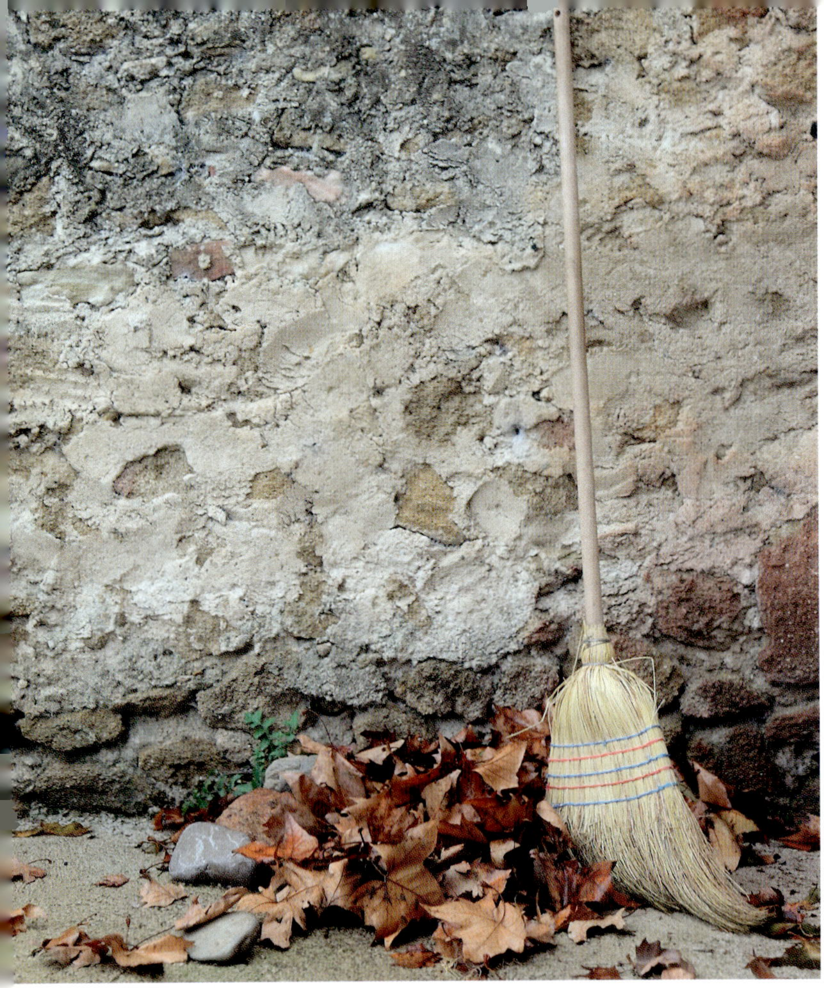
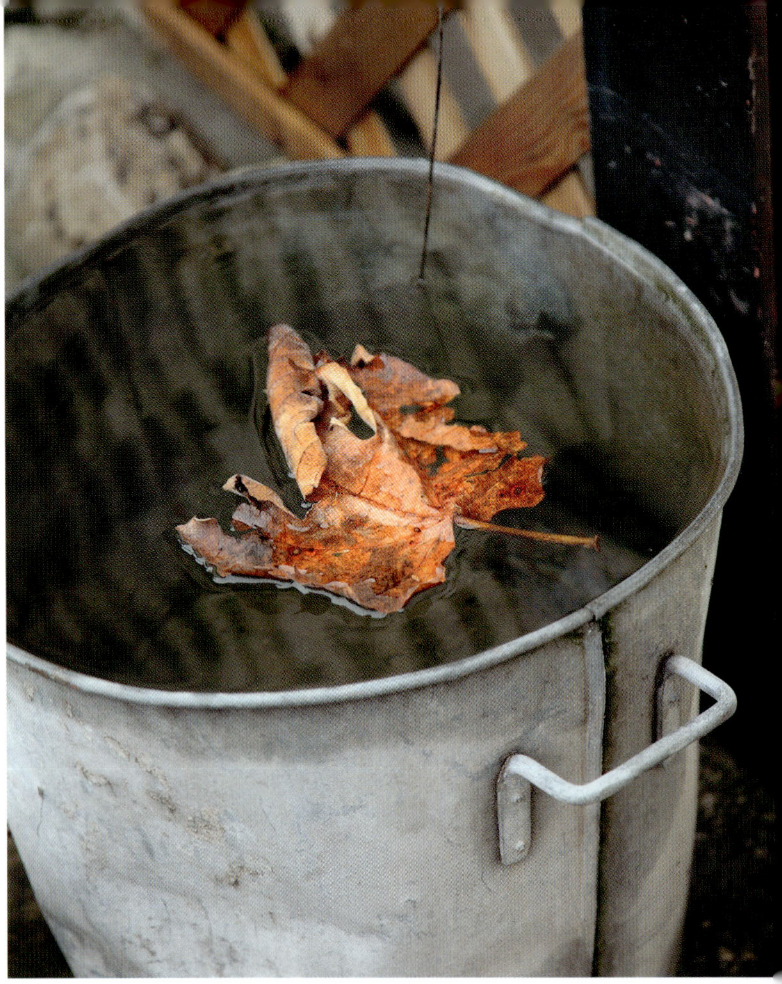
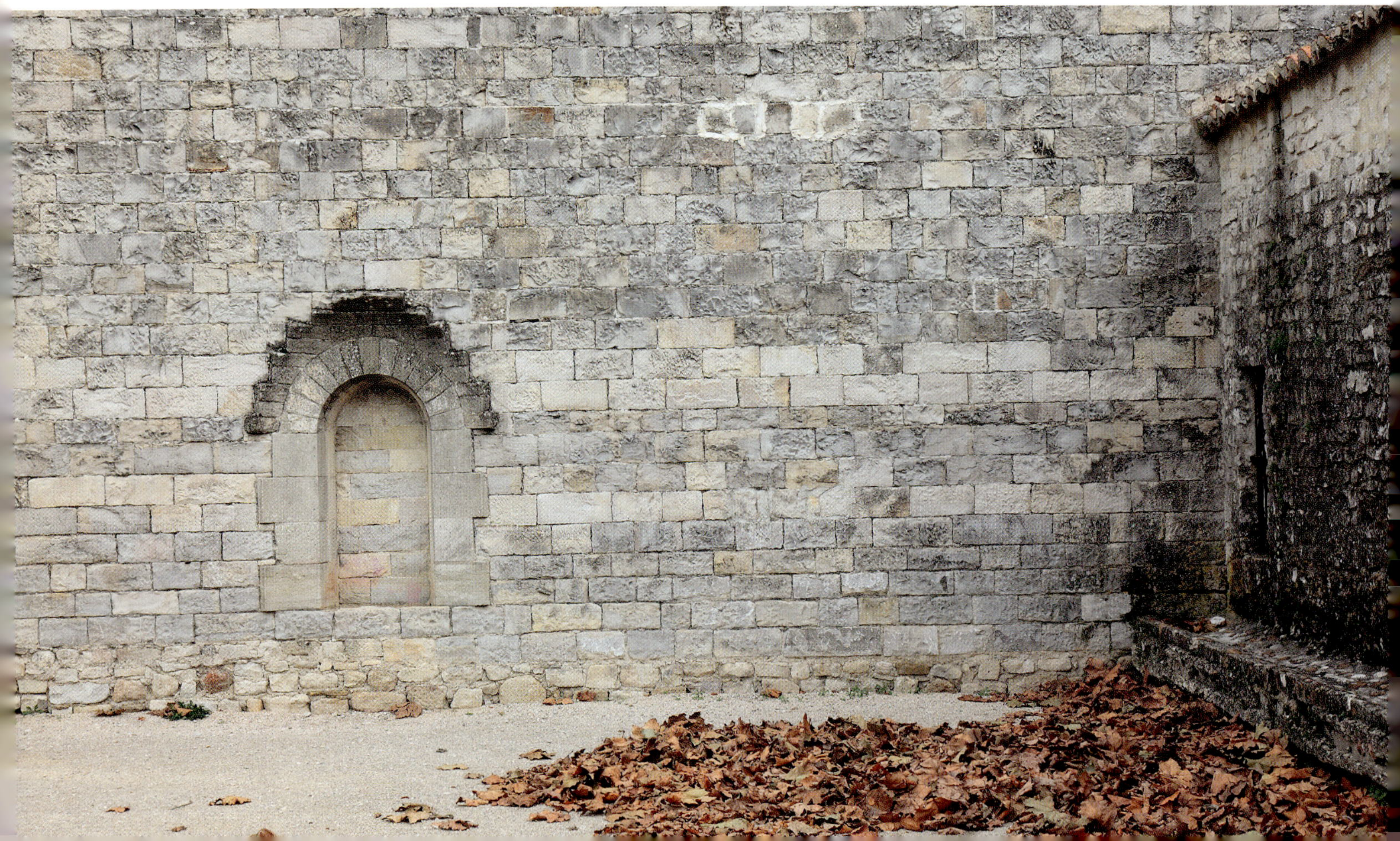

cook even more sensibly to make the most of the limited variety of fresh produce. During the colder months we use fewer herbs, for instance, because fresh herbs are difficult to find and the dried stuff just isn't the same. Fortunately there are other ways of livening up winter food: grey salt and yellow saffron and a wealth of spices, lemon juice and citrus zest, good-quality vinegar and a little wine, various types of onions and last but certainly not least, that old standby, garlic – what would a French kitchen be without garlic?!

There is, however, something that has changed since last we met. All three of our sons are now old enough to have moved out and our "little" Mia is a lanky teenager.

The boys still visit us on weekends and during the holidays, often bringing their friends, girlfriends and various hangers-on with them, which means we still need a roomy house and large pots to accommodate and feed the ravenous hordes. But during the week we no longer have to cater on such a large scale. And it is so much easier putting food on the table that only one child is going to moan about, instead of having to consider the wide-ranging tastes of four offspring at every meal.

Because one still does not eat cauliflower or broccoli, another will not touch mushrooms or pork, a third isn't partial to salad greens or raw tomatoes – and all four still refuse to eat Brussels sprouts. That is why you will not find any recipes for sprouts in this book, although the parents do enjoy them when the children are not at home. Oh, and I forgot to mention that not one of the four has learned to appreciate truffles. Not that you will hear me complaining about this, because truffles remain a scarce luxury in our house, and if the children will not eat them it means more for us.

Some luxurious French delicacies were avoided in our previous recipe book because they are difficult to obtain in South Africa and elsewhere – and because you will really feel it in your wallet if you do strike it lucky and happen to track them down. But writing a book about winter food without including truffles and foie gras simply would not work. They are after all every Frenchman's idea of the most prized winter foodstuffs. So we will be chatting about truffles and foie gras and wild mushrooms and shellfish and various other French delights that cannot reasonably be regarded as cheap. But, like the last time, we will try to suggest more readily available or economical alternatives where possible.

Our aim is still for you to be able to attempt most recipes outside France without too much effort or expense. We hope to provide inspiration for Provençal, Mediterranean and French food that nourishes more than just the body, and will, as it were, warm the very soul, wherever in the world South Africans find themselves these days. Soul food, hearty food, honest food. "*À table!*" thunders Alain from the kitchen, over the music that always plays full blast when he is cooking. "The food's on the table!"

So do come and sit down with us. And *bon appétit – encore*.

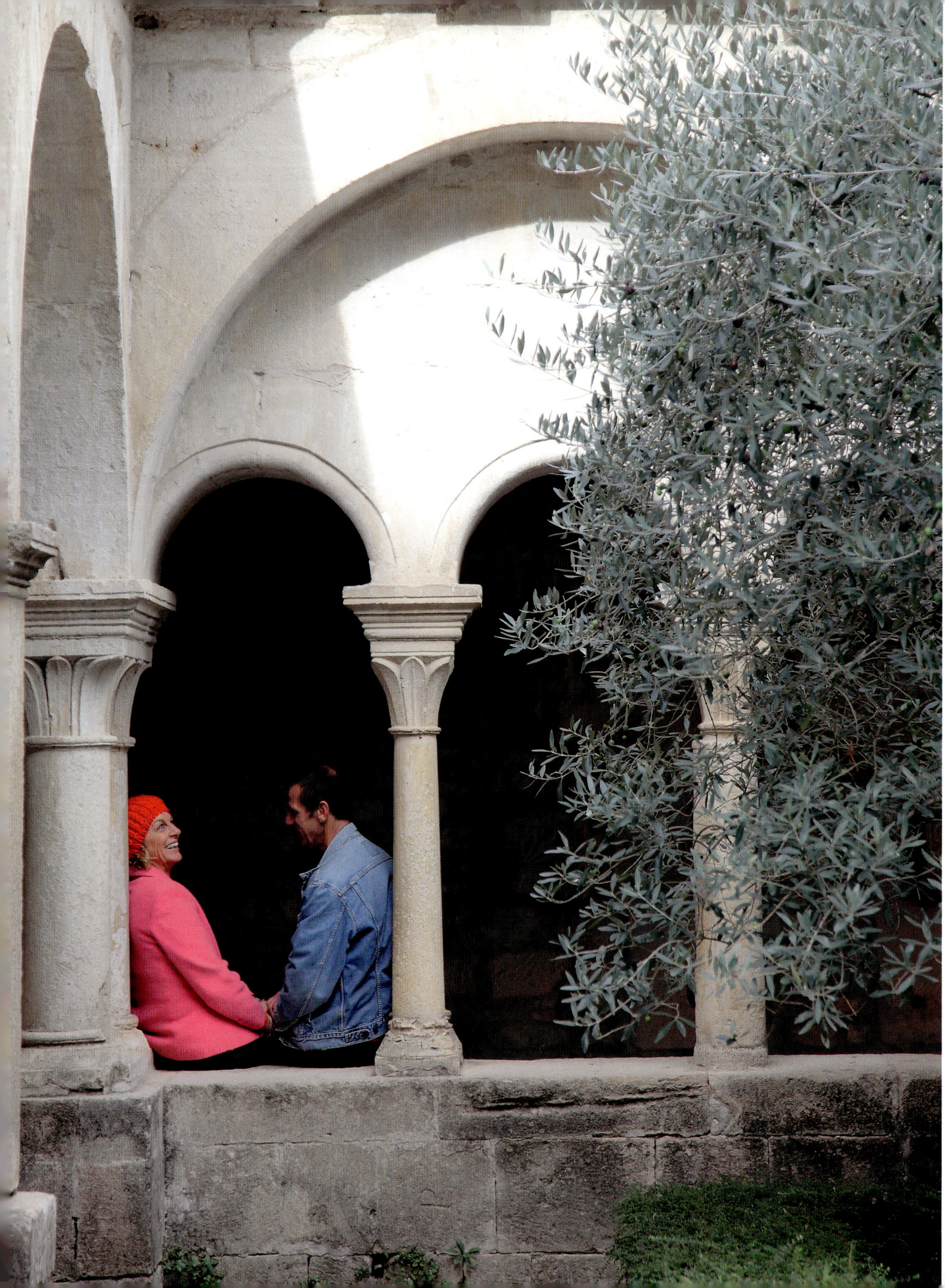

FOR THE LOVE OF AN OLIVE TREE

"EXCEPT THE VINE, THERE IS NO PLANT WHICH BEARS A FRUIT OF AS GREAT IMPORTANCE AS THE OLIVE."

PLINY THE ELDER, ROMAN WRITER (23-79 AD)

Buying a house is never an entirely rational affair. Some people buy a house simply because they fall in love with the view from an upstairs window, or a neglected old garden, or an impressive wooden staircase. The house in which our family has lived for the past few years had all these when I saw it for the first time – the view from what would become a bathroom window, the wildly overgrown back garden, the beautiful Art Deco staircase – but it was the olive tree next to the kitchen door that clinched the deal.

Years ago we decided that one day we wanted to swap our stone house in the village for a more rustic spot among the vineyards. By "we" I mean mainly Alain and I. Our three teenage sons were thoroughly unimpressed with this plan. As if we did not already live far enough away from the pleasures of city life, they grumbled. Now the old folks wanted to drag them even further into the sticks. Even further away from shops and transport and friends and everything that made a teenager's life worth living.

So we waited until they were older and wiser.

Fortunately their *laatlam* little sister had always been more of a child of nature than her brothers. Perhaps because she was not born in a city as they had been, and had lived her whole life in a sleepy village close to nature. Whatever the reason, Mia was not averse to moving deeper into the countryside. The only problem was finding a farmhouse we could afford – without necessarily buying the farm along with the house. Because we definitely did not want to go farming: we knew our limitations. We simply wanted to enjoy the advantages of a farm life, without the disadvantages. As the French would say, we wanted the butter *and* the money for the butter.

As the boys outgrew their teenage moods, we began patiently searching for that dream house in the vineyards. Until one day I came across a dilapidated double-storey house, part of what used to be a mill, that had stood empty for some years. From the moment the estate agent unlocked the heavy, dark wood front door with iron trelliswork, using an enormous old-fashioned key that belonged in a fairy tale, I looked past the mustiness and peeling paint in the hallway and saw my future home. In the cramped kitchen I immediately knew which wall I would break out to create a large open-plan room filled with light. But it was only when glimpsing the bent trunk of the old olive tree through the kitchen window, its leaves bathed in a silver late-afternoon glow, that I knew for sure that this was *our* house.

In our stone house in the village we had spent a decade eating under a large plane tree. From now on, I just knew, we would eat alongside an olive tree. I could not have wished for a more appropriate "sign". Didn't the Biblical dove bring Noah an olive branch as a sign that the flood was over? Isn't the legendary olive tree a symbol of peace, wisdom, light, purity, immortality and goodness knows what else?

Glimmering silver olive groves are as much part of the Provençal landscape as vineyards, lavender and sunflowers. Perhaps even more so than any other type of plant because, unlike the vines that grow pale and naked in winter, and the purple lavender and yellow sunflowers that are on show for scarcely two months of the year, the evergreen olive can be admired throughout the year. In the coldest months, when most other trees struggle to survive until spring, shivering in their nakedness, the olive trees are heavy with their wondrous fruit. In early autumn green olives cling firmly to the branches; by late winter black olives fall to the ground like blessed rain.

And nowhere in all Provence are olives as ever-present and part of the landscape as down our way, in the area around the town of Nyons. That is why it feels so entirely appropriate that these days we eat alongside an olive tree in summer and pick our very own olives in winter. You could say that we have finally truly come home in Provence.

Ordinary into extraordinary

Do you want to turn a jar of ordinary shop-bought black or green olives into something special? *Très facile,* Madame Voisine would assure you – it's easy. For approximately 300 g olives, heat ¼ cup decent olive oil with 2-3 cloves of garlic (finely chopped), 3 stalks of fresh thyme, the leaves from a stalk of rosemary and the zest of a small lemon (cut into thin strips) over moderate heat for 2-3 minutes, until you really begin to smell the herbs. Then toss the olives into the pan and stir to cover them all in the oil. Remove from the heat as soon as the olives are heated through. Decant into a sterilised jar and allow to cool. Close the jar and leave to stand in the fridge for a few days so the olives can continue marinating. You can eat them straight from the fridge but the flavour is better at room temperature, and the olives are perhaps at their tastiest when you warm them in a pan again, place in a serving bowl and sprinkle with the remaining warm oil.

Pickle your own olives

It took two winters of testing and many inedible olives before we developed a flop-proof method of pickling our own olives. If you are fortunate enough to have access to an olive tree but haven't known how to make them edible, follow these simple instructions. A word of warning before you start: Be careful when working with caustic soda; it is an extremely corrosive chemical that could leave your skin with nasty burns.

5 kg olives | 1 litre lye/caustic soda (30% solution)

Saumure: *300-500 g salt | 1-2 bay leaves | a few stalks of thyme and rosemary | peel of 1 orange or lemon, cut into strips | a pinch of aniseed a little imagination*

Place the olives, green or black, in a plastic bucket (do not use metal), preferably with a lid, and cover with 1 litre lye (caustic soda) solution, mixed with 9 litres water. Put the lid on or use a tray as a lid and leave to stand for about 2 hours – stir from time to time. After 90 minutes, test an olive by cutting it in half with a sharp knife. If the colour of the flesh has become lighter almost to the pit, the olives are ready. (Black olives become green and the green ones a light green.) Rinse the olives well and cover with fresh water. Stir every 2 hours for the first day. After that, rinse the olives at the same time every day, replace the water and keep the bucket covered. Continue for 7-10 days or until the water is clear when you replace it. Make sure you wash the olives well during the final rinse.

Now prepare the *saumure* or brine. Use the same bucket and cover the olives with water. Add 100 g salt for every litre of water. For 5 kg olives you will need about 3 litres water and 300 g salt. Flavour the brine with the bay leaves, thyme, rosemary, citrus zest, aniseed and a little imagination. (If you do not trust your imagination, stick to the ingredients suggested here.) Close the bucket and leave to stand for at least a week. Check once or twice that the salt has dissolved properly. If not, give it another stir.

After about 10 days you can start tasting the olives. Once they taste right, you can leave them in the brine for weeks in a cool, dark place like a cellar or garage, scooping out a few at a time for eating. (Do not panic if a white scum develops on the surface of the brine; simply skim it off.) And voilà, you have pickled your very own olives!

Right: Pickle your own olives

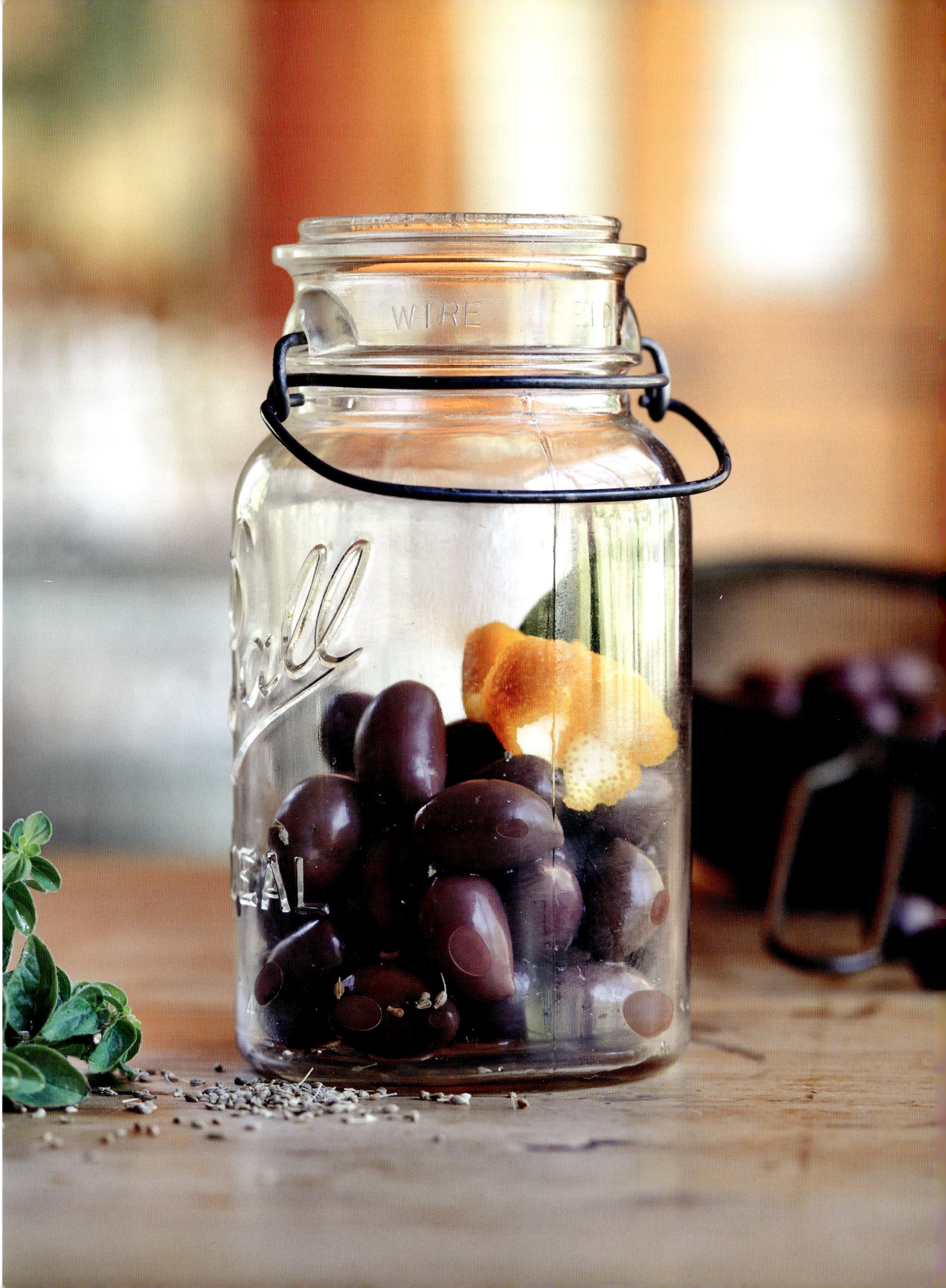
WIRE

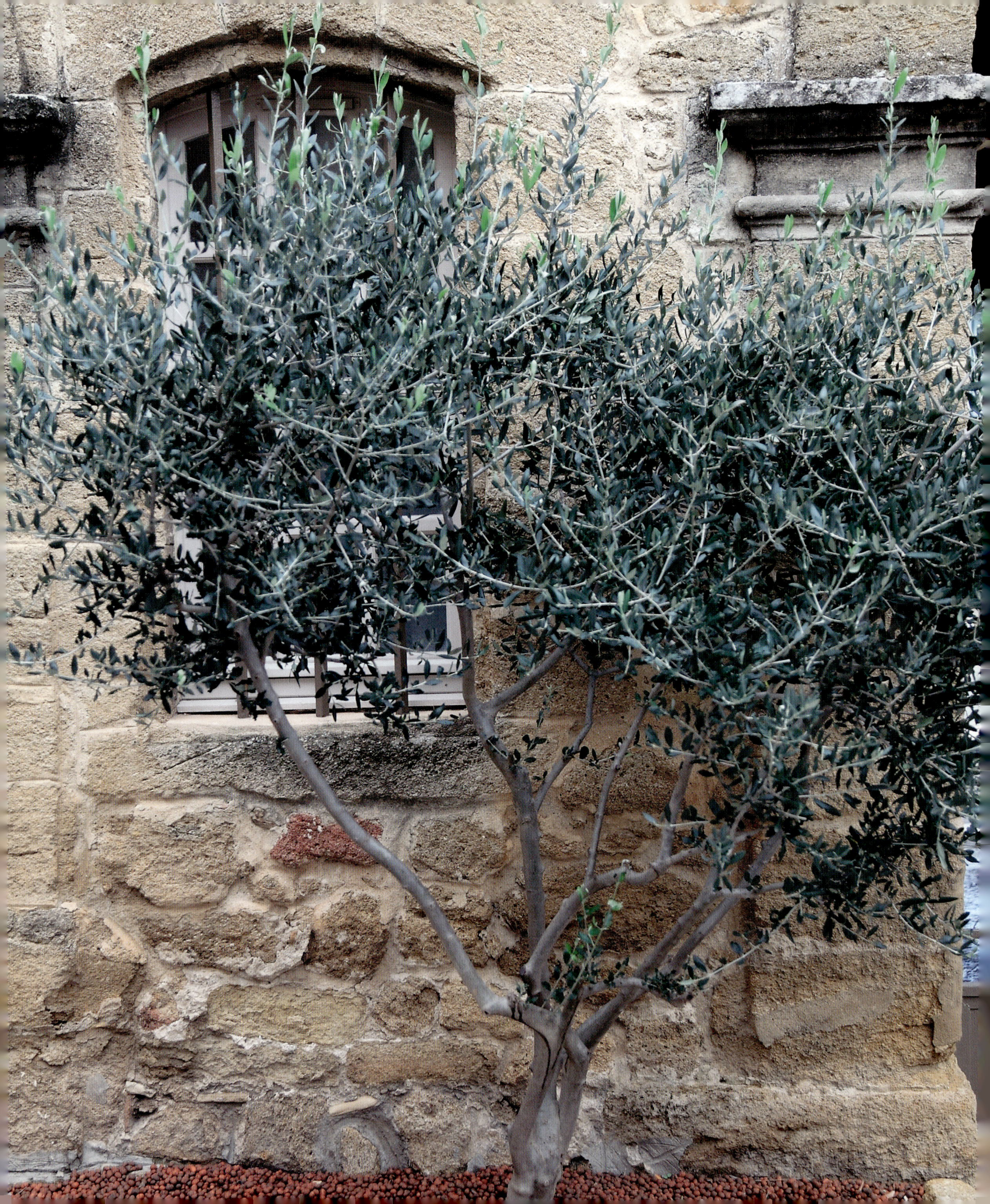

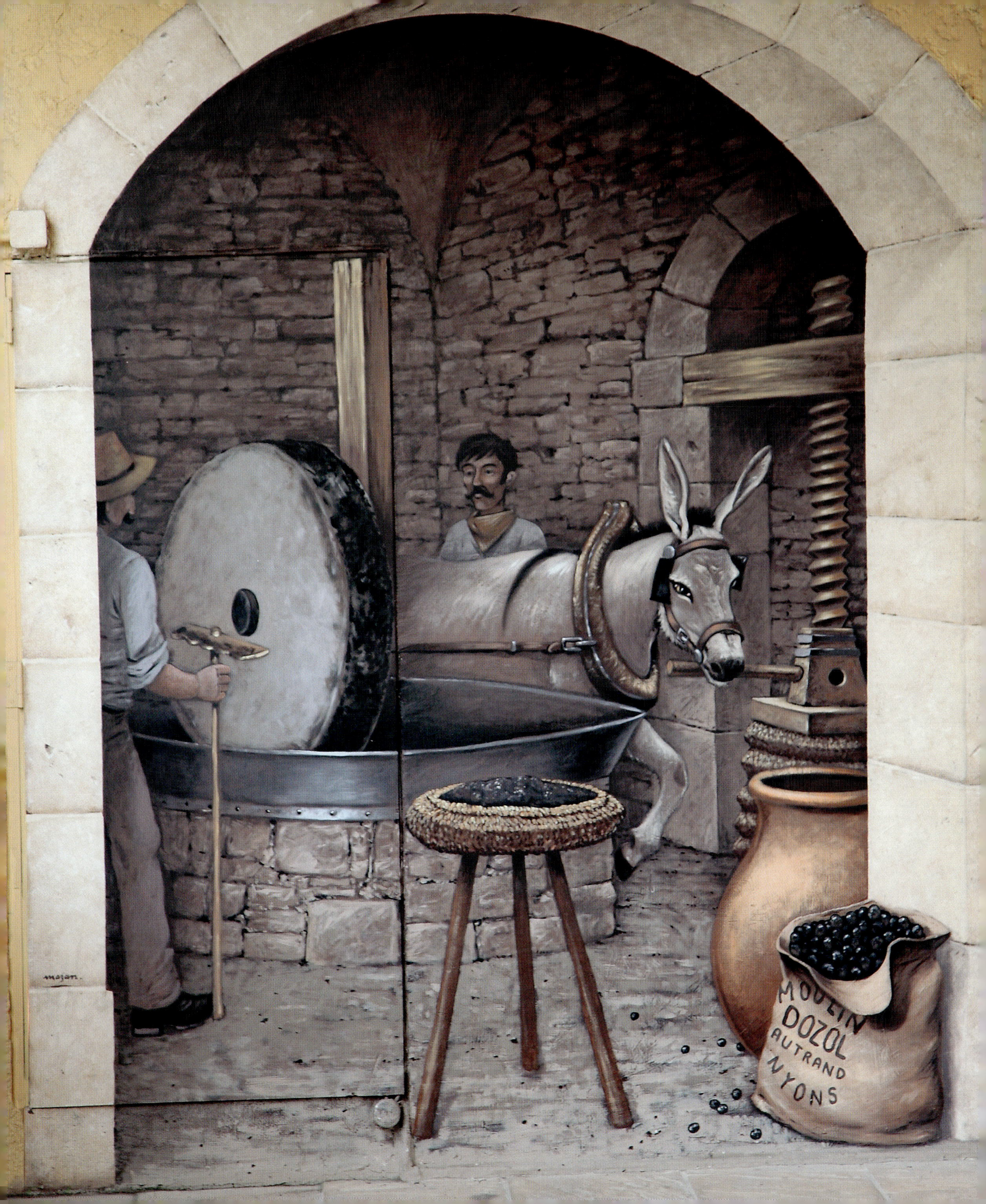
mojan.
MOULIN
DOZOL
AUTRAND
NYONS

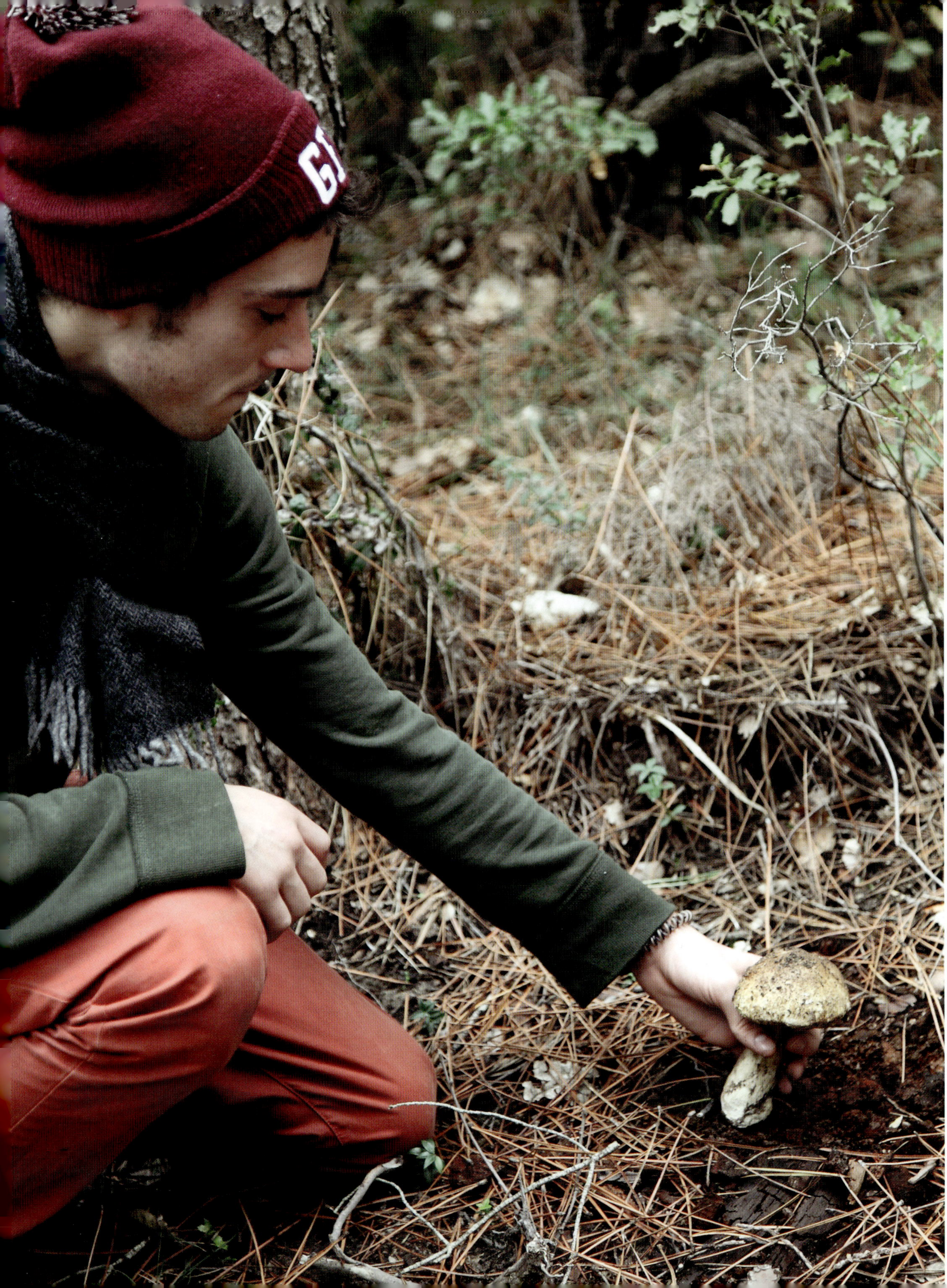

WILD ABOUT MUSHROOMS

"IF ONLY ONE COULD TELL TRUE LOVE FROM FALSE LOVE AS ONE CAN TELL MUSHROOMS FROM TOADSTOOLS."

KATHERINE MANSFIELD, NEW ZEALAND WRITER (1888-1923)

Like the first crop of asparagus heralds the joyous arrival of spring for our family, so too the first mushrooms hint at a change of season. The sun is weaker, there is a nip in the air and, sadly, our days of eating outdoors are numbered. Mushrooms bring rumours of autumn, the smell of damp earth and the rustle of falling leaves, and we start gathering firewood for the grate.

And by mushrooms we do not mean the pale, anaemic button mushrooms (*Agaricus bisporus*) that are grown throughout the year and sold in the shops in plastic containers. Oh no, what we are talking about are the mesmerising shapes and colours of the wild mushrooms that accompany the autumn rains. That enormous, meaty-flavoured favourite the *cèpe* (*Boletus edulis*), often found at the market with the damp soil still clinging to its fat stems, is called *porcini* in Italy, apparently because the young mushrooms look like piglets. Or perhaps just because pigs, like people, know what tastes good and love to nibble on *cèpes*. Remember that until fairly recently, here in Provence black truffles (which are simply an especially luxurious type of mushroom) were hunted for using specially trained pigs. But we can talk about truffles later. For now let's concentrate on ordinary wild mushrooms.

Although "ordinary" is hardly the right word to describe a fungus that can appear literally overnight, induce (desirable) hallucinations, be deadly, features in traditional fairy tales as the home of assorted pixies and other fairy folk, and is used in heraldry as the symbol of fertility and sexual prowess!

There are colours, flavours and varieties for every taste: the cheerful orange caps and delicate stems of the *chanterelle* and *girolle*; the knobbly *pied-de-mouton* (hedgehog mushroom) and the snow-white beauty of the *pleurote*; the strange spongy appearance of the *morille*; the blue-black horn of plenty with the terrifying nickname "trumpet of death" – which is a total misnomer by the way, as the only way this edible mushroom could kill is if you were to die of pleasure at the taste. Even the youngest in our house, who would never touch button mushrooms, was tempted after a recent mushroom hunt in a dark wood to sample the *girolles* she had found herself – and is now fast becoming a fungi connoisseur.

In the dry land of my birth, mushrooms are obviously not as plentiful as in damp European climes, but if you know where to look they can be found. My first mushroom hunt was undertaken with friends on the Meerlust wine estate while I was a young student at Stellenbosch University. And no, we were not poaching. The expedition was led by the farm owner's son, the only one of us who knew the difference between a sheep and a mushroom at that stage. Or the difference between an edible mushroom and a poisonous one at any rate.

Fortunately you can buy a fair variety of fresh and dried mushrooms in South Africa these days. Besides mature button mushrooms, which go by the pretty name of portobello, there are Italian porcini, Japanese shiitake, white oyster mushrooms... And remember, there is nothing wrong with farmed or dried mushrooms. They may not offer the same taste sensation as the fresh wild varieties, but they compensate for this by being readily available. A dish of ordinary button mushrooms prepared with respect and love and butter and cream – or with garlic and fresh herbs, or stirred into a risotto with some wine – is a delicious meal all year round.

Who remembers *Superwoman* Shirley Conran's phrase from the Seventies: "Life's too short to stuff a mushroom"? Well, here in France I have learned that this is not true. Firstly because it is not terribly difficult at all to stuff a mushroom – and the bigger the mushroom, the less hassle it is – and secondly, well, because even if it *were* as "difficult" as making a proper cassoulet or bouillabaisse, my French friends would still do it. If cooking always had to be "easy", some of the greatest dishes in French cuisine would never have been invented.

Right: Superwoman's stuffed mushrooms

CÈPES À LA BORDELAISE
4 SERVINGS

Bordel means brothel in French, but there is no need to panic, these mushrooms are perfectly respectable. *Bordelaise* refers to the region of Bordeaux, where the most famous of all French mushroom recipes originates. The secret lies in a slow cooking process so that the oil is clear when the mushrooms are cooked, and not brown or watery from the liquid given off by the *cèpes*.

1 kg medium cèpes (or large portobello mushrooms) | 1 cup olive oil 3 shallots, finely chopped | 1 clove garlic, finely chopped | a handful of chopped parsley | salt and pepper

If you are fortunate enough to get hold of *cèpes*, do not wash them as this can make them slimy. Simply wipe with a damp cloth, cut off the bottom of the stalks if they look a bit off and throw the offcuts away, wiggle the rest of the stems loose and put them aside.

Heat the oil in a heavy-based pan over high heat until it begins to smoke. Place the mushrooms in the pan with undersides down and fry for 5 minutes to dry out the bottoms quickly. Then turn the mushrooms over and reduce the heat.

Chop the stalks into pieces and toss them into the pan as well, along with salt and pepper to taste. Cook the *cèpes* gently for about 30 minutes. (Portobellos should be cooked sooner.) Add the shallots and garlic about 5 minutes before removing the mushrooms from the heat. Remove from the heat, sprinkle with parsley and serve with a nice juicy steak.

SUPERWOMAN'S STUFFED MUSHROOMS
4 SERVINGS

Use this recipe as the basis to create your own stuffings. For instance, you could leave out the first step with the tomatoes, replace the goat's milk cheese with blue cheese and stuff that into the hollows of the mushrooms. Then crumble walnuts over the top before popping the mushrooms under the grill. Or what about pieces of sundried tomato and mozzarella as a lovely light Mediterranean filling? The possibilities are truly endless.

200 g cherry tomatoes | 4 T olive oil | 3 cloves garlic, crushed | 1 T thyme leaves | 250 g large portobello mushrooms (about 12) | 1 T lemon juice | 100 g soft goat's cheese 1 T chopped parsley | a sprinkling of thyme, origanum and other herbs to taste | salt and pepper

Preheat the oven to 180 °C. Combine the tomatoes with 1 T olive oil, 2 of the crushed garlic cloves, the thyme and salt and pepper to taste. Place the mixture on a baking sheet lined with tinfoil and bake for 20-25 minutes, until the tomatoes start to wrinkle.

In the meantime, snap off the mushroom stalks neatly by wiggling them back and forth. Scoop out the gills from underneath the mushrooms using a teaspoon. (Don't throw away the stalks and the gills – they are perfect for adding to soup or a pasta sauce.)

Place the mushrooms on a baking sheet lined with tinfoil, hollowed-out side down. Brush with a little olive oil and the lemon juice. Place the baking sheet under the grill set to moderate heat and grill for 3-5 minutes, until the mushrooms start to look nice and juicy.

Heat the oven to 180 °C again (or leave it on after taking out the tomatoes). Fill the hollowed-out mushrooms with the roasted tomato mixture. Scatter pieces of goat's milk cheese on top and sprinkle with the herbs. Bake for about 10 minutes or until the cheese starts to melt. Brush the mushrooms with a little more olive oil so they shine beautifully and serve immediately.

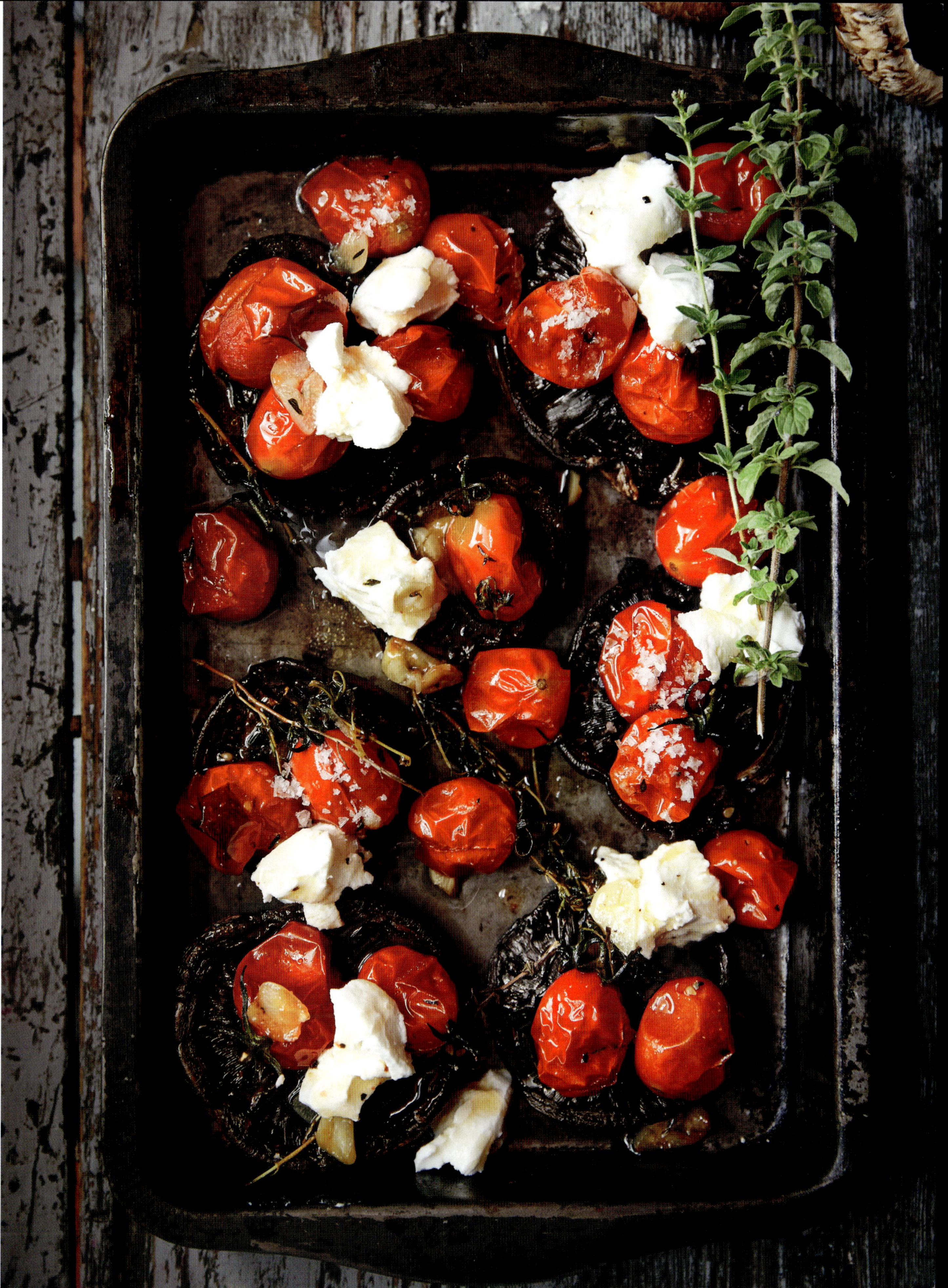

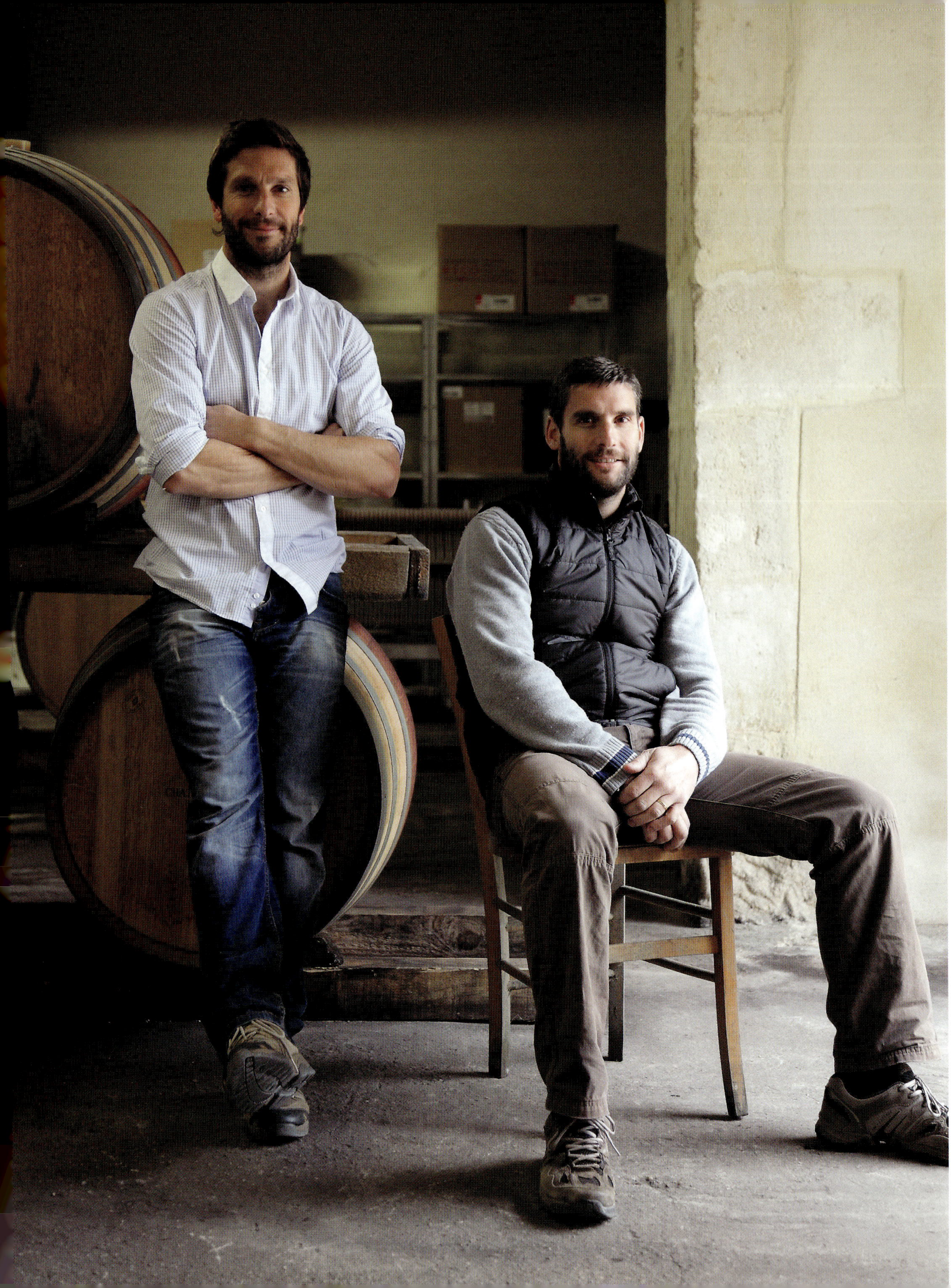

THROUGH THE GRAPEVINE

"THE VINE BEARS THREE KINDS OF GRAPES: THE FIRST OF PLEASURE, THE SECOND OF INTOXICATION, THE THIRD OF DISGUST."

DIOGENES, GREEK PHILOSOPHER (C. 412-323 BC)

It is impossible to ignore the grape harvest in this neck of the woods. Every time you hop in your car to drive somewhere quickly, you are reminded once again that no-one gets anywhere quickly in September. September is when gigantic harvesters resembling space ships invade the roads between the vineyards, when old-fashioned tractors transport loads and loads of grapes to the cellars all day long, and when the rest of us in normal vehicles are forced to crawl along behind the farm machinery and tractors at a proverbial snail's pace.

Getting impatient is pointless. No-one ever hoots at a tractor during the *vendange*. Except an ignorant tourist, perhaps. We locals resign ourselves to gnashing our teeth and try to imagine how wonderful the juice from those tractor-loads of grapes will taste one day after being turned into wine …

Provence's Côtes du Rhône wines are the second most important French products of the vine to carry the prestigious AOC label (*Appellation d'Origine Contrôlée*), after their famous cousins from Bordeaux. One of the world's greatest wines, Châteauneuf-du-Pape, which was praised by the writer Alphonse Daudet as "the wine of kings and the king of wines", has boasted the AOC appellation since 1929. Other great wines of the region had to wait longer: Vacqueyras, for instance, received AOC certification only in 1990 – although the actress Sarah Bernhardt had raved about the village and its wines many decades before.

The point is that it has never been easy to become an AOC wine. Winemakers have to comply with a slew of rules and regulations. In the Châteauneuf-du-Pape region, for instance, only thirteen varieties of grape may be cultivated for red wine (over ninety per cent of the production) plus a small amount of white wine, but no rosé is permitted. In Tavel, just a little further south down the Rhône, on the other hand, rosé takes pride of place – it was even popular in the court of Louis XIV. The pink wine of sun kings, you could say I suppose, and the sun king of pink wines.

A mere stone's throw from our house you could indulge in the golden colour and unique bouquet of Beaumes-de-Venise's sweet wine, served ice cold with a morsel of foie gras or a strong, salty blue cheese; or in the robust ruby-red liquid of Cairanne, which makes stews and other comfort food taste even better; or in Rasteau's sweet white or red wine, which is divine with chocolate at the end of a long repast …

The variety is truly staggering. When I moved here, I made a valiant attempt to get to know just the products of the cellars or *caves* in my immediate area. After dropping my son at preschool in the morning, I would stop at a different *cave* every day to taste their wines. While I did spit out a fair amount of it, as any proper wine taster should, I still managed to consume enough to leave me sleepy and lazy for the rest of the day. Before long I realised that keeping this up would mean never writing another book again – and that I would need at least nine lifetimes to taste all the wine Provence has to offer.

These days I tend to stick to the devil I know. We buy our weekly stock of Côtes du Rhône from the local cellar *en vrac*, which means that the wine is tapped straight from a massive tank – via a kind of hose that looks not unlike the one on a petrol pump – into the plastic jerry can I bring along. At home I decant it into airtight glass bottles, as my kind neighbours have taught me. In this way we are able to drink decent AOC wine every day without having to fork out for the bottle and the cork and the label. A very practical example of the renowned French reason, *n'est-ce pas?*

Boeuf à la Bourguignonne
6 SERVINGS

If I asked you to think of a classic French dish that combines red meat and wine, beef bourguignon is likely to spring to mind.

1 kg beef (chuck or rump), cubed | 1 large onion, sliced | 2-4 bunches parsley | 3-4 stalks thyme | 1 bay leaf | 2 T brandy | 350 ml red wine | 2 T olive oil | 50 g butter | 150 g diced bacon | 24 pickling onions, peeled | 500 g button mushrooms, halved | 1 T flour | 300 ml beef stock | 1 clove garlic, crushed | 1 bouquet garni (e.g. thyme, bay leaves, parsley, rosemary and sage) salt and pepper

Place the meat, onion rings, parsley, thyme and bay leaf in a dish and pour over the brandy, red wine and olive oil. Stir before covering and leave to marinate for at least 4 hours.

Then melt the butter in a heavy-based saucepan over moderate heat, add the bacon and fry until crisp. Remove the bacon with a slotted spoon and set aside. Add the onions and fry until golden brown. Remove with a slotted spoon and set aside. Add the mushrooms and fry for 1 minute. Remove with a slotted spoon and set aside.

Remove the meat from the marinade, put the liquid through a sieve and reserve the sauce. Put the meat in the saucepan and cook quickly until evenly brown. Sprinkle over the flour and cook for 1 minute. Gradually stir in the liquid from the marinade. Add the beef stock, garlic and bouquet garni and season with salt and pepper. Put the lid on the saucepan and simmer over low heat for about 2 hours or until the beef starts to become tender.

Skim the fat from the surface and add the bacon, onions and mushrooms. Put the lid on again and cook for a further half an hour over low heat. Remove the bouquet garni and serve with baguettes or rice.

Provençal daube

For a more Provençal version of beef bourguignon, cut 1 kg stewing steak into cubes and marinate it overnight in the following: 1 onion and 3 carrots, sliced, a strip of lemon zest, a bay leaf, a few peppercorns and 350 ml red wine. The next day, remove the meat (reserve the marinade with the vegetables and herbs) and heat a little fat or butter in a large saucepan. Braise the meat, remove from the pan with a slotted spoon and set aside. Add 3 crushed garlic cloves and another sliced onion to the saucepan and cook over moderate heat until golden brown.

Return the meat to the saucepan along with the reserved marinade and the marinated vegetables and herbs, and toss in a handful of black olives. Pour over 300 ml beef stock, season with salt and pepper and, once it comes to the boil, put the lid on. Now you can choose between leaving it to simmer on the stove for at least 2 hours or putting it into a preheated 160 °C oven until the meat is tender. Once the meat is done, remove it from the saucepan and keep warm, then turn up the heat and reduce the sauce by half. Return the meat to the pan and scatter a few snipped basil leaves over the top to bring out the Provençal flavours. (If fresh basil is unavailable in winter, parsley will do.) Serve the *daube* in the pan along with some crusty bread so your guests can mop up all the delicious sauce left on their plates. They will be forever in your debt.

Right: Boeuf à la Bourguignonne

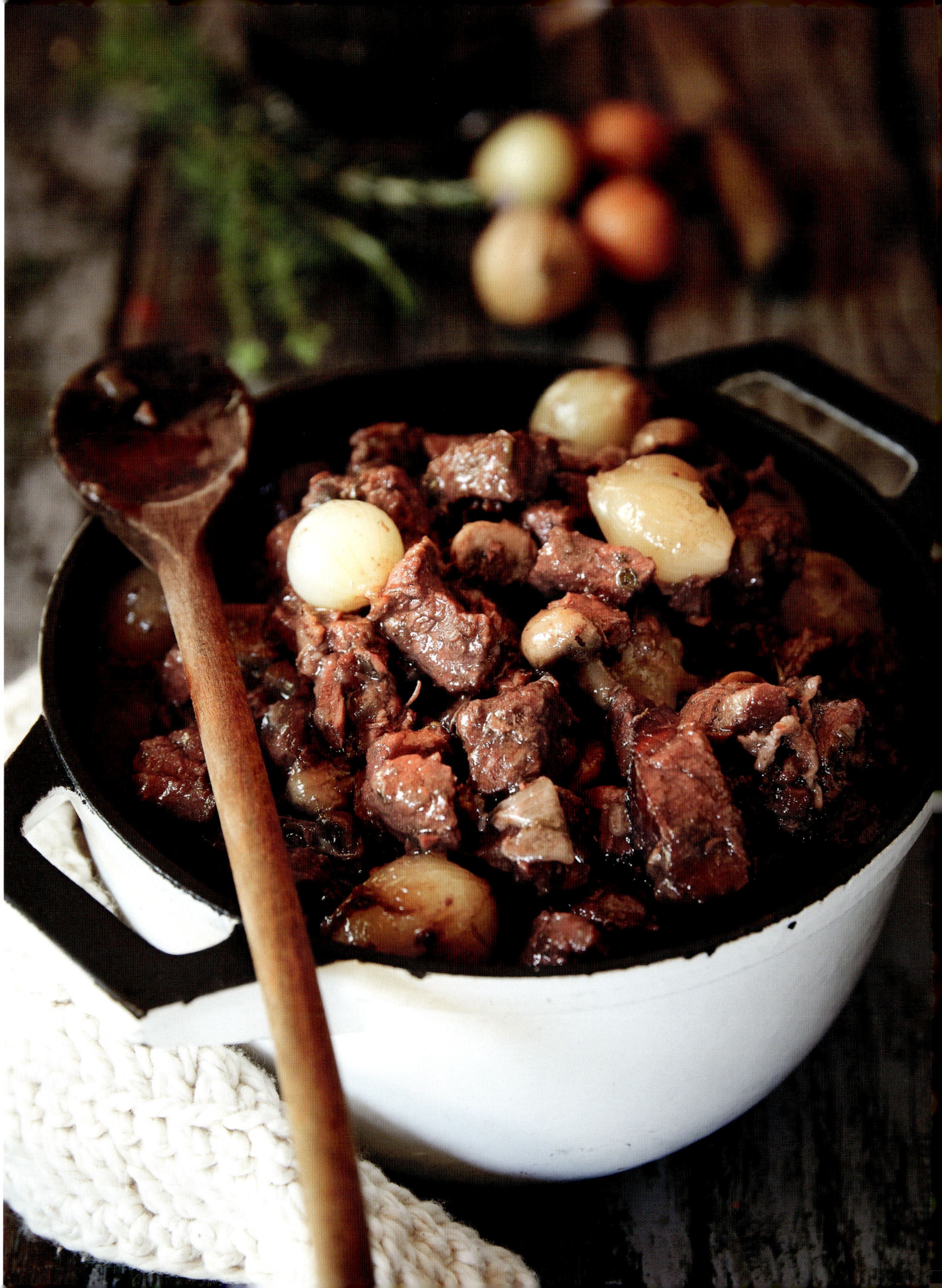

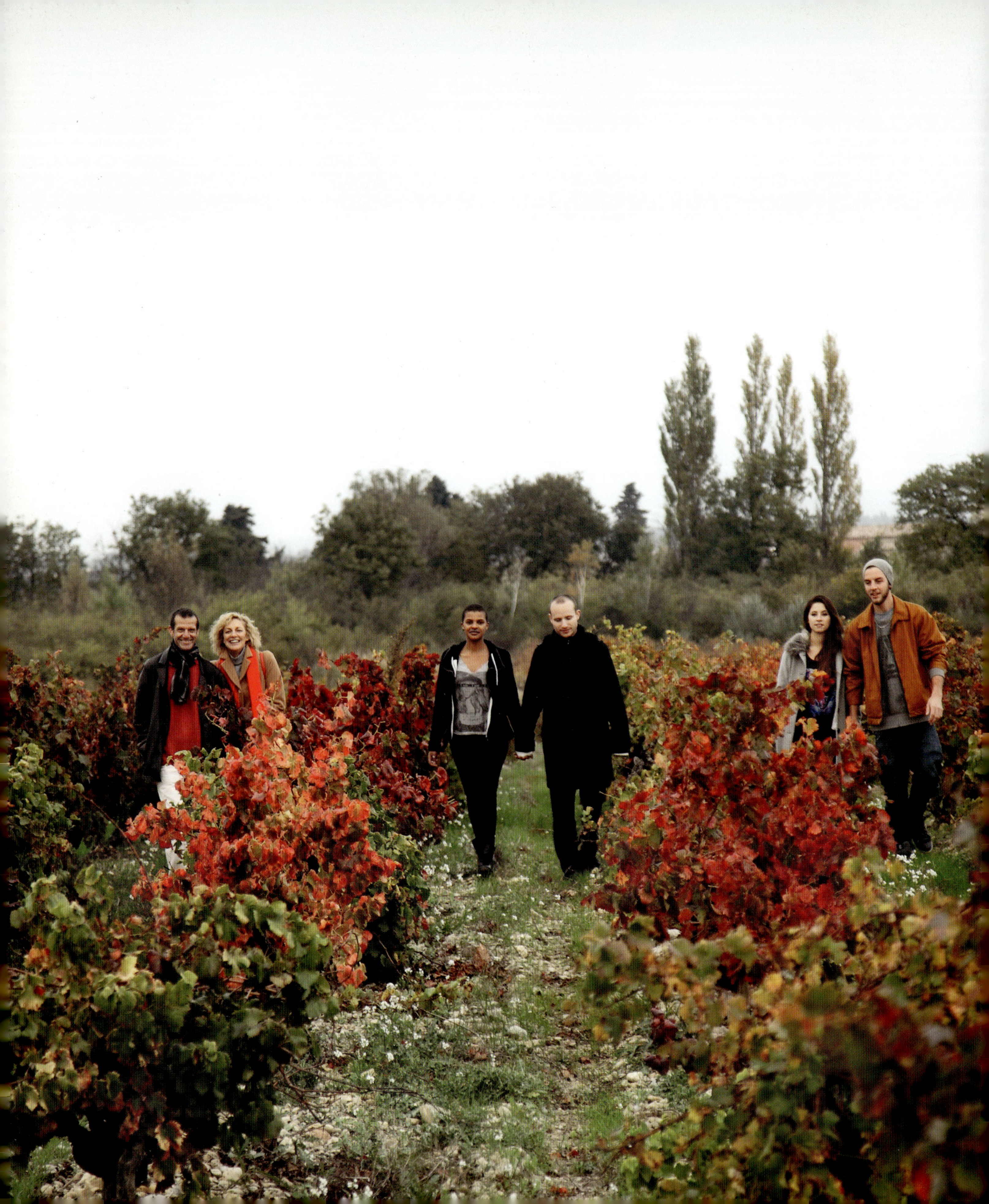

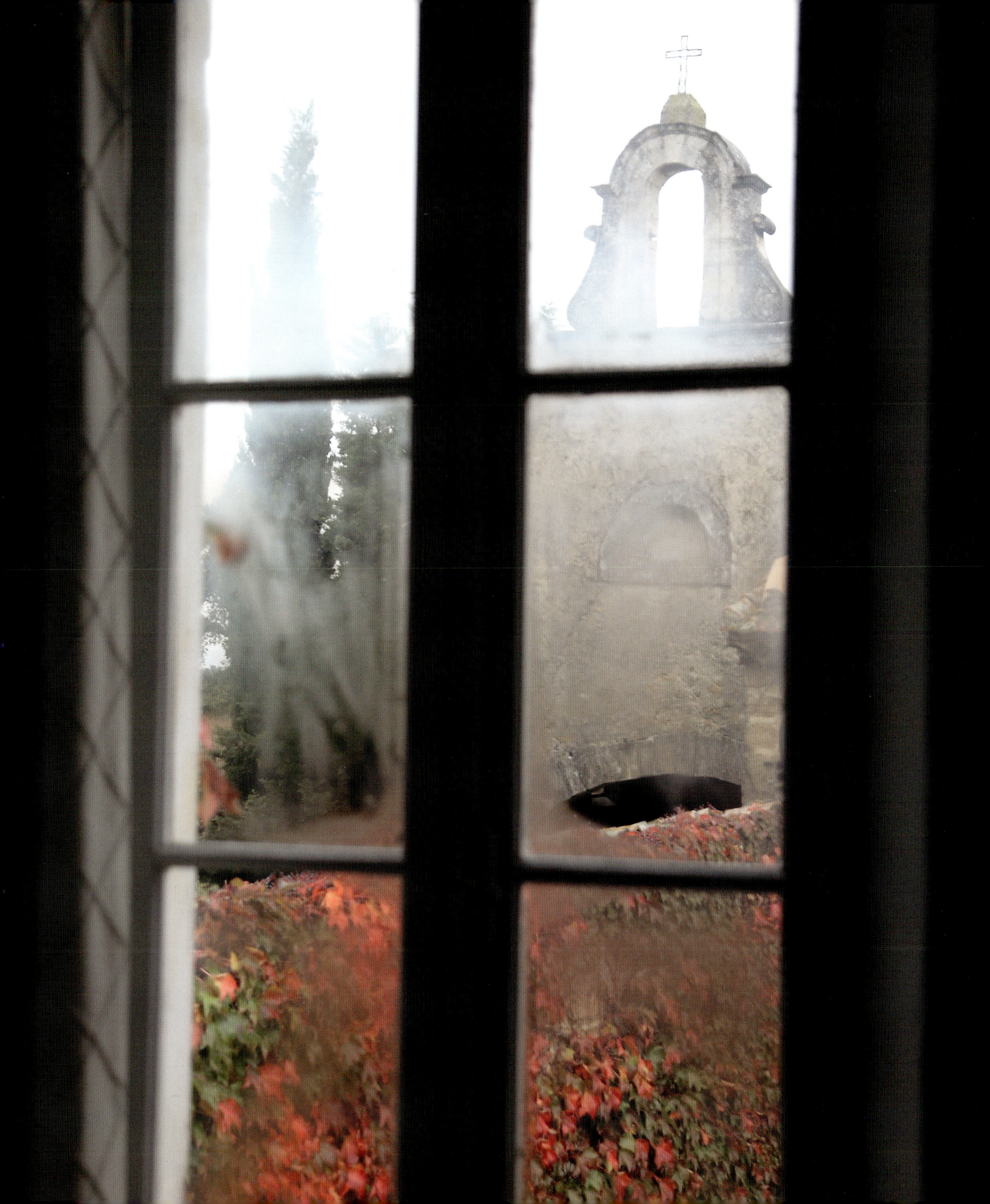

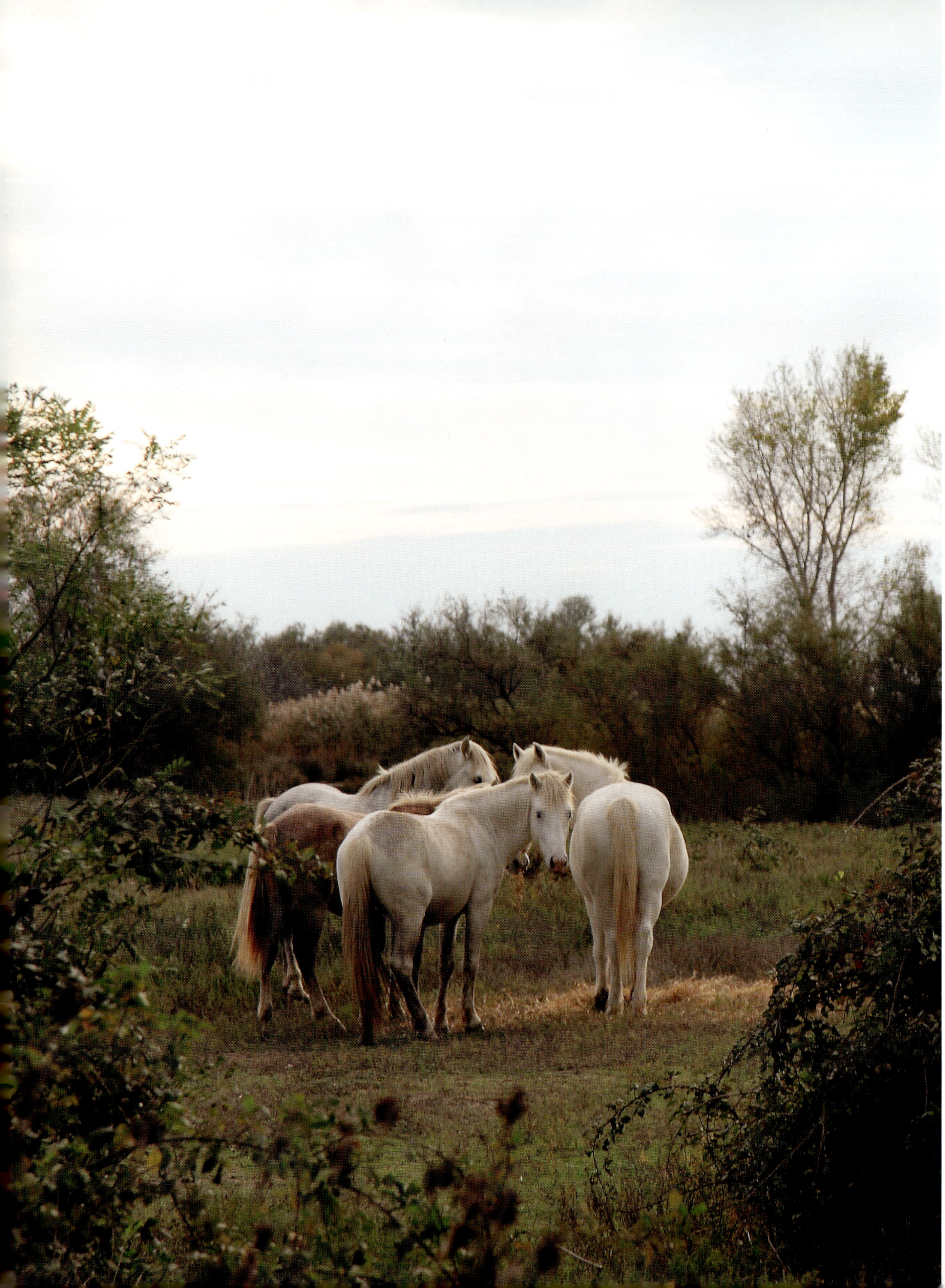

RICE RULES!

"COARSE RICE TO EAT, WATER TO DRINK, AND MY BENT ARM FOR A PILLOW – THEREIN LIES HAPPINESS."

Confucius, Chinese philosopher (551-479 BC)

It is not just grapes that are harvested in autumn. September is also the time of the rice harvest and the annual rice festival in the city of Arles, with bullfighting, a horse festival, street music, sangria and – as you would expect – enormous dishes of paella wherever you look.

The Spanish influence is strong in this western region of Provence, a stone's throw from Spain. And paella is a firm favourite at village and town festivals and other festive gatherings, probably because, like *couscous royal* – that other French "bazaar food" I wrote about last time – it contains a variety of white and red meat and, in the case of paella, seafood as well. So if there is something you don't like, you simply ignore that bit – and the tasty savoury rice mixed with vegetables will even satisfy vegetarians.

Rice paddies may not be as characteristic of the landscape of Provence as vineyards and olive groves, but rice is an important agricultural product of the region – as well as being essential in the kitchen. It is said to have been Henry IV who established rice farming in the marshy Carmargue during the sixteenth century. The same king who, perhaps not coincidentally, expressed the famous desire that even the poorest French family be able to eat chicken on a Sunday. Because what goes better with *poule au pot* than a generous serving of rice over which to pour the juices from the pot?

With this culinary aim, the marshes were drained and the ground levelled, and even today seventy per cent of rice produced in France comes from the Camargue. This relatively wild region with its legendary white horses and black bulls and pink flamingos offers the ideal conditions for cultivating rice.

Because rice is a plant that likes to have its feet in the water and its head in the sun, the seed is sown just before the spring rains cause the Rhône to overflow its banks and the summer sun really starts to bake. If the sun is not hot enough, the seed rots and the crop will fail. But once the seed has germinated, the rice paddies steam in the most wonderful green glory all through the hot, hot summer – until the rice blooms for scarcely two hours on just one day in August. Believe it or not! That is why, after more than fifteen years in Provence, I have never seen the elusive rice flowers. (Not to be confused with the Australian plants with pink or white flowers that also go by the name of rice flowers.) What I am talking about are "proper" rice blossoms.

By the way, I live a good hour and a half's drive from the nearest rice fields. But if someone were to phone one day to tell me that the rice was flowering right this very minute, I would be prepared to jump in my car and race there, on the off chance I would be in time to experience the final half an hour of that briefest of flowering seasons.

Until then, our family is quite happy to use the "fruit" of these fair flowers in the kitchen. The traditional short-grain rice of the Camargue is a japonica variety, like Italian arborio and carnaroli, and therefore perfect for a creamy risotto on a cold evening. Long-grain rice of the indica variety, like many of the most popular Asian rices, is however becoming more popular among local rice farmers – and we are not complaining, because it tastes so good in a festive paella.

We are especially fond of the nutty taste, firm texture and obviously also the characteristic red-brown colour of the Camargue's unique *riz rouge*. This delicious hybrid of cultivated white rice and a variety of indigenous red wild rice was "discovered" not much more than thirty years ago and is appreciated by gourmands around the world. Not so easy to get hold of if you live far from the Camargue – but definitely worth trying when you visit the region. And take a packet home with you too. Along with a packet of the local coarse grey salt, it is undoubtedly the easiest way to bring the taste of the Camargue to your own kitchen.

Red-rice risotto with mixed mushrooms

If you have a variety of wild mushrooms and a packet of *riz rouge*, you can whip up the most delicious autumnal risotto imaginable. If not, replace the wild mushrooms with imported or dried ones such as shiitake, porcini, oyster or button mushrooms, and the red rice with a mixture of short-grain and wild rice. Cut the largest mushrooms into pieces and the medium-sized ones in half. Heat a little butter in a large pan and fry all the mushrooms over medium heat until just cooked. Remove the mushrooms from the pan and keep warm.

Fry a finely chopped onion in the same pan, add 400 g red rice and stir the lot for a few minutes. Pour in a glass of red wine. Once the wine has been absorbed, add 1,5 litres beef stock little by little, stirring continuously. (Keep the stock hot on another plate on the stove.) After about 20 minutes the liquid should have been absorbed and the rice should be cooked, but if the rice is creamy and cooked with a slight bite in the middle before you have used up the stock, do not worry about it. Remove from the stove, stir in the mushrooms and 100 g grated Parmesan cheese, and serve. Garnish with a few Parmesan shavings. The bite of the rice and the creaminess of the mushrooms are a match made in heaven.

Easy Provençal paella
6 SERVINGS

Paella is marvellous festive fare when entertaining a crowd – but you could just as easily throw together an easy version for your family on an ordinary weeknight. Like most people, we do not have space in our kitchen for an enormous paella pan that is used only once or twice a year – mine was mislaid years ago during one of my many moves over two continents, and I never replaced it – so this recipe can also be made in an ordinary large pan. Feel free to use frozen mussels in the shell if you are in a hurry.

4 T olive oil | 1 green pepper, finely chopped | 1 red pepper, finely chopped | 1 red onion, finely chopped 2 cloves garlic, finely chopped | 400 g red rice from the Camargue (or a mixture of wild rice, brown rice and white rice) | a pinch of saffron 1,5 litres fish stock | 3 calamari tubes, sliced | 6 large mussels in the shell (or 12 small ones) | 200 ml white wine | 12 slices chorizo sausage | salt and pepper

Heat half the olive oil in your largest, sturdiest pan and fry the peppers, onion and almost all the garlic until soft and fragrant. Add the rice and saffron, then gradually stir in the fish stock. Simmer over low heat for about half an hour or until the rice is cooked (soft but still firm).

In the meantime, fry the calamari and remaining garlic in the rest of the olive oil for a few minutes in a smaller pan. Season with salt and pepper to taste. Place the mussels and the wine in a saucepan, put the lid on and simmer over low heat until the shells open.

When the rice is cooked, stir in the calamari, mussels and chorizo. Carry the pan to the table once all the ingredients are heated through. One of the pleasures of paella is that it saves on the washing up. Hooray!

Right: Easy Provençal paella

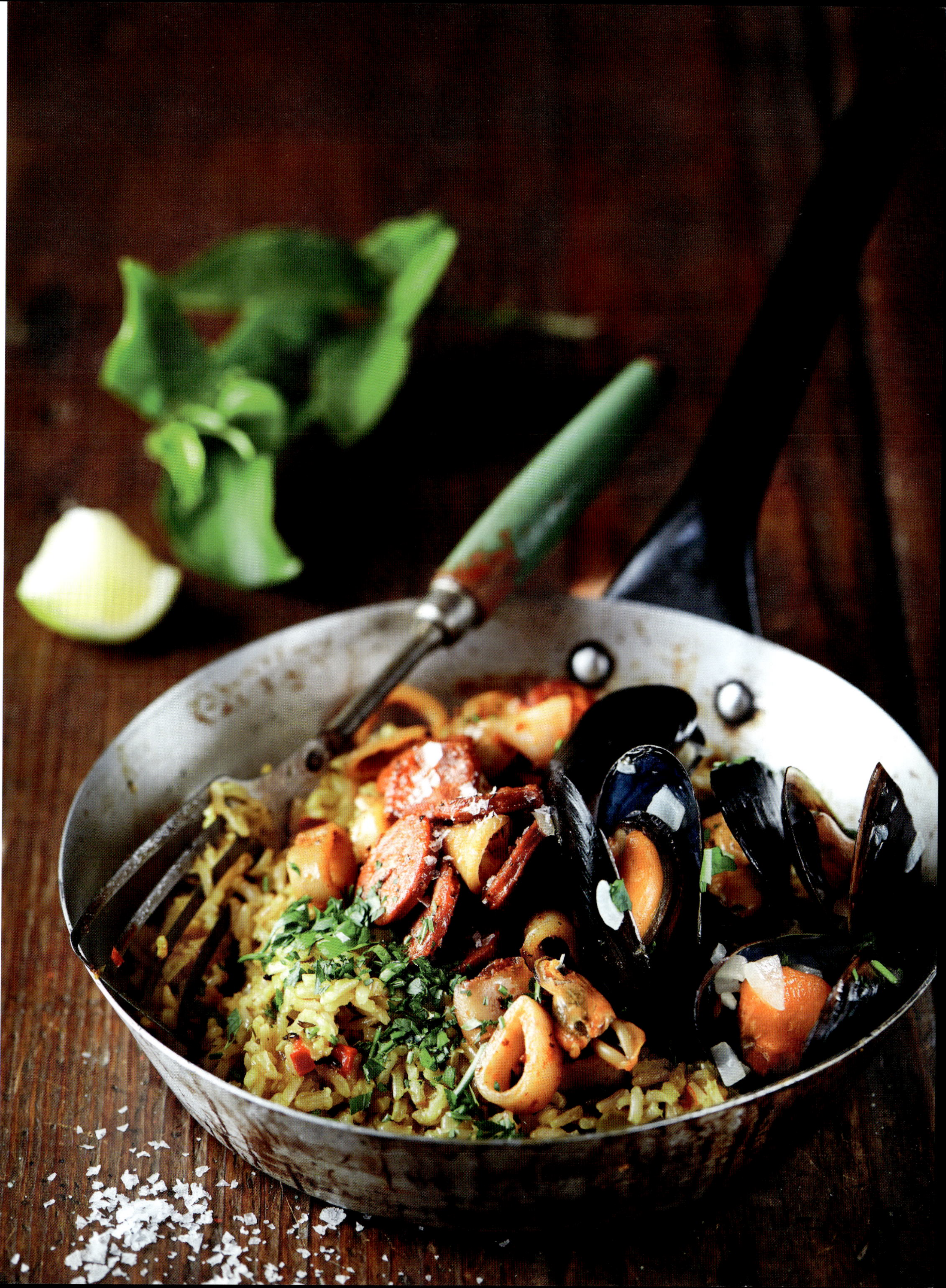

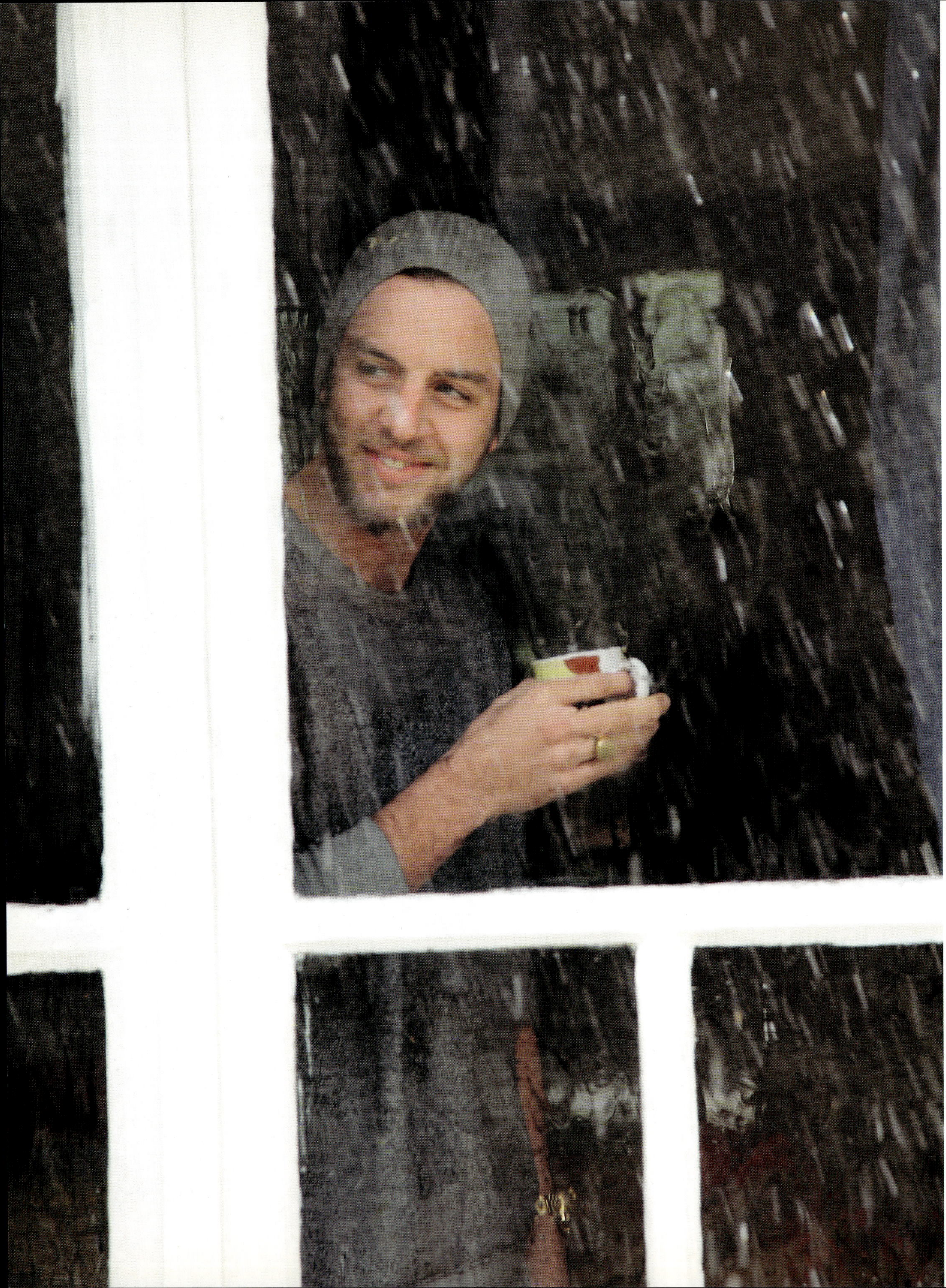

SALT OF THE EARTH

"GIVE NEITHER COUNSEL NOR SALT TILL YOU ARE ASKED FOR IT."

Traditional Italian proverb

Not too long ago a friend and I met for lunch at a bistro. There we were, chatting away, when the woman at the next table started scratching around in her capacious handbag and plucked out … a salt grinder. We must have stared at her a little too curiously, our conversation having suddenly dried up, because next thing she asked us in a friendly way whether we would like to borrow her salt grinder. I declined her offer because our food was already salted, but was nosy enough to ask why she had brought along her own salt when eating out.

She gave me a look that said this was the silliest question she had heard in a long time. Because it is *fleur de sel de Camargue*! Why would you sprinkle ordinary white factory salt on your food if you could carry the best salt in the world around in your handbag?

Why, indeed.

Fleur de sel means "the flower of the salt", a typically poetic French name for that most basic of food products formed by water and wind. After so many years in this country I still marvel at how lyrical the language can sound in the kitchen. French food is never simply cooked, it is "made to jump" (the word for sauté is the same as for jump), sweated, drowned in wine or drizzled with butter or oiled, bound or trussed (*trousser*), or handled in other ways that lend the kitchen a faintly erotic S & M atmosphere. Or is it just me seeing sex in everything? Perhaps just more proof that I have become more French than I originally intended.

But let us forget about sex and concentrate on salt. This "white gold", which has been produced in the Camargue since Roman times, was for centuries so precious that soldiers were paid partly in salt rather than gold. (This is in fact where the word salary comes from; derived from the Latin *salarium*, meaning salt wage.) Still today, every spring sees huge quantities of sea water being pumped into the salt flats, where it lies throughout the summer months and dries out into a thick crust. In autumn, shortly before the first heavy rains melt it all away, the precious crust is removed from the salt pan piece by piece using machinery, almost like slices of cake being lifted with a giant cake lifter. Then it is washed and dried again, and graded according to the size of the salt crystals.

The characteristic grey colour of the slightly damp *gros sel* or coarse salt is the result of the clay beds of the salt pans, making it an exceptionally pure, mineral-rich product that can be found in posh food emporiums the world over. My sister lived in New York for a few years where she would buy very expensive French *gros sel*. She could not believe her luck when she discovered it was available dirt cheap in any supermarket here. After her first visit to Provence she went home with a suitcase crammed with small packets of grey salt as gifts for appreciative foodie friends.

The "flower of salt" or *fleur de sel* can be seen as the cherry on the salt cake, and is therefore more expensive than ordinary grey salt. The flower is formed by salt crystals being blown to the edges of the salt pans by the legendary Provençal winds – the mistral and the tramontane – where it gathers. The delicate flowers are harvested by hand, left to dry in the sun for a few hours without any further processing, and sold in small quantities. In bags, tins or mills that you can carry around in your handbag.

A word to the wise: Any cook will be offended if a guest spoils a dish by adding too much salt – and reaching for the salt cellar before you have even tasted the food, is plain bad manners. But if the food needs a little salt, then I suppose you could say it with flowers?

Of salt crusts

I understand that some families almost come to blows around the dinner table over the crisp, golden brown skin of a roast chicken. Don't ask me why, but since they were little the four children under our roof have turned up their noses at the skin. All four only wanted the juicy white meat. (Which also almost resulted in blows being exchanged when the chicken was smaller than the appetite.) Even though I am partial to a piece of crisp, fatty skin, being fully aware that it is certainly not the most nutritious part of the chicken, in the interests of family harmony I had to find other ways to roast our weekly chicken.

An old French recipe for chicken baked in a salt crust came to my rescue. No crispy skin, only the most delicious, juiciest white flesh imaginable. And it is a recipe that works as well when you have guests over. It is like carrying a surprise package to the table: You break open the salt crust with the back of a knife and relish the sight of all those rapt faces when the flavoursome "gift" inside appears. The same technique can be used to prepare fish, red meat and even vegetables in a succulent and healthy way. Fresh beetroot is especially good – and looks amazing too as it emerges crimson and steaming from its salt blanket.

Potatoes "in dressing gowns" with coarse salt

This dish can also be eaten cold as a delicious potato salad, but in winter it is at its best served piping hot. Cook 500 g baby potatoes for 5 minutes in their skins (or in their "dressing gowns", as the French would say), drain and spread on a baking tray. Cut 2 red onions into slices vertically almost down to the bottom (so the slices remain attached) and place them among the potatoes on the tray. Add a few stalks of rosemary, drizzle everything with olive oil and bake for 45-60 minutes in a preheated 200 °C oven, until the potato skins are golden. Fry 100 g diced bacon in a small pan until crisp, add 3 T red-wine vinegar and cook quickly to deglaze the pan. Pour this over the potatoes, stir to combine everything and sprinkle with the best coarse salt you can afford. The better the salt, the better the dish will taste – that's a promise.

Chicken with sage in a salt crust
6 servings

2 kg coarse salt | 2 egg whites
1 chicken | a handful of sage leaves
a bunch of parsley | a few stalks of
thyme and rosemary

Mix the salt and egg whites in a bowl until the salt is damp throughout and can be worked like clay in your hands. Fill the cavity of the chicken with the herbs.

Choose a roasting pan that is only slightly larger than the chicken. (This helps keep the crust snugly around the chicken.) Line the bottom of the pan with tinfoil. Put a few layers of absorbent kitchen paper on the foil to absorb any liquid that may escape from the crust. Place a thick layer (about 2 cm) of the salt mixture on the paper. Place the chicken in the pan, breast side down, and use the rest of the salt mixture to cover the chicken well all over. (This is easier if the legs are trussed to the body with string first.)

Put the chicken in a preheated 200 °C oven and bake for at least an hour and a quarter (longer if the chicken is bigger than average). When the crust has hardened completely and becomes golden brown, the chicken should be cooked through – a soft, succulent, flavourful gift when you break open the crust.

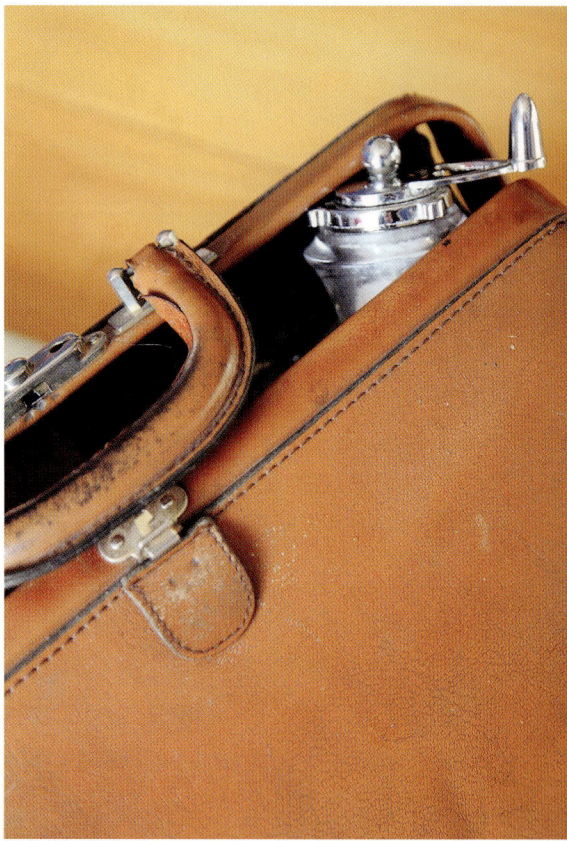

Right: Chicken with sage in a salt crust

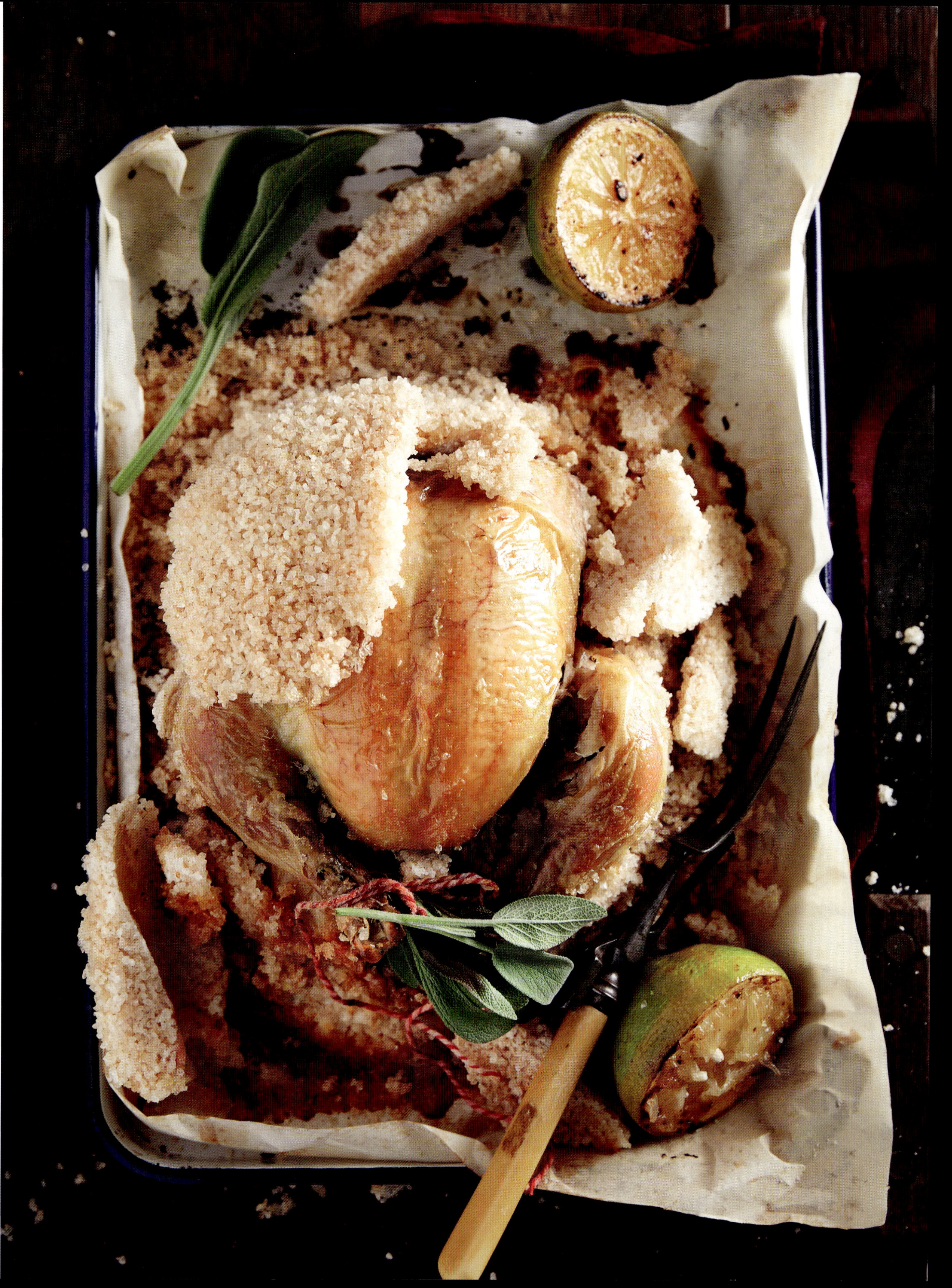

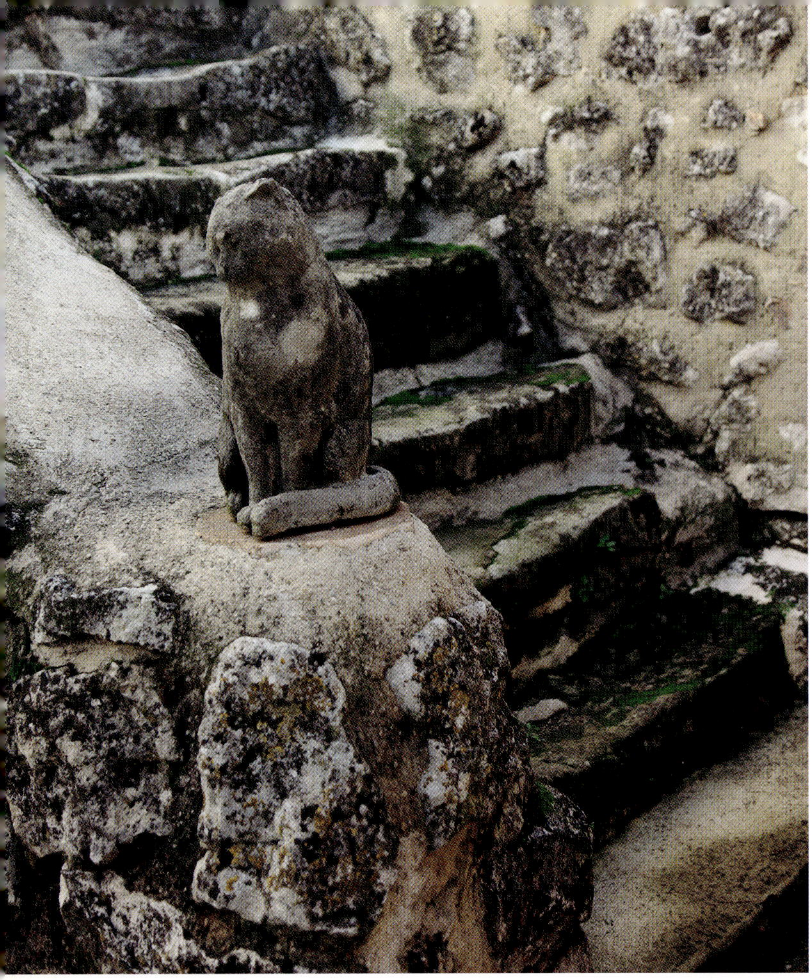
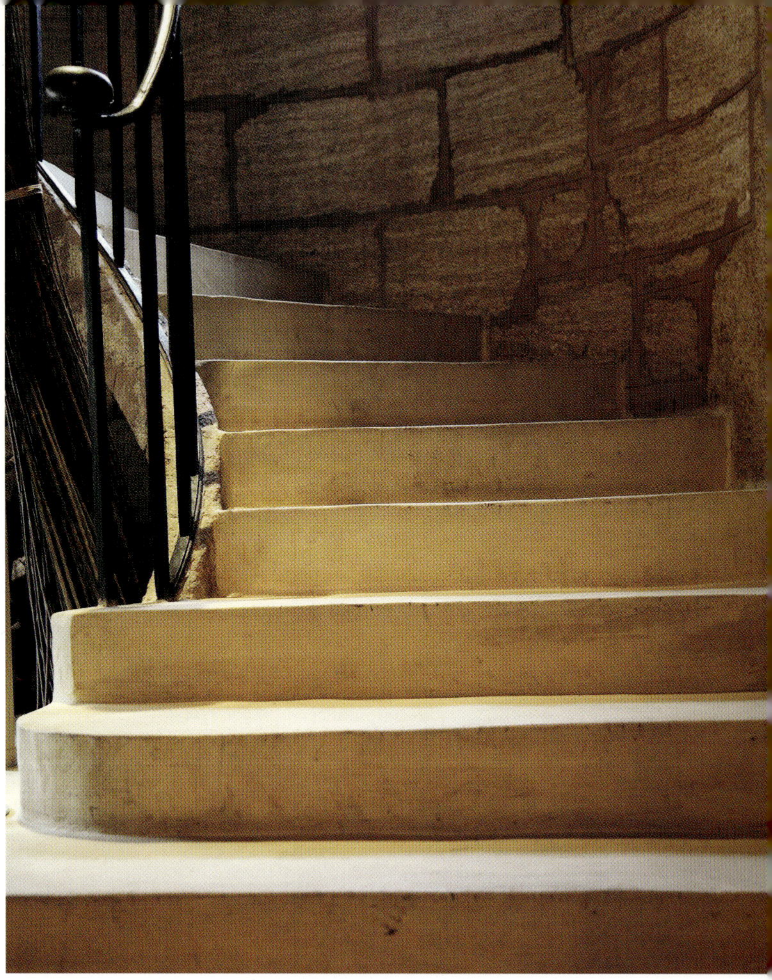
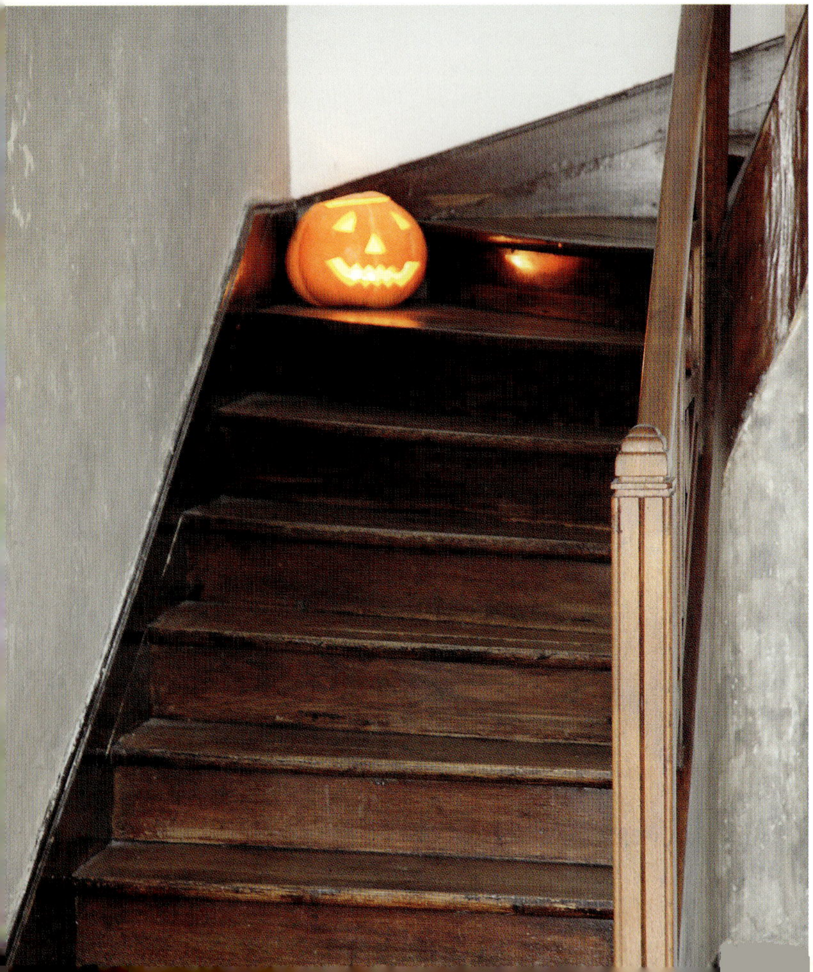
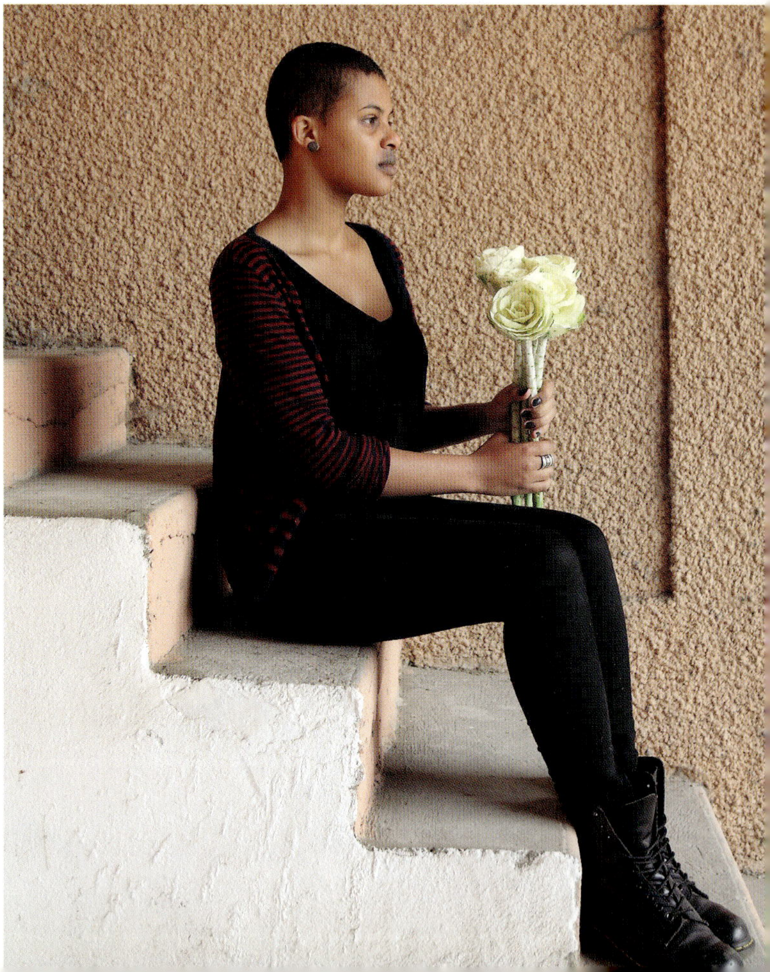

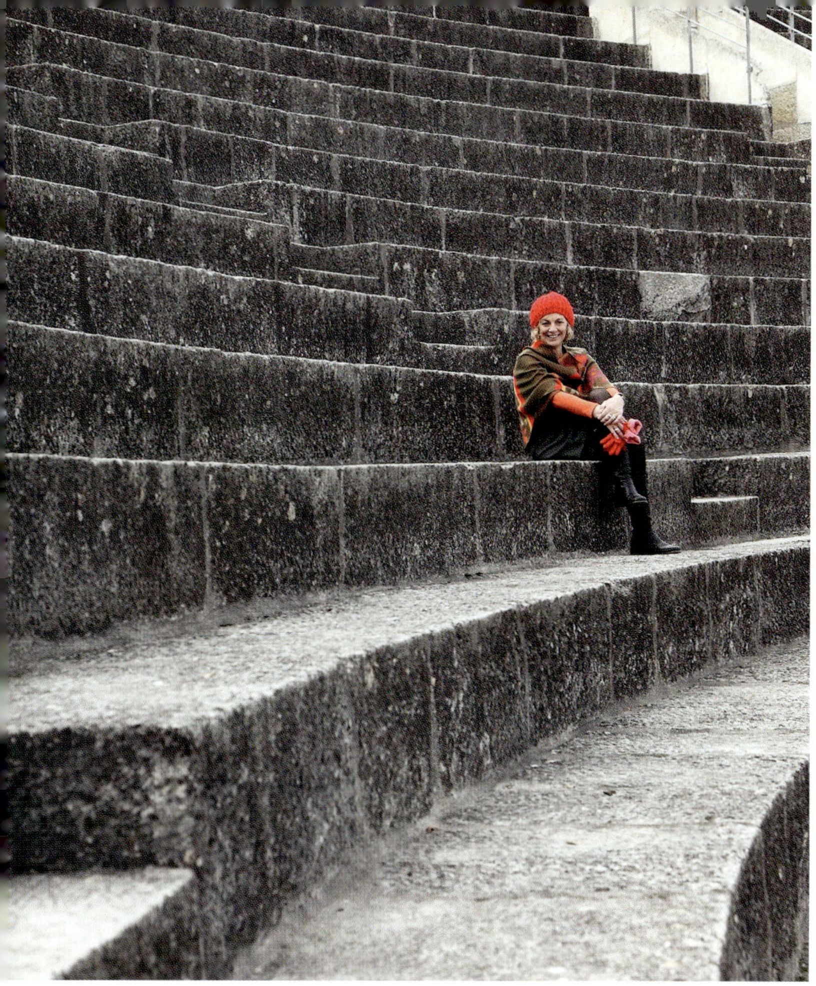
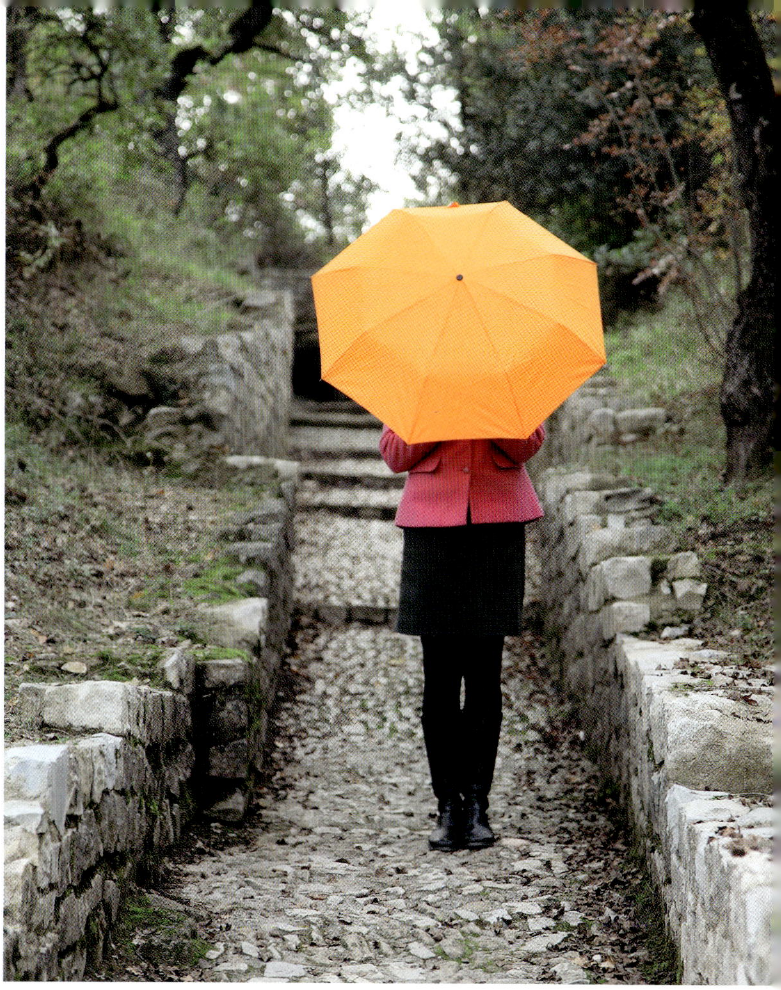
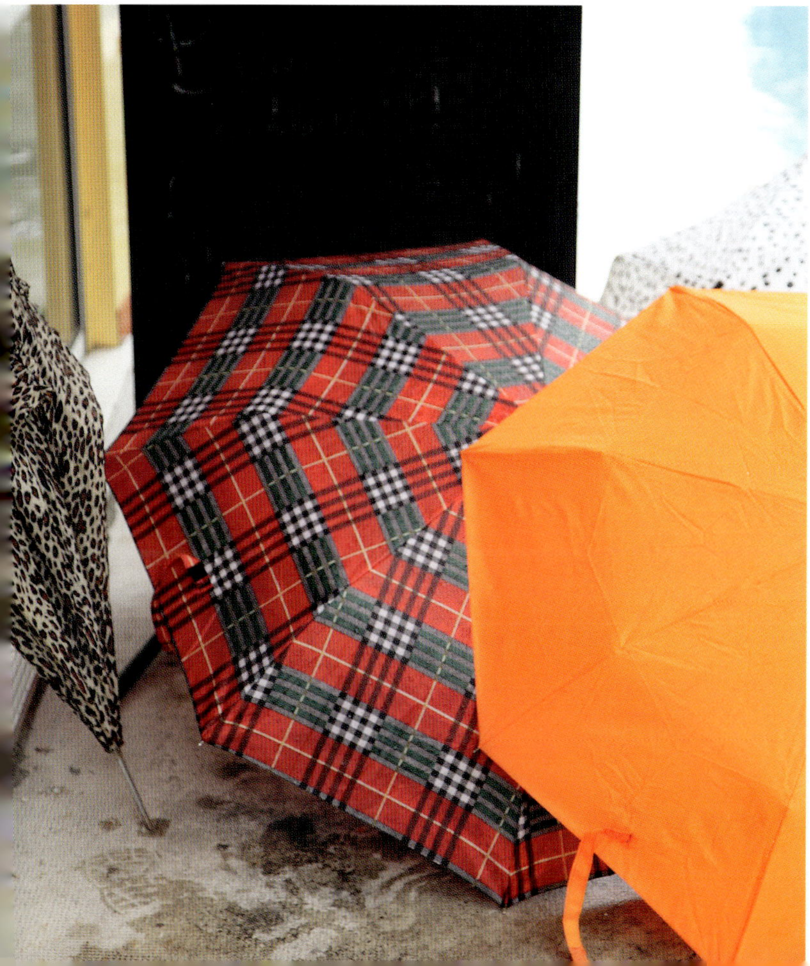
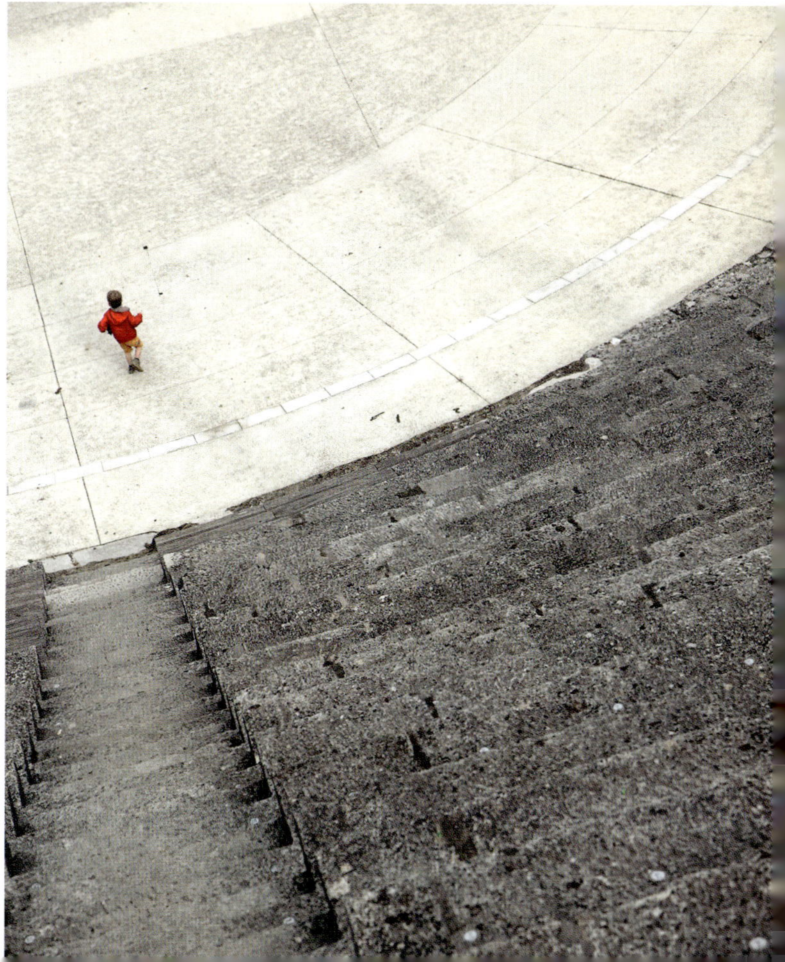

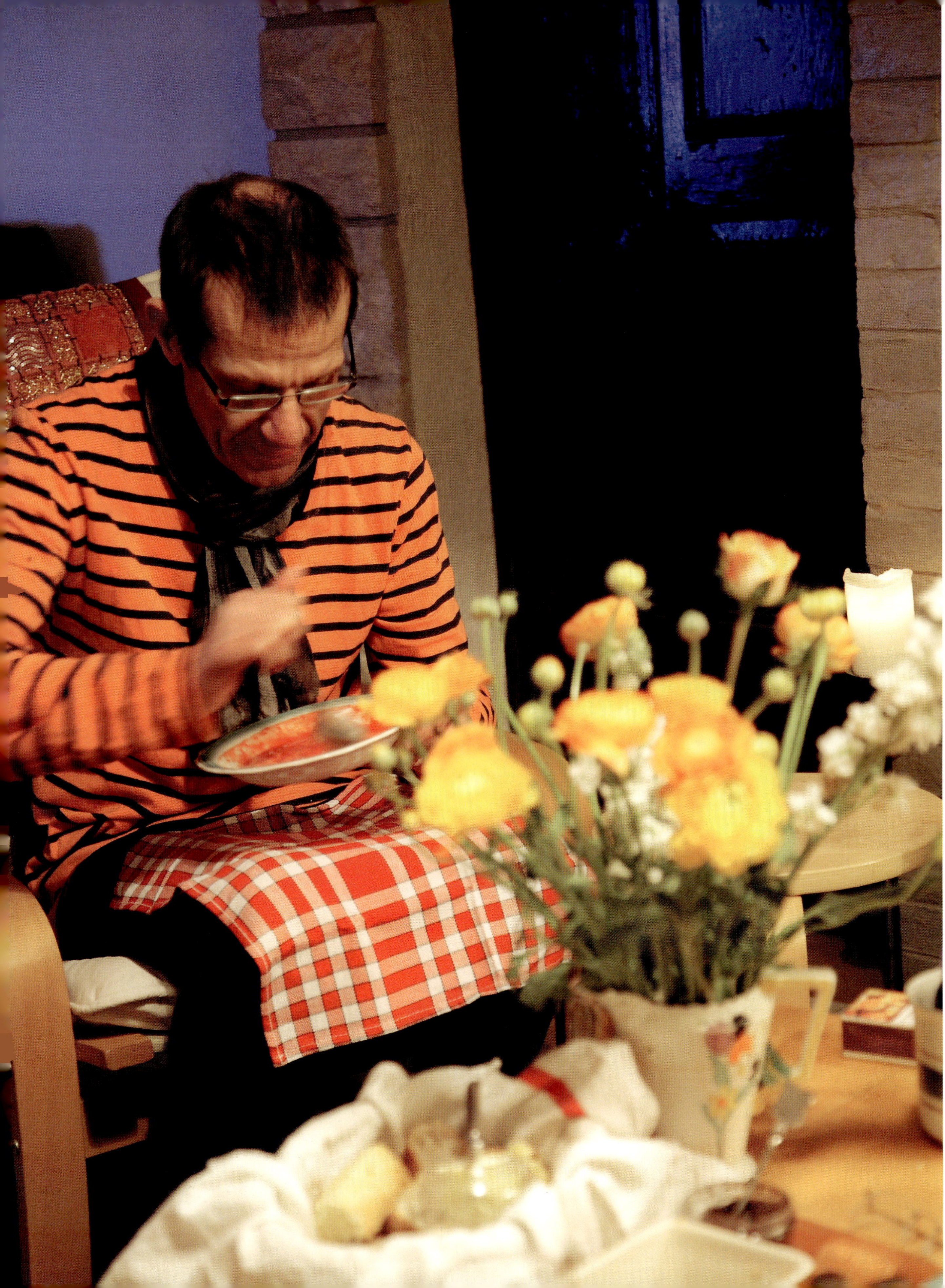

THE BRILLIANCE THAT IS BEETROOT

"WE DO NOT SEEM TO HAVE HAD MUCH SUCCESS WITH THE BEETROOT IN THIS COUNTRY. PERHAPS THIS IS PARTLY THE BEETROOT'S FAULT."

JANE GRIGSON, BRITISH FOOD WRITER (1928-1990)

During my South African childhood beetroot was something I knew only in its pickled form, that jar of tangy salad that was always kept in the fridge. On our groaning Sunday lunch table, among the sweet potatoes and mashed pumpkin and cauliflower with cheese sauce and at least three types of meat, a jar of beetroot or bean salad was often the sole representative of that slightly suspicious phenomenon called "salad". Something that had been blown in from overseas, according to older members of the family.

Beetroot in fact developed from wild sea beet many centuries ago in the Middle East and the area around the Mediterranean, being cultivated for the leaves rather than the root initially. The Romans started cooking beetroot with honey and wine, and the great Roman gourmand Apicius recommended it in recipes for healthy soups and, would you believe, as a salad with mustard, oil and vinegar. I could never have imagined that the bottles of beetroot from my childhood had such an ancient history.

What would have surprised me less, is the fact that until after the Middle Ages beetroot was used principally for medicinal purposes, to treat anything from fevers and constipation to skin problems. The pickled stuff was always too sour for my taste, but I had to eat it because my mom said it was good for me. Pumpkin makes your hair curl, carrots are good for your eyes, beetroot gives you rosy cheeks, and so on, and so on.

It was only years later while backpacking through Europe that I got to know *Beta vulgaris* in another form – and what a delicious introduction it was! In a Russian restaurant in Helsinki – the closest I would ever get to Russia, I imagined in those days of the Soviet Union and the Red Peril – I slurped down a large bowlful of velvet-smooth, dark pink borscht. It was love at first taste. So *this* was what could be done with the modest beetroot!

After the Iron Curtain was torn down at the end of the eighties, I did indeed make it to Russia and there tasted the famous Russian soup again. Strangely enough, it did not make as profound an impression on me as that first time in Finland. Then again, perhaps it is not so strange. Food experiences can be as emotionally intense as love affairs – and in both cases it is often the first time that stays with you.

The "superfood" health benefits of beetroot – and raw beetroot juice in particular – are fairly common knowledge these days, but we would do well to remember that the Romans also emphasised the erotic properties of beetroot. They knew all about such things, did those clever Romans. During the Second World War, Field Marshall B.L. Montgomery is said to have encouraged his soldiers to "take favours in the beetroot fields" – in other words, to visit prostitutes – and even today a *soupçon* of the erotic surrounds beetroot. Perhaps it is simply the unusually dark red colour, but beetroot is without doubt "the most intense of vegetables", as Tom Robbins put it in *Jitterbug Perfume*: "Tomatoes are lusty enough, yet there runs through tomatoes an undercurrent of frivolity. Beets are deadly serious."

Despite my intense love affair with borscht, it took landing up in France and falling in love with a Frenchman for me to buy raw beetroot for the first time in order to attempt the soup and other beetroot dishes for myself. That is how things are done here. You would never buy a tin or jar of something if you could buy it fresh at the market. And then the Red Peril developed a whole new meaning for me. Working with beetroot is indeed a peril to any clean kitchen – a messy business that stains your kitchen cloths and leaves your nails looking grubby for days – but the result is undoubtedly worth all the cleaning. Home-cooked beetroot has the irresistible aroma of iron and rain, and a rich, mellow taste that you will never find in a jar of bought beetroot salad.

Beetroot salad with broccoli and goat's milk cheese

Winter salads can be just as tasty, fresh and healthy as their summer counterparts. The red, green and white colour combination also makes this one a feast for the eye. Boil or bake 500 g beetroot and leave to cool. Peel and dice. (Remember the rubber gloves to keep your nails clean.) Steam 500 g broccoli briefly so that it is still crunchy, leave to cool and cut into florets. Combine the beetroot, broccoli and ½ cup chopped walnuts. Make a vinaigrette from olive oil, red-wine vinegar, a clove of crushed garlic and 1-2 t Dijon mustard, and drizzle over the salad. Scatter pieces of soft, white goat's cheese or crumbled feta over the top.

Beetroot soup with orange and thyme
6 SERVINGS

Orange juice and thyme give traditional borscht a sunnier, Mediterranean flavour. If you want your soup thicker and redder, use a little more beetroot.

600 g beetroot, scrubbed and leaves removed | 5 T olive oil | 1 onion, finely chopped | 2 cloves garlic, finely chopped | the leaves of a few stalks of thyme | a splash of balsamic vinegar | the juice of 1 orange 1 T grated orange zest | 1 litre chicken stock | 6 T crème fraîche (or sour cream) | salt and pepper

Cook the beetroot in boiling water for about an hour until just soft enough to cut. Leave to cool, peel and cut up. (This is the messy part of the operation. Pretend you are a surgeon and wear rubber gloves.)

Heat the olive oil in a saucepan and fry the onion, garlic and thyme over moderate heat for a few minutes. Add the beetroot along with the balsamic vinegar, orange juice and zest, and chicken stock. Season to taste with salt and pepper and simmer for 10 minutes.

Liquidise in a blender or food processor and serve in soup bowls. Stir a spoonful of crème fraîche into each serving and your soup will look as good as it tastes.

Roasted beetroot with wild rice

This is a delicious side dish to serve on a cold day. Roast 2 large, cleaned beetroots in the oven until just soft enough to cut, then peel and dice. Combine with ½ cup chopped hazelnuts and set aside. Heat a little olive oil in a large saucepan and fry a chopped shallot until soft and transparent. Add a cup of wild rice, fry for a few minutes, pour over a glass of red wine and cook rapidly until the wine has been absorbed. Add 3 T vegetable stock and enough boiling water to cover the rice with 1-2 cm liquid. Cover the saucepan and bring to the boil. Reduce the heat and simmer slowly for about half an hour until the rice is cooked and the liquid has been absorbed. Just before the rice is ready, stir in the beetroot and nut mixture, and season with salt and pepper. Serve with a spoonful of creamy Greek yoghurt on each plate.

Right: Beetroot soup with orange and thyme

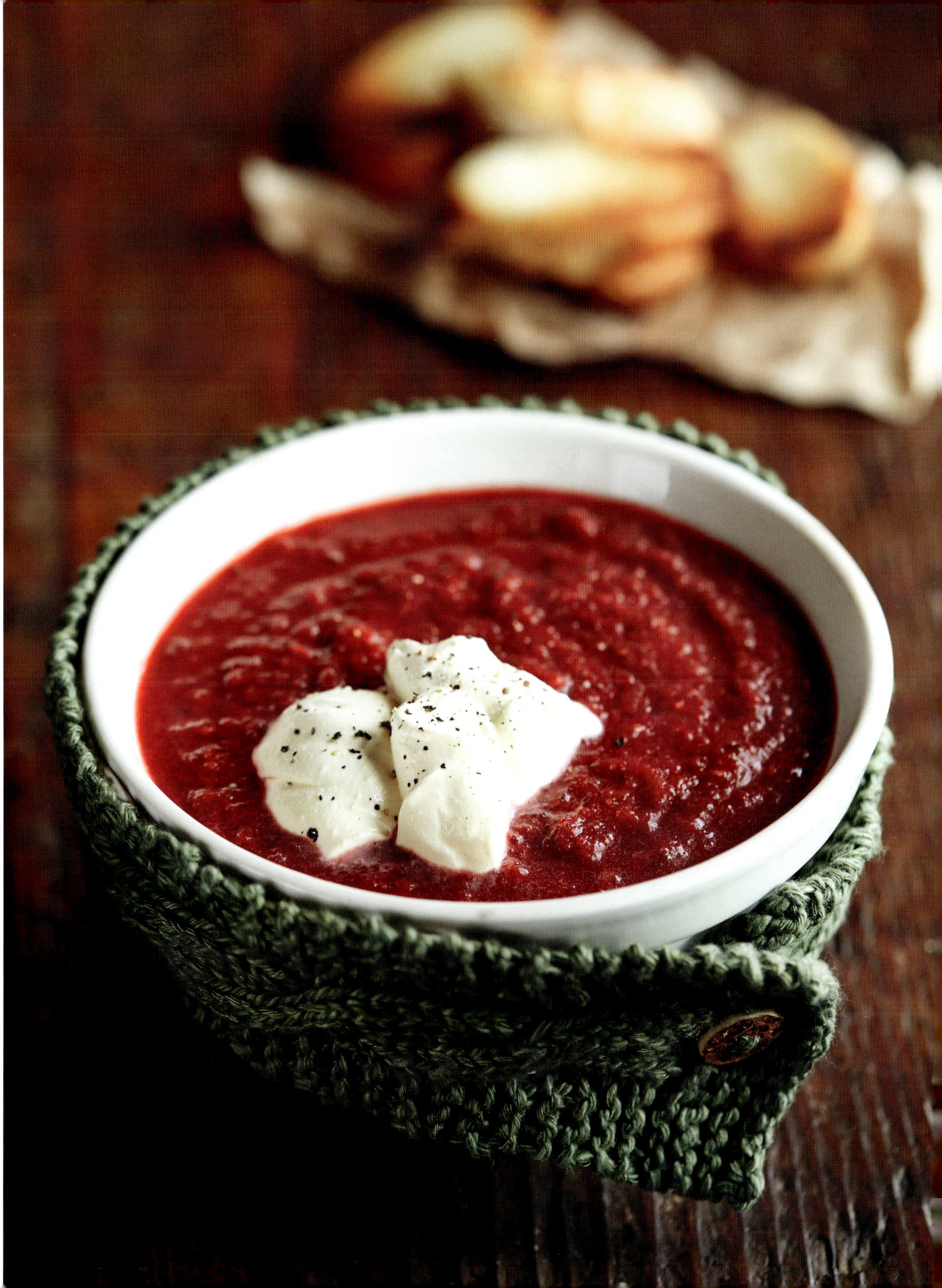

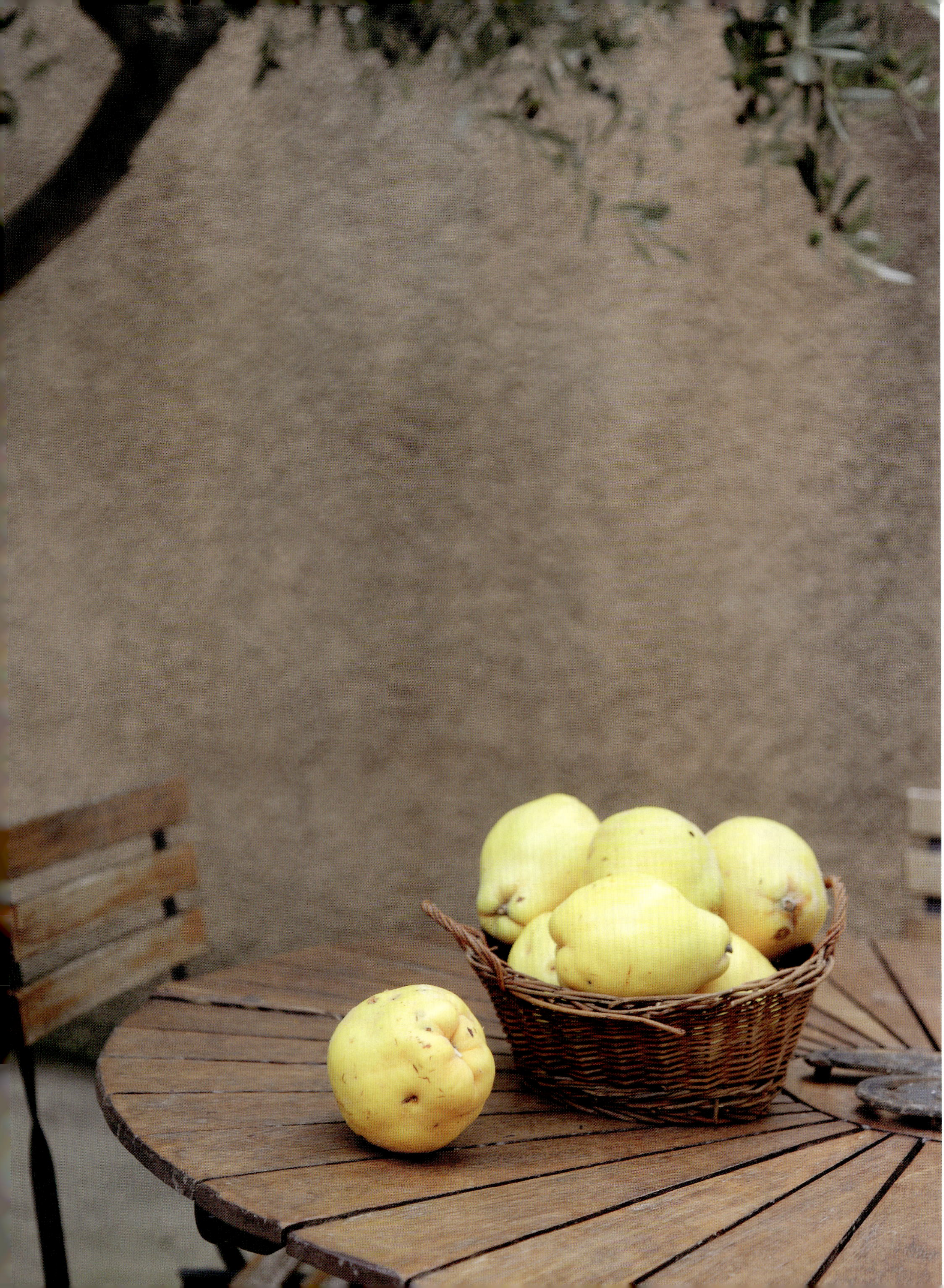

THE QUIRKY QUINCE

"THEY DINED ON MINCE, AND SLICES OF QUINCE, / WHICH THEY ATE WITH A RUNCIBLE SPOON; / AND HAND IN HAND, ON THE EDGE OF THE SAND, / THEY DANCED BY THE LIGHT OF THE MOON."

THE OWL AND THE PUSSYCAT, EDWARD LEAR (1812-1888)

The quince is a fruit that stirs the suppressed hunter-gatherer in me. Like fig trees and blackberry hedges, neglected quince trees grow along my country walking routes, and each autumn I get the distinct impression that the ripe yellow quinces are begging me to pick them. Otherwise they would just keep hanging there like forgotten decorations on a Christmas tree …

But after succumbing to their appeals and carrying the quinces home, I never quite knew what to do with them. This is an exceptionally fragrant fruit – a bowl of golden quinces will make an entire kitchen smell of roses and honey – but using a potential food source just as air freshener goes against my ecological and economic principles. Certain Middle Eastern varieties can apparently be eaten raw, but those along my Provençal walking paths are stubbornly hard and sour in their raw state. I know, I know, my grandmother would have told me to make jam with them, but I have already confessed that jam-making is not one of my talents. Consequently, until fairly recently quinces were to me a more or less useless fruit.

In the meantime I have learned more about the quince (*Cydonia oblonga*) – and now I am one of the biggest fans of this most ancient of fruit. Quinces are even older than apples and pears, and experts believe that this is in fact the first fruit mentioned in the Bible. That's right, the notorious one that Eve was not meant to touch. (Surely one of the softer and sweeter Middle Eastern ones that can be eaten straight off the tree, otherwise Eve and her Adam would still be living happily in their Garden of Eden.)

In Greek mythology too, the many references to apples are possibly errors in translation. The apple of discord that Paris gave Aphrodite (the one that resulted in the Trojan Wars), was probably in fact a quince of discord. And the so-called golden apples that the cunning Hippomenes used to distract the swift Atalanta in order to win his race against her, were also quinces. In this case the quinces did not lead to disasters on the scale of the Fall of Man or a decade of war, but Atalanta was forced to marry Hippomenes and they were both turned into lions. Not exactly a happy ending, is it?

But never fear, the quince has a wealth of good qualities too, like the golden colour of the flesh, which takes on a surprising orange-red shade when cooked for long enough. Or the fragrance that resulted in the ancient Greek custom of having a bridal couple nibble on a quince to ensure sweet breath for that all-important first kiss. The ancient Roman cookbook of Apicius contained recipes for heavenly stewed quince with honey – a combination that remains popular today – as well as the slightly odder pairing of quince and leeks.

It was Charlemagne who brought quinces to France at the beginning of the ninth century where they adapted so well, particularly in the milder southern regions, that sweet quince paste (*pâte de coings*) soon became one of the Thirteen Desserts in the traditional Provençal Christmas dinner. (More on the Thirteen Desserts later.) There is time for one more quirky quince story: Did you know that the word "marmalade", used worldwide for that famous British orange preserve, actually means quince preserve? The Portuguese word for quince is *marmelos*, and the story goes that in 1770 the thrifty wife of a Scottish shopkeeper decided to try and make something of a load of bitter oranges that no-one would buy, by cooking them using a recipe for a type of Portuguese confectionery. The rest of the tale of marmalade is culinary history.

It seems that the poor neglected quince is doomed to be omitted from the Bible, mythology and even preserve recipe books. Perpetually replaced by another fruit, poor thing. But in our kitchen in Provence we welcome it every autumn – and definitely not just as an eco-friendly air freshener.

Chicken with quince and honey
4 SERVINGS

In the fragrant world of Moroccan cuisine, *sarajalo* (the Arabic word for quince) is often used with chicken and other types of meat. If you have never cooked with quince before, this simple Frenchified version of a Moroccan tagine is the perfect place to start.

2 T olive oil | 4 large-ish portions of chicken | 2 large quinces, peeled and cut into chunks | 2 t cinnamon 2 t nutmeg | 2 T honey | 500 ml hot chicken stock | a few coriander leaves | salt and pepper

Heat the olive oil in an ovenproof frying pan (with a lid) and cook the chicken over moderate heat until golden brown. Remove from the heat and remove the chicken with a slotted spoon.

Place the quince in the pan, sprinkle with half the cinnamon and nutmeg, and season with salt and pepper. Stir to combine. Place the chicken pieces on the quince mixture. Sprinkle with the remaining cinnamon and the nutmeg.

Dissolve the honey in the hot chicken stock. Pour into the pan to cover the chicken pieces and the quince. (Reserve any remaining liquid and pour it over if the chicken dries out during cooking.)

Cover the pan and place in a preheated 180 °C oven for about an hour. Remove from the oven as soon as the chicken is cooked and the quince is soft, but not mushy. If there is too much liquid, leave in the oven for another few minutes with the lid off. Snip coriander leaves over the dish and serve with couscous or rice.

Quince cheese (pâte de coings)

To make traditional Provençal quince paste (often called quince cheese), all you need is a few quinces, lots of sugar, a little lemon juice – and the patience of Job. The paste needs to dry out for at least two weeks before you can cut it into blocks and enjoy the sweet treat.

Peel the quinces and remove the pips. Cut into pieces and place in a bowl of lemon juice to prevent the fruit discolouring. Put the peels and pips in a saucepan (these are the healthiest bits, you know), cover with water and boil until the skins soften. Pour through a sieve and reserve the liquid, because this is what you are going to cook the quinces in. Simmer the quinces gently in the liquid until soft. Remove, drain well and process in a food processor. Weigh the processed fruit so that you know how much sugar you need (as much as the weight of the quince). So, for 1 kg quince you will use 1 kg sugar. Put the quince and the sugar into the saucepan and cook over low heat for about an hour – stir frequently to stop the mixture sticking to the pot.

When the sticky paste starts pulling away from the sides of the saucepan, it is ready to be transferred to a rectangular baking tray that has been lined with baking paper. Leave in a cool, dry spot for 15 days or until the paste is dry enough to cut into blocks. Roll the blocks in icing sugar just to make them look pretty – they are quite sweet enough as they are. If your family does not gobble it up in a day, quince cheese will last for weeks in an airtight container.

Right: Chicken with quince and honey

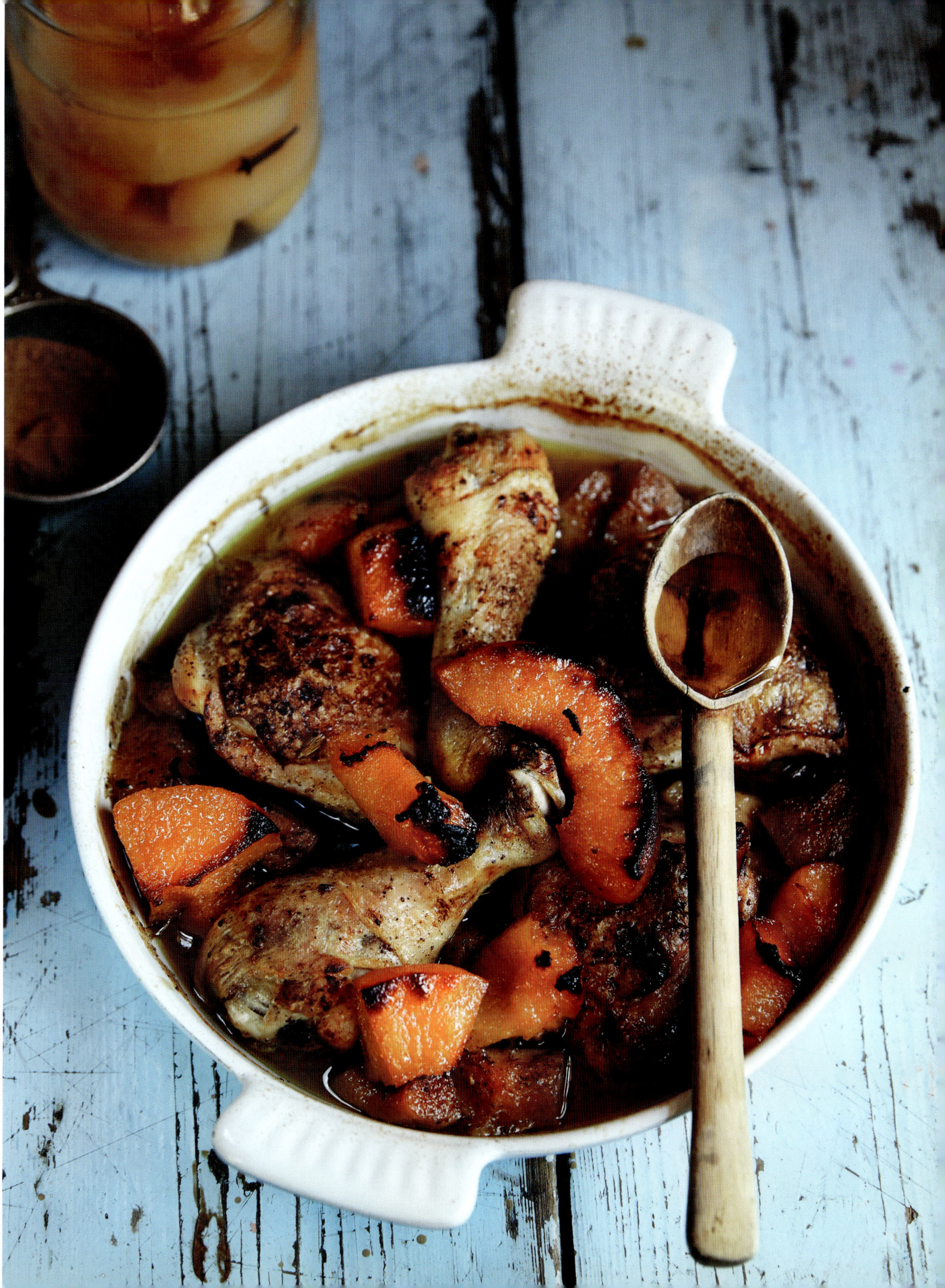

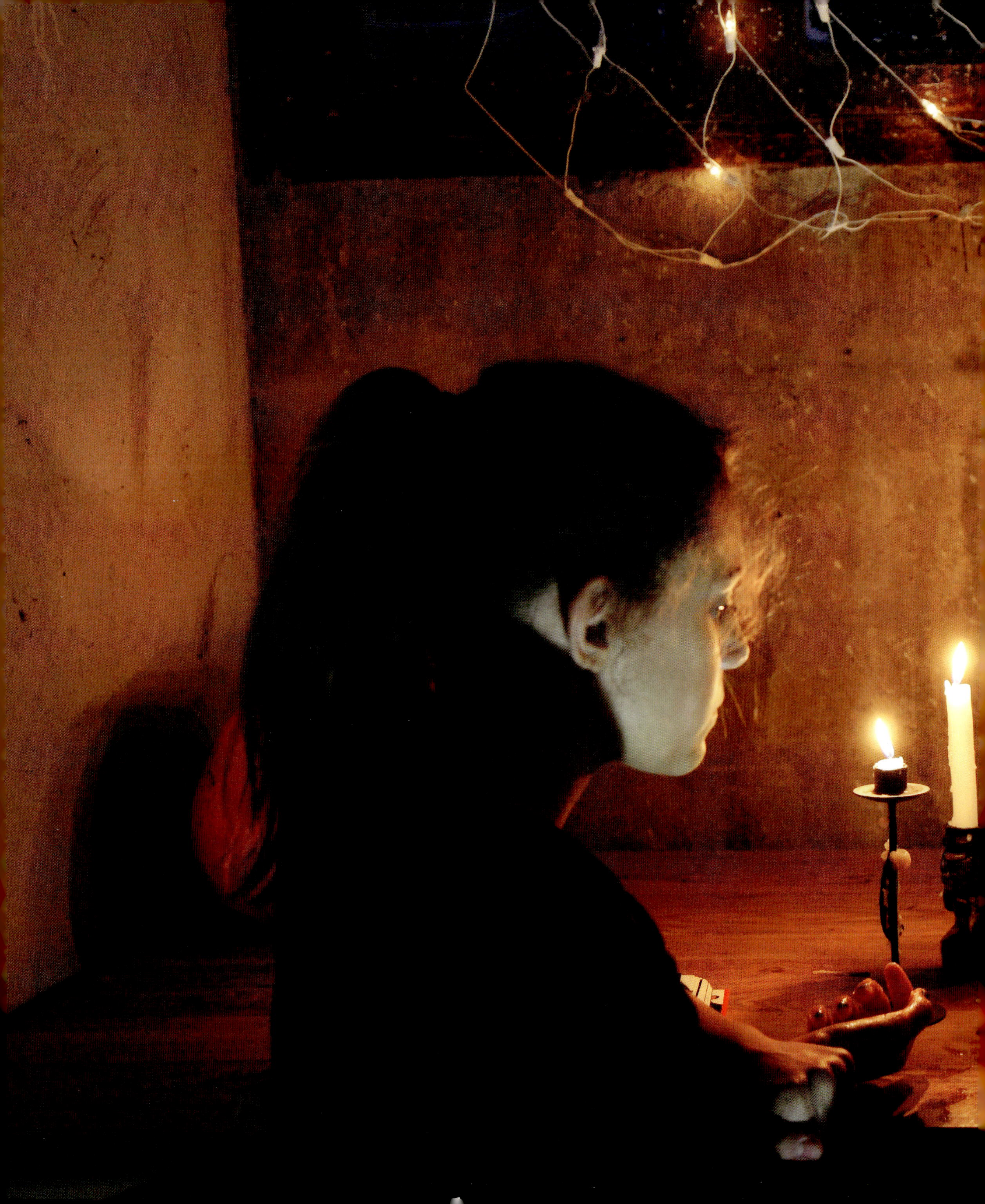

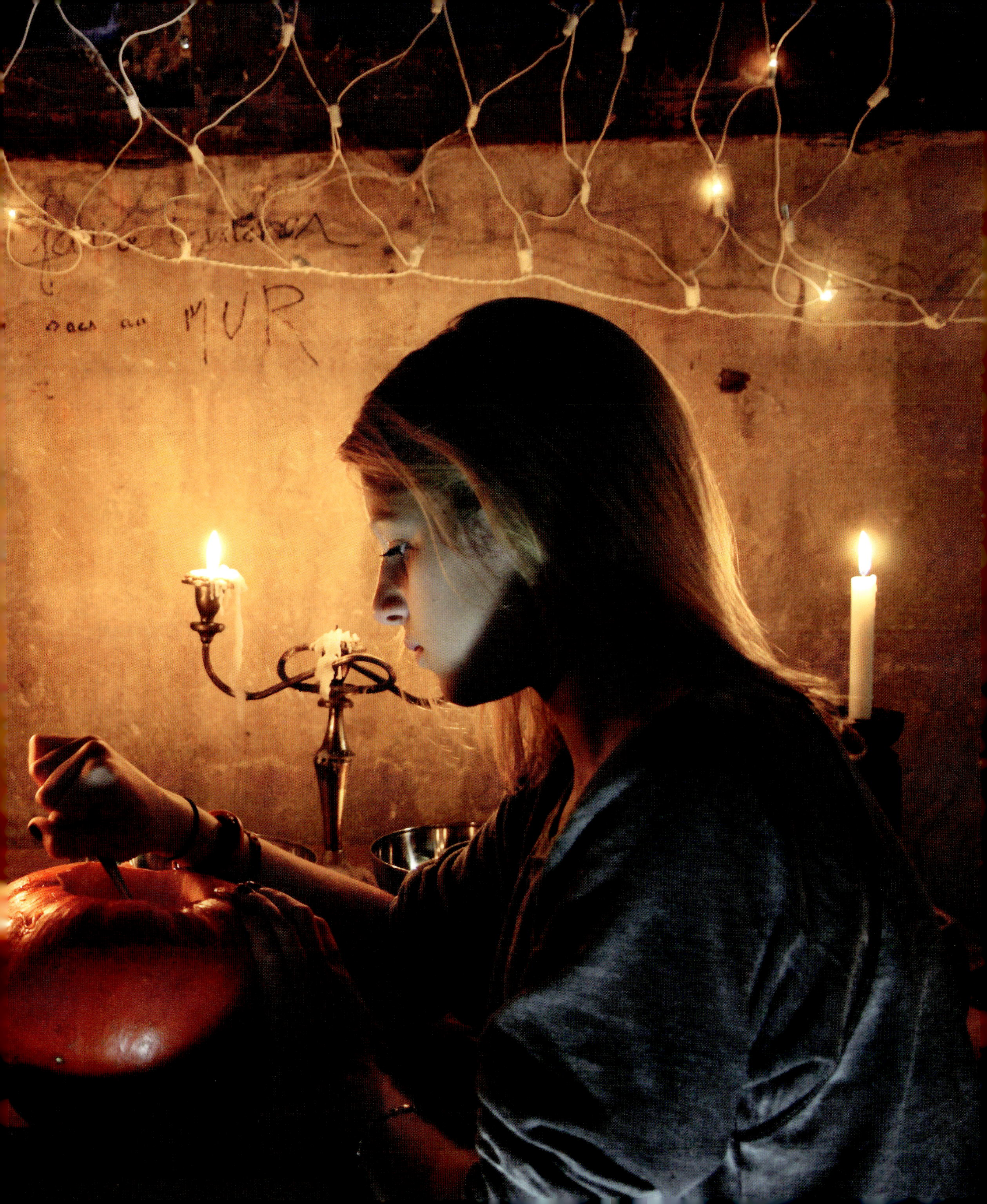
MUR

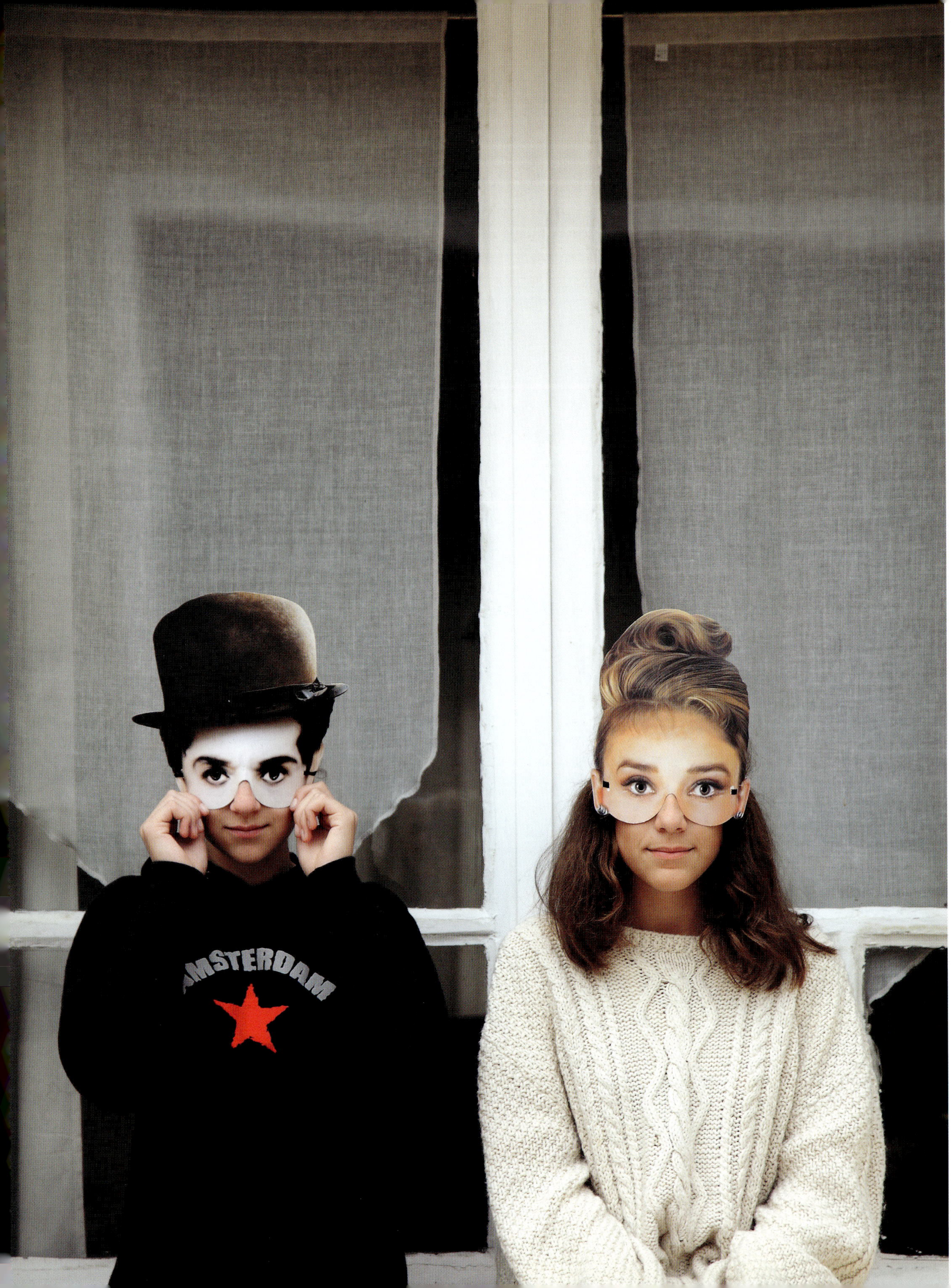
MSTERDAM

THE PLEASURES OF PUMPKIN

"WE HAVE PUMPKINS AT MORNING AND PUMPKINS AT NOON, /
IF IT WERE NOT FOR PUMPKINS WE SHOULD BE UNDOON."

AMERICAN PILGRIM RHYME (CA. 1633)

Pumpkin may not be a traditional Provençal product, but like even the most "traditional" vegetables – tomatoes and aubergines, for example, without which ratatouille and other typically Provençal dishes would be impossible – it was brought here from far-off lands many hundreds of years ago. (And like tomatoes, pumpkins are technically a fruit, but let's not split hairs about such delicious foods.) The point is that today you can find the most wonderful French *potirons*, such as the large, round *rouge vif d'Étampes*, truly a pumpkin among pumpkins.

The orange "fruit" (which can also be white, yellow or green) is one of the oldest agricultural products in America, where Native American tribes cultivated it centuries ago as one of the Three Sisters. Pumpkin (squash), beans and maize (corn) were usually sown together so that the maize provided something for the beans to climb, while the large pumpkin leaves offered shade and protection for the shallow roots of the maize, and the beans ensured there was enough nitrogen in the soil. Truly an example of sisterly symbiosis. The Native Americans also knew how to use every last part of the pumpkin plant. The flesh, pips, leaves and even the flowers were eaten, the hollowed-out shells used as food and water containers, and the flesh was carved into long strips that were woven together and dried as food for the long, hungry winter months. This "pumpkin biltong" could be kept for years – and the bone-dry pumpkin strips were even used for weaving mats.

The early English Pilgrims learned from the local tribes to appreciate the value of *pompion* – what this strange-looking produce was originally called. In winter especially, pumpkin was often all that stood between a Pilgrim family and starvation, as the anonymous verse quoted above will attest. However, the seeds that Columbus brought back from the New World were anything but an overnight sensation in Europe. Pumpkin was mainly used as feed for pigs and other livestock, and was long regarded as a poor man's food.

By the seventeenth century a French cookbook did contain a number of recipes for pumpkin soup with cream, butter and nutmeg – which do not sound terribly meagre – but the best evidence that squash was fairly well known in French vegetable gardens by that time, is probably Charles Perrault's tale *Cendrillon*. A good fairy asks the poor downtrodden Cinderella to fetch a pumpkin from the garden and, with a wave of her wand, transforms it into a fabulous coach – possibly the most original advertising campaign ever created for a fruit or vegetable.

These days a wide variety of pumpkins and squashes are a colourful autumn feature of market tables in Provence. The cheerful orange "fruit" are especially popular around *Toussaint* or All Saints' Day on 1 November, still a public holiday in France, when the graves of loved ones are adorned with orange, yellow and white chrysanthemums. Although Provençal pumpkins are not hollowed out and used as candleholders like the American Halloween tradition – here *potirons* or *citrouilles* are cultivated for food, not as silly stoep decorations – Halloween celebrations have started to make inroads in the French countryside over the past decade. Children in fancy-dress costumes going trick or treating door to door, festivities involving witches and monsters held in town squares, pumpkin soup and pumpkin pies and other pumpkinny dishes that are sold at these events …

In our kitchen too we start conjuring with pumpkin around *Toussaint*. Our children do not like mashed pumpkin or pumpkin soup. Even those favourites of my Afrikaner childhood, sugary pumpkin fritters, leave their French taste buds cold. We tried pumpkin stew and pumpkin curry, we tried everything, believe me, but they refused to take our pumpkin bait. After numerous failed attempts we finally hit on a couple of dishes they would eat with as much relish as those bags of Halloween sweets they go and cadge off the neighbours. And that, as any exasperated parent will tell you, is almost as unbelievable an achievement as turning a pumpkin into a fairy-tale coach!

Right: Sweet pumpkin pie

Roast pumpkin couscous
4-6 SERVINGS

800 g pumpkin (or butternut), peeled and seeds removed | 5 T olive oil | coarse salt and freshly ground pepper 1 onion, finely chopped | 2 cloves garlic, crushed | 500 ml vegetable or chicken stock | 400 g instant couscous | 100 g raisins or sultanas 100 g almonds, chopped and toasted fresh coriander leaves

Preheat the oven to 200 °C. Cube the pumpkin and spread the cubes evenly on a baking tray. Drizzle with 2 T olive oil, season with salt and pepper, and give the tray a good shake to mix everything together. Roast for 30 minutes or until the pumpkin is soft and golden brown. (Shake the pan once or twice during the cooking time.) Keep warm if the pumpkin is cooked before the couscous is ready.

In the meantime, heat the remainder of the olive oil in a saucepan and fry the onion and garlic over moderate heat for only a few minutes, until soft but not brown. Pour over the stock and bring to the boil. Stir in the couscous. Remove the pan from the heat, put the lid on and leave to stand for at least 10 minutes to allow the couscous to swell up.

Remove the lid and fluff up the couscous using a fork. Season to taste with salt and pepper. Add the raisins, almonds and the hot, roasted pumpkin, combine well and snip over the coriander leaves. Serve immediately as a light vegetarian meal or as a side dish with meat – or even the next day as a very tasty pumpkin salad.

Sweet pumpkin pie
6-8 SERVINGS

Pumpkin pie, as American as baseball, has become a sneaky way to turn pumpkin haters into pumpkin eaters in our Provençal kitchen. Our recipe has been Frenchified, which simply means that we use real pumpkin instead of canned American mashed pumpkin, and real milk or cream instead of the cans of evaporated or condensed milk recommended in virtually every American recipe, goodness knows why. Our only short cut is that we usually do not make the shortcrust pastry ourselves – the pastry you can buy here is just too delicious and convenient – but there is nothing to stop you making it yourself.

2 eggs | 2 cups cooked and mashed pumpkin | ¾ cup brown sugar | ½ t each cinnamon, ginger and nutmeg | a pinch of salt | 350 ml full-cream milk (or 150 ml milk mixed with 200 ml cream, for a richer, more decadent flavour) | 250 g shortcrust pastry, bought or home-made

Preheat the oven to 220 °C. Beat the eggs in a large bowl and add the mashed pumpkin, sugar, cinnamon, ginger, nutmeg, salt and milk. Mix well together.

Roll out the pastry into a circle slightly larger than your pie dish, line the dish with the pastry and spoon in the pumpkin mixture. Fold over the overhang of the pastry to form a neat edge right round. Cover the edge with a narrow strip of tinfoil.

Place the pie in the oven and bake for 10 minutes before reducing the heat to 180 °C. Bake for a further 45 minutes or until a toothpick inserted in the middle comes out clean. Remove the foil strip a few minutes before the end of the baking time to enable the crust to brown.

Leave the pie to cool – place in the fridge overnight if you have the willpower and it will taste even better – and serve with whipped cream.

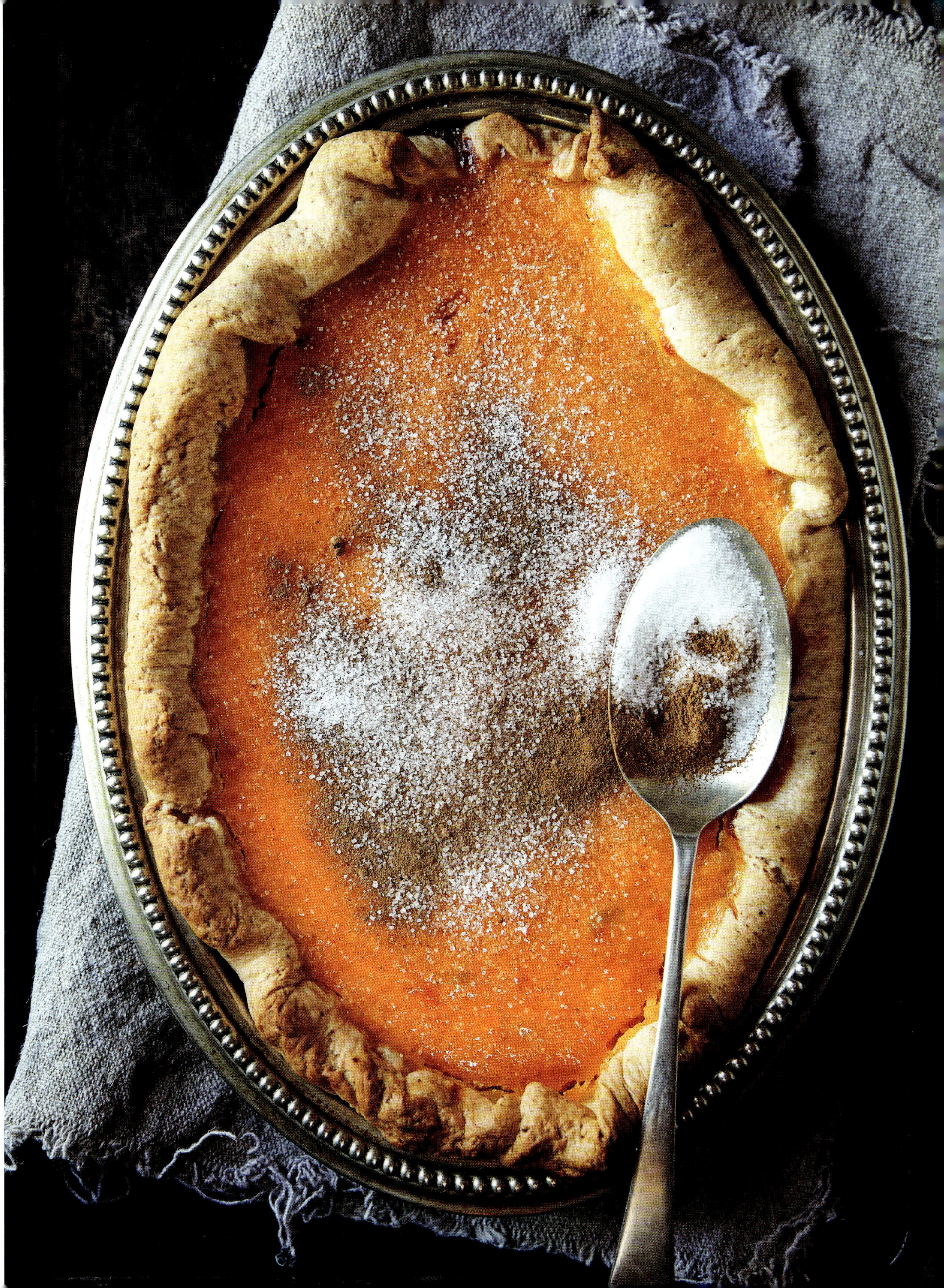

GISELE FREUND
portraits d'artistes
GALERIE LWS
3 NOV - 31 DEC 2011   6 rue Bonaparte 75006 Paris

SAY "PRUNES"!

"PAPA, POTATOES, POULTRY, PRUNES AND PRISM, ARE ALL VERY GOOD WORDS FOR THE LIPS."

CHARLES DICKENS, ENGLISH AUTHOR (1812-1870)

"Anglo-Saxons often treat prunes as little more than a laxative; the French regard them as a jewel in their gastronomic crown." In response to this assertion in the highly entertaining book *1001 Foods You Must Try Before You Die*, all I can say is "Amen!".

The most famous prunes in France, if not the world, are the *pruneaux d'Agen*. While prunes from South Africa and other countries in the New World such as Australia and Argentina have become worthy competitors for the noble prunes of Agen, any Frenchman will assure you that Agen's have that little extra *je ne sais quoi* that trumps all the others. Bigger, juicier, shinier, prettier, sweeter, you name it, these *pruneaux* are the princesses of prunes.

Or perhaps dowager queen would be a more appropriate name. In their younger incarnation, as the beautiful purple-blue plums of the Ente variety, they are pleasingly plump and smooth of complexion like fairy princesses. But after being dried to become prunes, they are covered in wrinkles like noble old ladies.

As is so often the case with food stories – you only have to think of the fruit in the Garden of Eden – this one also had its origins in religion. It was the crusaders returning from the Holy Land who brought the first plums to France, and it was in all likelihood monks who first started drying the fruit, transforming it into heavenly shiny, black prunes. Agen, a city near Bordeaux in the west, has a port on the Garonne River through which the region's prunes were transported to the rest of the country and much further afield. From the church to the ship, that is the story of French prunes; or from crusaders to mariners. During the seventeenth and eighteenth centuries, the latter valued this dried fruit as a welcome sweet treat during long voyages – a treat that also protected them from scurvy.

As the clever Charles Dickens noted, prunes were good not only for your health but also "good for the lips". In the early days of photography, photographers would call out "Say prunes!" from behind their enormous cameras to ensure that their subjects' lips maintained a flattering pout during the long posing process. It was only when automatic cameras speeded up the process considerably – and dental health was so greatly improved that subjects were prepared to have their image recorded for posterity with a broad smile – that the modern "Say cheese!" came into common use.

Nowadays these jewels of the French crown are steeped in Armagnac and other types of alcohol, stuffed with marzipan and used in a number of classic desserts. In our kitchen, where we like to keep things simple, we bake clafoutis with prunes. This is the most delicious but unbelievably simple cherry flan that originates in the Limousin region, though strictly speaking it is no longer a clafoutis if you do not use cherries – then it becomes a *flaugnarde*, another type of traditional fruit-based dessert – but who wants to be pedantic when you are talking about something so delicious? My French relatives and friends make clafoutis using whatever fruit is available.

You are actually not supposed to remove the pips from cherries for clafoutis, because the baked pips contribute to the special taste, but our children refuse point blank to eat a tart with pips in it. To my mind this is one of the biggest advantages of rather using prunes – it is so much easier to remove the pips. You just wiggle the prune back and forth between your fingers and the pip comes out almost by itself. And if you want to make things even easier, you can buy pitted prunes in the first place.

And prunes are not only delicious in puddings. Try our recipe for *porc aux pruneaux* – and if someone at the table wants you to pose for a photo, remember to say "prune". It works in any language, and not just when there are prunes on your plate.

Right: Clafoutis with prunes

Porc au pruneaux de Tours
4 SERVINGS

Even guests who are not too fond of pork usually cannot get enough of this classic from the city of Tours. You can replace the redcurrant jelly with a more local sweet and tangy flavour, such as quince jelly or even plain old apricot jam. The sauce will be a little less French and slightly paler, but taste almost as good.

300 g pitted prunes | 450 ml white wine | 4 thick slices of pork fillet (called filet mignon in France) 2 T flour | 4 T butter | 150 g button mushrooms | 2 T redcurrant jelly 200 ml crème fraîche | a bunch of parsley | salt and pepper

Soak the prunes in the white wine overnight. Place the prunes in a small saucepan along with 300 ml of the wine they were soaked in, and cook over low heat until the prunes are soft.

Roll the pork in the flour, which has been seasoned with salt and pepper. Heat the butter in a large pan and brown the pork lightly on all sides. Add the rest of the wine in which the prunes were soaked to the pan along with the mushrooms. Put the lid on and simmer for about 30 minutes (Turn the meat after 15 minutes.) Remove the meat and keep warm.

Once the prunes are soft, remove from the saucepan using a slotted spoon. Keep warm. Pour the liquid used to cook the prunes, into the pan with the mushrooms. Add the redcurrant jelly and cook rapidly to reduce the sauce. Turn down the heat and stir in the crème fraîche gradually until it is hot. Season with salt and pepper to taste.

Divide the meat and prunes among four plates, pour over the sauce and garnish with chopped parsley. The sweetness of the prunes brings out the best in the creamy mushroom sauce – making this a meal to remember.

Clafoutis with prunes
6-8 SERVINGS

6 eggs | 6 T sugar | 1¼ cups milk 1 t vanilla extract | a pinch of salt ¾ cup flour | 2 cups pitted prunes 2 T icing sugar

Preheat the oven to 180 °C. Beat the eggs, sugar, milk, vanilla and salt together in a bowl. Add the flour and mix well to form a smooth, liquid batter.

Pour the batter into a buttered flan dish and spread the prunes evenly on the top. Bake for approximately 30 minutes, until a golden crust has formed. Stick a toothpick in the middle – if it comes out clean, the clafoutis is done.

Dust with the icing sugar and serve warm with crème fraîche. If there is any left the next day – which does not happen very often in our house – it is just as delicious eaten straight out of the fridge.

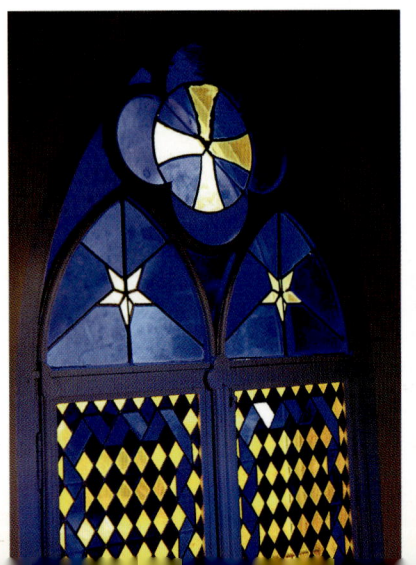

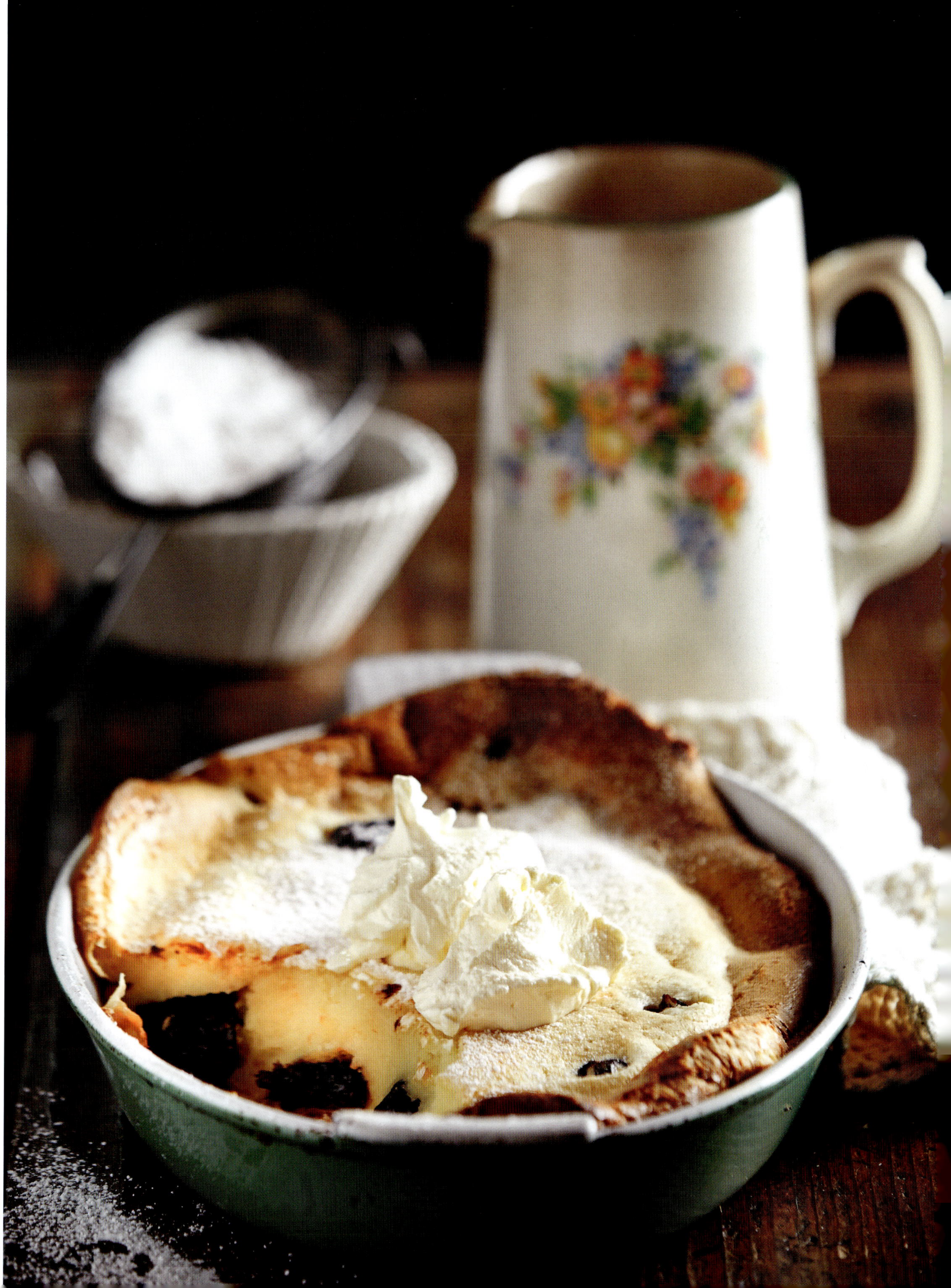

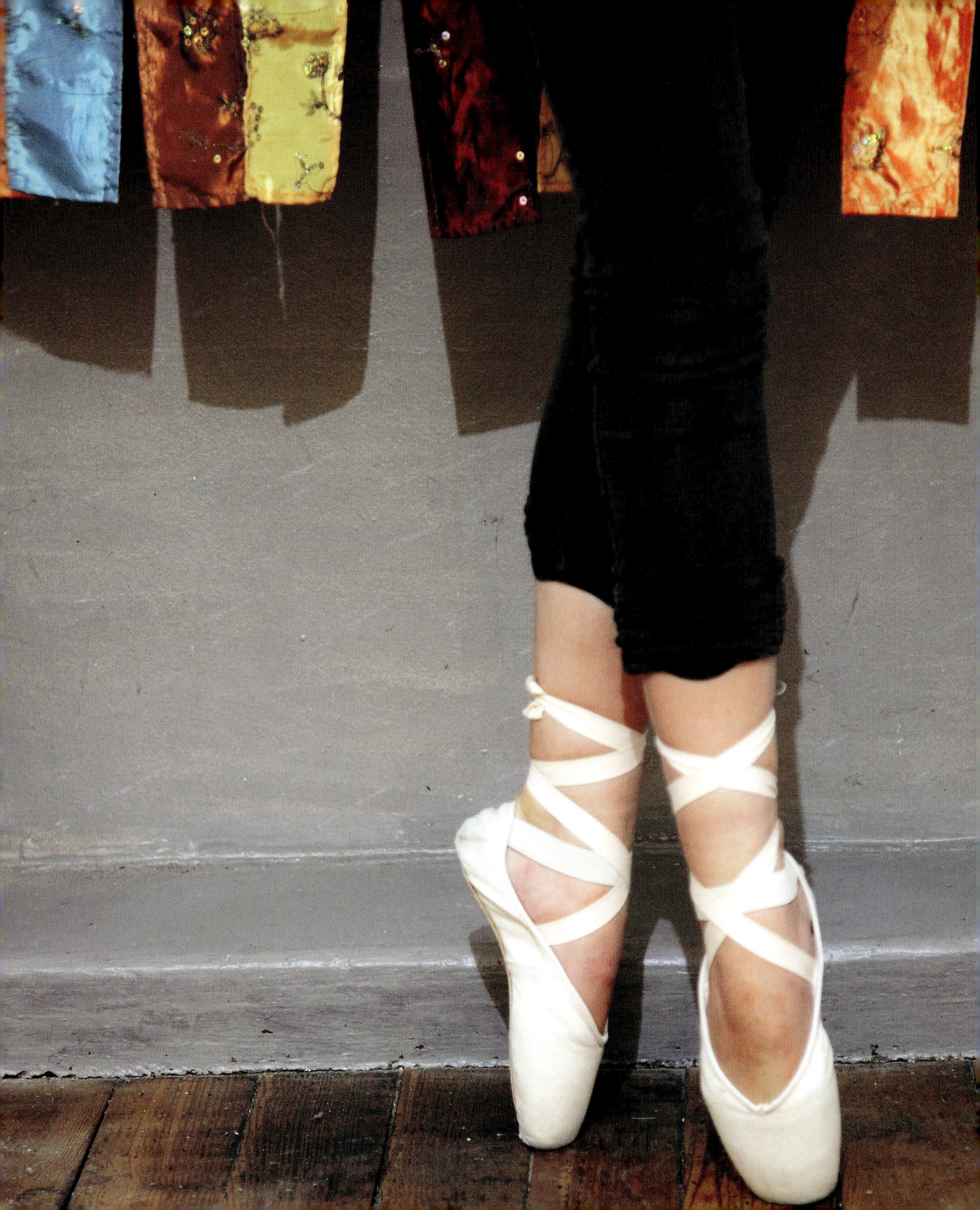

MICHEL BOUQUET
JULIETTE CARRÉ

LE ROI SE MEURT

UNE PIÈCE DE
EUGÈNE IONESCO

MISE EN SCÈNE
GEORGES WERLER

L'ATELIER MUSICAL

VENTE NEUF ET OCCASION
LOCATION / RÉPARATION

andré brunel
FACTEUR DE PIANOS

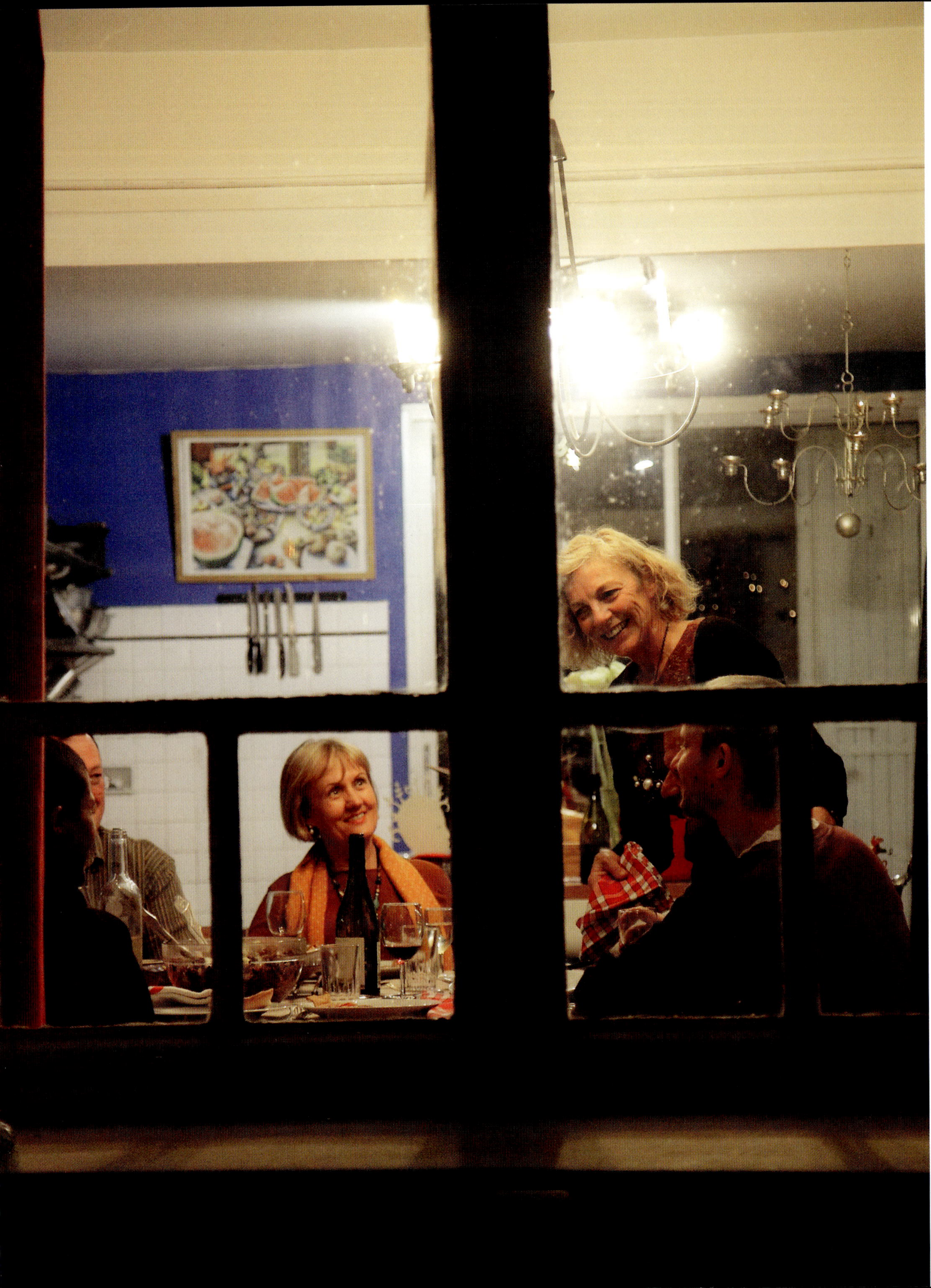

THE BIG CHEESE

"WHEN MY BRAIN BEGINS TO REEL FROM MY LITERARY LABOURS,
I MAKE AN OCCASIONAL CHEESE DIP."

JOHN KENNEDY TOOLE, AMERICAN NOVELIST (1937-1969)

Our friends from other countries are always slightly surprised to learn that even cheese is eaten according to the seasons in France. There are summer cheeses and winter cheeses, just like there are summer vegetables and winter vegetables. The season of the cheese depends on where the cows, goats and ewes graze and what they eat there – because this determines the taste of their milk and ultimately the taste of the cheese made from that milk – as well as on the length of the maturation process.

The most popular winter cheeses are the creamy blues, Roquefort and the like, and the firm sheep's milk cheese such as Ossau-Iraty. Then there are the cow's milk cheeses from the previous year's summer milk that have been allowed to mature gently for a long time (Comté or Beaufort for instance), and the versatile goat's milk cheeses, which can in fact be enjoyed whatever the season. A good example of the latter are the small round cheeses from the town of Banon that are wrapped in chestnut leaves like little gifts.

And then there is the special Mont d'Or (golden hill), available only from autumn until early spring. This fantastic cheese can be spooned like soft and runny ice cream from its round container to conclude a festive meal in the appropriate manner.

Besides these, any kind of melted or baked cheese is a winner when the temperature starts to fall. A firm favourite when the French want to offer their friends a relaxed meal, is Raclette. This is a pale yellow, salty cow's milk cheese with an orangey brown rind, but has also become the name of a social meal during which slices of cheese are melted on an electric grill in the centre of the communal table. Guests melt their own slices of cheese, which are then spread on cooked potatoes and eaten with smoked ham, gherkins and other vegetables and smoked meats.

The idea is similar to the Swiss fondue, but it is easier and above all, less messy. (No bits of meat and breadcrumbs landing in the pot and turning it into a lumpy, unappetising mess.) Tradition has it that this type of meal developed in the French-speaking part of the Swiss Alps, among shepherds and cowherds who would spend the night outside with their animals. Pieces of cheese that happened to be left on stones close to the campfire, started to melt, and because the herdsmen had no wish to waste food, they scraped it off the stones. And so a star meal was born, with a readymade name, because raclette is simply a derivation of the French verb *racler* (to scrape).

Like most French families we have an electric raclette grill, which comes with cute little wooden spatulas so that each guest can *racler* to their heart's content. But if you're a South African without such a grill, bear the origins of raclette in mind next time you're gathered with friends around a large campfire on a cool evening. Wrap some potatoes in tinfoil to bake in the coals, open a jar of gherkins or pickled onions, and melt slices of any firm, salty cheese on clean, flat stones around the fire. This is a welcome variation on the eternal braai – and for those who cannot fathom a fire without a bit of meat to go with it, you could always serve some biltong on the side, I suppose.

In our kitchen we have a repertoire of melted cheese that is second to none. It is very seldom that a good cheese becomes too old to eat; firstly because Alain and the boys demolish cheese faster than I can buy it, and secondly because a cheese really has to become stinkingly off before a Frenchman regards it as "too ripe" for his taste. But on those rare occasions when Alain doesn't fancy a particularly elderly piece of cheese, he would definitely not throw it away. Absolutely not, because it can be melted and used as a filling for a savoury tart or pancakes, or in a rich sauce for steak or pasta, or on a pizza, or …

We also always have grated cheese on hand in the fridge to sprinkle in an omelette or over soup, or as a gratin to top a baked dish, or in white sauce, or … In short, we cannot imagine life without melted cheese. Especially not in winter.

Baked cheese wheel with olives

For an easy starter or snack, press about a dozen green olives, a few stalks of fresh rosemary and thyme and pieces of finely chopped garlic into a round of Camembert cheese. Place on a sheet of baking paper in a shallow baking tray, grind over some pepper and drizzle with olive oil. Bake for a few minutes in a preheated 180 °C oven, until the cheese begins to melt. Serve with baguettes so that each guest can break off a piece of bread and spread the tasty cheese on top.

Baked cheese croquettes with red jam
4 SERVINGS

1 Camembert cheese (or 250 g Brie or similar soft cheese) | 1 T butter 3 T flour | 5 T hot milk | 1 T brandy (optional) | freshly ground pepper | 1 egg | 3 T dried breadcrumbs oil | a little raspberry or redcurrant jam (or mixed red fruit jam)

Cut off the outer rind of the cheese thinly and mash the rest of the cheese with a fork until it has the consistency of soft pâté.

Make a white sauce by heating the butter in a pan and stirring in 2 T flour. Cook over low heat for 1-2 minutes without letting it brown. Stir in the milk and the brandy (if you are using it), and mix well until it forms a thick, smooth sauce. Add a little pepper and leave to cool.

Mix the mashed cheese with the sauce. Dust your hands with flour before rolling small amounts of the cheese mixture between your palms to form about 12 plump croquettes. Beat the eggs with a splash of water and roll the croquettes in it. Mix 1 T flour with the breadcrumbs on a plate or work surface and roll the croquettes in the crumbs.

Heat enough oil in a saucepan to cover the croquettes and deep-fry briefly until golden brown. Drain on a few layers of absorbent kitchen paper. Serve the croquettes with a dollop of red jam on the side as a delicious warm starter.

Quick "cheesecake" with nuts

This is a similar idea to the cheese wheel with olives, but this time you turn a baked round Camembert or Brie into a sweet treat to be enjoyed at the end of a meal. It is a practical and fun way to combine the traditional French cheese board and the dessert that follows into a single course. Combine a variety of roasted chopped nuts, as well as raisins, sultanas, pieces of dried figs or dates or whatever takes your fancy, with enough runny honey to make a sticky mixture. Cut the cheese in half horizontally, spread a thick layer of the nut mixture on the bottom half and replace the top. Push some more nuts and dried fruit into the top of the cheese, drizzle with a little honey and bake for a few minutes at 180 °C until the cheese starts to soften. Pure melted pleasure.

Right: Baked cheese croquettes with red jam

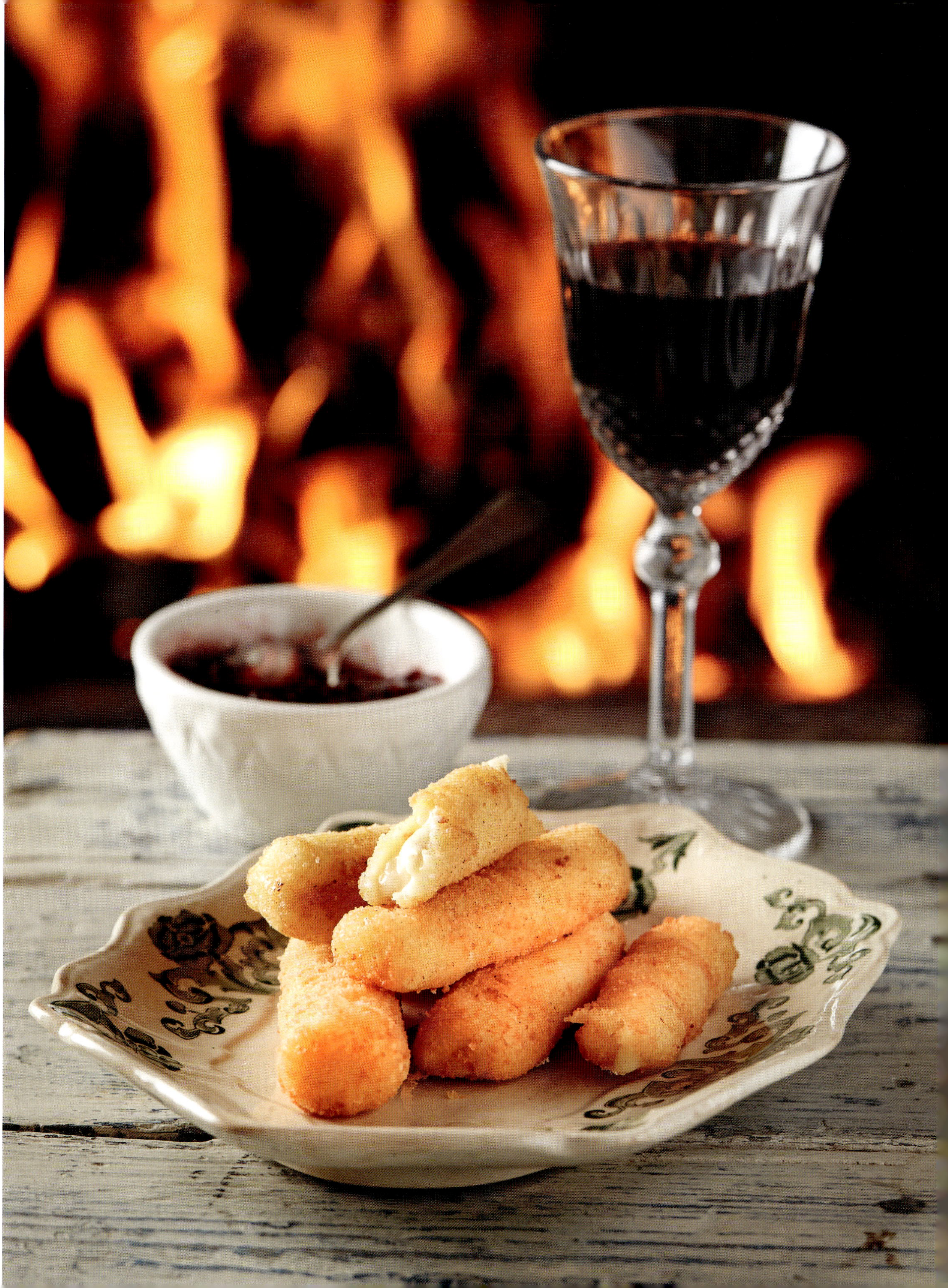

MAIRIE

HIDDEN TREASURES

"WHOSOEVER SAYS TRUFFLE, UTTERS A GRAND WORD, WHICH AWAKENS EROTIC AND GASTRONOMIC IDEAS."

Jean-Anthelme Brillat-Savarin, French food writer (1755-1826)

Every Saturday morning from mid-November to mid-March, one of our sleepy neighbouring villages is transformed into the busiest truffle market in the country. Richerences is an experience on such a winter's market day when the aroma of black truffles hangs in the cold air like incense and deals worth thousands of euros are done between truffle sellers and truffle seekers. The buyers are often professional chefs and restaurant owners from across France – and even further afield in Europe – drawn there by the region's "black gold".

But what is all the fuss about truffles anyway? Are truffles really so special that you would be prepared to pawn your wedding ring to get your hands on them? These are the questions I am often asked by friends who are not from around here. The easiest answer is that I don't have a wedding ring to pawn. Like all couples in France, Alain and I had to get married in our local *mairie* or town hall, and as is always the case if you venture anywhere close to an administrative building in France, there was so much bureaucracy and paperwork involved that we were just too exhausted to bother about rings as well. And once the ceremony was over, we could immediately think of better things to do with our money than to buy rings. Like buy enough fresh truffles for a magnificent once-in-a-lifetime meal …

But on a more serious note. Because truffles are a deadly serious business around here. Recently someone was shot on sight for trespassing on a farmer's truffle grounds – and all the locals took the murderer's side.

What you need to remember though, is that not all truffles are created equal. The black summer truffles from Provence, for instance, are nothing to write home about. The truffles of Burgundy have an agreeable taste but not nearly enough aroma. The white Italian truffles have an unbeatable aroma but not enough taste – or so it is alleged in Provence. (The Italians might not necessarily agree with this view, as you may expect.)

And then you have the renowned Périgord truffle (*Tuber melanosporum*) which, name notwithstanding, has always been more prolific in Provence than in the region of Périgord. In fact, in Provence they have a pet name for it, *rabasse*, the champion truffle in terms of both taste and aroma. By aroma I mean a pungent, earthy, aromatic cloud that can penetrate walls, is virtually impossible to describe, and almost as impossible to forget once you have smelt it. It is almost like sniffing at the underworld, with a hint of sulphur and the deep stirrings of the devil. And yet, it is not an unpleasant smell. Not at all.

In one of my previous books I went so far as to compare *rabasse* to cannabis – not only because of the unmistakable smell that both emit, but also because so many myths and legends have arisen around both that trying them for the first time could be a bit of a disappointment.

If you do not want to spoil your first experience of truffles, do yourself a favour and forget about canned or bottled truffles. You could just as well taste one of those sickly-sweet glacé cherries out of a little plastic container and try to imagine what a fresh cherry from the tree tastes like.

The best way to eat *rabasse* is still the simplest: fresh and raw, cut into slivers and sprinkled with *fleur de sel*. (From the Camargue, of course.) And for this the preserved article simply will not do. For some French truffle recipes you could even use fresh Kalahari truffles rather than canned French ones. Although these South African "desert truffles" may not be stocked in every local supermarket, they are becoming more widely available. If you do replace the *rabasse* in a French recipe with South African truffles, the dish is not going to taste the same, of course. And the aroma will definitely not be the same. But as Alain always exclaims so enthusiastically when we toss together recipes and ingredients from different countries: "*Mélangeons les cultures!*" Let's mix the cultures, indeed. We South Africans certainly are not afraid of multicultural food, are we?

The secret of truffle eggs

Usually I am not a culinary dictator, but for traditional scrambled eggs with truffles you must use the best, freshest farm eggs and the best butter you can lay your hands on. No exceptions. Keep the cheaper eggs and margarine for something else; this is a dish that brooks no compromises. The secret is to store the fresh truffles with the unbroken eggs in an airtight container in the fridge for a few days to allow the aroma of the truffles to permeate the porous eggshells. In fact, we usually pop a few extra eggs in the container as well. A couple of days later we are able to turn the eggs that were not used for the scrambled eggs into a luxurious omelette steeped in the fragrance of truffles – without even a sliver of truffle in the pan.

Or what about truffle honey?

I recently tasted a crèpe filled with Brie and flavoured with truffle honey – and what a delightful experience it was too! The heavenly sweetness of the honey combined with the earthy flavour of truffles was such a surprising taste sensation that I am definitely going to make my own truffle honey as soon as I lay my hands on a truffle again. Follow the instructions for truffle oil, replacing the oil with honey, if you want to give your taste buds a wonderful surprise.

Deluxe scrambled eggs
4 SERVINGS

1-2 fresh truffles | 12 eggs | salted butter | freshly ground black pepper

Remove the truffle(s) from the container in which it was stored for a few days with the eggs. Rinse, brush clean, dry and then peel off the hard outer skin using a vegetable peeler. (Reserve the peels for making your own truffle oil.) Shave or slice the truffle(s) into paper-thin slices.

Break the eggs into a bowl with a lid, beat, add the truffle slices, a few knobs of butter and a little ground pepper. Mix well to combine before putting the mixture in the fridge for a further 1-2 hours so that the eggs become even more fragrant. (Put the lid on to prevent tomorrow's milk and tomatoes from smelling like truffles.)

Heat a knob of butter in a heavy-based pan. Add the egg mixture and stir with a wooden spoon over a very low heat. Remove from the heat as soon as the eggs start to set, but are still moist and creamy, and serve immediately with fresh baguette.

Make your own truffle oil

And use it to make a simple green salad taste like a million bucks. Or add a few drops to a bowl of ordinary cauliflower or pumpkin soup if you want to taste something incredible. Just remember to use truffle oil sparingly. In much the same way that a few drops of French perfume are better than clouds of cheap fragrance, so too just a drop or two of truffle oil will impart a flavour that is far superior to lashings of other flavourings.

If you are fortunate enough to get hold of a fresh truffle or two, keep the pieces of hard skin that you have to peel off and pop them into some of your very best olive oil. (The less oil you use, the stronger the scent of truffles will be.) Pour into a bottle with a tight-fitting lid. Filter the oil after about two weeks to remove the pieces of peel before bacteria can develop – and then you can enjoy your own truffle oil sprinkled over your food.

Right: Deluxe scrambled eggs

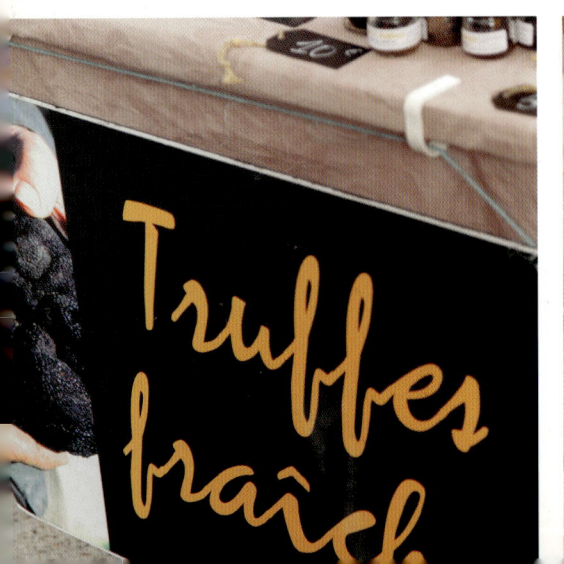

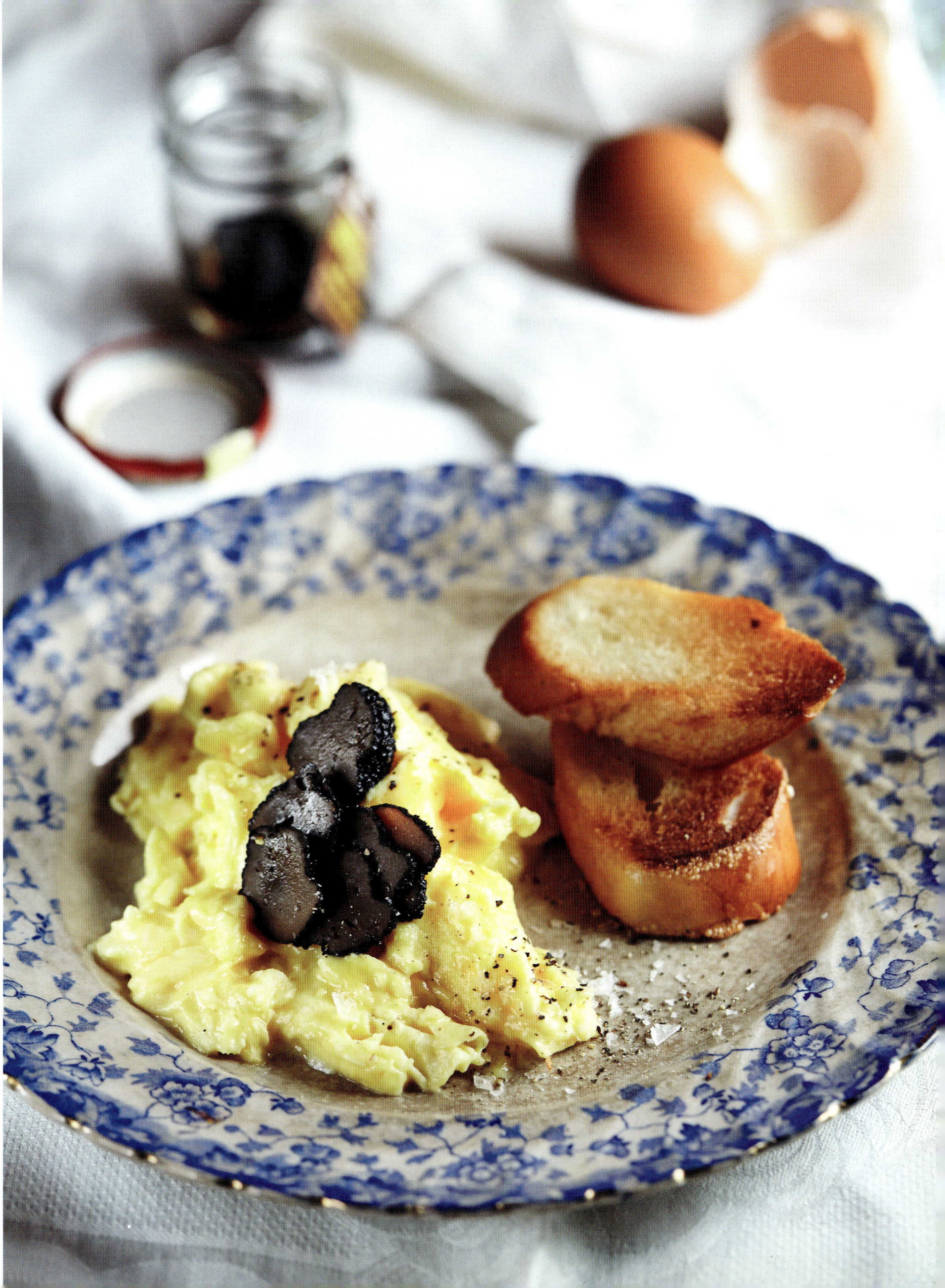

VEND VÉLO ENFANT
16 pouces (4-6 ans)
40 €
contrôle technique OK

KAKI

LE COMPTOIR DE MATHILDE

ÉPICERIE FINE

COMESTIBLES

HUILE d'OLIVE
OLIVES de BOUCHE
NOUGÂTS
DRAGÉES
CARAMELS

Tous les jours sur vos Marchés

Spécialité BABA au Rhum de Mathilde

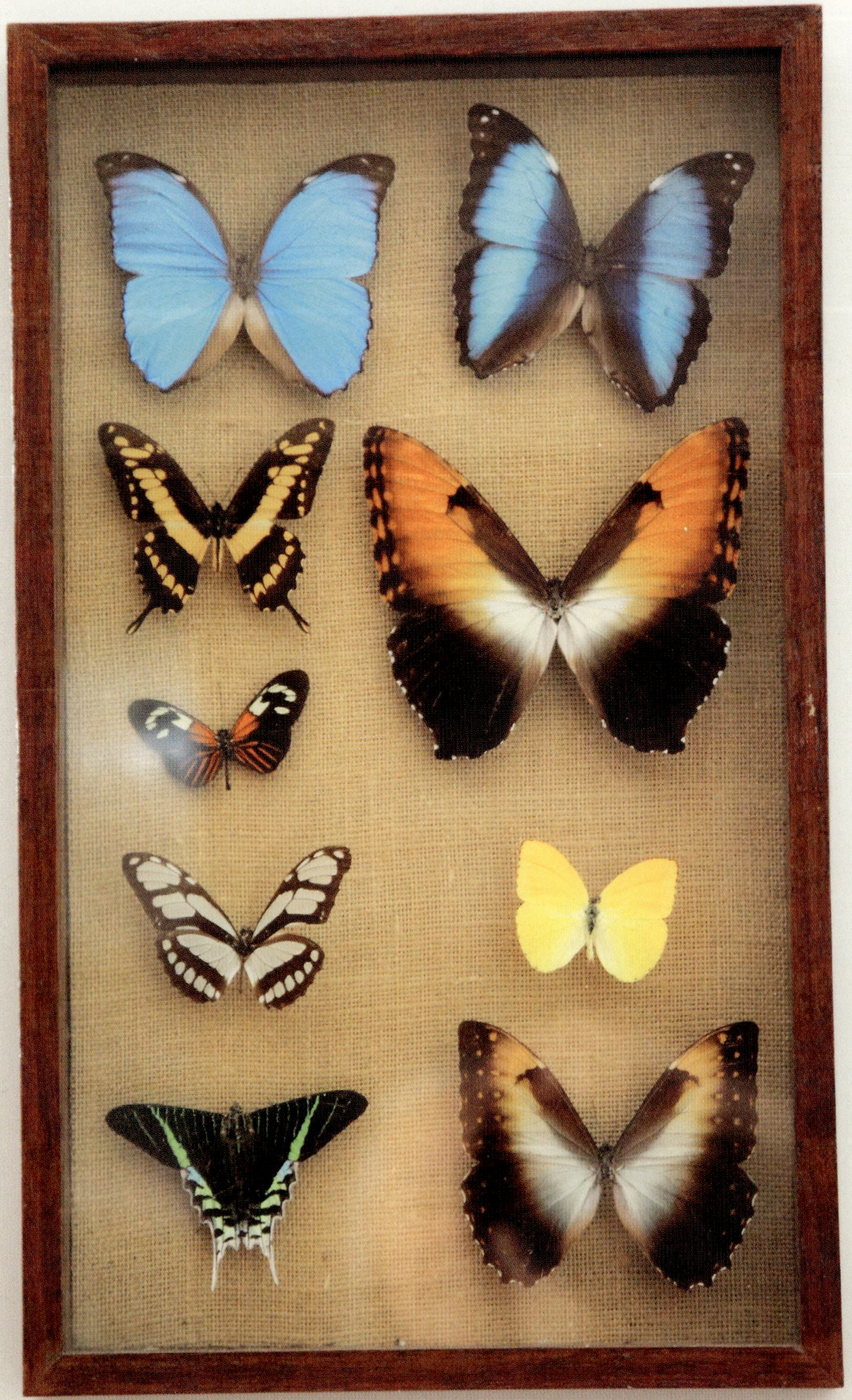

GAME ON

"PEOPLE NEVER LIE SO MUCH AS AFTER A HUNT, DURING A WAR OR BEFORE AN ELECTION."

OTTO VON BISMARCK, GERMAN STATESMAN (1815-1898)

Soon after landing up in Provence almost twenty years ago, I was awoken early one Sunday morning to the sound of ear-splitting gunshots. Like any normal paranoid South African, I immediately assumed criminal activity and leapt out of bed. While my common sense tried to convince me that bloody gang warfare was extremely unlikely in a sleepy little French town, I peered terrified out into the street. No sign of bloodshed in the narrow cobbled streets. No sign of life either, to tell you the truth. The other townsfolk had slept peacefully through the massacre.

Later that day I realised that there had indeed been a massacre, only not of human beings. It was only the start of the French hunting season. Hunting is principally a winter sport here, as it is in South Africa, but unlike South Africans, French hunters shoot buck, wild pigs, rabbits, birds; in short, anything that flies, jumps or scurries and is stupid enough to cross a hunter's path.

Since moving out of town, it no longer sounds like gang warfare in the neighbourhood on Sunday mornings. Now it sounds like we are trapped in Sarajevo or Syria, as if full-scale war is being waged in the vineyards surrounding the house. On those mornings I prefer to lure the cats indoors so the hunters don't confuse them with small game – and I always wear a bright red scarf on my walk so that I am not mistaken for big game.

We are not a family of hunters but our hunting neighbours sometimes give us a pheasant or other type of game bird. To apologise for disturbing our sleep every Sunday morning, I would like to believe, but probably because they hunt so indiscriminately that they do not know what to do with all the kill. The first time it happened, I hadn't a clue what to do with the beautiful feathered offering on the kitchen table in any case. As a child of the city I had never even plucked the feathers of a common or garden chicken. And how was I supposed to know that a pheasant is meant to be hung for days by the neck, apparently to improve the flavour and texture of the meat, before its lovely feathers are removed?

Mia on the other hand, scarcely eight years old at the time, pulled the bird towards her and calmly started plucking. It must have been her French grandmother's genes, I immediately concluded. If it had been a gift from the Afrikaans side, then it had skipped a generation, straight over me, who could only stare open-mouthed in admiration at my child.

Just for the record: We cooked the pheasant gently in wine until the pale breast meat was almost creamy with deliciousness – even though we did not hang it beforehand. The flesh of game birds is usually so tasty that you do not need complicated recipes or fancy techniques. And fortunately, smaller game birds like quails are bred quite widely these days so you can buy them ready plucked.

Although my biggest culinary objection to quails has nothing to do with feathers: It was all those tiny bones that put me off cooking quails for guests for years. The French generally do not like eating with their hands – and quails, like crayfish, are something I can eat only with my hands. But my friend Lynn, another *Boeremeisie* who lost her heart to a Frenchman, assured me that she regularly served quail to guests in her stylish guesthouse – and then proceeded to demonstrate with great style how much easier and more sociable it was to eat such a dish with one's hands. And guess what? They would take to the idea fairly easily.

Lynn's quails with dried fruit
4 SERVINGS

For our TV cookery series, Lynn made this dish with dried cranberries, ensuring fantastic flavour, but it will still be a hit if you replace the cranberries with raisins, sultanas, chopped dried apricots or a mixture of dried fruit. You can also stuff the quails with a mixture of breadcrumbs, fried shallots, a handful of cranberries and whatever takes your fancy before putting them in the pot.

200 g bacon, cubed | 2 onions, finely chopped | 2-3 cloves garlic, finely chopped | 4 quails | 200 g dried cranberries | 250 ml white wine (or apple cider) | 500 ml vegetable stock salt and pepper | parsley

Fry the bacon in a heavy-based saucepan until it crisps up. Add the onion and garlic and cook until soft but not brown. Add the quails (with or without the stuffing) and the cranberries, pour over the wine and enough vegetable stock to make sure everything is nicely moist. Season with salt and pepper and chopped fresh parsley.

Simmer gently for about an hour over low heat. Add a little more stock if it starts looking dry. Once the quails are cooked, remove from the saucepan and place on an ovenproof tray. Roast the quails under the grill element of your oven for about 5 minutes until they are golden brown. Spoon the berry sauce over the quails and serve with rice or couscous.

En papillote with herbs and garlic

The simpler, the better – this remains the best advice for preparing small game birds. The meat is so flavourful that it really does not need complicated or pretentious sauces. Stuff a partridge or young pheasant with herbs and garlic, wrap a rasher or two of bacon around the body to make sure it does not dry out, and wrap snugly in tinfoil or baking paper. If the pheasant looks a bit big to be parcelled up *en papillote*, cut the bird in half (or ask your butcher to do it), lie the portion on its side and press the herbs and garlic into the hollow on top before wrapping up the parcel. Then bake in a moderate oven until the meat has cooked in its own juices. The cooking time will depend on the age and "gaminess" of the bird. In France this could be less than half an hour, but according to my South African cooking friends, it needs an hour or two – probably because, like almost anything I can think of, birds in Africa are just a bit wilder and gamier than in Europe. The juices that remain in the foil package after the birds are removed, should be poured over the meat before it is served. And feel free to use your hands so you can suck every last little bit of meat off the bones!

Right: Lynn's quails with dried fruit

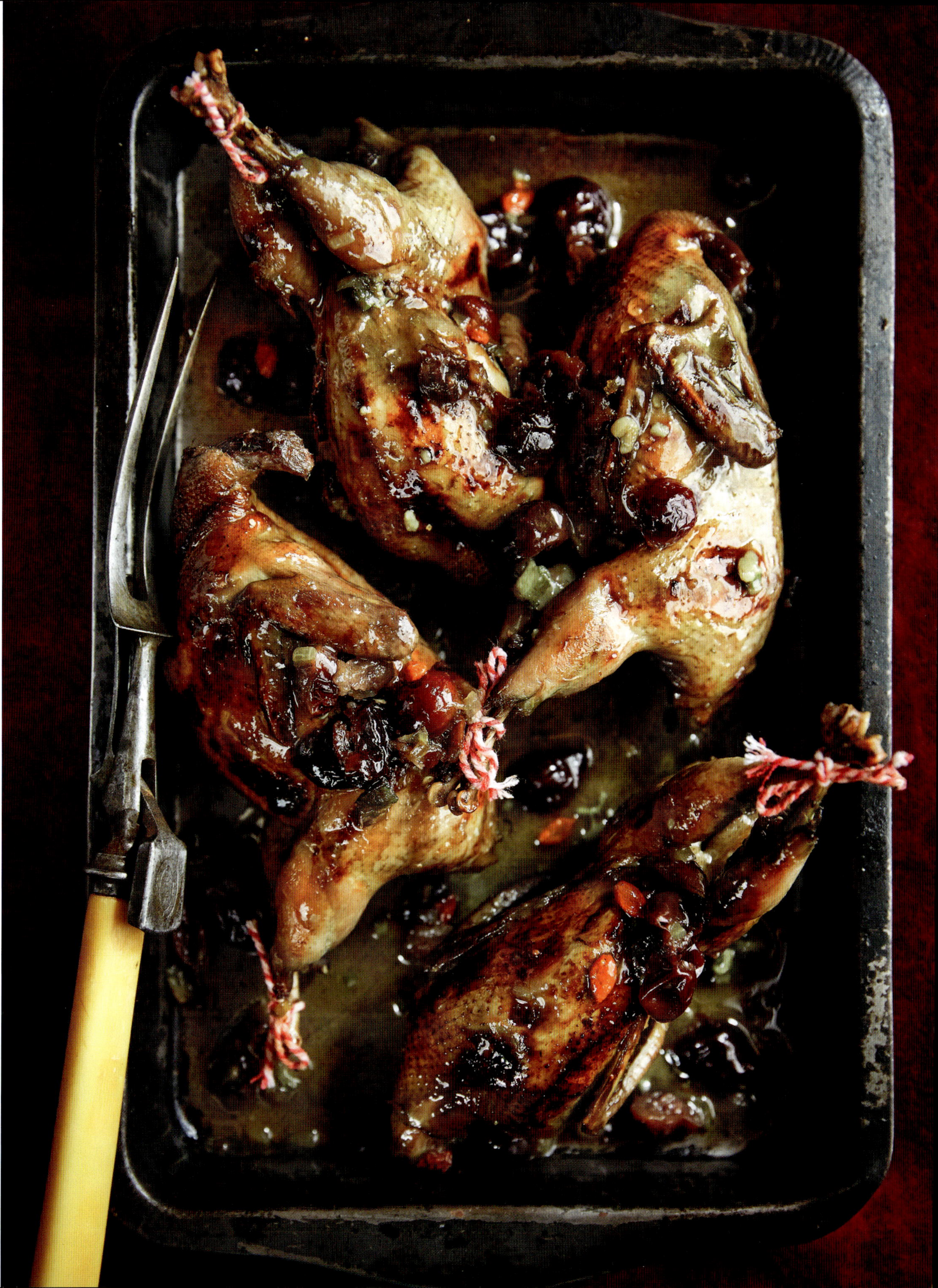

OIGNONS
GARNITURE
2€ le Sachet 300 gr
AMANDINE
AMANDINES NON TRAITEES

AIL ROSE de LAUTREC
1Kg 12€
ECHALOTES
AMANDINE
CITRON
SPUNTA DES CEVENNES
RATTES
BINTJE

PROUD OF POTATOES

"WHAT I SAY IS THAT, IF A FELLOW REALLY LIKES POTATOES, HE MUST BE A PRETTY DECENT SORT OF FELLOW."

A.A. MILNE, BRITISH AUTHOR OF CHILDREN'S BOOKS (1882-1956)

Potatoes have caused fierce arguments in our home. And it has nothing to do with the pronunciation – "You like potato and I like potahto" – that Ira Gershwin wrote the well-known song about.

Every time we start preparing a meal and I ask what vegetables we should serve with the meat, Alain or one of the children will point at the potatoes next to the meat: "But we already have vegetables!" But as far as I am concerned potatoes count as starch (like bread, rice and pasta) and not as one of the five vegetables one is supposed to consume every day. I know that botanically the potato is classified as a vegetable, but like most mothers I am on the side of the dieticians, who regard it as a starch. End of story.

Well, not really. It is an argument I cannot win. The other five members of the family form a democratic majority – and they are all more French than I am. The French have for generations regarded the potato as an exceptionally versatile *vegetable*. Not starch. And when you see what French cooks can do with this modest tuber, you begin to understand the love affair.

But like most other types of food introduced from the New World, it was not exactly a case of love at first sight. On the contrary, until the eighteenth century it was illegal to cultivate potatoes because this malicious plant was believed to cause leprosy, syphilis, sterility, lust and all sorts of other unmentionable evils.

Until one Antoine-Augustin Parmentier (1737-1813) – pharmacist, dietician and later also health inspector for Napoleon – saved the reputation of the potato almost single-handedly.

As a Prussian prisoner of war, Parmentier had had to eat potatoes to survive, and on his return to France he became a lifelong campaigner for the honour of the potato. His marketing techniques could teach modern advertising companies a thing or two. For instance, he gave Queen Marie-Antoinette potato blossoms to wear in her hair – which naturally soon led to a new fashion at court. The story also goes that he would have his potato crops protected by armed guards during the day – to convince the locals that this was an extremely valuable crop – only to call off the guards at night so that any acquisitive or inquisitive person could come and "steal" the desirable potatoes.

Today, Parmentier's name lives on worldwide in gastronomy, with many potato dishes named after him. *Pommes Parmentier* are potatoes that are cubed and fried in butter; *potage Parmentier* is a thick potato and leek soup; and *hachis Parmentier*, similar to the English shepherd's pie, is a dish of savoury mince that is cooked, covered with a layer of mashed potato and baked quickly to give the potato a delicious golden crust.

In France it is virtually impossible to say *pomme de terre* without thinking of Parmentier.

But just as a chicken is never just a chicken in a land of gastronomes, a potato can never simply be a potato. There are ordinary chickens that can be found in any yard, and then there is the aristocratic Bresse chicken, which the best cooks regard as the undisputed king of chickens. So too with potatoes. Of the hundreds of varieties of potato grown around the world, the French *ratte* has been singled out for gastronomic glory for more than a century.

Ratte gets its name from the nasty rodent that its long, narrow shape may remind you of, but there is certainly nothing ratty about its taste or reputation. The texture is firm enough not to disintegrate on cooking, but silky smooth on the tongue with a slightly nutty taste. This is the noble potato recommended by great chefs for classics such as *gratin dauphinois*. Our family regularly enjoys this dish – even though it is not always made with the prince of potatoes – and sometimes I enjoy it so much that I do not even mind if there are no "real vegetables" on my plate.

Right: Gratin dauphinois

Which potatoes for which dish?

A potato is never just a potato. An important distinction is made between floury potatoes and waxy ones. The former contain more starch, making them fluffy and liable to break up when boiled, and are therefore more suitable for making mashed potatoes, baked and fried potatoes, as well as potato chips or *frites*. Waxy potatoes, on the other hand, contain less starch, retain their shape better when boiled and are ideal for dishes like *gratin dauphinois* in which potato slices need to remain whole and firm. If you are not sure, a simple test is to place the potato in a solution of one part salt to eleven parts water. Floury potatoes will sink, while waxy ones will float.

Gratin dauphinois
6 SERVINGS

1 clove garlic, peeled and cut in half 80 g butter | 1 kg waxy potatoes, peeled and thinly sliced | freshly grated nutmeg | 350 ml hot milk 250 ml pouring cream | salt and pepper

Rub the inside of an ovenproof ceramic casserole dish with the garlic clove. Also grease the dish with a little of the butter. Cover the base with a layer of potato slices. Season with salt, pepper and nutmeg. Place another layer of potato slices on top of the first and season again. Continue layering until you have used all the potato slices.

Mix the hot milk and cream. Pour it over the potatoes until they are almost covered with the liquid. Dot with butter and bake in a preheated 180 °C oven for at least an hour, or until the potatoes are soft when tested with a sharp knife.

Increase the oven temperature to 200 °C and bake for a further 5-10 minutes, until the top becomes golden brown. Serve in the casserole to remain true to the name of the dish, a *gratin*. The idea is to *grater* (scratch or scrape) the dish to get at the last bits of food on the bottom.

Provençal potato salad
4-6 SERVINGS

This salad is perfect for a cooler day when a hungry body craves carbohydrates. Toss in a tin of tuna and it becomes a delicious light meal.

1 kg baby potatoes (with different coloured skins if possible: brown, purple and red, to make the salad look prettier) | 1 clove garlic, crushed 1 T capers | ¼ cup green olives, pitted and halved | a handful of chopped parsley

Cook the potatoes in their skins in a large pot of salted water for about 15 minutes until cooked but still firm. Drain and leave to cool just long enough so you can touch them without burning your fingers. If the potatoes are small enough, leave them whole; otherwise cut them in half or into quarters.

Put the hot potatoes into a large glass bowl with the rest of the ingredients and pour over a Provençal vinaigrette (add mashed anchovies to ordinary vinaigrette). The potatoes absorb the dressing better while they are warm, but after that you can leave the salad to cool and serve it at room temperature. If you want to add the tuna, do so just before you serve the salad.

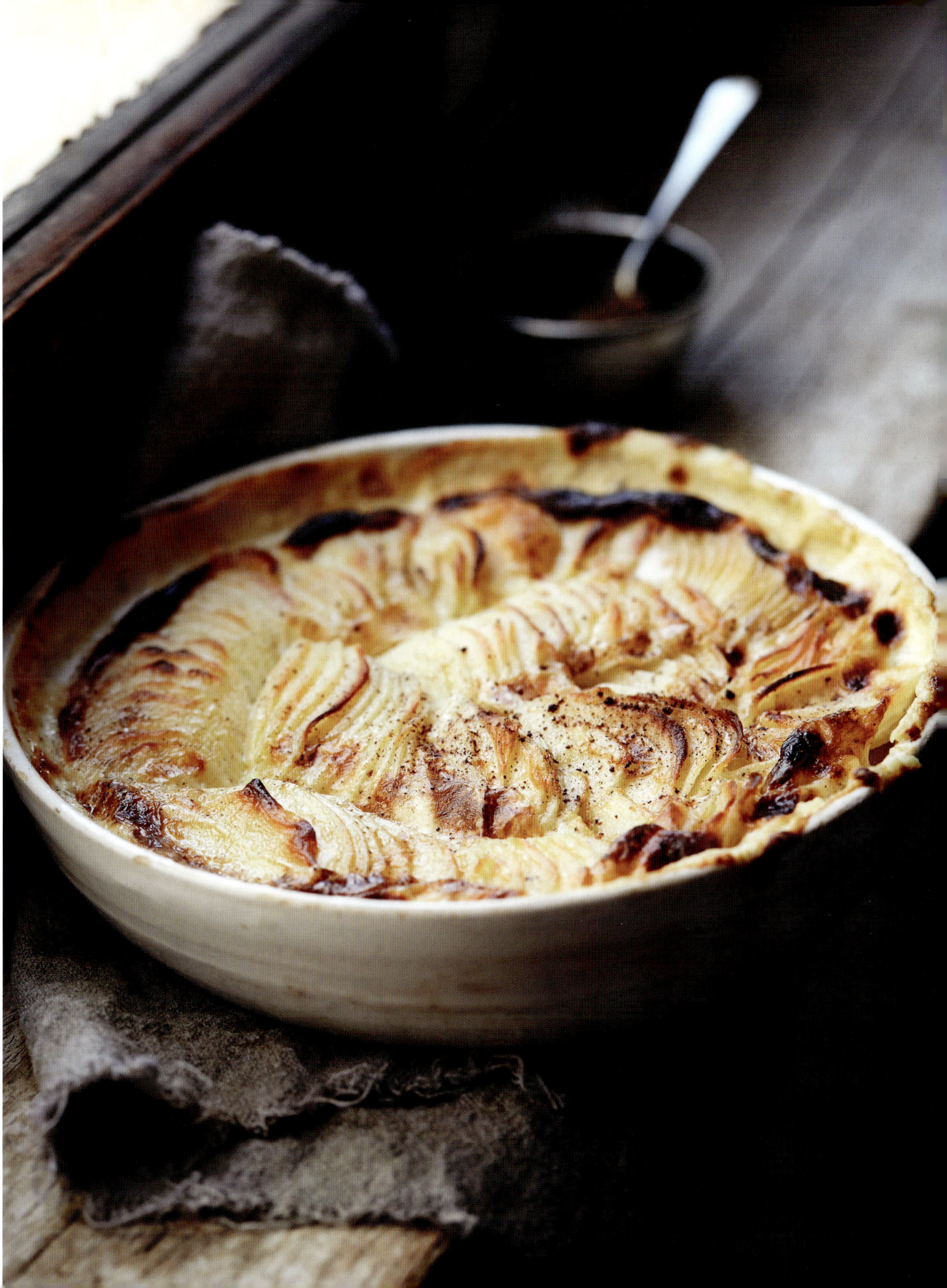

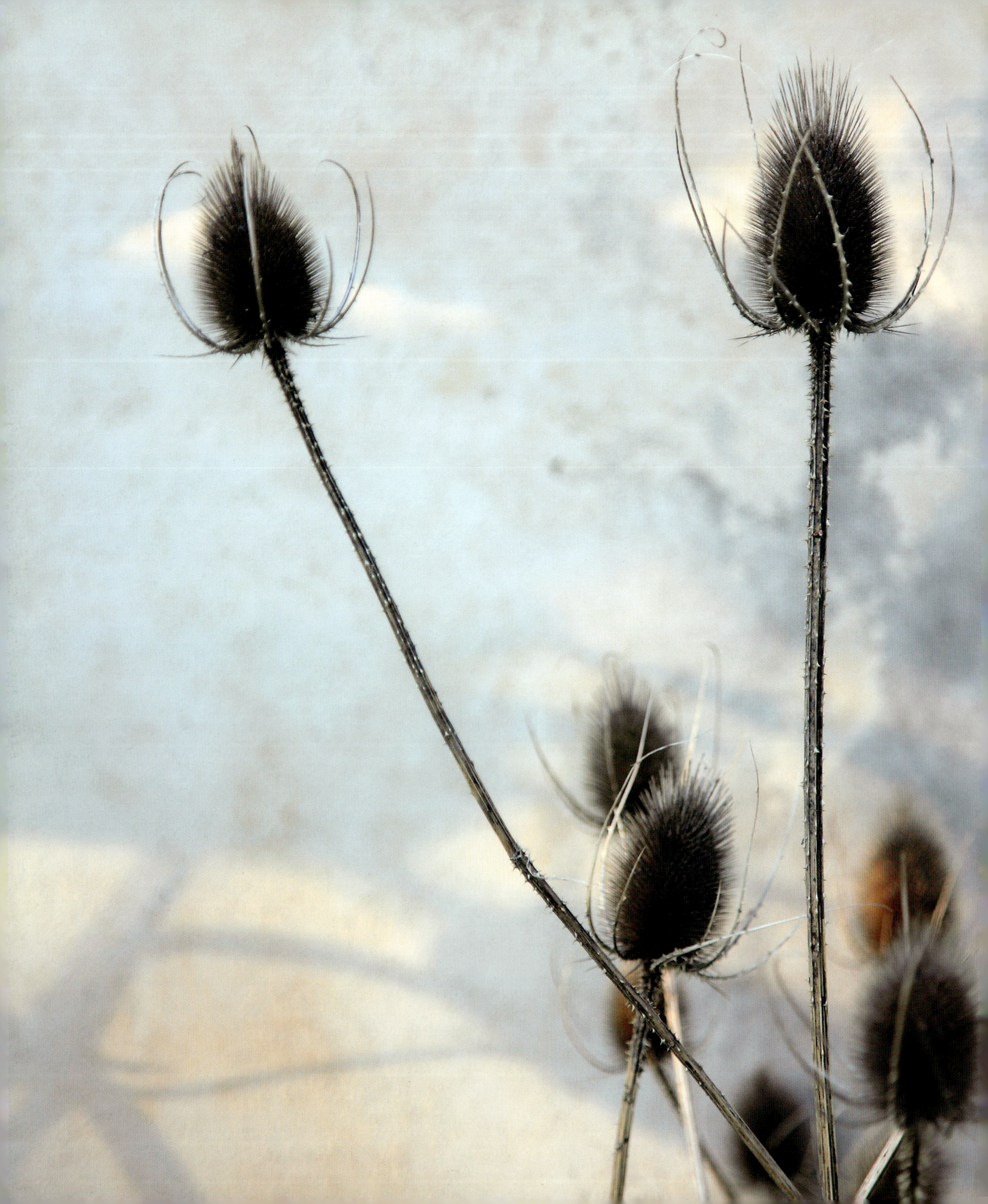

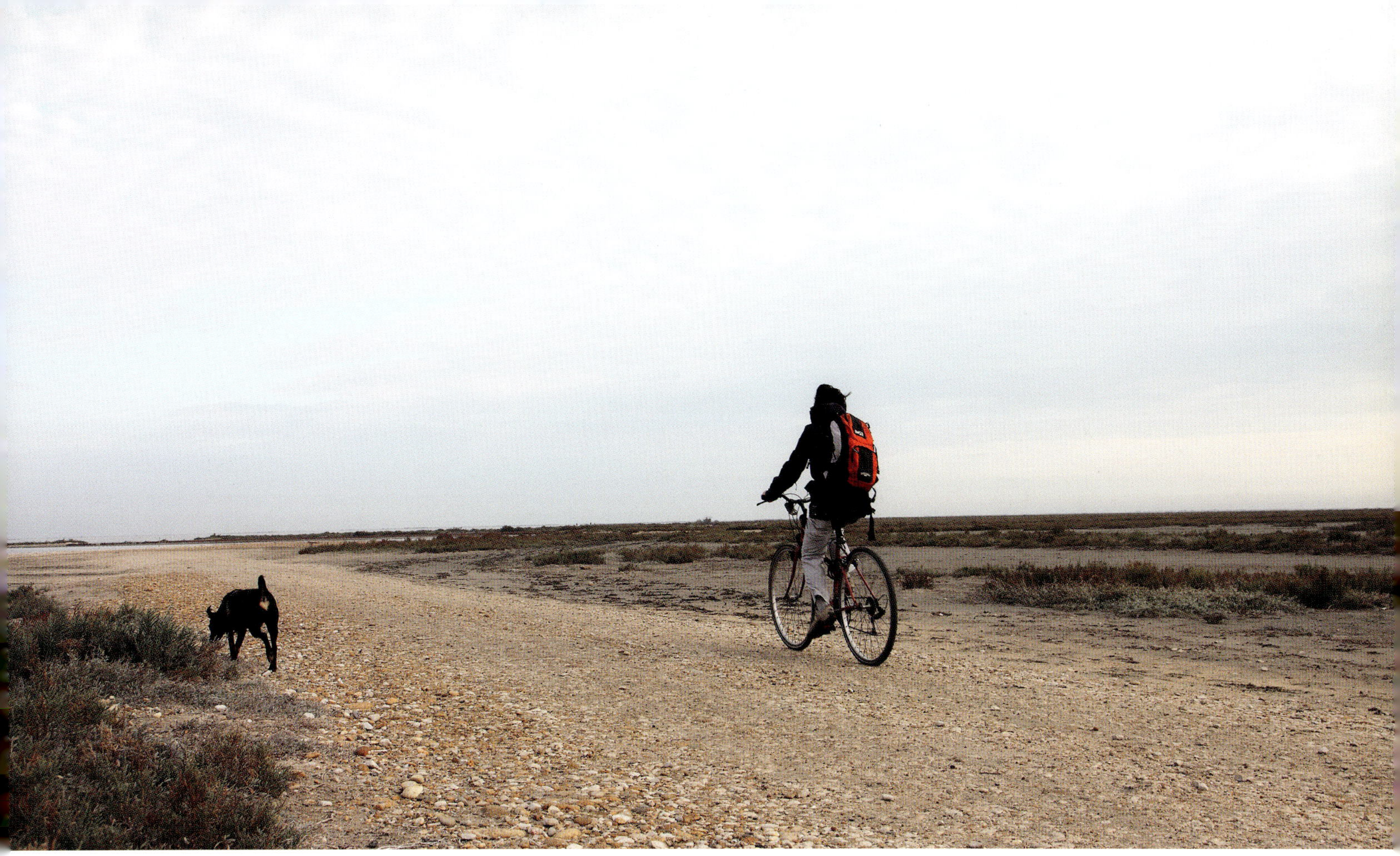

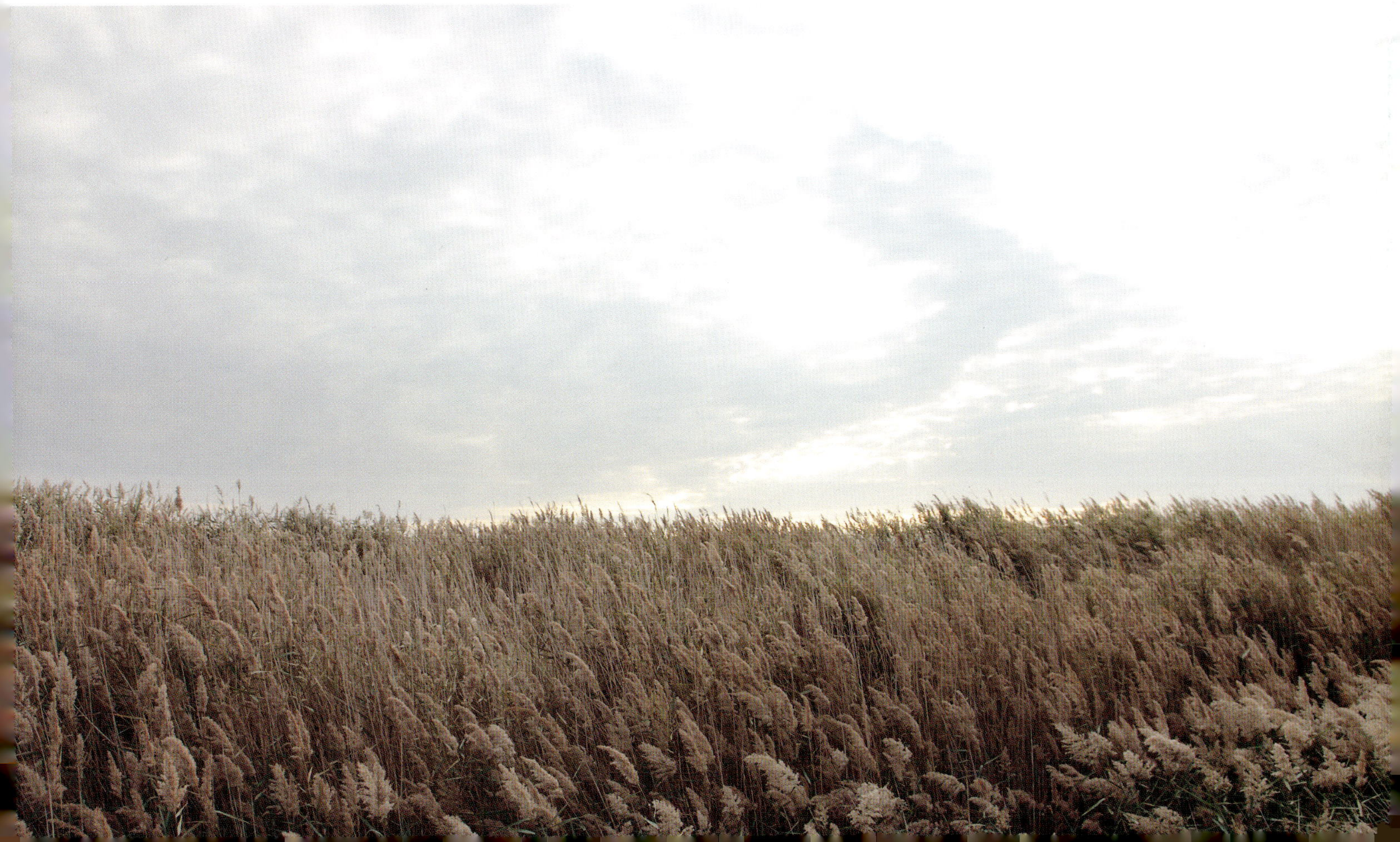

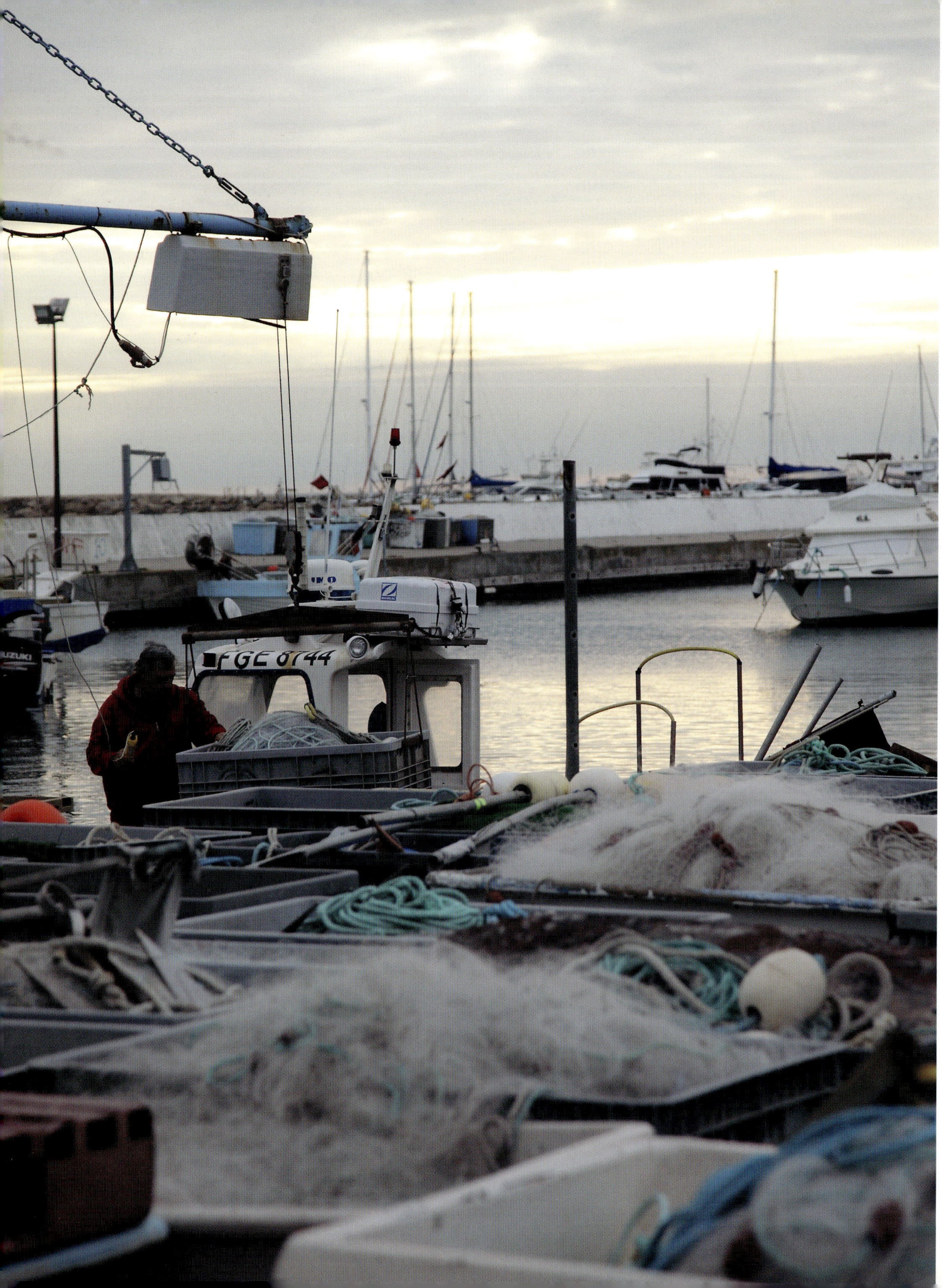
FGE 8744
SUZUKI

A COD BY ANY OTHER NAME...

"MANY MEN GO FISHING THEIR ENTIRE LIVES WITHOUT KNOWING IT IS NOT FISH THEY ARE AFTER."

HENRY DAVID THOREAU, AMERICAN WRITER (1817-1862)

European cod is central to Mediterranean kitchens. The Portuguese boast of (at least) 365 cod recipes, one for every day of the year, summer and winter. In France it is called *cabillaud*, and it was just about the only fish I "recognised" when I moved here, simply because the name sounded virtually the same as it is pronounced in South Africa: *ka-bee-yo*.

But I soon learned that the French kabeljou and my South African namesake are not even related. *Cabillaud* is the European cod, which belongs to the Gadidae fish family and lives in the deep, cold oceans of the Northern Hemisphere. Our South African kabeljou (sometimes called kob in English), as I have known since childhood, occurs close to the coast and even in river mouths. With this little lesson behind me, I immediately forgot the old saying that a little knowledge can be a dangerous thing, and decided that I was quite clever enough to buy fish at the market without Alain's help, thank you very much.

Imagine my consternation to discover that the dried, salted form of *cabillaud* is not called "dried cod" or "salted cod", but something else entirely: *morue*. And that *cabillaud/morue* gets yet another name when it is turned into a creamy pâté. *Brandade* is the name given to this cod pâté, a delicacy that is eaten cold or hot, or used to make the most delicious savoury tarts, for instance. I still do not understand why an ordinary fish needs three different names, but am willing to accept the opinion of our neighbour Jean-Pierre on the matter: *C'est comme ça*.

In Afrikaans, dried cod is called *klipvis*, but whatever you do, don't confuse it with the little fish that swim around in rock pools along the coast. The word *klip* (stone) probably refers rather to the rock-hard texture of the dried fish in this case. The Norwegians, who began drying and salting cod more than a thousand years ago, still call it *klippfisk* to this day. The other very important nation in the story of dried cod are the Portuguese, who know it as *bacalhau* and have based dozens of traditional dishes on it.

Whatever you call it, prepared correctly the modest dried cod can be turned into a fantastic meal. *Morue* is as much part of Provence as *bokkems* are of the West Coast, and it is the main ingredient (along with obscene amounts of garlic) in the well-known Provençal festive dish of aïoli. Aïoli is usually served in summer with fresh vegetables, but many of the preferred ingredients such as potatoes, carrots, beetroot and broccoli, are also available in winter – or especially in winter, for some of them.

According to that old father of gastronomy Auguste Escoffier, your *morue* should preferably come from the icy waters of Iceland but, what can I say, these days you take what you get. You then soak the rock-hard fish in water for at least twelve hours, replacing the water regularly to get rid of the salt. It is such a time-consuming process that I asked Alain in all innocence what the point was of *salted* fish that was so much hassle to *desalt*. Wouldn't it have been easier simply to buy fresh cod?

The expression on my husband's face made me realise that I had made a faux pas – once again. My only excuse was that I was new to the area and ignorant. Now that I am older and wiser, I *know* that for aïoli you use desalted salted fish. Anything else would be sacrilege. Don't ask why. *C'est comme ça*.

If you want to make aïoli in South Africa, you can use fresh fish. What you are looking for is a neutral taste like hake, to allow the garlic mayonnaise to shine. Our lovely dried snoek probably has too strong a taste – thank goodness! – to be overshadowed by garlic. Just don't tell my Frenchman I said you could use hake.

Winter Food in Provence

Right: Alain's tarte à la brandade

Alain's tarte à la brandade
6 SERVINGS

250 g shortcrust pastry (bought or home made) | 200 g brandade (we buy it in a tin or make our own – see page 177 – but in South Africa you could replace it with snoek pâté) 3 eggs | 1 lemon, thinly sliced 1 tomato, thinly sliced | salt and pepper

Preheat the oven to 180 °C. Roll out the dough and place in a tart pan that has been lined with baking paper. Prick several holes in the dough with a fork and bake for 10 minutes.

In the meantime, mix the *brandade* or snoek pâté and the eggs in a bowl and season with salt and pepper.

Remove the par-cooked pastry from the oven and spoon in the fish mixture. Arrange the lemon and tomato slices in alternating patterns on the fish.

Bake for 20-25 minutes, until the tart crust is golden, and serve hot, warm or cold. Any way is delicious.

Winter aïoli

To perk up your winter aïoli a little, you can roast the vegetables instead of boiling them. Yes, I know, aïoli purists would have a fit, but that is their problem. If you are not familiar with aïoli, a plate of boiled vegetables could be rather boring – even with all that garlic mayonnaise spooned on top. And the great thing about aïoli is that it allows improvisation. All that absolutely has to be there is the garlic mayonnaise (see page 177) and the desalted salt cod – or ordinary hake if you have to.

Start, perhaps, with baby potatoes that you have boiled quickly beforehand and spread them on a large, flat baking tray. To this add carrots, cut into thin strips, winter vegetables like cabbage or red cabbage, also cut into strips, and florets of cauliflower or broccoli. If your baking tray is large enough, you could also add strips of pumpkin or sliced mushroom – or use more than one tray if your oven is large enough. Season the vegetables with coarse salt and freshly ground pepper, and drizzle with olive oil. Bake for about 15 minutes in a preheated 180 °C oven, until the vegetables are just cooked. (Shake the pan a couple of times during cooking and remove any vegetables that are cooked sooner.) In the meantime, poach your desalted *morue* or hake flavoured with a few drops of lemon juice.

Another advantage of this dish is that it can be eaten at room temperature or even cold, although you won't want to let your food get too cold in winter. So do not wait too long before serving. Each plate gets a piece a fish and a serving of vegetables with a generous spoonful of garlic mayonnaise on the side. The idea is to dip each mouthful in the aïoli. Put a dish of aïoli on the table for those guests who cannot get enough of the delicious garlicky taste. We usually also provide a bowl of plain mayonnaise, preferably home made, for children and other souls who are scared of too much garlic in their food, poor dears.

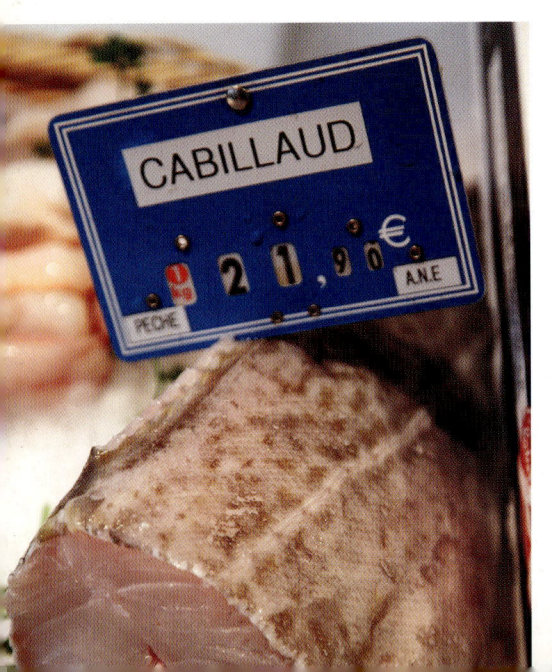

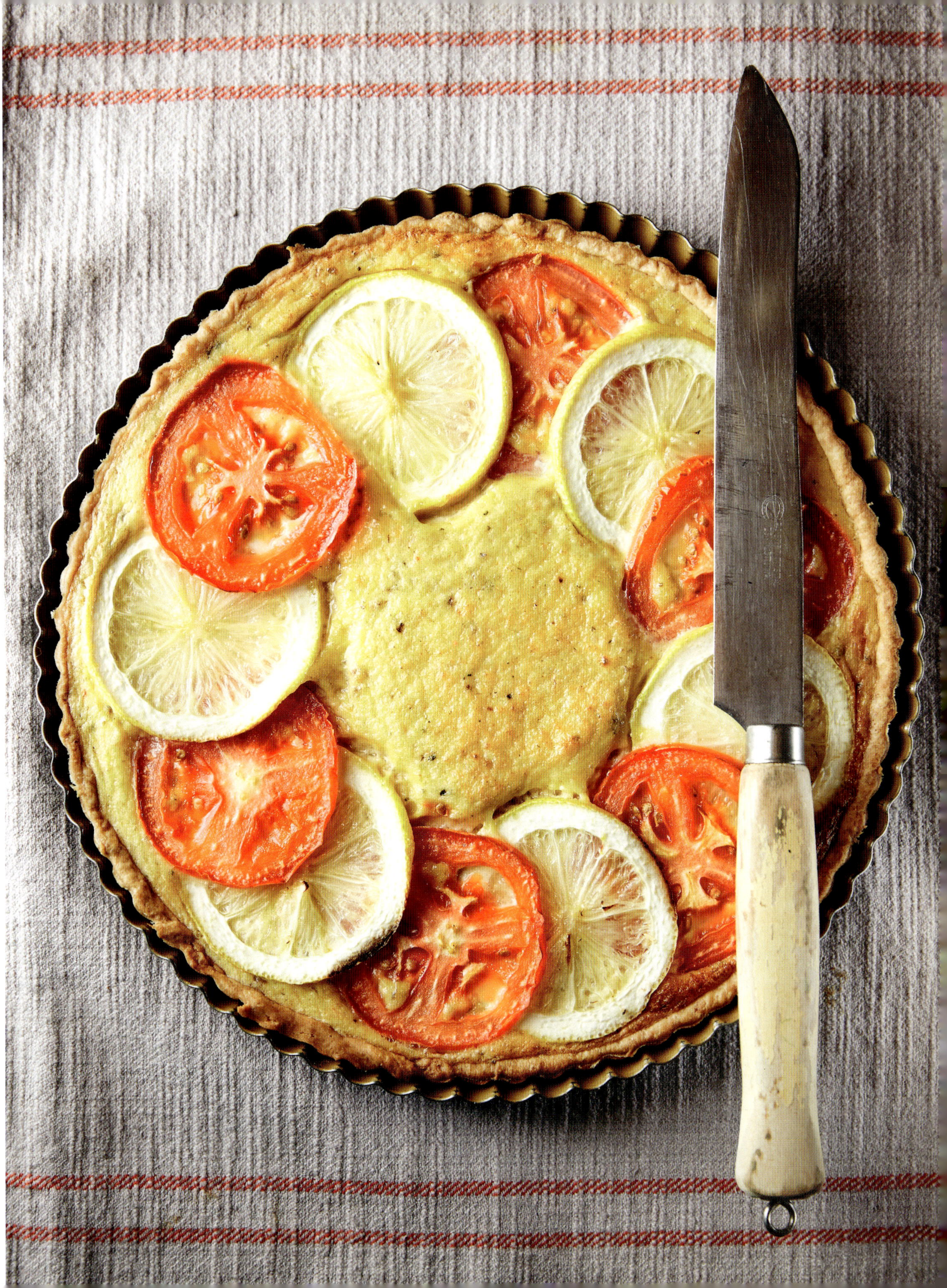

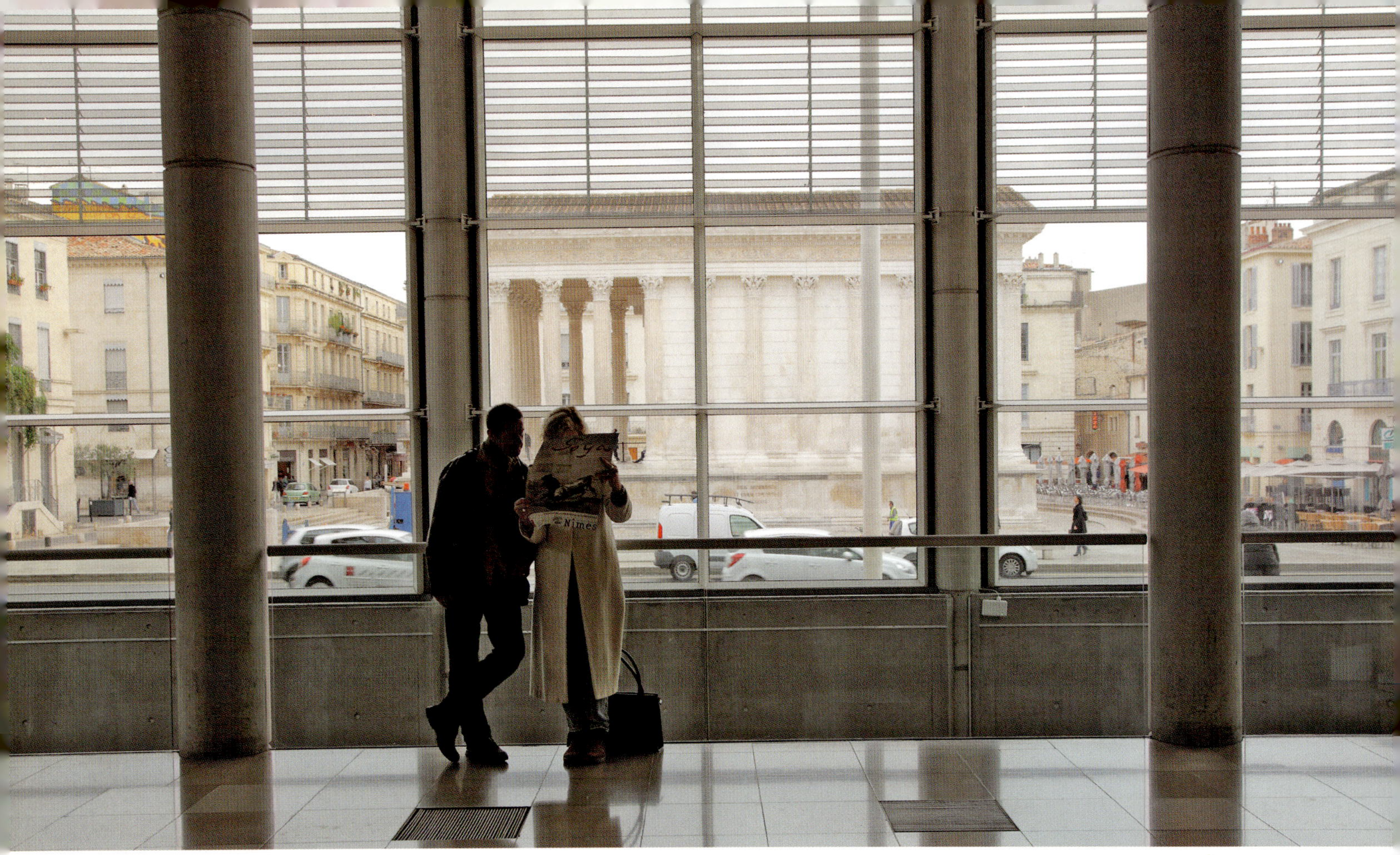
Nîmes

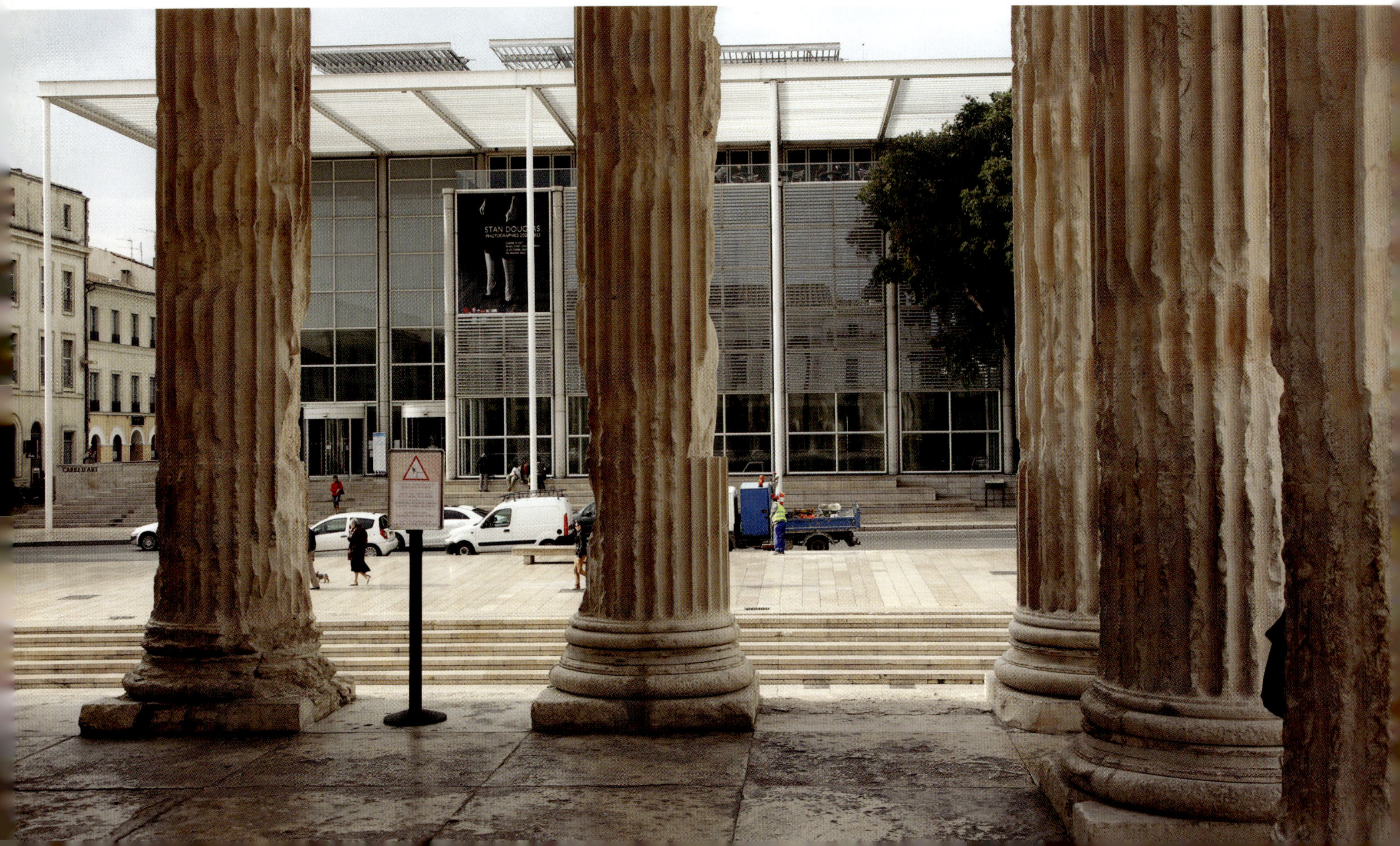

JULIE

e eighties, Stan Douglas has been producing films, photographs and
that make further inquiry into certain places and events from the past,
codes and techniques already existing in the movies, television or press

ow is devoted to the various series of photographs produced in the years
(*Midcentury Studio, Disco Angola, Crowds and Riots*). They deal with
sm, the rhetoric of the reportage, documentary fiction, the media, and
the news is being turned into a spectacle. The return to the past in all
aphic series is a way of making a break with the immediacy
ke a critical look at history. The show lets us elaborate
aesthetic and political aspects of image making in va
ng makes the complex "fictionalization" of reality a
ant devices in order to understand what is real.

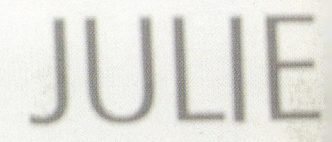

orn in Vancouver in 1960. He has had many exhibitions, including
rtembergischer Kunstverein and the Staatsgalerie Stuttgart,
ence Biennales and three Documenta.

d in partnership with the Centre Culturel Canadien, Paris

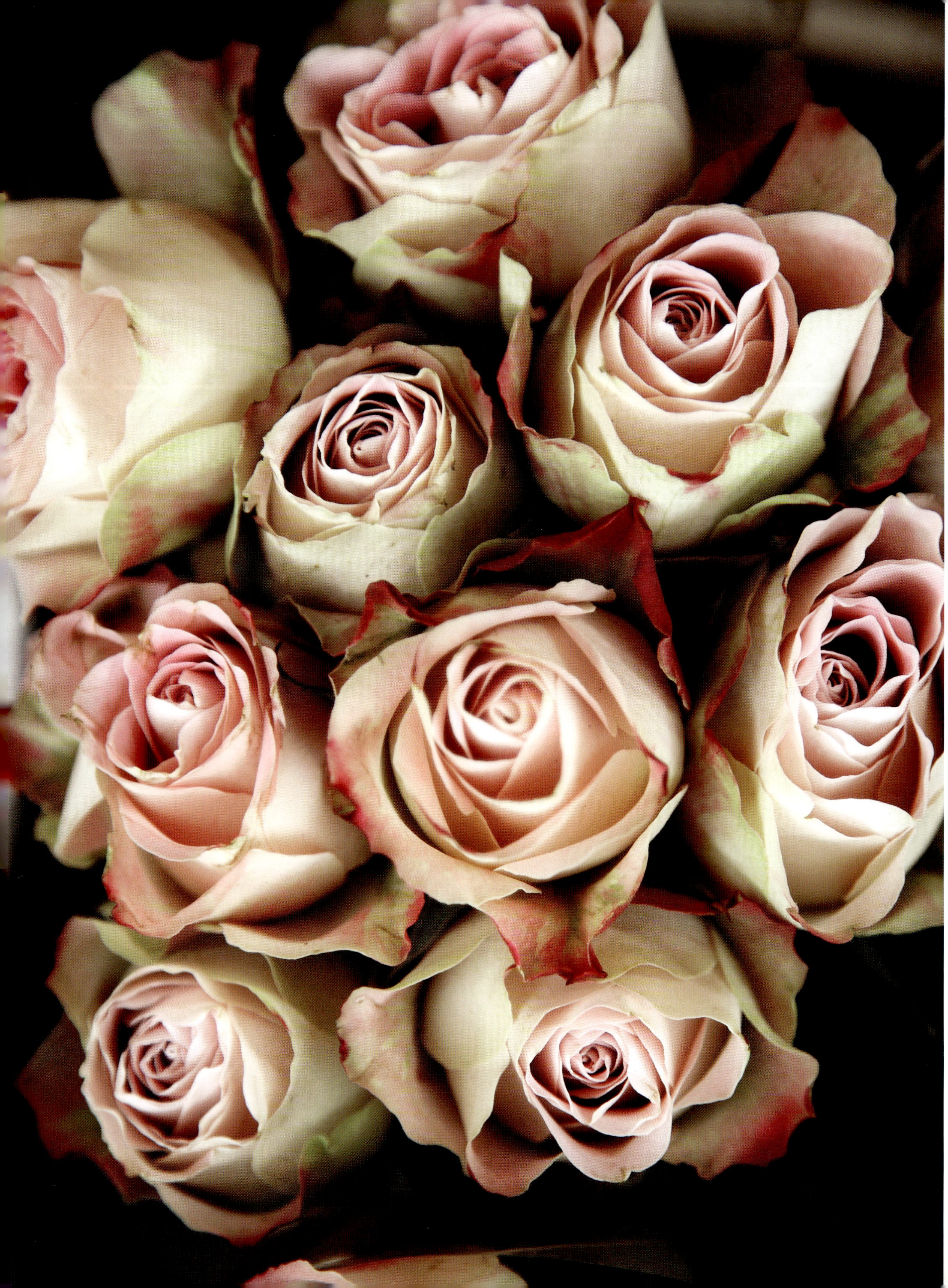

OF CABBAGES AND KINGS

"AN IDEALIST IS ONE WHO, ON NOTICING THAT A ROSE SMELLS BETTER THAN A CABBAGE, CONCLUDES THAT IT MAKES A BETTER SOUP."

BERTRAND RUSSELL, BRITISH PHILOSOPHER (1872-1970)

If vegetables were movie stars, poor old cabbage would never be cast as the romantic lead in a Hollywood blockbuster. Cabbage is simply not a glamorous vegetable, and certainly not a star who sets hearts aflutter like Brad Pitt or George Clooney. No, Mr Cabbage is what one would term a character actor. Solidly built, interesting rather than drop-dead gorgeous, a quiet guy with an undeserved bad-boy reputation.

He comes from the ancient and respected Brassica family, like his cousins cauliflower, broccoli and Brussels sprouts, with early ancestors found in Europe as long ago as 1 000 BC. The original family name was Cruciferae because the pattern on the flower was said to remind Europeans in the Middle Ages of a cross. (That said, those pious crusaders saw crosses in almost everything.) Cabbage's current family name is derived from the old Celtic word for cabbage (*bresic*), because one of the oldest branches of the family originates in Ireland.

But one of Mr Cabbage's younger relatives, the Savoy cabbage, which was developed in the Alpine region between Italy and France only in the sixteenth century, proves that even unattractive ancestors can produce beautiful offspring. The loose, frilly leaves and bright green colour of the Savoy cabbage are so attractive that it is sometimes used for a purely decorative purpose – almost like the bikini girl in a James Bond movie – as a gorgeous pot plant during the European winter, when most other plants succumb to the cold.

Because Miss Savoy is much hardier than her lovely appearance would have you believe. She thrives in icy weather and is truly worth her weight in gold in the kitchen during winter, because she cooks faster than ordinary smooth cabbage and also does not give off that nasty sulphurous odour that has turned so many of us off the entire cabbage family since childhood. One of my earliest memories is in fact of the two old ladies who lived next door in a dark, double-storey house that always smelled of boiled cabbage, cat pee and damp carpets. Fortunately I have since learned that the notorious cabbage odour is sulphur compounds that form when the vegetable is cooked for too long. And since we tend to under-cook rather than over-cook all vegetables in our Provençal kitchen, smells like this are never really a problem.

These days I have a particularly soft spot for cabbage because *chou farci* (stuffed cabbage) is a traditional favourite in various regions of France. Sometimes it reminds me of old-fashioned South African cabbage frikkadels – savoury mince wrapped in cabbage leaves – although the French usually prefer minced pork rather than lamb or beef. On other occasions it looks and smells like a far more exotic dish. In regions such as the Auvergne, the head of cabbage is served whole, with layers of pale pork meat arranged among the light green leaves, creating an extremely attractive picture when the cooked cabbage is cut in half at the table. In Poitou-Charentes, on the other hand, the leaves are removed from the head of cabbage in order to cover the meat, but not to make individual parcels. *Chou farci poitevin*, as it is called there, is instead one big meatball that is tucked away neatly under cabbage leaves and cooked in a round dish.

Obviously there is also a Provençal version, with its own Provençal name (*lou fassum*), that is thought to have originated in the perfume city of Grasse. An appropriate home town for such a dish, I suppose: with all the gorgeous floral fragrances permeating the air in Grasse, no one would notice the smell if someone cooked the cabbage for too long and it developed a pong.

In healthier, more modern versions of stuffed cabbage, the meat is sometimes replaced with fish. The beautiful pink colour of salmon is such a lovely contrast to the frilly green leaves of a Savoy cabbage that it has become a fancy dish fit for heads of state. President François Mitterrand's personal chef regularly spoiled him with *chou farci au saumon*, it is said. But the biggest attraction for an ordinary mother like me who fortunately never has to cook for presidents, is that it makes our children forget that they do not, in fact, like cabbage.

Chou farci au saumon
4 SERVINGS

This elegant version of stuffed cabbage is useful for entertaining because you can prepare the cabbage parcels ahead of time. Then, at the last minute, while you are making the sauce, fry the parcels briefly so they turn a lovely golden colour.

300 g salmon | 2 egg whites | 150 ml cream | 1 large Savoy cabbage | 50 g chopped bacon | 1 onion, finely chopped | 100 g butter | 300 g Cantal cheese, grated (Cantal is a pale yellow cow's milk cheese with an exceptionally creamy taste, though you can replace it with Cheddar) | 100 ml white wine | 1 shallot | 200 ml crème fraîche | salt and pepper

Mash the salmon with a fork and combine with the egg whites and cream to form a soft mousse. Season with salt and pepper.

Remove the leaves from the Savoy cabbage and blanch for 5 minutes in salted boiling water. Choose eight of the best-looking whole leaves and set aside. Chop the rest of the leaves finely. Fry the bacon and onion in half the butter and add the finely chopped cabbage. Leave to cool before mixing with the salmon mousse.

Place a cabbage leaf on a sheet of tinfoil and spoon about 30 g of the grated cheese onto the leaf. Cover the cheese with a little of the salmon filling. Wrap the cabbage leaf and filling in the foil to make a neat, round parcel. Fold over the foil tightly at the top. Make another seven parcels in the same way. Use all the salmon filling, but reserve about 60 g of the cheese.

Steam the stuffed cabbage for 20 minutes and leave to cool slightly before removing the foil. Heat a little butter in a frying pan and fry the parcels until golden brown.

Heat the white wine and shallot in a small saucepan, add the crème fraîche and cook rapidly to reduce the liquid by half. Stir in the reserved cheese until it melts to form a thick sauce. Serve the creamy cheese sauce with the cabbage parcels.

Gratin de chou
6 SERVINGS

As I have mentioned, our children are not mad about cabbage – show me a child who is – but like most children they do like mashed potatoes. This side dish combines cabbage and mashed potatoes so ingeniously that even the youngest in the house will eat it.

1,5 kg cabbage | 150 g butter | 225 g chopped smoked bacon | 150 ml chicken or beef stock | freshly grated nutmeg | 1,5 kg potatoes | 150 ml milk | 2 egg yolks | salt and pepper

Cut the cabbage in half and blanch for 8-10 minutes in salted boiling water. Drain well and cut into pieces. Heat a little of the butter in a saucepan and fry the bacon until crisp. Stir in the cabbage, pour over the stock, and season with salt and pepper and nutmeg. Leave the cabbage to simmer over low heat for 30 minutes, stirring occasionally.

In the meantime, boil the potatoes in their skins. Peel the cooked potatoes and mash with a fork. Mix with 100 g butter and the milk to form a firm mash. Season with salt and pepper. Stir in the egg yolks.

Place the cabbage in an ovenproof dish that has been greased with butter. Cover with a thin layer of the mash and dot with a few knobs of butter. Bake in a preheated 210 °C oven for about 20 minutes until the top is golden brown.

Right: Chou farci au saumon

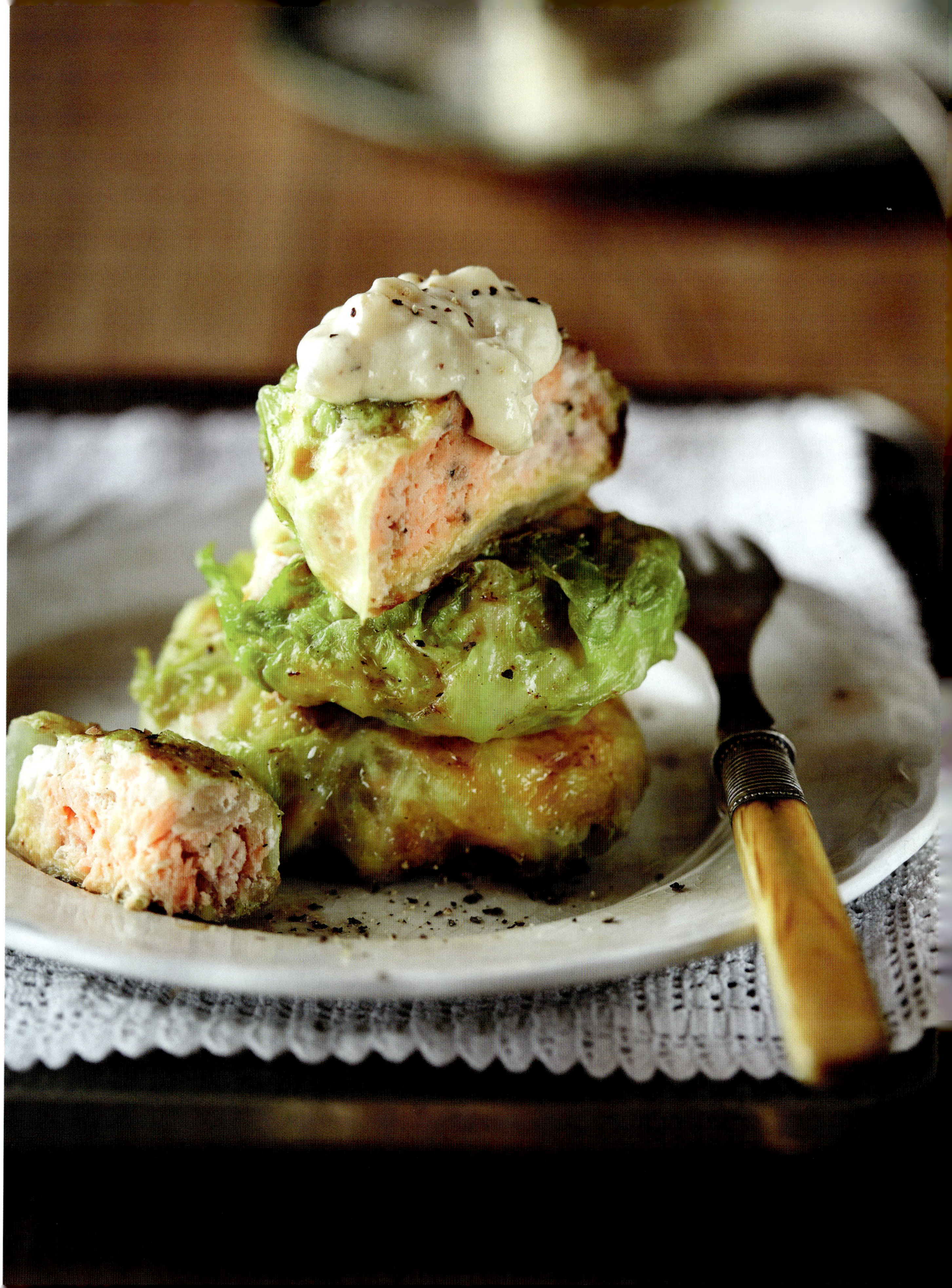

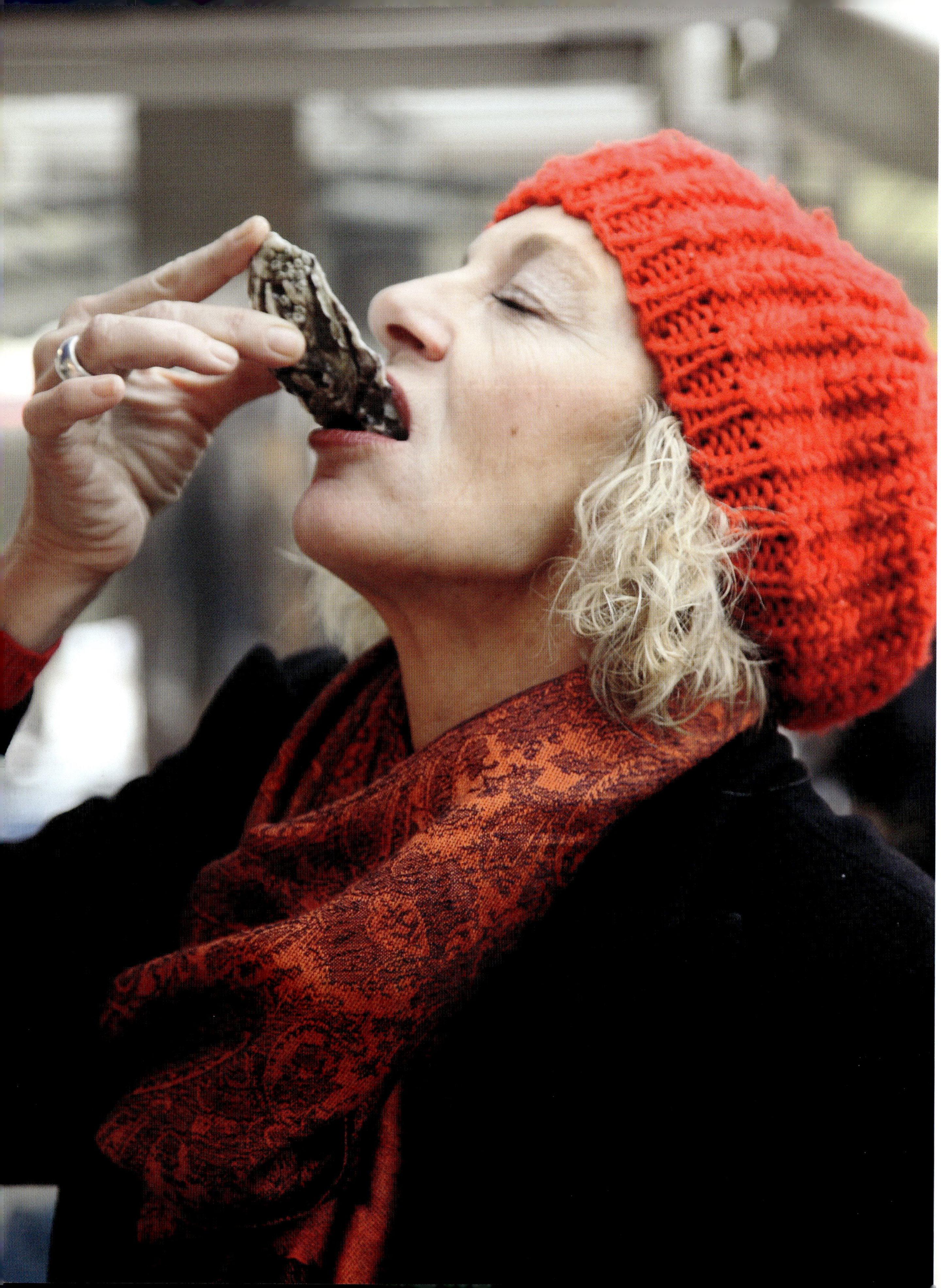

OH SHUCKS, IT'S SHELLFISH!

"HE WAS A BOLD MAN THAT FIRST EAT AN OYSTER."

JONATHAN SWIFT, IRISH WRITER (1667-1745)

During my childhood days spent barefoot, exploring the coast around Franskraal, I grew to love shellfish: mussels, winkles and especially abalone or perlemoen. Alas, the closest I ever get to abalone in France are the empty shells I brought with me from the land of my birth to use as ashtrays outside in the summer. Much to the astonishment of my French friends. Even those who have tasted abalone somewhere before are amazed at the size of the shells. Then I assure them, with a seemingly modest smile, that perlemoen is not the only thing that is bigger and better in South Africa.

My only consolation when I crave a slice of meltingly tender perlemoen like I knew as a child, is that it has become almost as unobtainable in South Africa too. (Unless you have a contact in a poaching syndicate.) And that is certainly a bitter consolation.

Happily I have discovered other types of seafood here, such as the juicy white morsel to be found in the scallop. In France they are called *coquilles Saint-Jacques* in honour of the saint whose body, according to legend, was transported by boat from Jerusalem to the northern coast of Spain. He is said to be buried in the present-day city of Santiago de Compostela; hence the scallop having become the symbol of the popular pilgrimage of the same name. But for a non-Catholic romantic like me, the scallop is just as irresistible because it is the shell on which Botticelli's Venus arose so evocatively from the foam.

In France I have also come across old favourites like oysters in new guises – and what a pleasant rediscovery it has been. Like chickens and potatoes and just about anything eaten by the French, oysters are of course graded, and the undisputed king of oysters is the *spéciale Gillardeau* with its plump, almost sweetish flesh. Named after the Gillardeau family, who have farmed them near La Rochelle for more than a century, these are the ones you will find in the gourmet emporiums of Paris like La Grande Epicerie, as well as served in the most famous seafood restaurants, including Le Dôme Montparnasse.

Although oysters are available throughout the year these days, winter – and around Christmas in particular – is when the French really indulge in this delicacy. The oysters sold at the Christmas markets down our way may not always come from the Gillardeau family, but you won't hear us complaining. Even "ordinary" oysters are a gastronomic delight when they are shucked in front of you, so you can devour the slippery morsel straight off the shell.

To appreciate their unique sea taste, oysters must be enjoyed raw and fresh. I could never understand why anyone would want to do anything more with an oyster. We recently had dinner with friends and the entire meal consisted of enormous silver platters crammed with raw oysters, slurped down with (excellent) white wine and concluded with a rich and creamy Brillat-Savarin cheese on slices of (excellent) fresh bread. Once again, a lesson in French simplicity, elegance and luxury. Yes, you can do all three at the same time.

Other types of shellfish are enjoyed in more democratic and less elegant ways. La Grande Braderie, the largest street market in Europe, is held in the northern city of Lille each autumn. Anyone can come and sell their wares that weekend, and there among all the stalls, mountains of *moules frites* are consumed, washed down with copious amounts of beer. And I am not exaggerating when I say "mountains". Restaurant owners pile up the empty shells in huge mounds outside their front doors so that everyone can see where the most mussels have been consumed.

Moules frites in fact originates in Belgium, and is the most popular dish on the menu when the Belgian national day is celebrated in our neighbouring village in July, but Lille's *braderie* mussels in September are definitely tastier. And I am not just saying this because my husband comes from Lille. Although mussels are also enjoyed throughout the year these days, they are unavoidably less meaty during the breeding season in the summer. Just another food that should rather be eaten during the colder months. Long live winter food!

Moules frites
4 SERVINGS

Right: Moules frites

For a juicier taste, choose the smallest mussels you can find. Remember, fresh mussels must be shiny and black with a pleasant sea smell, and preferably still be tightly closed. Discard any mussels that smell off, look dry or remain open when you place them in water or tap the shell.

2 kg mussels | 5 T olive oil
4 shallots, finely chopped | 2 onions, finely chopped | 4 cloves garlic, finely chopped | 2 sticks celery, finely chopped | 2 stalks thyme | 2 bay leaves | 300 ml dry white wine
4 T crème fraîche | a generous handful flat-leaf parsley

Wash the mussels in a bowl of water and remove the beards.

Heat the oil in a heavy-based pan and fry the shallots, onion and garlic for 1-2 minutes until soft. Add the celery, thyme, bay leaves and mussels, and stir well to combine. Pour in the wine, give it another stir and cook for 1-2 minutes until the wine has reduced by half. Put the lid on and cook for about 5 minutes.

Decant the contents of the pan into a large colander over a dish that is deep enough to take all the liquid. (Mussels that are still closed should be prised open with a sharp knife before serving.) Pour the strained liquid back into the pan, reheat and stir in the crème fraîche and parsley. Season with salt and pepper if necessary. Return the mussels and vegetables to the pan and stir a couple of times to ensure everything is properly reheated. Serve the mussels in large soup plates with a generous amount of the wine sauce and crisp potato chips (*frites*) – and a bowl of mayonnaise if you want your meal to be authentic.

Fabulous frites
The *frites* should be thin and crisp, unlike the *slap* chips we know in South Africa, and to do this they must be fried twice. Here is how you do it: Cut floury potatoes into thin fingers. Rinse, dry very well, and deep-fry in oil that has been heated to 150 °C. (For this you need one of those handy immersion thermometers; otherwise you are going to have to guesstimate.) As soon as the potato chips begin to soften, lift them out of the oil using a sieve and drain on kitchen paper. In the meantime, cook the mussels – alternatively, prepare the *frites* to this point in advance. Just before the food goes to the table, reheat the oil, to 185 °C this time, and fry the chips for about 3 minutes until golden brown and crisp.

Velouté de moules
Use the liquid remaining in the pan after you have eaten the *moules frites* to make a velvety-smooth mussel soup. Pour about 500 ml of the wine sauce through a coffee filter to remove even the smallest impurities. Chop up 2 leeks and sauté in butter. Add 2 T flour and cook, stirring, for a few minutes. Add the filtered wine sauce and stir over low heat until the sauce "binds". Add 1 litre fish stock and simmer for a few minutes. Add 200 ml crème fraîche and bring to the boil. Remove from the heat and season with salt and pepper. If you have a few leftover mussels, put them in the soup bowls and pour the deliciously smooth soup over them.

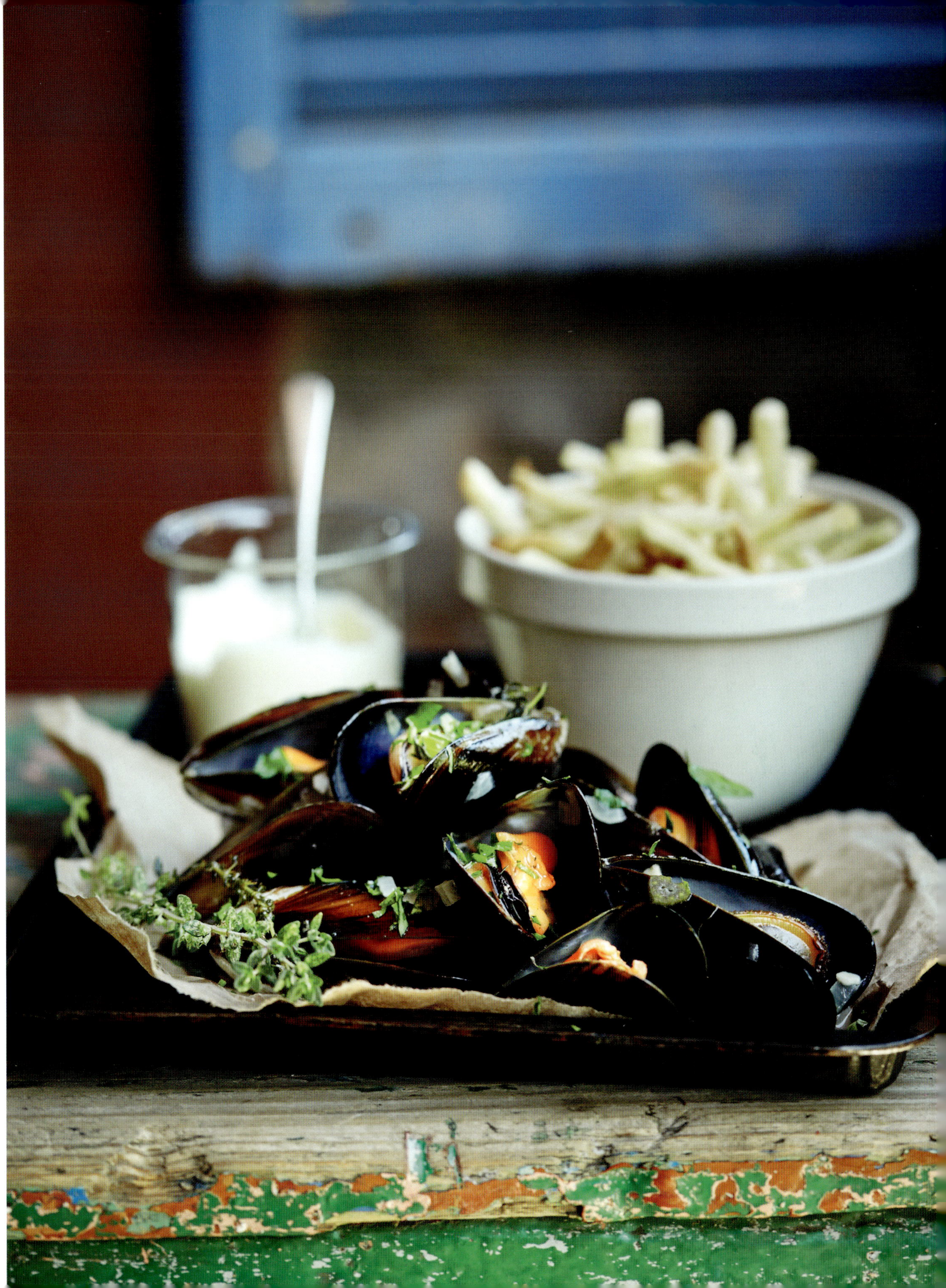

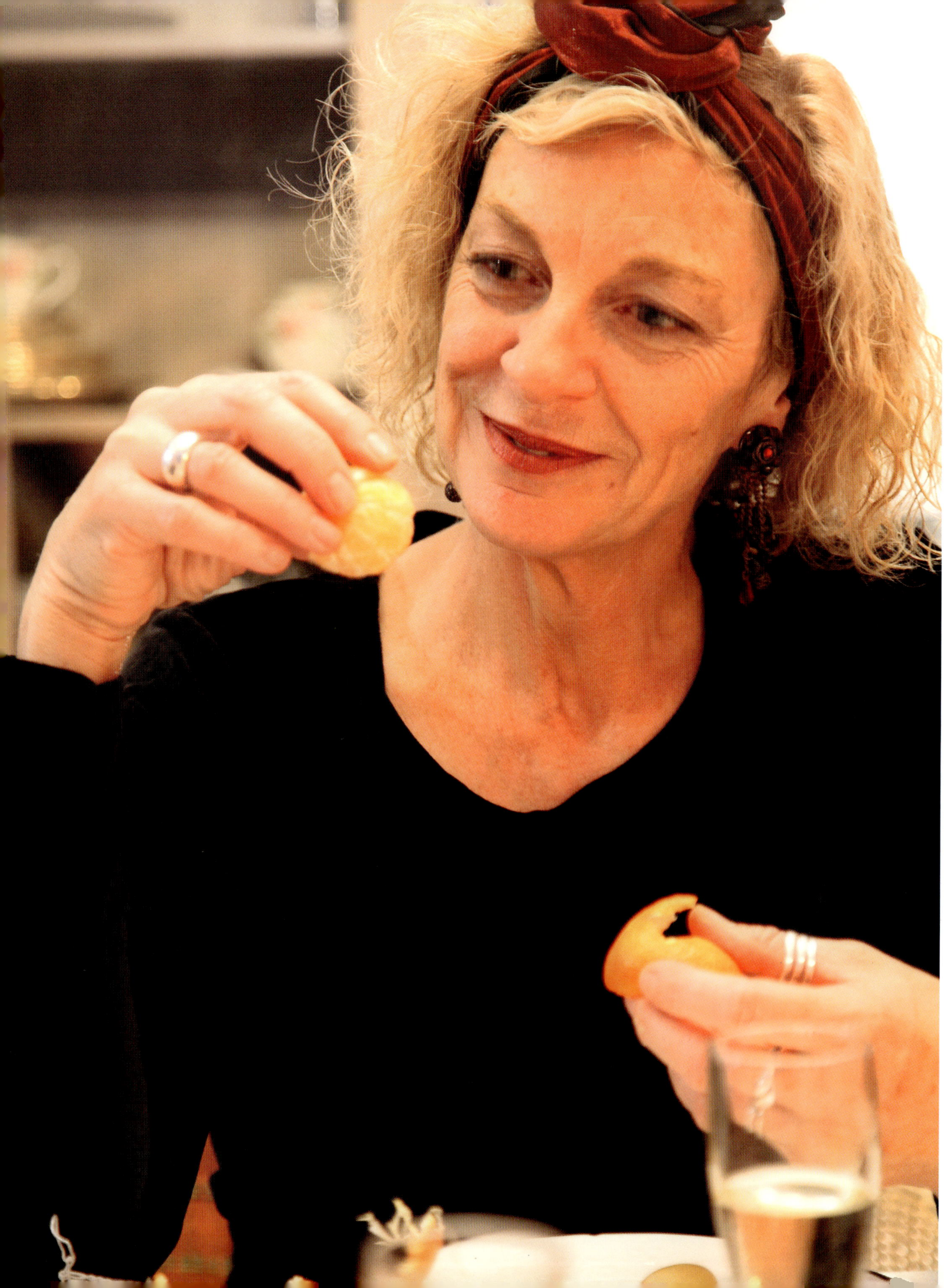

FESTIVE FARE

"CHRISTMAS IS THE SEASON FOR KINDLING THE FIRE OF HOSPITALITY IN THE HALL, THE GENIAL FLAME OF CHARITY IN THE HEART."

WASHINGTON IRVING, AMERICAN WRITER (1783-1859)

"What do you eat at Christmas in Provence?" people always want to know. The honest answer is: Whatever we feel like, whatever we like, within the limits of our budget, of course. Usually a few bites of French tradition combined with a good shot of Anglo-Saxon or South African enjoyment.

But sometimes we are brave enough to tackle the traditional Provençal Christmas meal. Or rather, a pared-down version of the traditional spread with its twenty dishes (yes, you read that correctly, twenty), because to do that justice you really need a hoard of guests and ours is usually just a modest family feast. Our extended family, on both sides, live too far away to come and help us eat it all.

I should add, however, that the twenty dishes are not the eat-until-you-fall-over type of food that characterised the Christmas meals of my childhood. No stuffed turkeys, legs of lamb and so on. The genuine, traditional Provençal Christmas meal is meatless, believe it or not. (And that alone is enough to ensure that my meat-loving Afrikaans family is unlikely to make the trip to spend Christmas with us.) But still it is anything but a shabby meal. Cooks in Provence can do amazing things with fish and vegetables – and no one said this meal could not include delicacies like snails or truffles.

Le gros souper is served on Christmas Eve to satisfy the hunger of the body before attending midnight mass to quench the spiritual thirst. At least that is how the tradition arose centuries ago, and even today everything has a symbolic religious meaning, from the table cloth and the candles to the food. For instance, you lay three white table cloths one over the other to represent the Holy Trinity, and three candlesticks for the same reason. I must admit to not following the table cloth tradition myself, for the simple reason that three dirty table cloths are just too much work for a non-Catholic, non-industrious woman who does not fancy spending her entire Christmas doing washing and ironing.

The meal is made up of seven meatless main courses (for the seven sorrows of the Virgin Mary) and thirteen desserts (for Jesus and the twelve apostles), which are all put out on the table at the same time. It is then up to each guest to taste a little of each dish – especially the thirteen desserts – to ensure prosperity in the coming year.

A place is also always set for an absent guest, to remember the poor and the hungry. Dishes vary from region to region and from family to family, but none of them requires hours of slaving over a hot stove. (My kind of Christmas meal, many of my slaving sisters in South Africa would probably sigh.)

One of the seven meatless main courses is almost always *morue* (dried, salted cod, as described in a previous chapter), but the remaining six can vary widely. The Provençal poet and Nobel Prize winner Frédéric Mistral recalls the six other dishes of his childhood as snails, mullet with olives, two different dishes made from Swiss chard, celeriac salad known as *rémoulade*, and fougasse, a type of flatbread baked with pieces of olive or bacon or other tasty morsels. If you want to adhere strictly to the meatless tradition, or if you have vegetarian tendencies, you could obviously replace the bacon with something else. But in our non-Catholic and non-vegetarian household, no one turns their nose up at a little bacon on Christmas Eve.

Then it is time for the *Treize Desserts* – written in capital letters just so you know this is no ordinary pudding – that I will explain in the next chapter. And once every guest has tasted every dish, you do not simply clear the table. You leave the dishes where they are so that the spirits of your ancestors can also come and eat during the night – but you knot the overhanging corners of the (three) table cloth(s) to prevent evil spirits gliding up the table cloth to reach the food. Now this is a practical tradition that I like to keep. Not that I believe in evil spirits, but who wants to stand around washing dishes on Christmas Eve?

Gratin de carde
6-8 SERVINGS

This baked dish of Swiss chard often forms part of a Christmas spread in Provence. You can replace the Swiss chard with cardoon or ordinary spinach – an easy way to turn any leafy winter vegetables into a tasty meal.

1 kg Swiss chard | 1 cube concentrated beef stock | 75 g butter | 2 T flour | 500 ml milk | freshly grated nutmeg | 125 g cheese, grated | salt and pepper

Cut the stems of the chard into small pieces (about 5 cm long) and cut the leaves into smaller pieces too. Bring 1½-2 litres water to the boil in a deep saucepan, dissolve the beef stock in it and add the chard. Cook for 15 minutes and drain well. (All types of spinach release moisture when cooked. To avoid sogginess under the crust of the gratin, make sure you squeeze out all the water with your hands or a wooden spoon.)

Make a white sauce: Melt 50 g butter in a small saucepan over low heat and stir in the flour. Add the milk a little at a time, stirring continuously. Season the sauce with salt, pepper and nutmeg.

Grease an ovenproof dish with the remaining butter and place the Swiss chard in it. Spoon over the white sauce and sprinkle with the grated cheese. Bake for 30 minutes in a preheated 180 °C oven until the cheese topping is golden. Serve immediately in the dish in which it was baked.

Creamy rémoulade

Celeriac is a well-known variety of celery and used to be the only type of celery available in winter. For this reason, one of the seven dishes of the Provençal Christmas meal is often made from it. The best thing to do with celeriac is to turn it into a creamy salad that goes by the name of *rémoulade*. Because this salad is sold at a reasonable price in French supermarkets throughout the year these days, we are usually too lazy to make it ourselves – but Christmas is the time to push the boat out. Here is how it's done:

Peel and grate the celeriac and immediately stir in the juice of half a lemon to prevent it discolouring. In a small bowl, mix 5 T of your finest mayonnaise (preferably home made – you can find our recipe in *Summer Food in Provence*) with 2 T smooth Dijon mustard, 2 T crème fraîche, 2 T finely chopped parsley and a little salt and pepper. Combine the dressing with the celeriac in a pretty bowl and pop it in the fridge for half an hour before serving. It's as easy as that.

In South Africa you can also replace the celeriac with sticks of celery, cut into the thinnest slices possible. It will taste more like celery than real *rémoulade*, but could be an interesting and refreshing salad for a southern summer Christmas.

Right: Gratin de carde

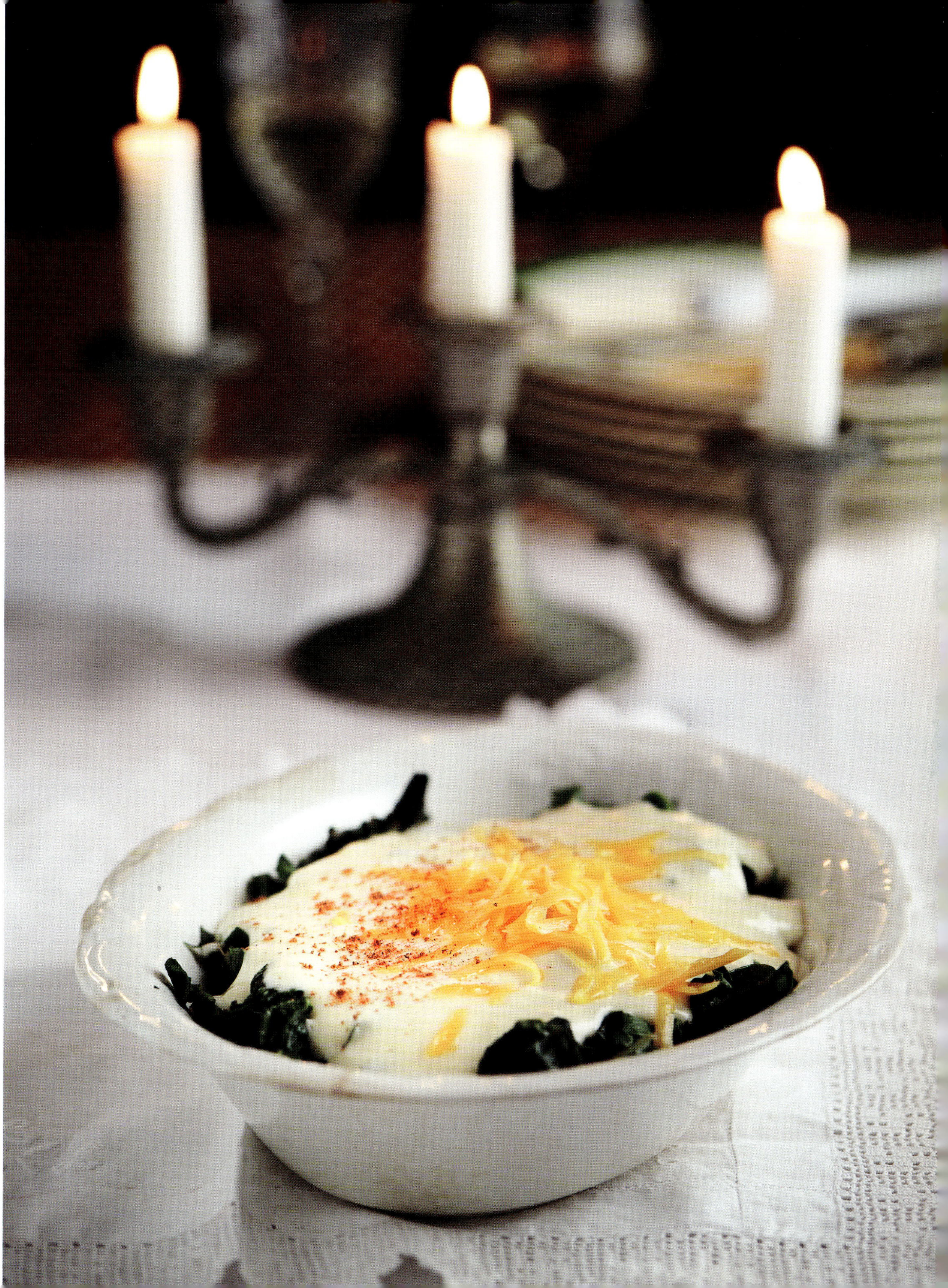

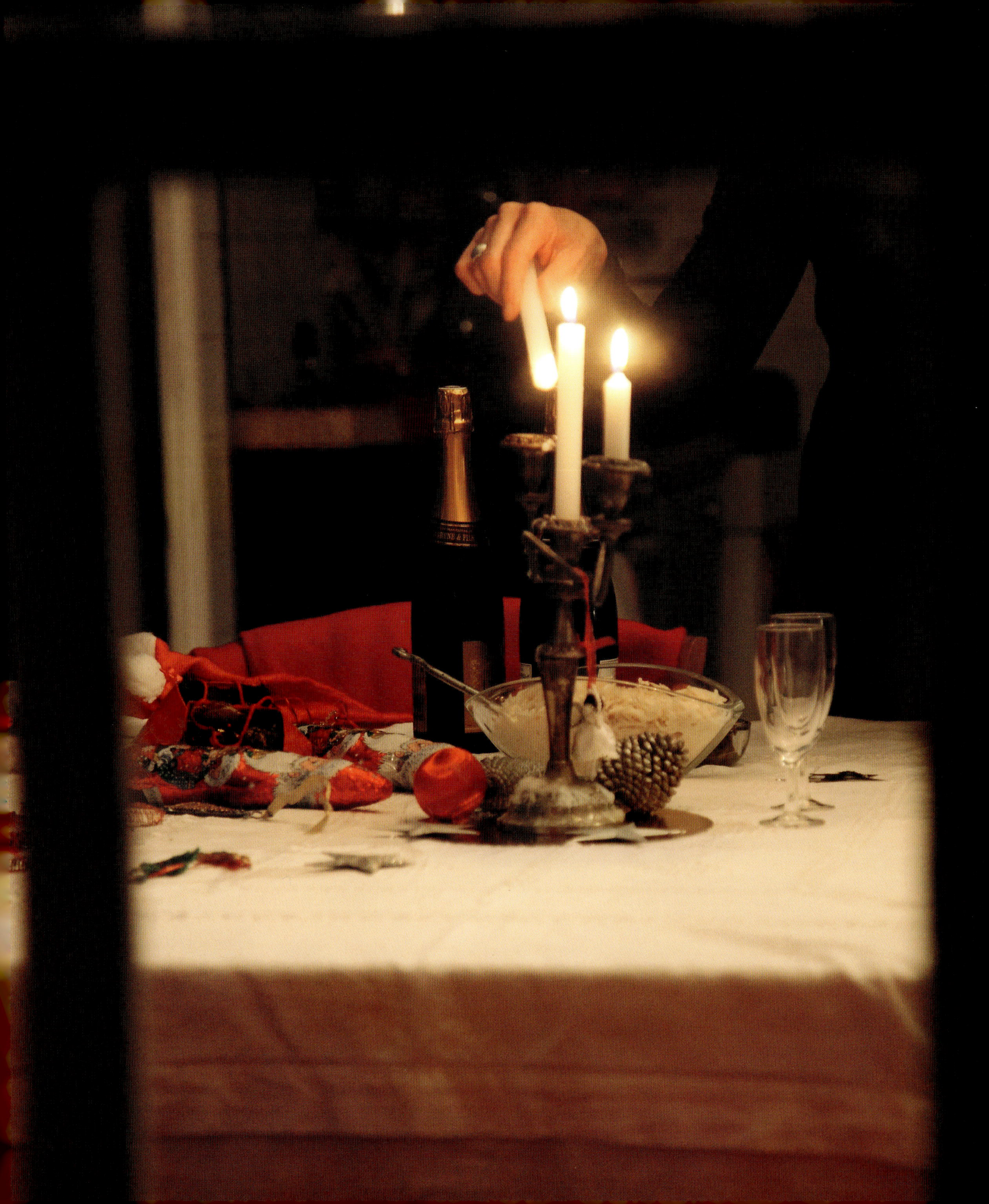

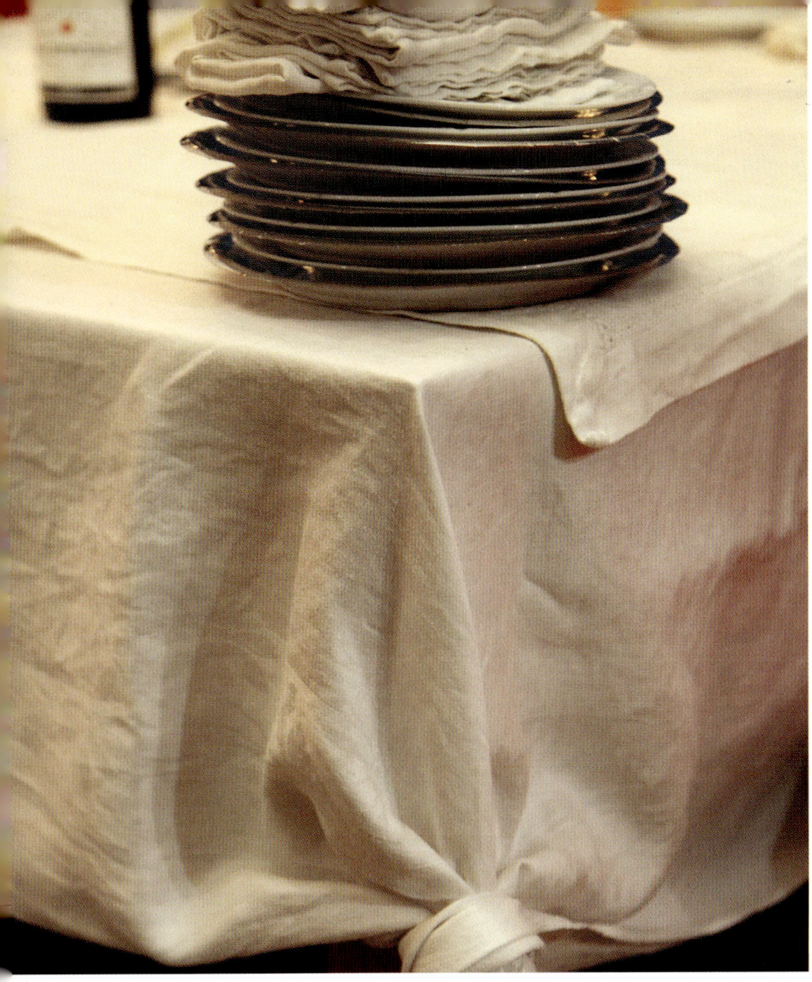
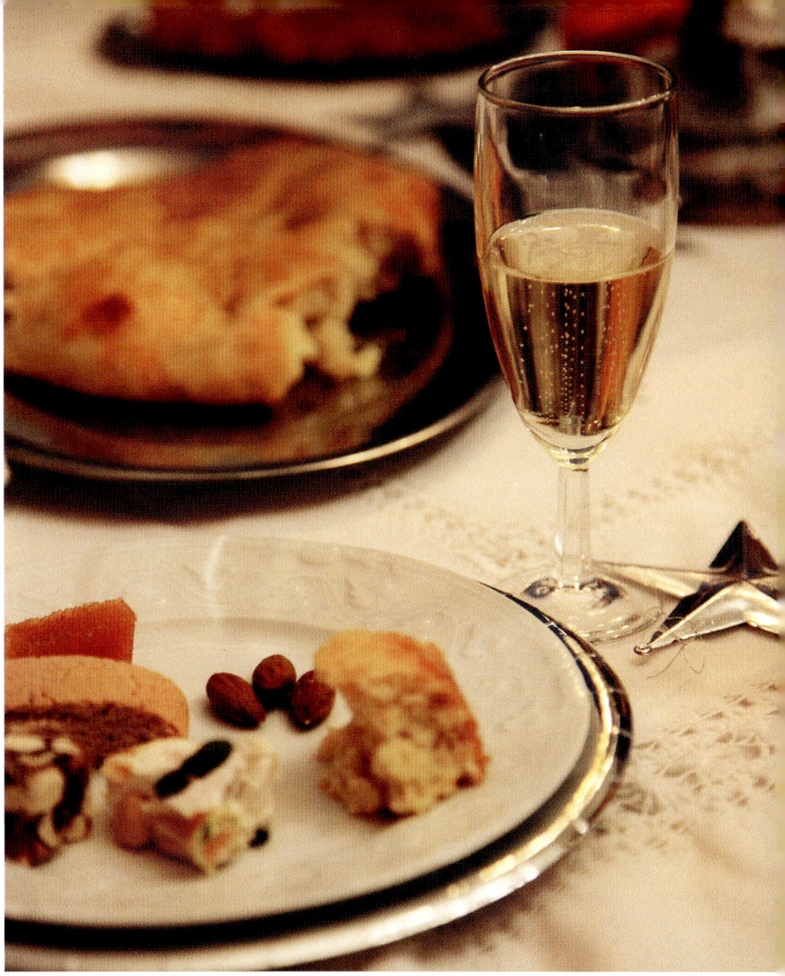
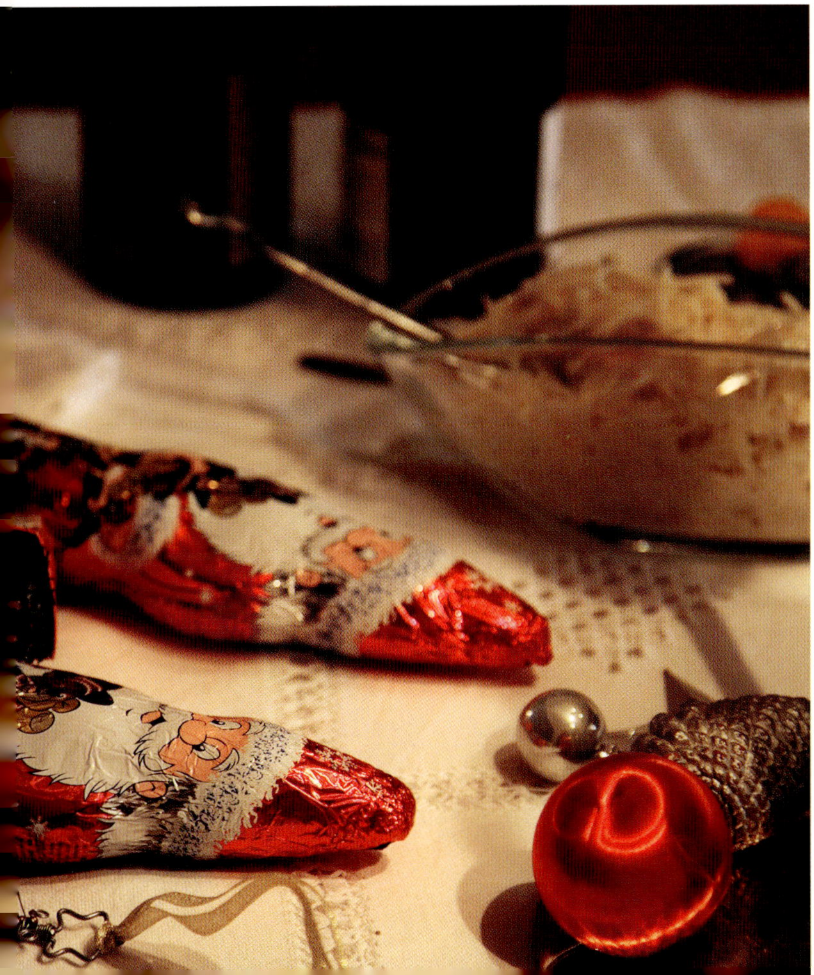
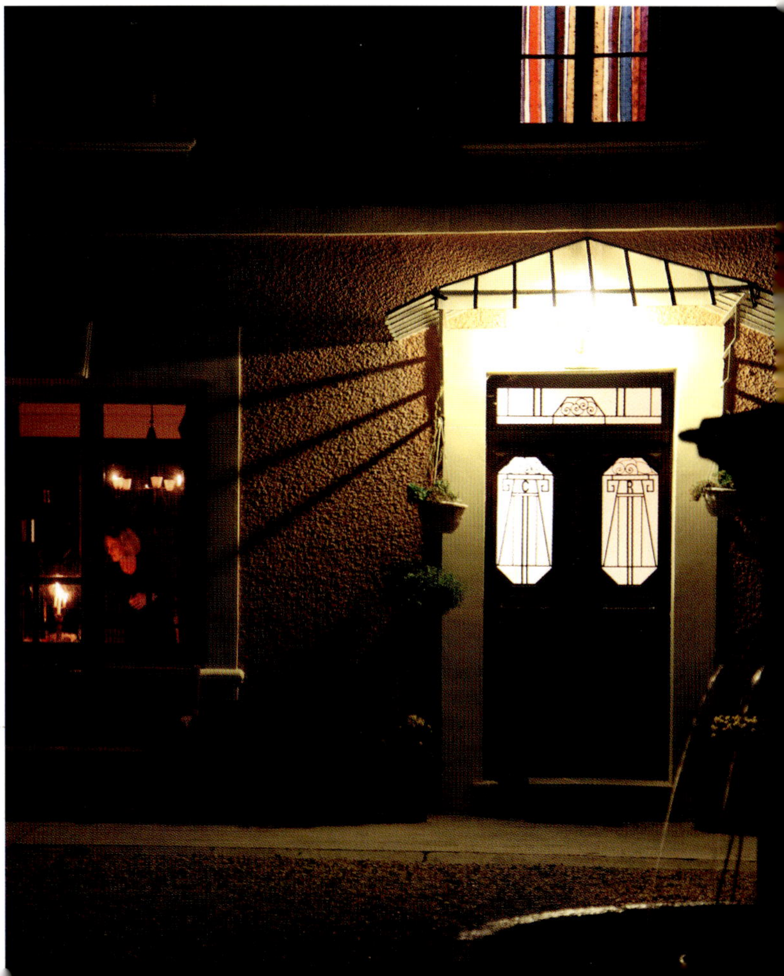

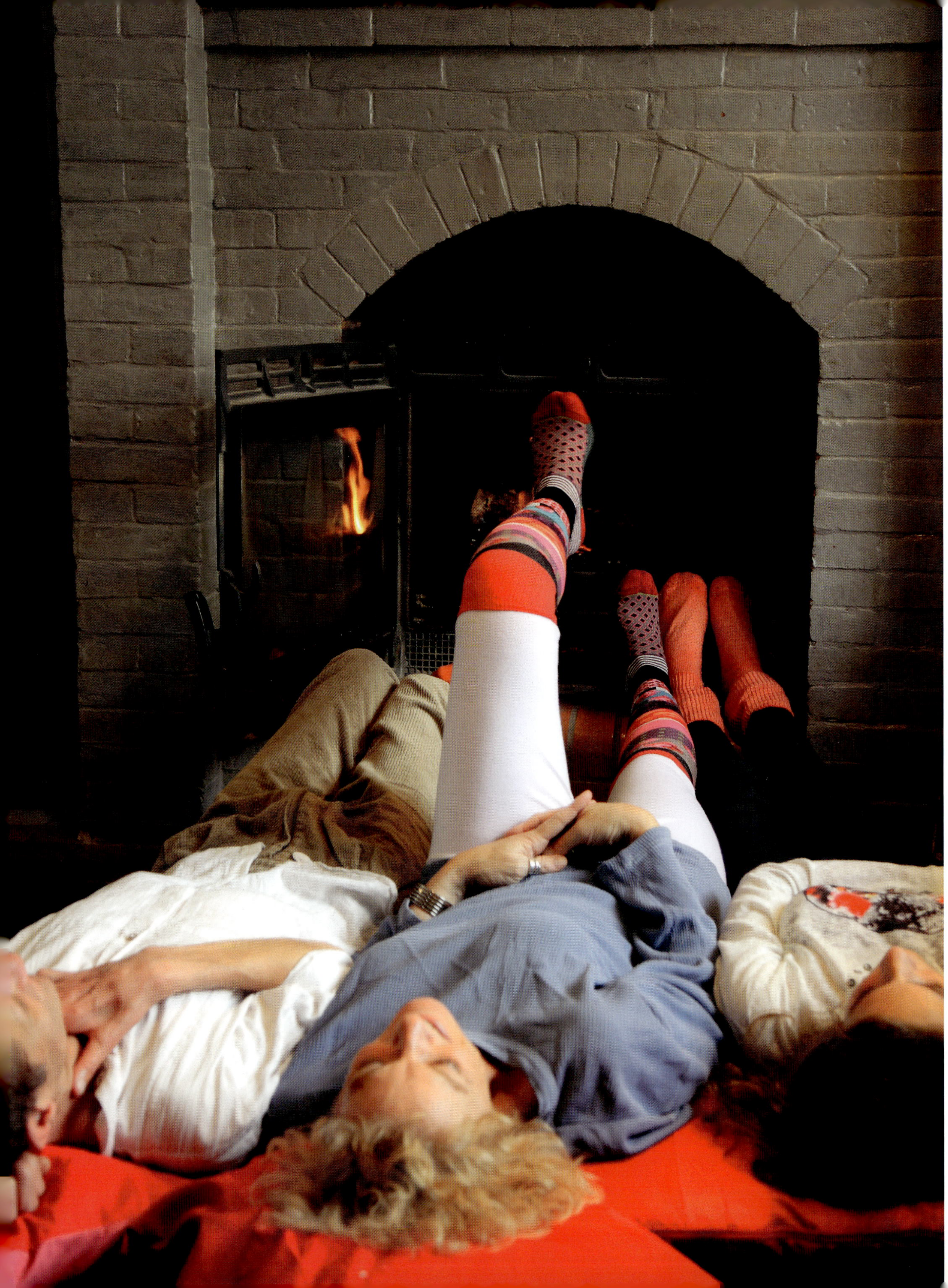

JUST DESSERTS, DEAR

"DESSERT IS PROBABLY THE MOST IMPORTANT STAGE OF THE MEAL, SINCE IT WILL BE THE LAST THING YOUR GUESTS REMEMBER BEFORE THEY PASS OUT ALL OVER THE TABLE."

WILLIAM POWELL, AMERICAN ACTOR (1892-1984)

On my first French Christmas Eve, a neighbour arrived bearing a gift of a log and said he was sorry we couldn't eat it. From the amused expression on his face I could see that it was supposed to be a joke, but I was too new to the country and culture to understand what he meant.

However, by my second Christmas I had learned that a *bûche*, which means log, is the pinnacle of French Christmas desserts. A type of rolled cake, a fancy version of what we know as a Swiss roll, it is decorated to look like a sawn-off log from a tree. It is said to symbolise the real log that, according to an ancient Celtic tradition, is burnt on the longest and darkest night of the year (21 December on our modern calendar) to celebrate the rebirth of the sun. Like so many other pagan customs, this one was later also incorporated into a Christian festival, and across Europe families would keep an enormous Yule log burning throughout the night to ensure heat, light and happiness in the coming year. In Provence, where the *bûche de Noël* naturally received its own Provençal name (*còssa de Nadau*), it was apparently customary to pour wine over the log and to predict the future by studying the patterns of the flames, coals and shadows on the wall.

But sometime during the nineteenth century the French started replacing the burning logs with symbolic edible logs – according to some sources, because one of Napoleon's many laws prohibited Parisians from using their fireplaces. Talented *pâtissiers* soon filled the gap with the most divine oblong cakes, covered with a layer of chocolate that is finished to look like the bark of a tree, and decorated with cute little mushrooms made of marzipan or meringue.

These days, ice-cream logs are popular among ordinary French families, while great chefs come up with their own imaginative versions of the *bûche* each Christmas. (Sometimes the person eating the cake needs even more imagination than the pastry chef to spot the modest log in these exotic creations.) So my neighbour was simply referring to the origin of the culinary tradition when he carried a real log into my house that evening.

In Provence the *bûche* is usually eaten on Christmas Day, because Christmas Eve is still devoted to the local tradition of *Treize Desserts*. The thirteen desserts will always include a *pompe à l'huile* – a sweetish round loaf baked with olive oil – as well as dried figs, almonds, raisins and hazelnuts or walnuts. These four ingredients represent the colours of the four most important Catholic orders. (I mentioned previously that even the table settings for the Provençal Christmas have a religious significance – so, here we go again.) There must also be two kinds of nougat: soft and white to symbolise purity and goodness, and hard and black for the opposite. If, like me, you prefer the hard black nougat to the soft white stuff, it is no reflection on your character.

Then you need three types of fresh fruit – easier said than done in the European winter – such as oranges, late harvest grapes, apples or pears. For the final three desserts you can use your imagination. Often this will be dates stuffed with marzipan, quince paste or quince cheese (see page 44), and something more decadent among all the virtuous fruit and nuts, like my own personal favourite, chocolate truffles.

And if the Yule log and scores of desserts sound like far too much trouble for one Christmas, you could always follow our family's lead and combine the two traditions. We make an easy *còssa de Nadau* from ice cream – even more appropriate for a hot South African Christmas – into which we mix pieces of dried fruit, shards of nougat and nuts, then decorate with grated chocolate to look like a log. And there is no Napoleonic law to prevent you enjoying it on any other day of the year.

WINTER FOOD IN PROVENCE   *Right: Our ice-cream còssa de Nadau*

MIA'S BÛCHE DE NOËL
8-10 SERVINGS

400 g dark chocolate (at least 50% cocoa butter), broken into pieces
5 eggs, separated | 200 g sugar | 1 T icing sugar | 150 ml crème fraîche

Melt half the chocolate in a bain-marie or microwave oven. Beat the egg yolks with the sugar in a mixing bowl and add the melted chocolate.

Beat the egg whites in a glass or metal bowl using an electric beater until stiff peaks form. Carefully fold the egg whites into the chocolate mixture.

Line a shallow baking tin (33 x 23 cm) with baking paper and spoon the batter into it. Smooth the surface and bake in a preheated 180 °C oven for 12-15 minutes, until the thin layer of cake is just firm to the touch. Remove from the oven, cover with a damp tea towel and leave to cool slightly.

Sprinkle the icing sugar on another sheet of baking paper and carefully turn out the cake on it. While the cake is still soft and flexible (before it has cooled completely), roll it up with the baking paper, like you would an ordinary Swiss roll.

Now make the ganache to fill the cake: Break up the remaining chocolate. Heat the cream in a small saucepan until bubbles start to form.

OUR ICE-CREAM CÒSSA DE NADAU

Allow a litre of good-quality vanilla ice cream to soften slightly, just so that you can mix in the other ingredients easily. While the ice cream softens, chop a handful of walnuts and almonds into small pieces and toast briefly in a pan. In a large bowl, mix 2-3 dried figs and 2 pitted and chopped dates with 25 g each soft white nougat and hard black nougat, also chopped. Add 2 T raisins (which you can soak in water or alcohol to make them soft and plump) and 1 T finely grated lemon zest. Toss in the toasted nuts, add the ice cream and stir well to combine.

Line a small loaf tin with baking paper, spoon in the ice-cream mixture and press down with the back of a spoon to remove the air bubbles. Place in the freezer for 2-3 hours. Take 1 cup large green grapes and the segments of a clementine (or ordinary naartjie), roll in icing sugar and spread on the base of a shallow plastic container, which you then leave in the freezer for as long as the ice cream. Grate 50 g good-quality dark chocolate and reserve for decoration.

Once the ice cream has frozen solid, remove from the loaf tin and place on a large silver platter. Cover the top and sides with the grated chocolate and arrange the frozen grapes and citrus segments around it, along with another traditional Provençal sweet treat such as quince cheese or marzipan mushrooms. And that gives you a "log" with two kinds of nuts, three kinds of dried fruit, two kinds of nougat, three kinds of fresh fruit (if you include the lemon zest), chocolate and something else sweet – 12 of the 13 "compulsory" desserts all rolled into one – with the ice cream as the all important thirteenth, of course.

Remove from the heat and stir the chocolate into the hot cream until it forms a thick sauce. Leave to cool.

Carefully unroll the cake again. Beat the ganache to make it even thicker and spread it on the flat cake. Roll up the cake again, this time without the baking paper. Then it is time to use your imagination to decorate the outside to look like a log. You could spread a little crème fraîche on it and stick pieces of Flake chocolate or grated milk chocolate all over to look like tree bark sprinkled with snow.

Or forget about the log idea, sprinkle with icing sugar or shards of nuts and enjoy throughout the year as a rich and decadent chocolate cake. Or serve it with ice cream as a memorable dessert.

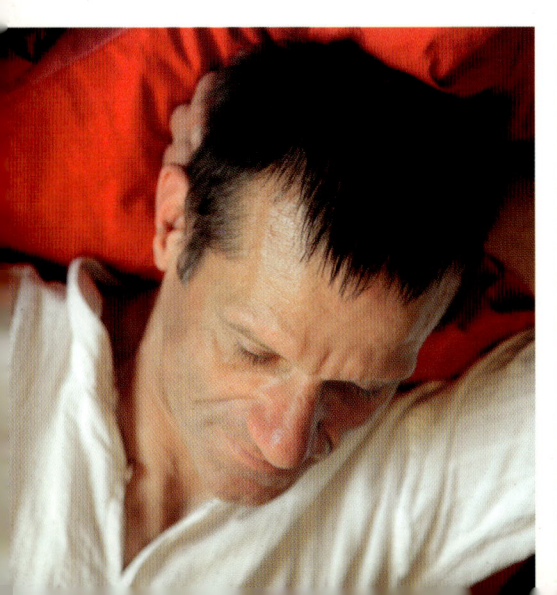

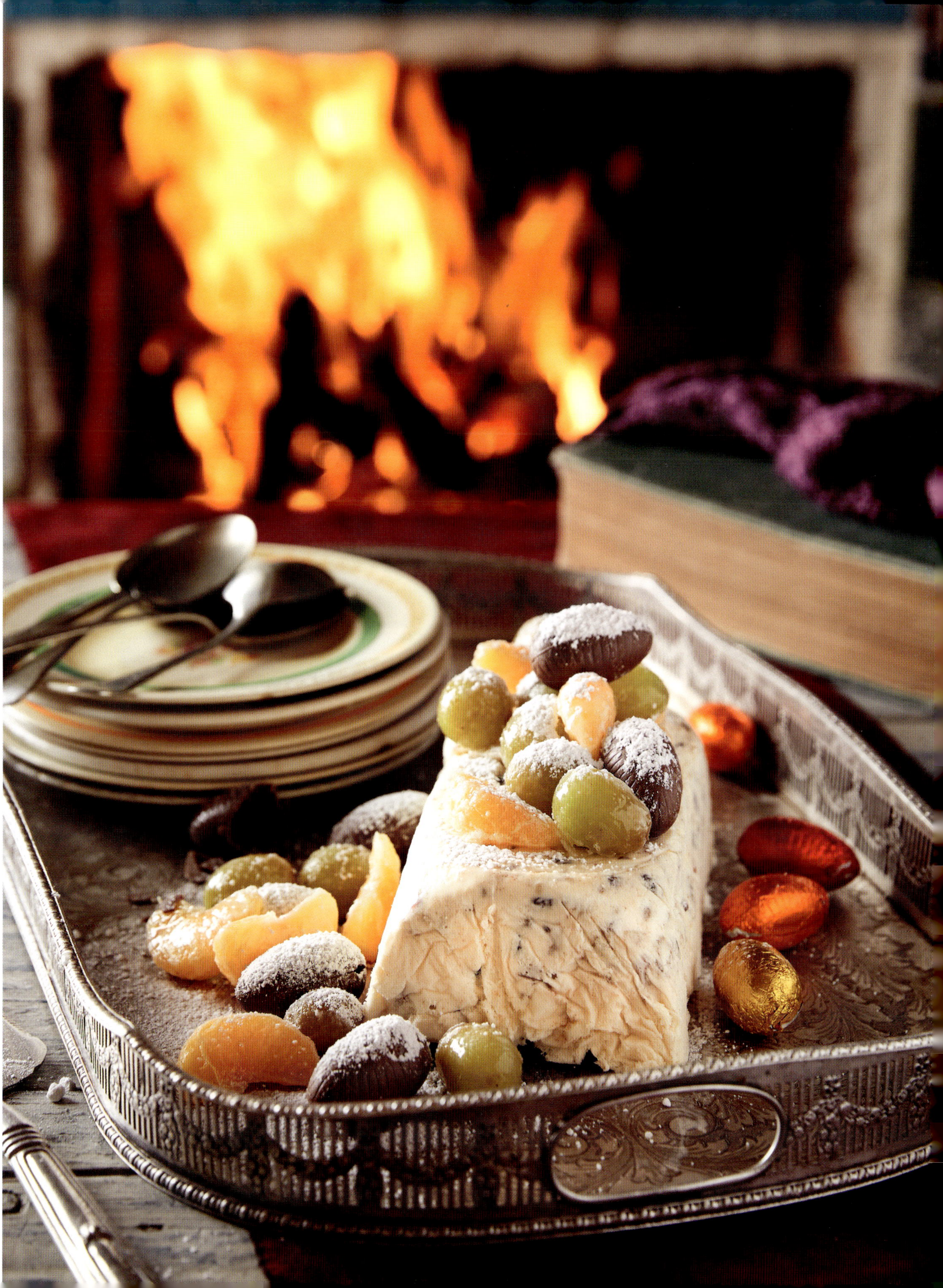

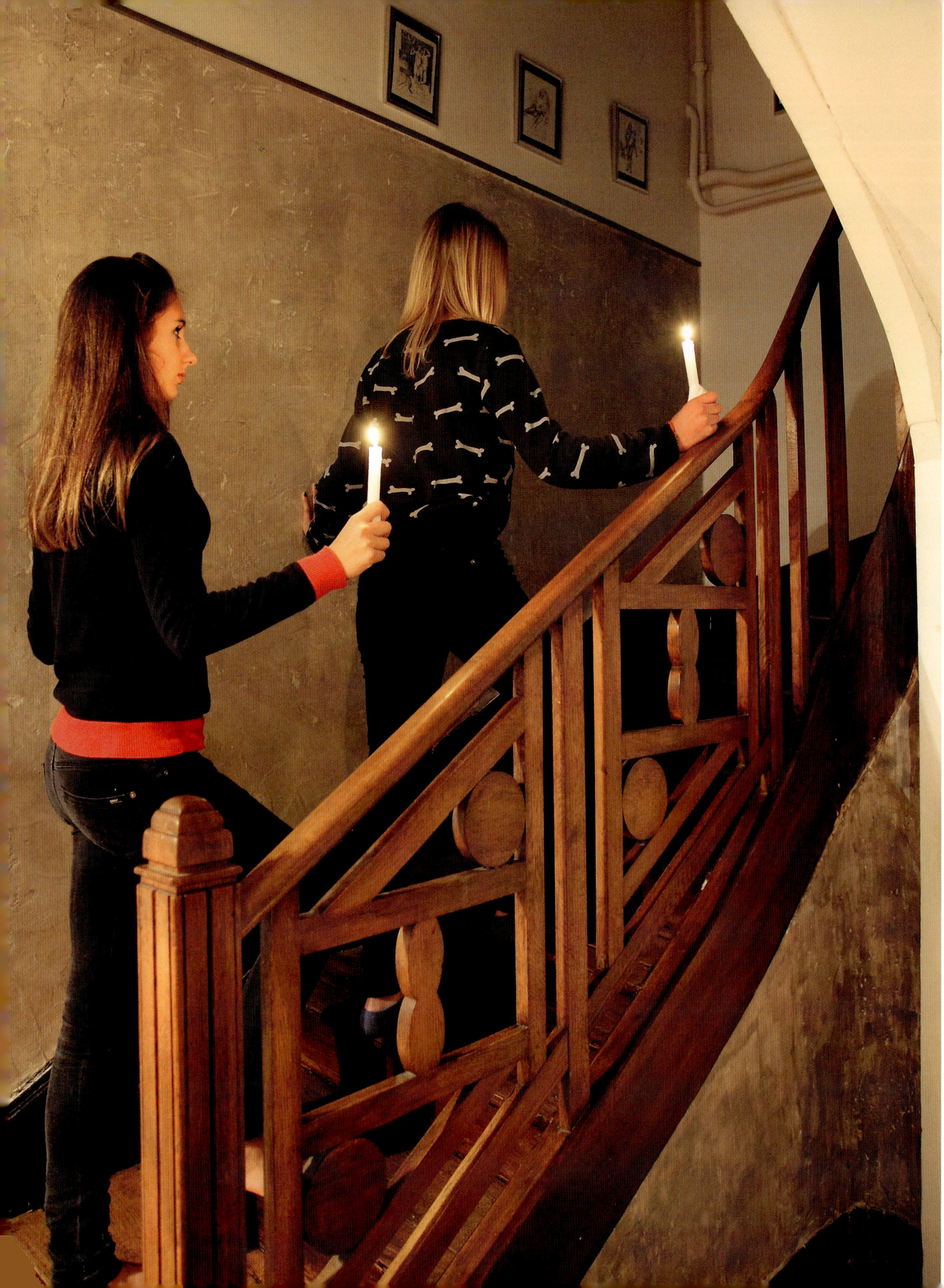

THE STUFF OF LEGENDS

"MY IDEA OF HEAVEN IS EATING PÂTÉ DE FOIE GRAS TO THE SOUND OF TRUMPETS."

SYDNEY SMITH, ENGLISH WRITER (1771-1845)

Foie means liver and *gras* means fat or oily. The evocative name of the delicacy that is foie gras is therefore plain old "fatty liver" in English – which certainly does not sound nearly as impressive as the French "fwhaghgaa".

Let me make one thing absolutely clear at the outset. Fatty liver is far too expensive to be an everyday dish on French tables – except perhaps in the south-western Périgord region where ninety per cent of French foie gras still comes from – although astronomical amounts of the stuff are consumed country-wide during the festive season at the end of the year. France produces nearly 20 000 tons annually – approximately eighty per cent of all foie gras sold globally – and still this is not sufficient to satisfy demand in the French market. That's right, foie gras is also imported into France from countries such as Hungary.

And yet there are French people who would not touch this luxurious liver even during the festive season, because they object to the way in which the poultry are force-fed to get their livers so nice and fatty. Whenever I sit down and consider the issue, I decide they have a point. What's sauce for the goose is sauce for the gander, so next Christmas I will also say no thank you. And then next Christmas comes round and all resistance crumbles …

Because, prepared correctly, foie gras is a very, very special dish. And I am not talking about the pâté, you understand. The pâté might be an extraordinary luxury for our rather ordinary family, but it is the lowest grade of fatty liver, far beneath that of the blocks of liver that you buy raw and cook yourself. With fresh black truffles it becomes a mythical dish, almost as irresistible as a drug that you *know* you should not be taking. After many French festive seasons I can sum up my moral standpoint as follows: I like geese and ducks, but I like foie gras more.

If you do not agree, please skip this chapter and head straight on to the one about garlic soup. To my knowledge, no living creatures – with the possible exception of vampires – are harmed by buying and eating garlic.

The practice of *gavage* or force-feeding did not, however, originate among the cruel and greedy French. Thousands of years ago, the Egyptians – possibly even crueller and greedier than the French – discovered that geese and ducks would overeat in a quite unseemly fashion before embarking on their long migratory flights. And that this gluttony actually made their meat and liver taste much nicer. So the ancient Egyptians reckoned, if the geese did it themselves, they could help them do it even better. And that is how the practice developed of forcing grain and other food down the birds' throats.

From Egypt the practice spread to the ancient Greeks and further afield, until Roman gastronomes shifted the focus from the meat of the goose to the highly prized liver. *Iecur ficatum* they called it, Latin for "liver stuffed with figs", because the geese fed with dried figs were said to produce the very best livers. This was the birth of a gastronomic delicacy that really came into its own at the French court of the seventeenth century. And this is why fatty liver was given the French name that it is still known by throughout the world today – despite the fact that no-one but the French is able to pronounce it properly.

These days French foie gras is almost exclusively duck liver – less than five per cent is the traditional goose liver – and because the fat content of duck liver is slightly lower, it is more suitable for shorter cooking times at higher temperatures. While goose liver should rather be prepared using a slower, more traditional method such as *au torchon* (in a cloth) in a bain-marie. But goose or duck, fatty liver remains fatty liver, a delicacy that can taste like a little piece of heaven on earth. No wonder it is so popular on New Year's Eve, when virtuous resolutions are made for the year that lies ahead. If you eat enough foie gras at New Year, you too will believe you can move mountains.

Foie gras in a sauce

Just in case you manage to get your hands on a block of cooked foie gras some day and want to do something with it besides scoff it on toast, you could use it to make a rich and creamy sauce to go with a juicy steak. Mix 50 g foie gras with a knob of butter to form a soft pâté. Heat another knob of butter in a small pan over moderate heat and fry a chopped shallot until soft. Add the foie gras along with 50 ml chicken stock and 3 T crème fraîche, and bring to the boil. Reduce the heat and simmer for a few minutes. Pour the hot sauce over steak that has been cooked to your liking and tuck in.

Creamy rillettes
6-8 SERVINGS

If you cannot get hold of foie gras there are fortunately more modest and affordable French pâtés with and without liver to be tried in the South African kitchen. *Rillettes* are not as well known as liver pâté, but are just as tasty – if not more so if you prefer a coarser texture – and much easier to make at home than you would think.

1 kg cheaper cut of fatty pork, without bones (such as pork belly)
1 T salt | 2-3 bay leaves | 3 stalks of thyme | 3 cloves garlic | sage, rosemary or other herbs to taste (optional)

Rub the salt all over the meat and place it in an ovenproof dish along with all the remaining ingredients. Put the lid on and place in a preheated 160 °C oven for 3 hours until the meat has roasted and softened in its own fat.

Remove the meat from the fatty juices. Remove the skin and shred the meat with two forks. Don't be tempted to use a food processor to do this, as the texture will be much too smooth and you will end up with pâté instead of *rillettes*. This part of the recipe requires no skill on your part, just patience.

Press the shredded meat into a ceramic or glass container, or into sterilised glass jars if you do not plan on eating it all at once. Pour some of the fatty gravy in the ovenproof dish over the *rillettes* through a sieve (just enough to cover the meat if you do not want it too fatty). Stir gently with a fork to ensure the liquid is absorbed and that only a thin layer of fat remains on top of the meat.

Leave to cool and place in the fridge for a couple of hours until the fat has set. Spread on slices of wholewheat bread and enjoy with olives or gherkins. Or store for a few weeks in airtight glass jars and enjoy snacking on it when the craving becomes irresistible.

Raw, semi-cooked and cooked

Raw foie gras, the most expensive of all, can be stored in the fridge for up to three weeks – provided you keep it in the vacuum packaging it is sold in. Once removed from the packaging, the foie gras must be eaten within a day or two. The semi-cooked version (*mi-cuit*) must also be kept in the fridge until it is cooked, but the cooked version (*cuit*) is usually sold in tins and lasts as long on the shelf as any other canned food. Pop it in the fridge the day before you plan to eat it and spread cold on triangles of hot toast.

Right: Creamy rillettes

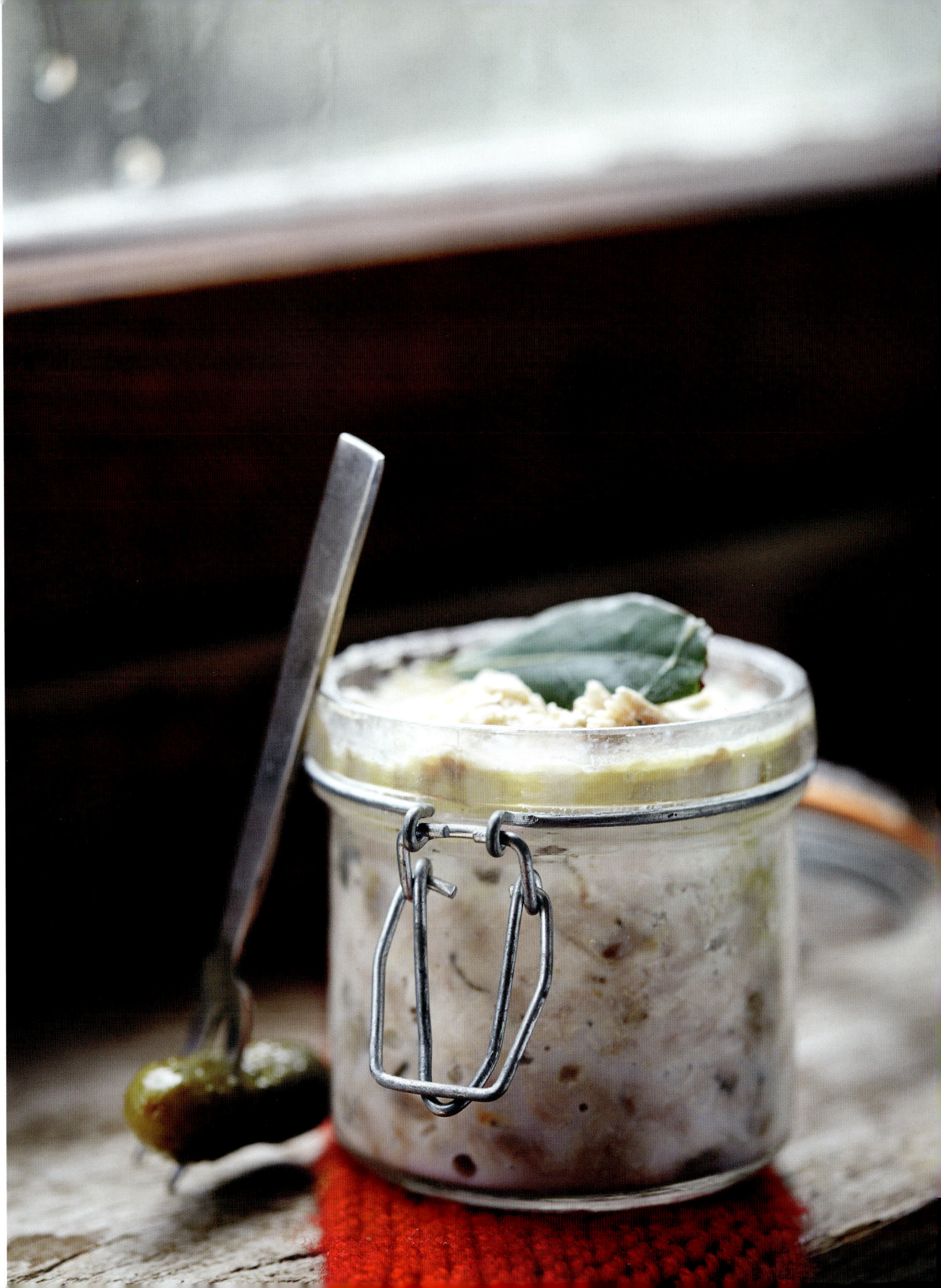

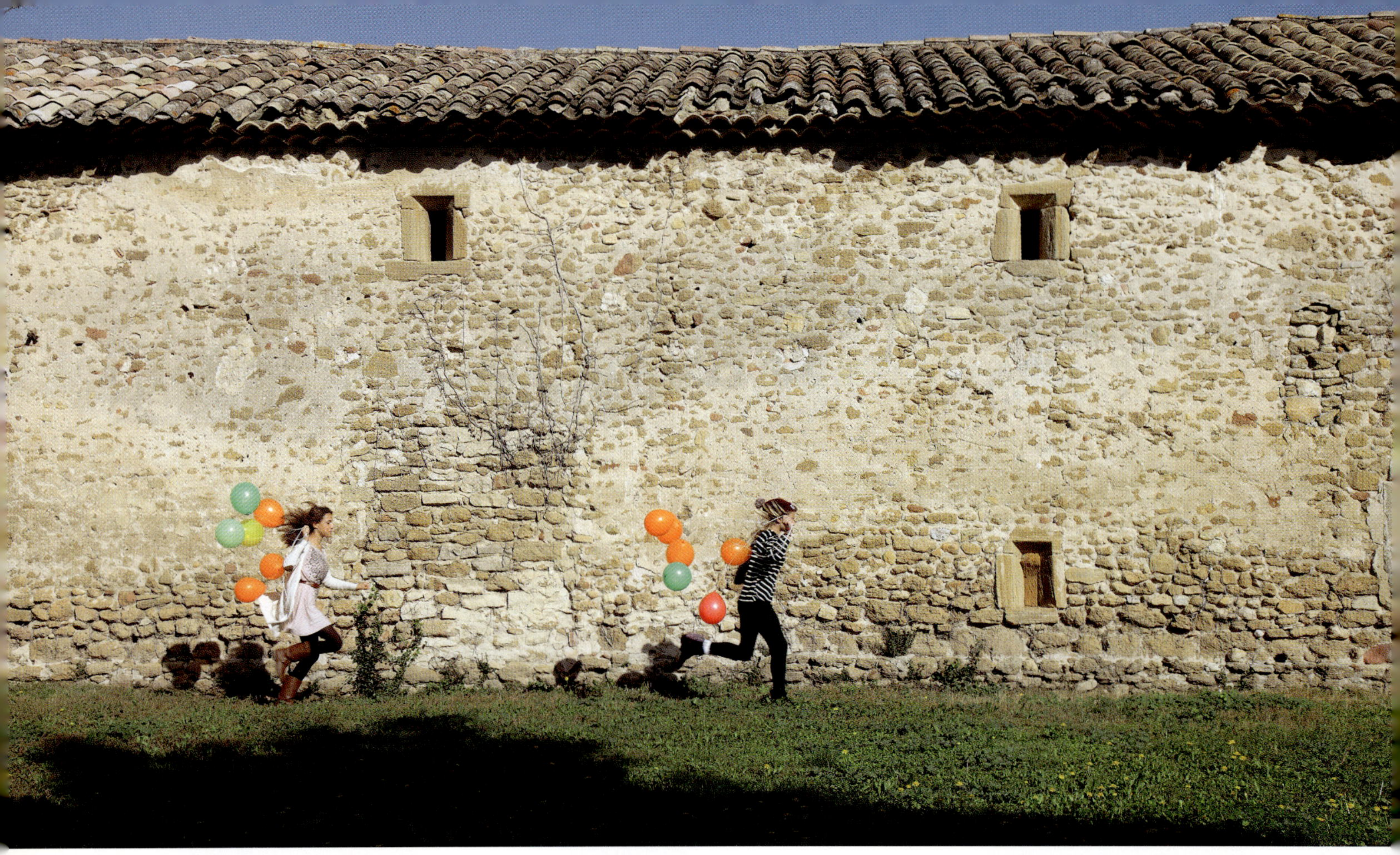

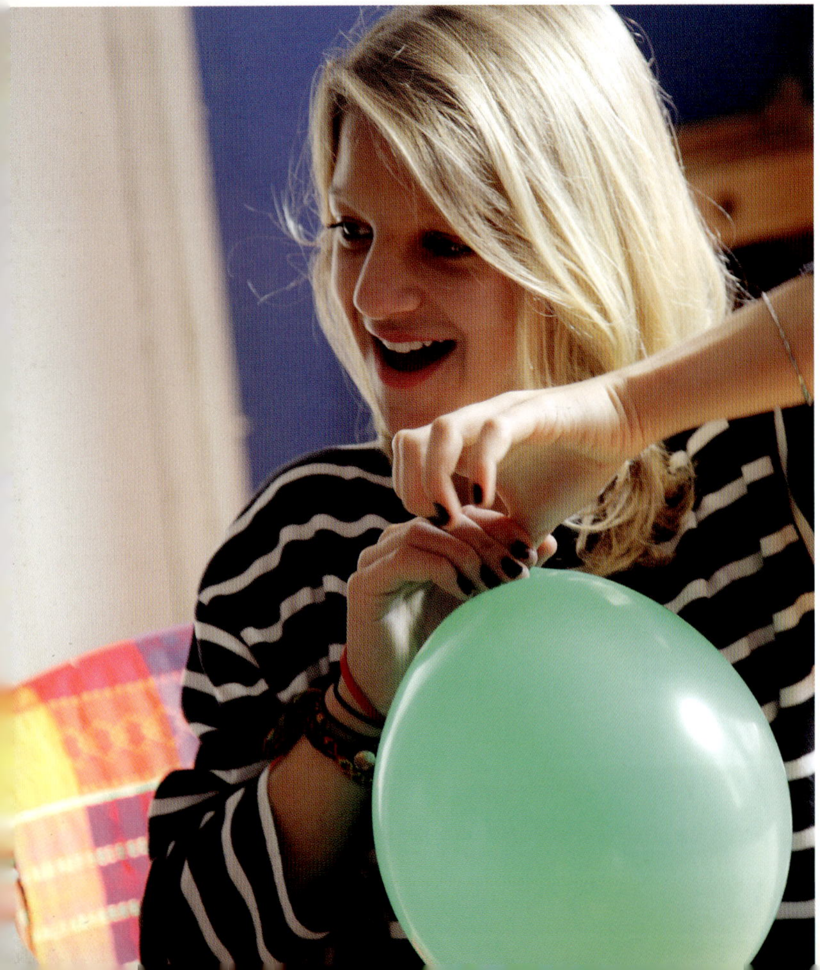

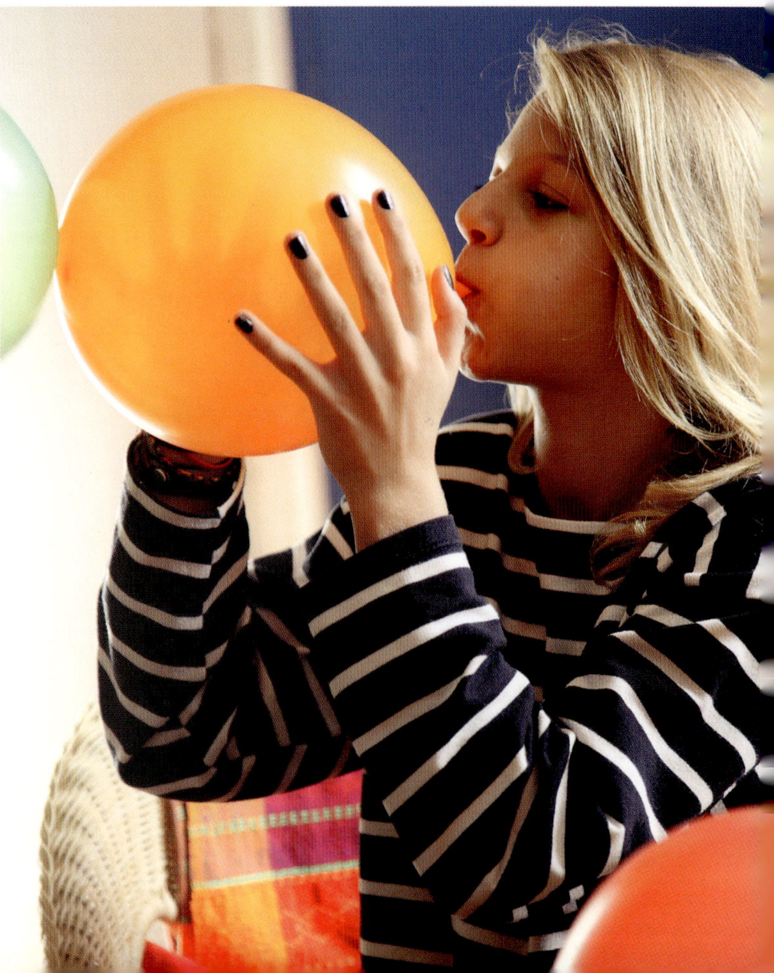

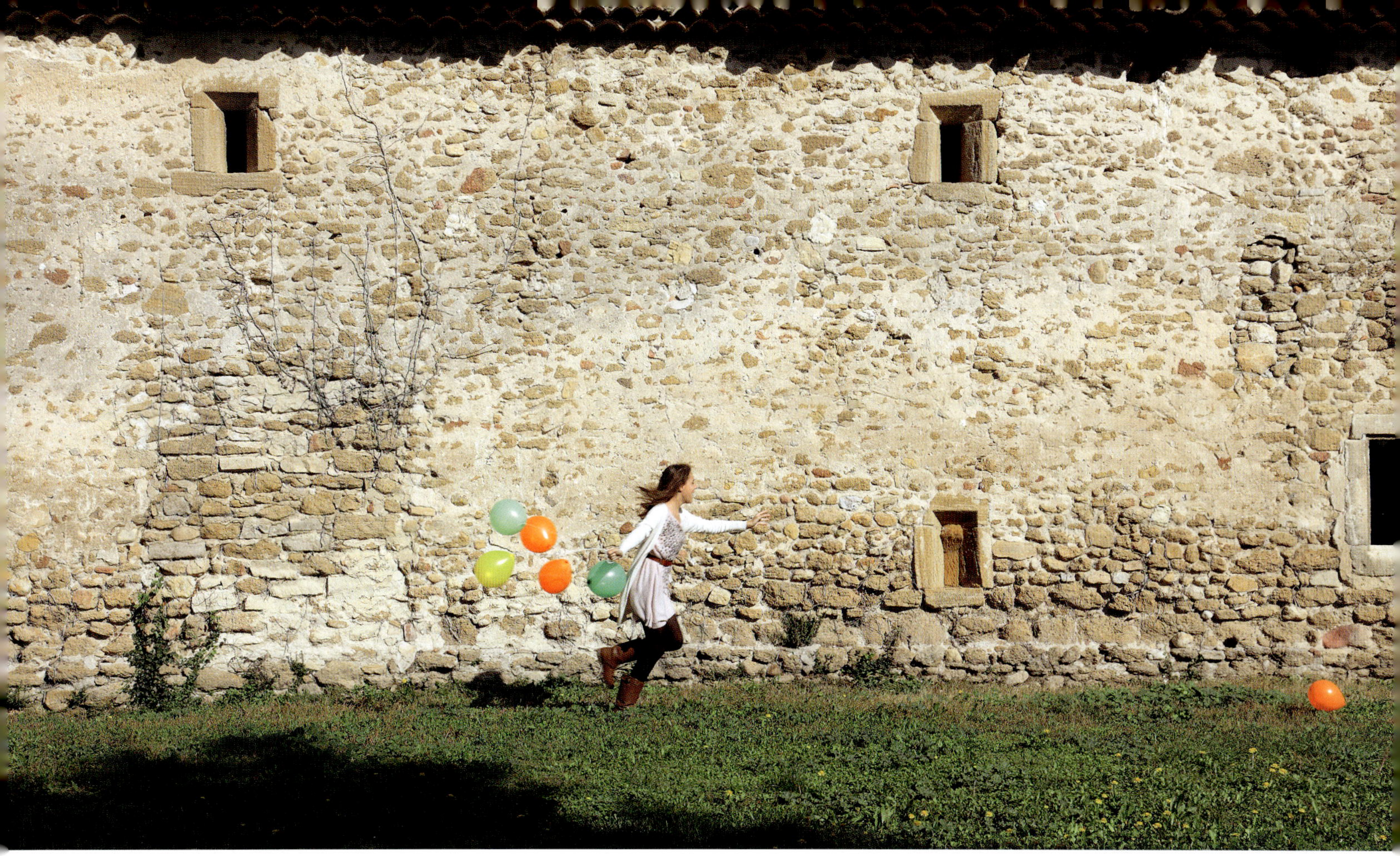
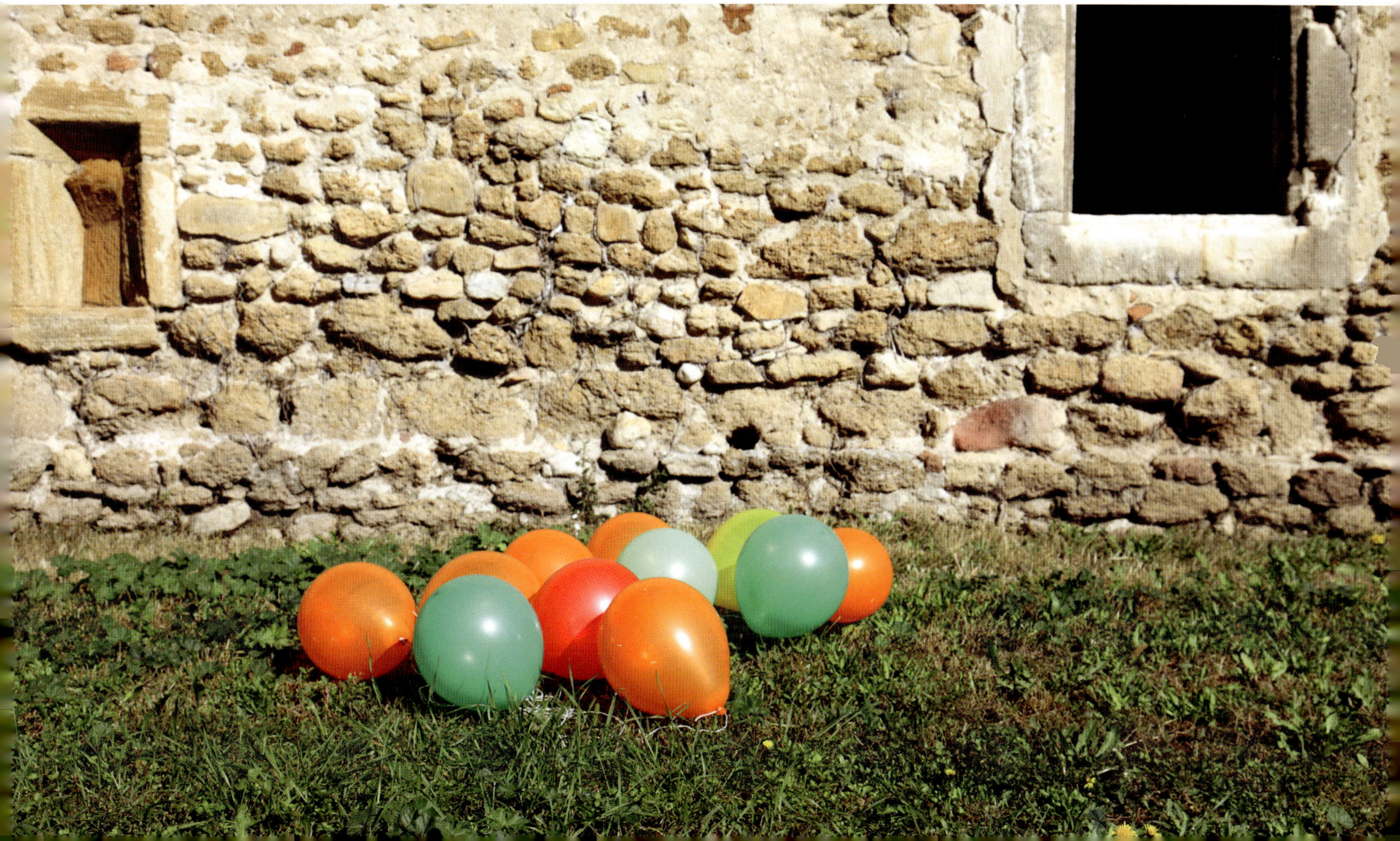

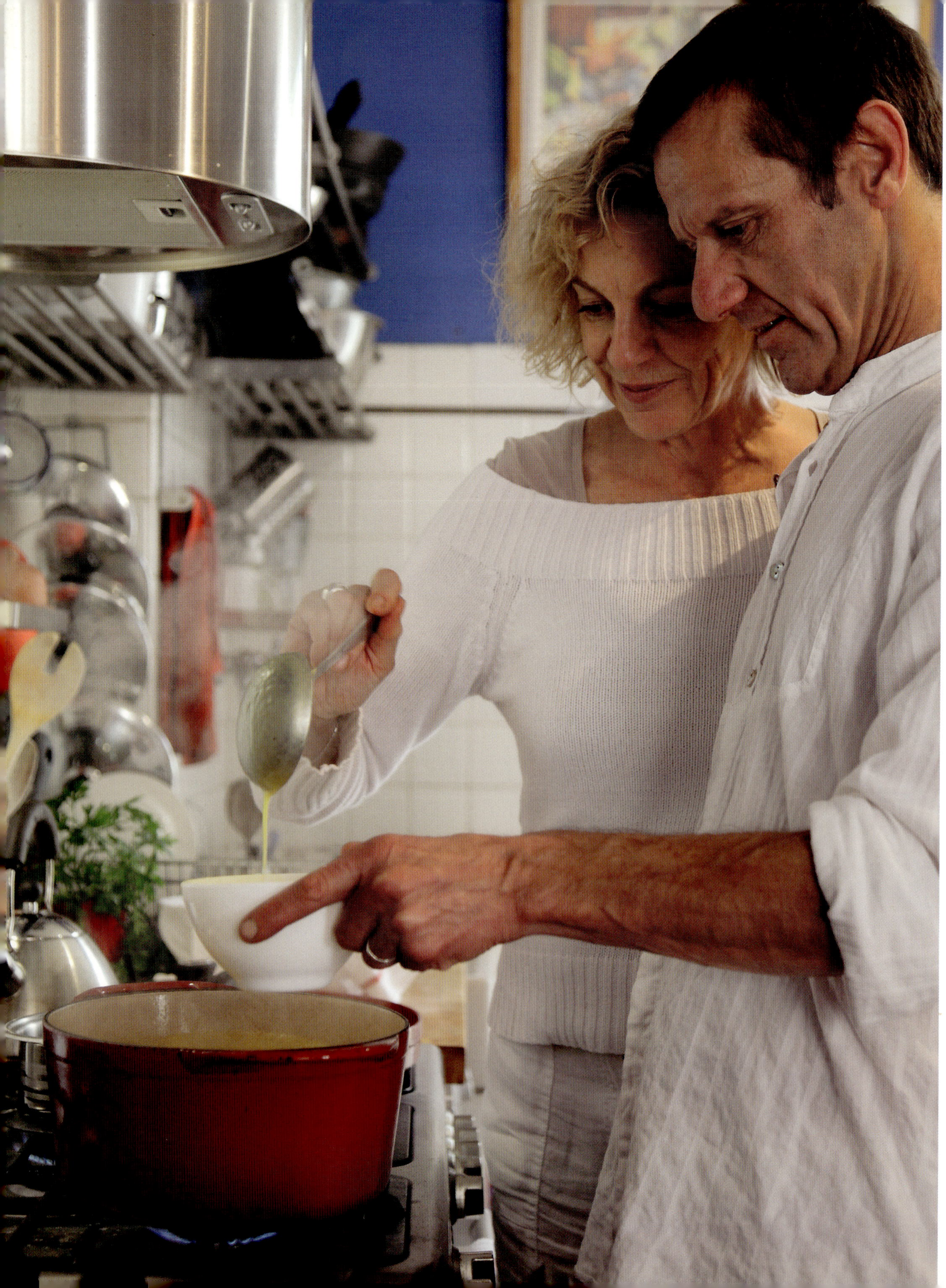

IN THE SOUP

"THE AIR OF PROVENCE WAS PARTICULARLY PERFUMED BY THE REFINED ESSENCE OF THIS MYSTICALLY ATTRACTIVE BULB."

ALEXANDRE DUMAS, FRENCH WRITER, ON GARLIC (1802-1870)

What could be tastier, simpler and healthier than a big pot of soup to ward off the winter cold? In our house we have been known to survive on soup and bread for days at a time. No, that is not strictly true. The parents of the house love soup but the children, like children everywhere I suppose, would soon start moaning if they had to eat soup all the time. Fortunately there are so many different kinds of soup – thick and thin, creamy and smooth, bouillons and *potages* and *veloutés*, and some so substantial you could eat them with a fork instead of a spoon – that our soup diet need never become boring. And among all our beloved winter soups there are some that even the children and the cats seem to like.

One soup that the children certainly did not appreciate when they were younger, is garlic soup. But now that the boys are old enough to party through the night on New Year's Eve (and many other nights too), they have started to understand why this healthy and tasty soup has been popular for centuries. According to an old French tradition, garlic soup is the first meal you should enjoy in the new year, usually in the early hours of the morning after a night of revelry, to cleanse and strengthen the constitution. Believe me, in France by New Year's Day your constitution will probably need it. It is not just the previous night's excesses; it is very likely an entire week's carousing catching up with you.

My French family and friends love to eat and drink the whole year long, but in the week between Christmas Eve and New Year the national obsession with food and drink reaches almost unimaginable proportions. This is a week in which your mouth is only empty when you are asleep – and sleep is a lot scarcer than food during the festive season. That is where the garlic soup comes in.

This relative of the onion and the leek was used for medicinal purposes by the Egyptians and Chinese thousands of years ago, and still plays an important part in homeopathic remedies for aches and pains ranging from the common cold to high cholesterol.

A number of cultures have even attributed supernatural powers to garlic. According to Korean mythology, a tiger and a bear begged the god Hwanung to turn them into human beings. He gave them twenty cloves of garlic and a bunch of mugwort as holy food, and commanded them to live in a cave for one hundred days and eat nothing else. The tiger left the cave after twenty days, but the bear persevered and was turned into a woman. (Am I the only one to detect a feminist lesson in this story?)

But it is in the kitchen that garlic really comes into its own. Alain strongly identifies with the *cri de coeur* of his fellow countryman Louis Diat (the famous chef who is honoured as the "father" of vichyssoise soup): "Without garlic I simply would not care to live!" Oh yes, the French certainly have a passionate relationship with this "mystically attractive bulb", as Alexandre Dumas described it. Note that Dumas did not complain about the notorious smell; he waxed lyrical about the "refined essence" that "perfumed" the air. Hear, hear, is all I can say.

Garlic soup offers not only a powerful combination of health, taste and aroma; it is also cheap and easy to make, traditional "poor man's food", and blissfully warming in icy weather.

The same can be said of another interesting soup that I discovered in France: lettuce soup. Before I moved here, I would never have guessed that lettuce leaves could be used for anything other than salad. Now I know that if you have bought too much lettuce for a big event, as often happens during the festive season, and a day or two later the leftover leaves are looking a little too limp for another salad, you simply cook the whole lot up in a green soup that roars with flavour.

As I have said before, in our house we hate throwing leftovers away. Think about the poor hungry children in Africa, I can still hear my dear late mother saying. Well, Mom would be very proud if she could taste our lettuce soup.

Right: Garlic soup

Garlic soup
4 SERVINGS

The taste – and the smell! – of France in your kitchen.

1 T olive oil | 50 g butter | 1 head of garlic (about 12 cloves), peeled and finely chopped | 1 litre chicken stock 5-6 slices stale baguette | 2 egg yolks salt and pepper

Heat the oil and butter in a large saucepan and fry the garlic over moderate heat until brown. Add the stock and bread, as well as salt and pepper to taste, and leave to cook over low heat for about 20 minutes.

Remove from the heat and liquidise the soup. Scoop out a large ladleful of the soup and mix it with the egg yolks in a bowl. Slowly stir the egg-yolk mixture into the soup.

Reheat if necessary and season with plenty of salt and pepper. Serve with fresh baguettes and a bowl of grated cheese for sprinkling generously over the soup. I like to melt a little cheese in mine, while my Frenchman prefers not to dilute the pure flavour of the garlic. To each their own, I say.

Lettuce soup
4 SERVINGS

Use any type of lettuce with bright green leaves, such as butter lettuce or Cos, or even different types of lettuce, such as watercress or lamb's lettuce mixed with frisée, to give the soup a lovely colour. And remember, wilted leaves are not a problem – it makes no difference to the taste.

50 g butter | 2 large heads of lettuce, washed, dried well and cut into pieces 1 litre beef stock | 1 large potato, peeled and chopped | 2 egg yolks 2 T flour | 200 ml crème fraîche or fresh cream | salt and pepper

Heat the butter in a large saucepan and add the salad leaves. Fry them gently, stirring, until all the liquid they give off has been absorbed. Do not allow the lettuce to colour.

Add the stock and the potato, season more generously than usual with salt (this is a soup that needs salt) and a little freshly ground black pepper, and bring to the boil. Reduce the heat and simmer gently for about 20 minutes.

Remove the soup from the heat and liquidise. Beat the egg yolks and flour together in a bowl. Slowly add 1 cup of soup to the egg mixture, beating continuously. Return the soup to low heat and very gradually stir in the egg mixture. (You want the egg to bind; you do not want scrambled eggs.)

Once the soup is hot, remove from the heat, taste to check the seasoning, and stir in the crème fraîche or cream. Serve with a generous spoonful of cream in each soup bowl. Pure green pleasure.

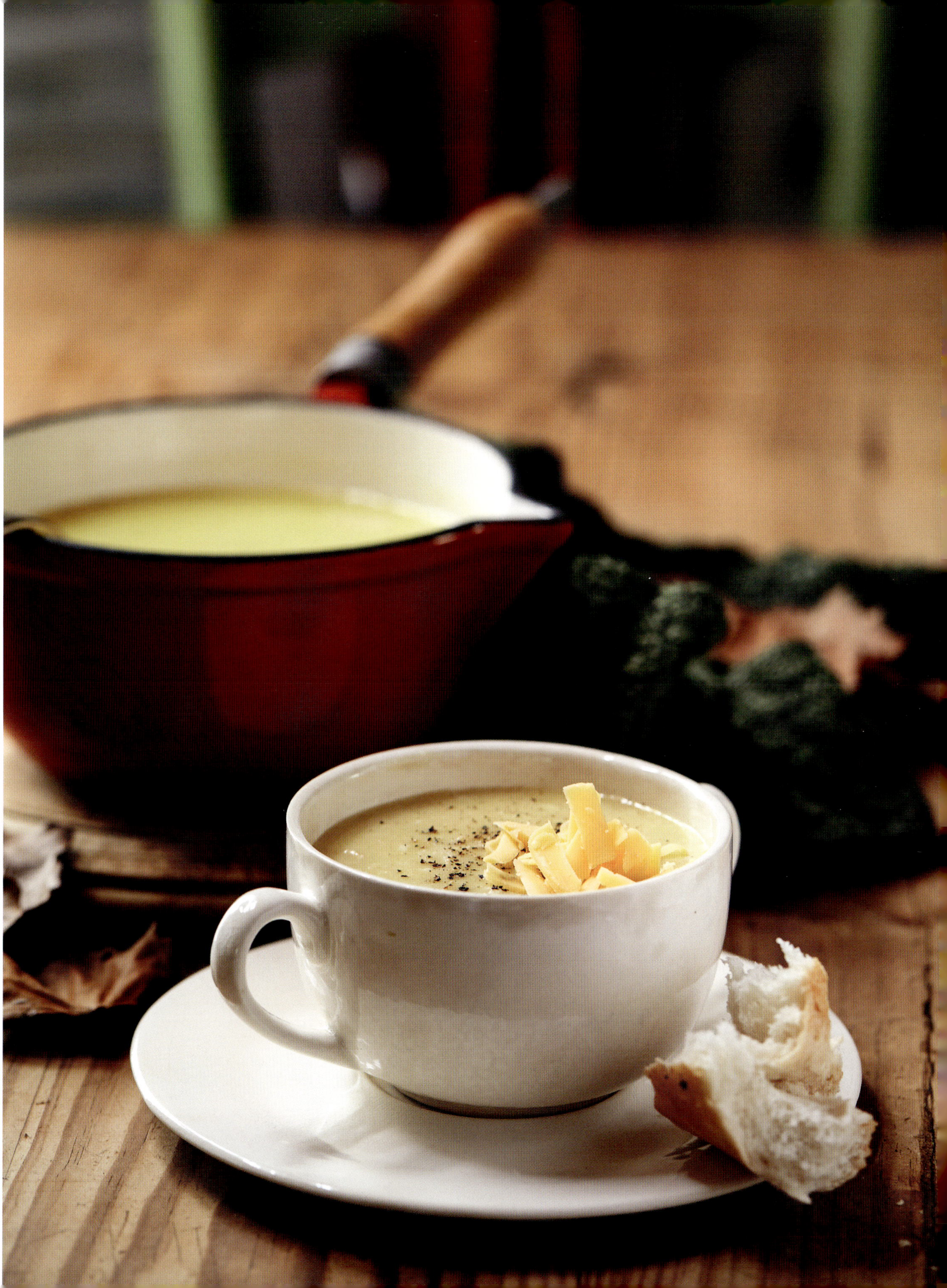

4 DECOUPAGES ANIMES

BOUCHERIE
CHARCUTERIE
Cyril et Béatrice
Usclat
NYONS (Drôme)

antjie krog fiona moodie
Tomi Ungerer

LE COMPTOIR DE MATHILDE
14 juin 2013
CHOCOLATERIE

Boîte de Coloriages
Marc Vidal Brunoy France marcvidal.com

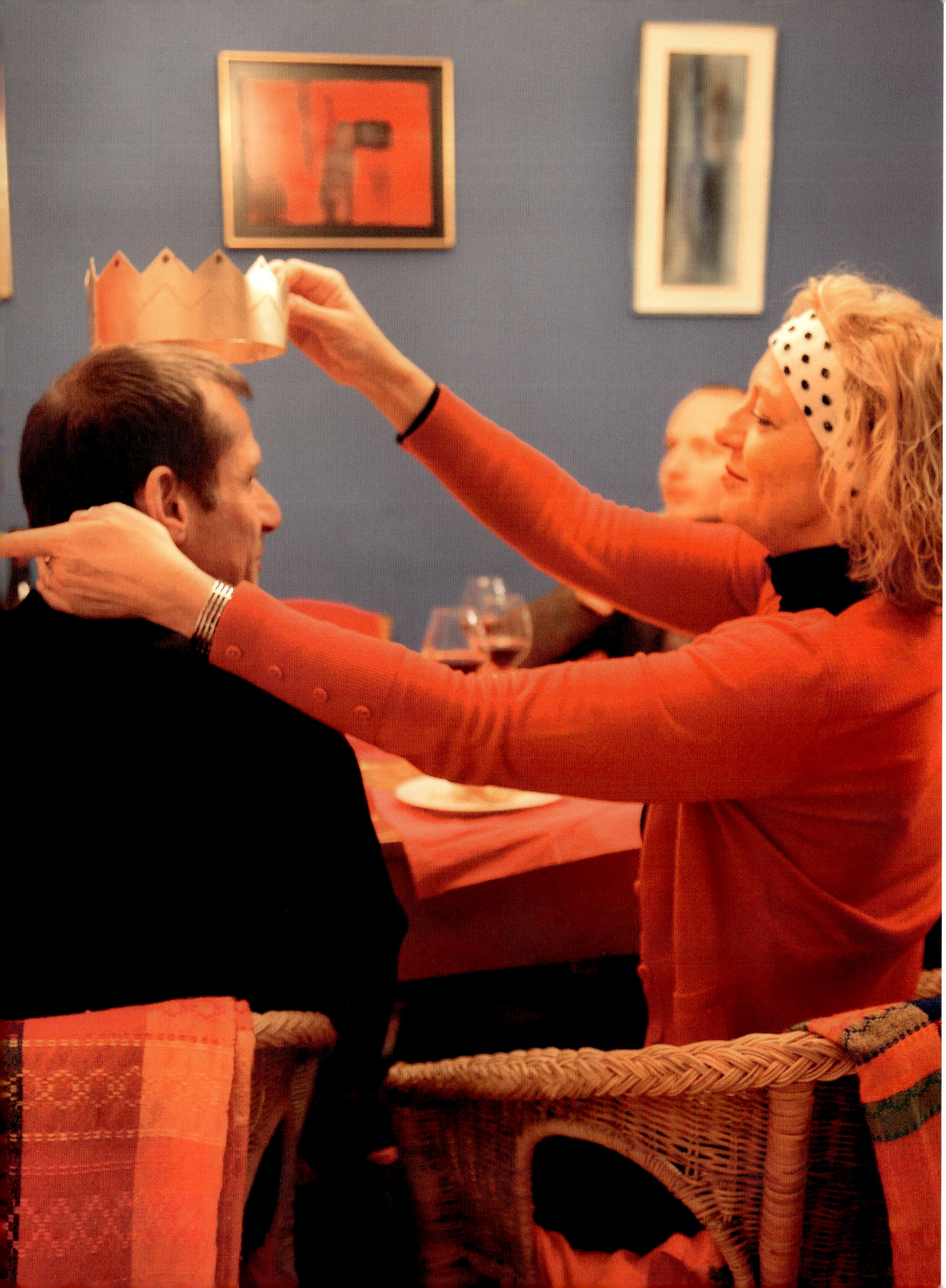

TRADITIONAL TARTS AND PRETTY PIES

"GOOD APPLE PIES ARE A CONSIDERABLE PART OF OUR DOMESTIC HAPPINESS."

JANE AUSTEN, ENGLISH AUTHOR (1775-1817)

In early January, when the poplars and plane trees stand shivering naked in the wind, you can buy a beautiful tart from your local baker with a porcelain or plastic *fève* (lucky charm) hidden inside. Along with the tart, the baker will give you a gold cardboard crown. Back home, with the fire crackling in the hearth, the tart is cut and divided among the company. If you find the lucky charm in your slice, you get to wear the golden crown and be king or queen for the day. That is how it is supposed to work anyway. I have heard of more than one greedy person who has swallowed the charm in their enthusiasm for the tart.

This was more or less how I described the ritual surrounding *galettes des Rois* or kings tarts in *Where The Heart Is* a decade ago – and exactly how one of our guests swallowed the charm again recently. His greatest fortune that day was that this time the lucky charm was not made of porcelain or plastic. Because we bake our own galettes these days, we hid a "real" *fève* in the form of a dried bean under the pastry. *Fève* is simply the French word for a type of fat bean used centuries ago as the original charm in these tarts – and when it comes to tradition, we like to do things properly.

The kings tart is in fact an old Catholic tradition that commemorates the visit of the Three Kings (or the Three Wise Men, as they are also known) to Jesus in the stable. The official feast day is *Épiphanie*, which falls on 6 January, but the tarts are so delicious that they are sold, baked and devoured countrywide throughout January. The older, Provençal version is a cake rather than a tart, a more bready kind of affair with glacé fruit, but the galette is more popular these days, even in the south and at our Provençal table.

By the way, now that we are talking about the difference between tart and cake, I should add that this galette is strictly speaking a pie rather than a tart. The correct translation of galette is "flat cake" or pancake, and although *galette des Rois* is regarded as a type of tart in France, most bakers would tell you that, unlike a pie, a tart does not have a layer of pastry on top. This distinction has long faded in America, where the word "pie" is widely used for the traditional pumpkin pie, for instance, which is in fact an "open" tart rather than a "closed" pie. (You can find the recipe for this traditional favourite on page 50.)

The *galette des Rois* is therefore a tart and/or a pie (you decide) that is eaten fresh and warm from the oven, comprising two layers of crispy, flaky puff pastry and a meltingly soft almond filling that goes by the lovely name of *frangipane*. A winner, believe me, even without the *fève* and the crown and the tradition of having the youngest child in the company crawl in under the table and from there decide who gets which slice. This ritual is supposed to ensure fair distribution of the tart, but the reason is not really important. It only goes to prove, as if one needed more proof, that French food traditions can be full of fun.

To add even more confusion to the distinction between tarts and pies, France has also produced the famous upside-down tart that goes by the name of *tarte Tatin*, which is baked like a pie (with a pastry topping), but when it comes out of the oven, it is unceremoniously turned upside down and eaten like a tart. Because the traditional "filling" (or bottom layer, which becomes the top layer!) is apples, it is the ideal winter dessert. Other autumn and winter fruits such as figs, prunes, pears and quinces also work very well in this tart. Even vegetables like tomatoes and onions are used to make irresistible upside-down savoury tarts these days.

Ultimately, it makes no difference what you call your baking. In the words of Shakespeare, a tart by any other name would taste as good. Well, perhaps not quite the Bard's words, but we know that is what he meant.

The Tatin sisters' foremost failure

Tarte Tatin is one of those legendary dishes that is said to have been created by accident. Sometime in the 1880s, Stéphanie Tatin, who ran the Hotel Tatin in a small country town along with her sister Caroline, made a mistake while baking an "ordinary" apple pie. Either she absentmindedly put the tart into the oven upside down, or she left the apples to cook in the caramel sauce for too long and tried to rescue the dish by covering it in pastry, or she ... The details do not really matter, as the result made culinary history. There are also sources that allege the tart is simply an improvement on *tarte solognotte*, a traditional baked dish from the Sologne region where the sisters lived. But who wants to spoil such a lovely story with boring facts?

Galette des Rois
8 SERVINGS

We tried a number of galette recipes – some had too much sugar in the filling, others too little butter – until we hit upon this version. It made us feel like Goldilocks when she tasted baby bear's porridge: It is just right. If you cannot find ground almonds, you can grind up blanched almonds in a food processor.

100 g butter | 100 g sugar | 125 g ground almonds | 2 eggs | a dash of bitter almond extract (optional) 2 x 250 g sheets readymade puff pastry | 1 egg yolk

Cream the butter and sugar until the mixture is smooth. Add the ground almonds and 2 eggs, as well as the optional flavouring, and mix well.

Roll out the pastry dough into two circles slightly larger than the tart pan. Line the tart pan with baking paper and place a dough round on it. Spread the almond filling evenly on the dough. Press a dry bean or a trinket of your choice into the filling before covering it with the remaining pastry dough. Press the two layers of pastry together all round the pan by pinching them between your fingers and make a pretty edge using the tines of a fork.

Dilute the egg yolk with a little cold water and brush it over the dough with a pastry brush. Use a knife to draw a latticework pattern on the top. Make a few small holes in the pastry with a fork. Bake in a preheated 200 °C oven for about 30 minutes, until the pastry is golden. If you insert a knife between the tart and the pan and the tart lifts easily, it is done. Enjoy immediately or reheat it before serving, as this galette should be enjoyed warm.

Tarte Tatin
6-8 SERVINGS

150 g sugar | 100 g butter | 1,5 kg apples (Granny Smith or similar), peeled and quartered | 250 g puff pastry (bought or home made)

Start with the caramel sauce. Add half the sugar to 3 T water in a saucepan and stir over low heat until all the sugar has dissolved. Turn up the heat and cook the sauce until golden brown. Remove from the heat immediately and stir in 75 g butter. Add a little water if the sauce is too thick – be careful you do not get splattered! – and pour into a deep tart pan.

Arrange the apple quarters on the sauce, tightly packed in concentric circles, to cover the bottom of the pan completely. Sprinkle with the remaining sugar and dot with knobs of the remaining butter. Bake for 20 minutes in a preheated 190 °C oven.

Leave the tart to cool slightly while you roll out the dough in the shape of the pan. Carefully place the pastry layer on the apples and press the edge onto the pan right round. Increase the oven temperature to 220 °C and bake the tart for a further 15-20 minutes, until the crust has risen and is golden brown. Leave the tart to cool slightly before inverting it onto a large plate. Serve warm with crème fraîche.

Right: Tarte Tatin

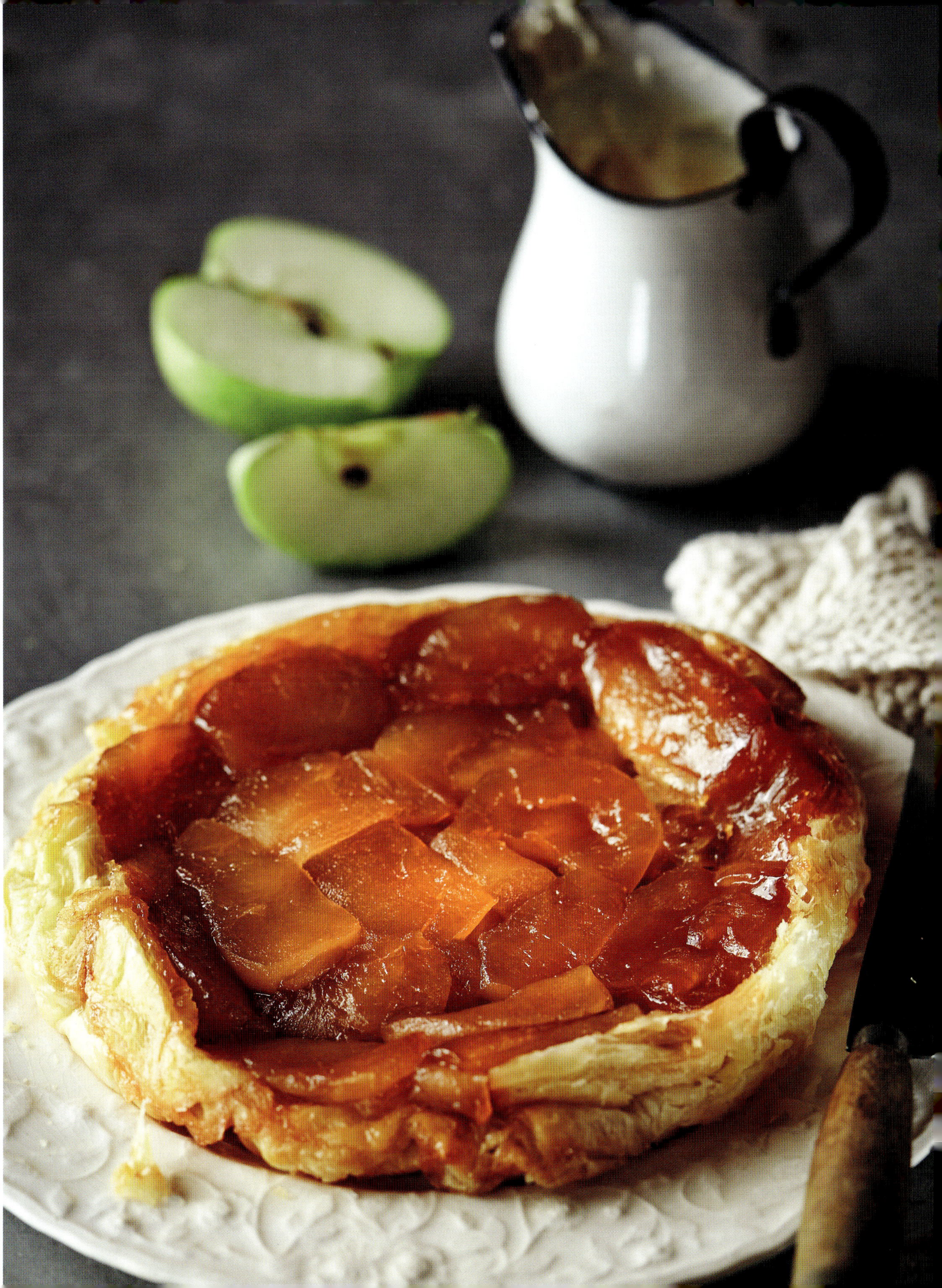

PICASSO

AH, ANCHOVIES

"LIFE IS RATHER LIKE A TIN OF SARDINES – WE'RE ALL OF US LOOKING FOR THE KEY."

ALAN BENNETT, BRITISH ACTOR AND WRITER (1934-)

The best processed anchovies in France – better make that the whole world, according to those in the know – come from the Mediterranean coastal town of Collioure near the Spanish border. Collioure, which was also a painting paradise for artists like Picasso in the last century, is not officially part of Provence, but is close enough to feel like family.

The flesh of these anchovies is plump and firm and dark brown with a unique flavour – less "fishy", closer to good cured ham – and was salted and preserved in Collioure as long ago as the Middle Ages, to preserve it as long as possible for eating in times of scarcity. Still today, the fish is processed fresh from the sea in the town's "salt houses": selected by hand, carefully cleaned and packed in barrels between layers of salt, then left to ripen for at least three months.

Thanks to this painstaking process, Collioure's anchovies have been rewarded with the European Union's prized PDO (Produce of Designated Origin) label, similar to the AOC status. Anyone who turns their nose up at anchovies (those poor, misguided souls who do not know what they are missing), would do well to taste the product from Collioure. It could just be the start of a beautiful friendship.

A plucky little fish that gives an instant savoury boost to any boring dish – pizzas and pasta and pies, sauces and salads and many more – anchovies are particularly well known as a partner to that ubiquitous Provençal morsel, the olive. The little fish is stuffed into the pitted olive or wrapped around it, and the pair play together very nicely, thank you very much, in traditional dishes such as *pissaladière*. But the most practical thing to do with anchovies is to make your own anchoïade or anchovy spread and keep it in the fridge as the basis for instant meals or snacks (See "Indispensable" on page 177.)

Anchovies also have a less luxurious sister, the sardine, that is sold in tins around the world. In France, canned sardines are not regarded as highly as bottled anchovies, but sardines preserved in the best olive oil can still be a quality food product. And just to sort out any confusion between sardines and pilchards: In Europe only a young pilchard of less than a certain length is called a sardine. In the USA, on the other hand, other small saltwater fish such as young sprat and herring are also regarded as sardines.

Fresh sardines are so plentiful at Provençal markets in summer – and so much tastier than the tinned version, especially if you simply roll them in olive oil and coarse salt and grill outdoors over an open fire – that we never bother with the tins. Along the coast near Marseille, sardine braais are such a popular activity they even have their own name, *sardinade*. And the best *sardinade*, the braaiers of Marseille will assure you, are over a fire scented with pine needles from the area.

During winter though, we usually do keep a tin of sardines in the food cupboard because, like canned tuna, it is great in an emergency. That Sunday evening when you return from a holiday and the fridge is empty and the shops closed. Remember, here in the countryside the shops close at midday on Sunday and only reopen at nine on a Tuesday morning. It can be a long and hungry wait if you do not have a tin or two of fish stashed away.

There is a type of sardine that can be eaten fresh in winter, but it is a rare delicacy with an almost legendary reputation that I have not had the chance to taste myself. *Poutine*, basically baby sardines that have not got their scales yet, are caught around Nice from January to March to put in soup and especially omelettes. The best way to eat them is apparently raw, with a drizzle of olive oil and lemon juice, which sounds so good that it has earned a place on my gastronomic bucket list. This is one Provençal winter delicacy that I definitely intend getting to know.

120 | Winter food in Provence

Right: Puttanesca sauce

Mediterranean salad with spinach, bread and anchovies

Salad is just as much part of our meals in winter as it is in summer. This one is made from spinach, which is available in winter, whole-wheat bread, which is nice and filling on a cold day, and various other Mediterranean standbys such as olives, garlic, capers and – obviously – anchovies.

Cut half a *pain de campagne* into small cubes. (Or use any decent old-fashioned whole-grain bread; ordinary brown shop bread will not do.) Spread the cubes on a baking tray, drizzle with olive oil and toast in a preheated 180 °C oven until you have crisp, golden brown croutons. Cut 6 ripe tomatoes into small pieces and put them in a bowl, along with the juices left behind on the cutting board after chopping the tomatoes. Add 2 crushed garlic cloves, ½ cup olive oil and ⅓ cup red-wine vinegar. Grind over some salt and pepper.

Once the toasted croutons have cooled slightly, carefully combine them with the tomato mixture. Add ½ cup pitted black olives and leave to stand for half an hour. Stir a couple of times to make sure the bread soaks up all those lovely juices. Place a few handfuls of spinach leaves, washed and dried and cut smaller if necessary, on a serving platter. Spoon the tomato and bread mixture onto the spinach leaves and sprinkle ¼ cup capers on top. Arrange 10 anchovy fillets or so in a crisscross pattern over the salad – the devil's in the detail, don't you know – and enjoy.

Puttanesca sauce
4-6 SERVINGS

2-3 T olive oil | 1 large onion, finely chopped | 2-3 cloves garlic, finely chopped | 500 g tomatoes, chopped 8-10 anchovy fillets | 3-4 T capers 100 g black olives, preferably pitted (if you are in a hurry, the family can always spit out the pips) | salt and pepper

Heat the oil in a large pan and fry the onion and garlic until soft. Add the rest of the ingredients and season to taste with salt and pepper. (If the anchovies were preserved in salt, you probably do not need more salt.) Simmer for about 20 minutes over low heat while you cook the pasta or fish or chicken (or whatever you want to serve with the sauce). It's as easy as that.

A delicious sauce with a saucy name

Puttanesca is derived from the Italian word for a whore, and therefore means "in the style of a whore". One explanation for this (as always when it comes to the history of food, there are a number of versions of the truth) is that it was an easy, tasty and economical pasta sauce that the busy prostitutes of Naples could prepare and eat between clients. For busy mothers it is an easy, tasty and economical sauce for a weekday evening that can be prepared between other tasks and served with pasta, fish fillets or chicken legs.

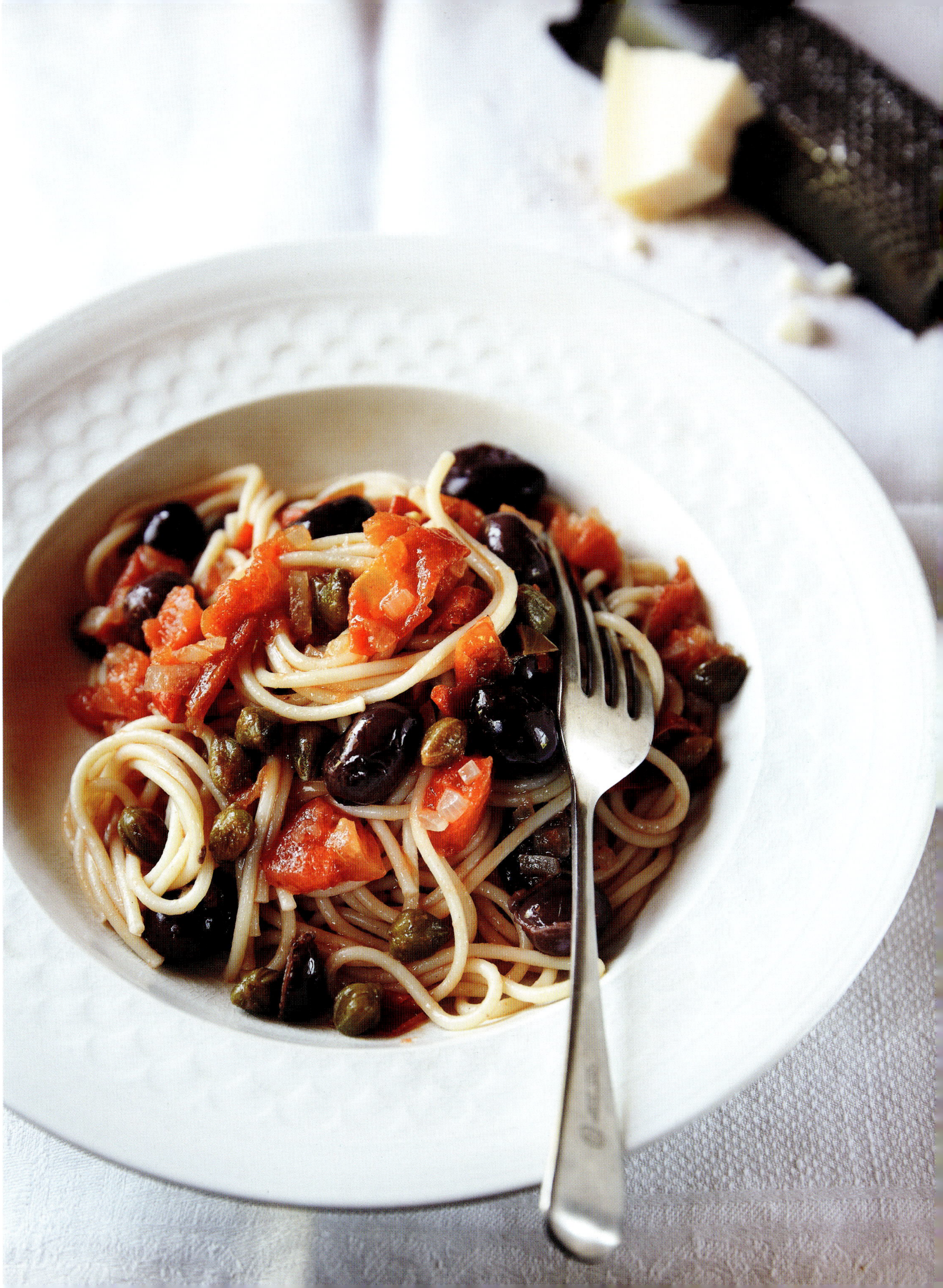

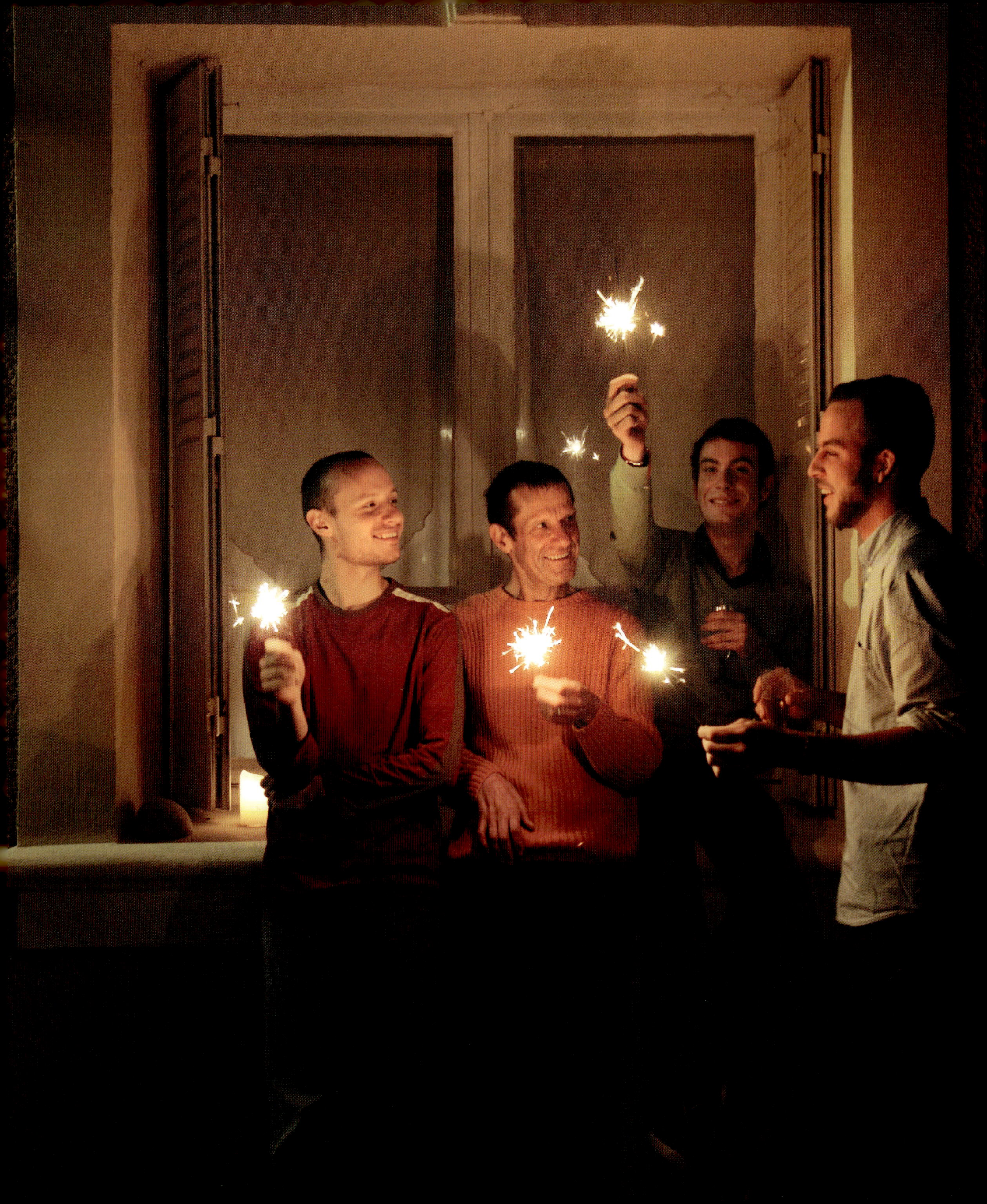

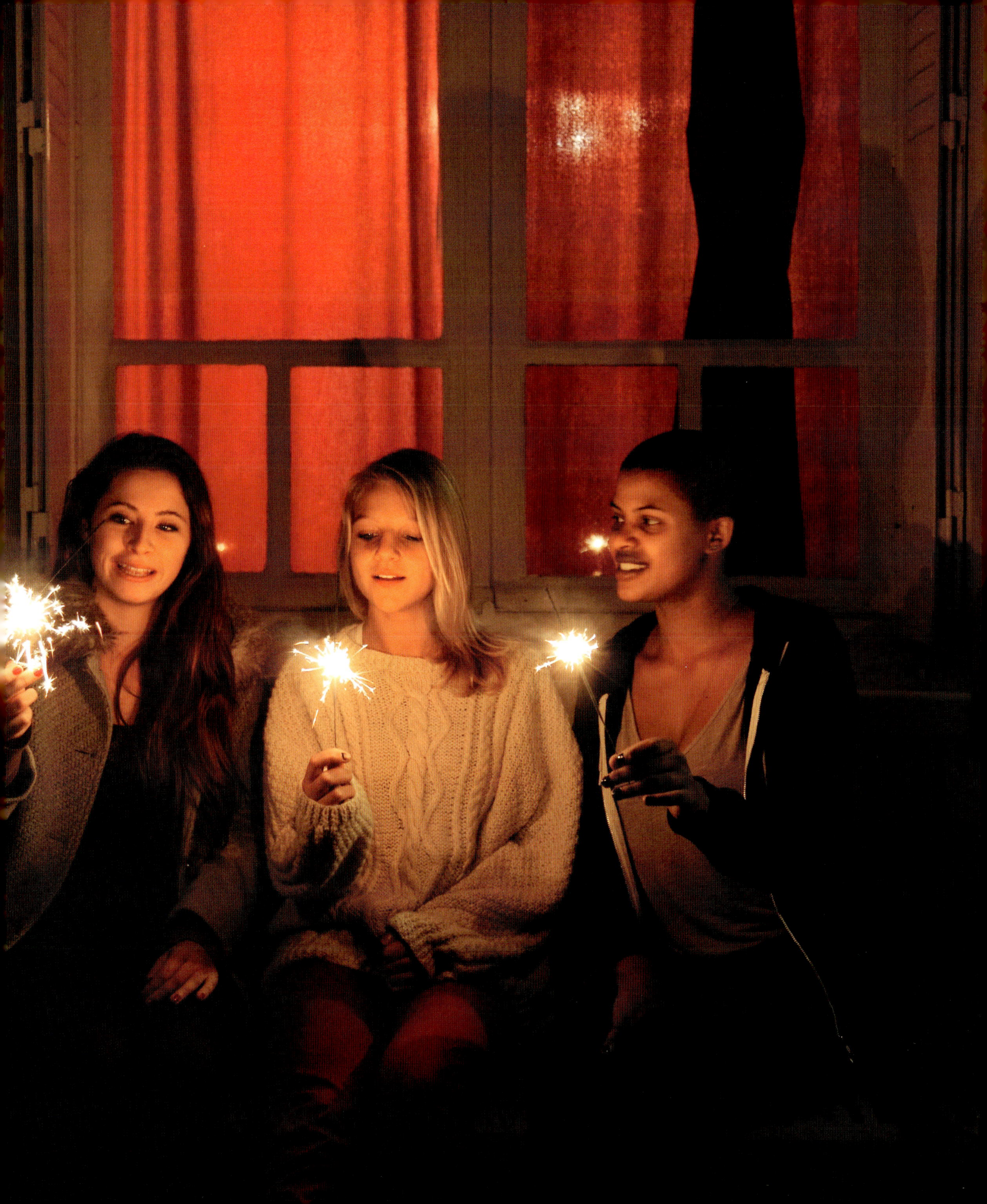

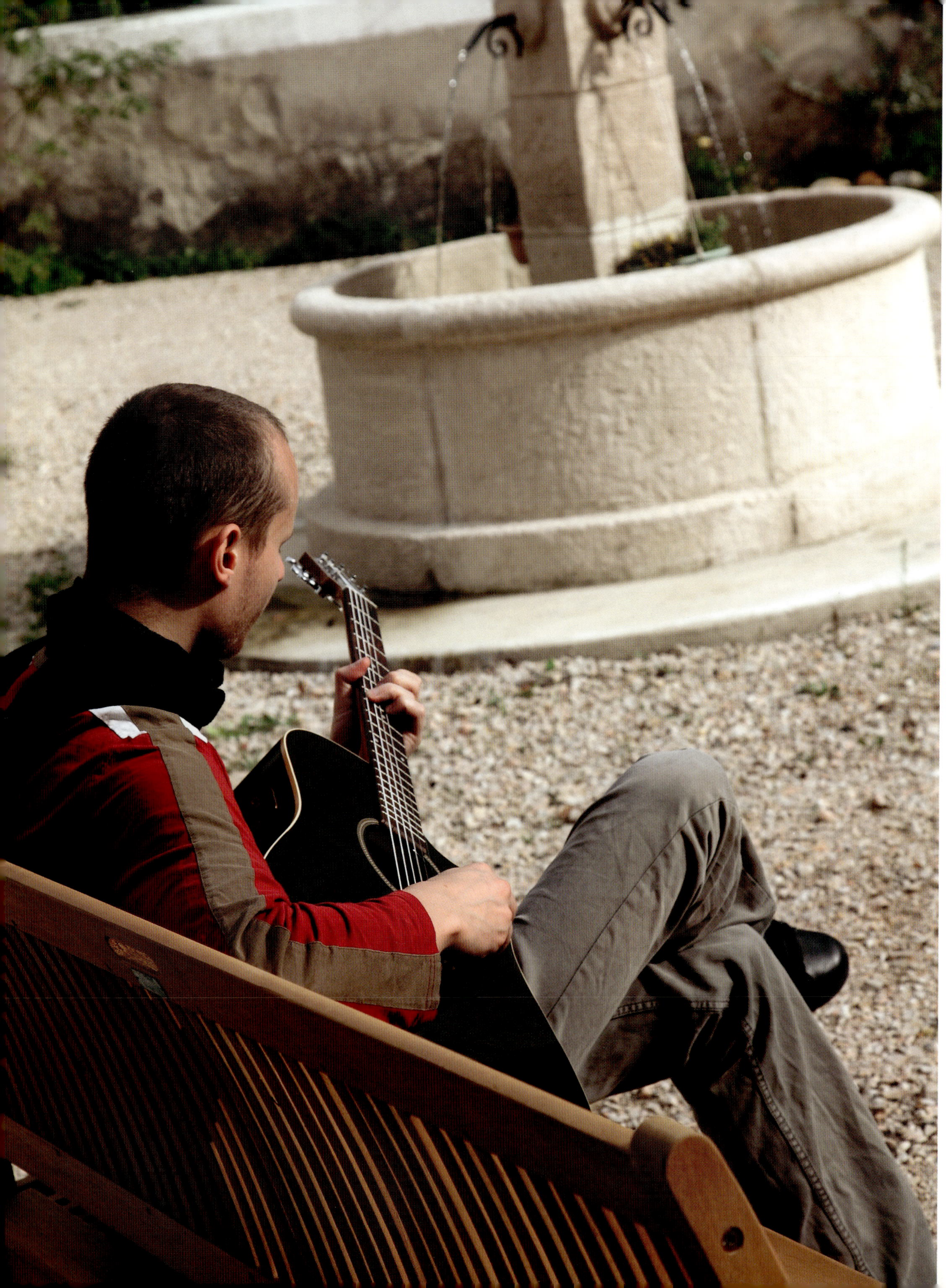

IN PRAISE OF PULSES

"LENTILS ARE FRIENDLY – THE MISS CONGENIALITY OF THE BEAN WORLD."

LAURIE COLWIN, AMERICAN FOOD WRITER (1944-1992)

What would we do in winter without dried pulses? Beans, lentils, chickpeas and split peas are indispensable when fresh vegetables are scarce, as our ancestors discovered thousands of years ago. These days we are also able to buy our legumes (not to be confused with *legumes*, the French collective noun for vegetables) in cans or jars, making preparation so much easier than it used to be.

In our house canned food is regarded with some suspicion. Fresh is always first prize, followed by dried and bottled produce, then food we have frozen ourselves, and right at the bottom of the list, as a necessary evil in any modern kitchen, comes canned food. But whenever we want to make a quick bean soup or a warm lentil salad or a Moroccan tagine with chickpeas, we are grateful for the convenience of a can. Life is so much easier when you do not have to soak the pulses for hours and then cook them for almost as long again.

The first time I came across lentils was as a child in Sunday school, when I heard the Bible story about Esau, who swapped his birth right for a bowl of lentil stew. I could not believe my ears! I could perhaps have imagined swapping my shiny new bike for a freezer filled with ice cream, but giving up everything you owned – for a pot of *lentils*? From that day onwards I regarded lentils as something mystical and magical.

Later I discovered that I was by no means the only one to be enthralled by the wonder of lentils. In Jewish culture, lentils are viewed as suitable food for those in mourning (apparently because the round shape symbolises the cycle of life and death) and in Italy, lentils are eaten on New Year's Eve to ensure a prosperous new year (again because of the shape, which resembles coins). And according to Shia stories, lentils are said to have been blessed by no fewer than seventy prophets, including Mohammed and Jesus, which is enough to make me suspect that old Esau might not have been as stupid as the Bible makes him sound.

Lentils come in a rainbow of colours, from yellow and orange-red to black, and from white to green with shades of blue, and have been a protein-rich substitute for meat since prehistoric times. In India, where they are called *dal* or *dhal*, lentils are an essential ingredient in many traditional dishes. But the queen of lentils, the noblewoman with AOC status, is the *lentille verte du Puy*. Thanks to the unique microclimate in this part of the Auvergne, these green lentils have thinner skins and less starch than other types, and a delicate almost sweet flavour that famous chefs like to use in gourmet dishes. Still, many residents of the Auvergne believe that their lentils are at their best in a simple regional dish like *petit salé*, cooked simply with salted meat and sausages.

Chickpeas were completely unknown to me as a child – not even in Bible stories or fairy tales did I encounter them – although these legumes have been appreciated in the Middle East at least as long as lentils. From there they gradually spread to Ancient Greece and the Roman Empire. Homer's *Iliad* mentions chickpeas, and Apicius's well-known cookbook also contains a number of recipes for them. The Romans also believed that chickpeas had magical properties – like helping them produce more sperm or milk!

Which again leads me to wonder whether Esau might not have had a hidden agenda. As I see it, any gourmand is sometimes prepared to make tremendous sacrifices for a beloved dish. But if Esau did not have a secret reason for his legendary exchange, he was without a doubt the most reckless food lover in Western history.

Right: Warm lentil salad

Warm lentil salad
4-6 SERVINGS

The "right" way to make this traditional French lentil salad, is using dried lentils that have been soaked and boiled. If you are in a hurry though, there is nothing stopping you reaching for a can.

375 g green puy lentils (or other preferably brown or black lentils that keep their shape during cooking), soaked in water for at least 3 hours (or use tinned) | 1 clove | 1 onion, peeled | 2 carrots, 1 just peeled and the other peeled and cut into thin rounds | 1 bay leaf | 1 stalk thyme 1 clove garlic, peeled | 1 leek, thinly sliced | 2 celery sticks, chopped 200 g chopped smoked bacon vinaigrette | 1 T chopped chives

Drain the lentils and place in a large saucepan. Stick the clove into the onion and put it in the pot along with the peeled carrot, bay leaf, thyme and garlic. Cover with hot water, bring to the boil and simmer for about half an hour. (If you are using tinned lentils, you can heat them in the liquid from the tin.) Remove the onion, carrot, garlic and herbs, and drain the lentils.

Place the sliced carrot, leek and celery in a pot of salted boiling water and blanch briefly. Drain well. Fry the bacon in its own fat until it is golden brown. Mix the fried bacon with the blanched vegetables and the hot lentils. Pour a little vinaigrette over the salad, stir to combine and sprinkle with chopped chives. Enjoy before it gets cold.

Catalan chickpeas
4 SERVINGS

This is a tasty and easy winter dish of Spanish origin – with just the right amount of heat in the chorizo to drive away the cold.

3 T olive oil | 1 onion, finely chopped | 100 g chopped smoked bacon | 350 g chorizo sausage, cut into thick slices | 3 carrots, thinly sliced | 2 large tomatoes, cubed 250 g tinned chickpeas | 1 cup beef stock (or less if the tomatoes are very juicy) | a few fresh origanum leaves (or a generous pinch of dried origanum) | salt and pepper

Heat the oil in a large heavy-based pan and fry the onion over moderate heat until almost golden brown. Add the bacon and fry for 1-2 minutes. Add the chorizo, carrots and tomatoes and cook for about 5 minutes.

Add the chickpeas and the beef stock. Sprinkle in the origanum and season to taste with salt and pepper. Put the lid on the pan, reduce the heat and simmer for at least half an hour so that the spices in the chorizo can infuse the entire dish.

Serve with rice or baguette to mop up the delicious gravy.

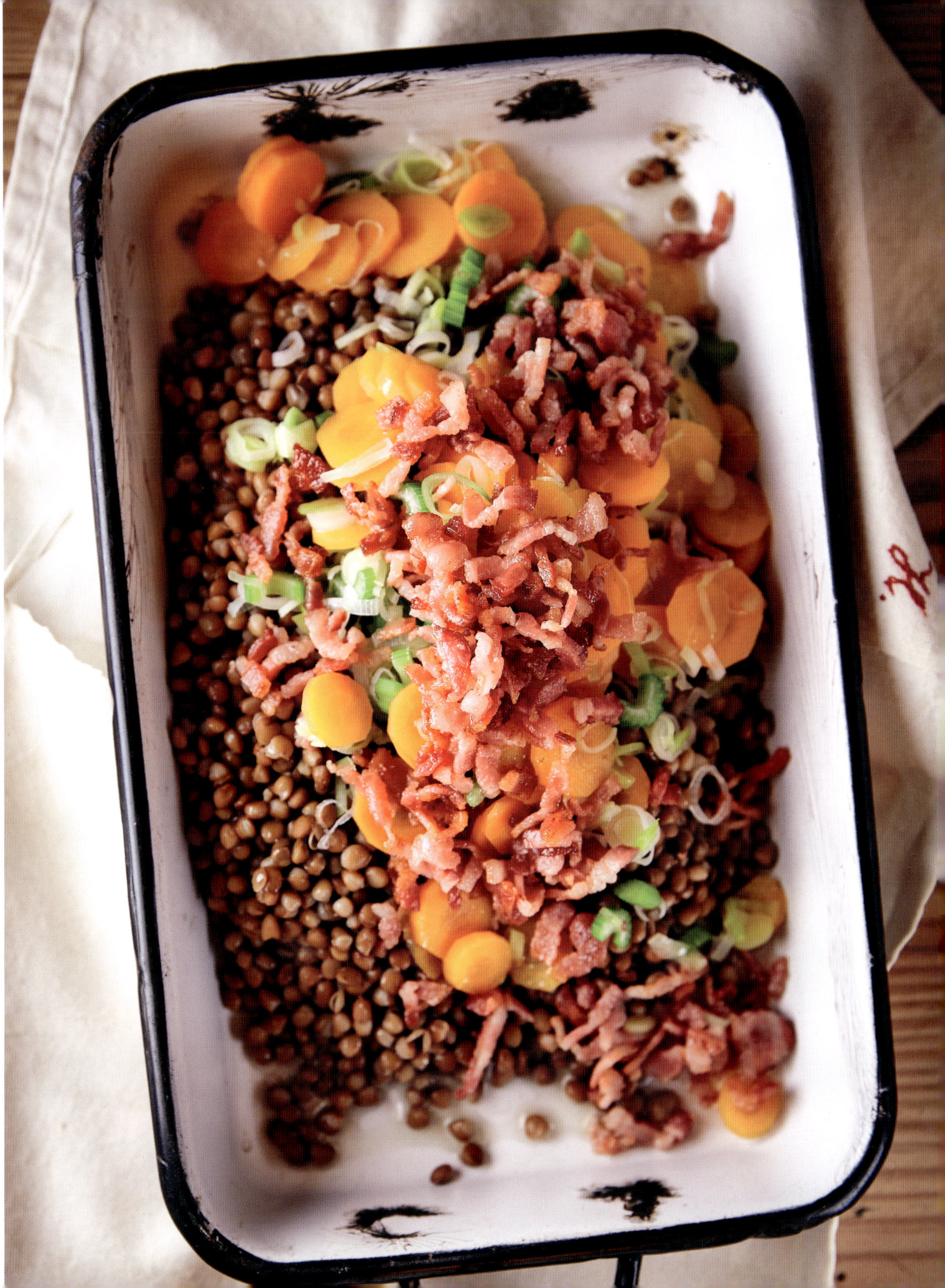

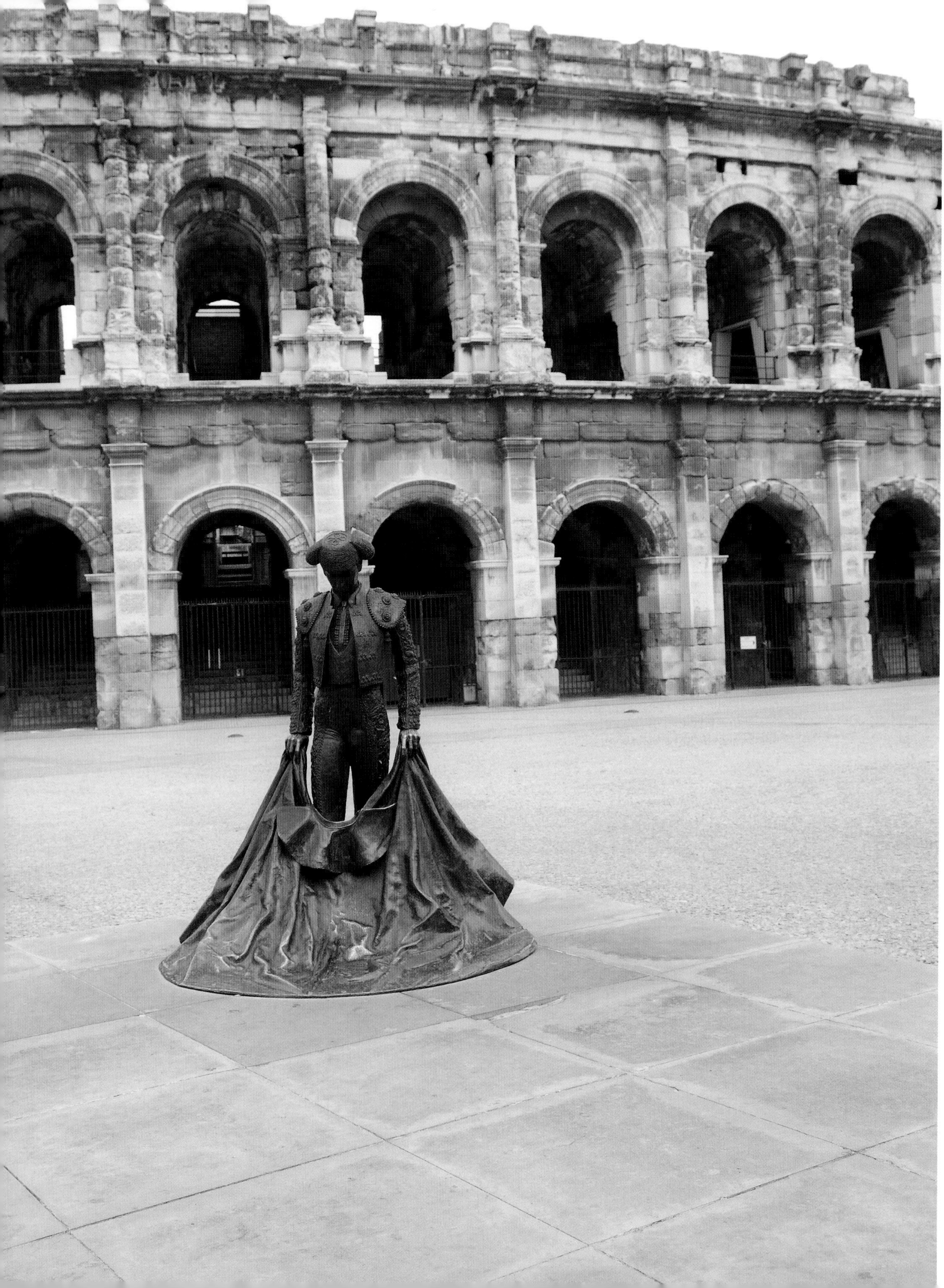

BULLS AND BEEF

"TO ME HEAVEN WOULD BE A BIG BULL RING WITH ME HOLDING TWO BARRERA SEATS ..."

Ernest Hemingway, American author (1899-1961)

The Camargue is the Wild West of Provence, and like the American Wild West, you also find cowboys and ranches there. *Gardian* is the name given to a mounted cattle herdsman in this neck of the woods, and *manade* refers to the farm on which he lives and works, as well as the cattle and horses he tends. Like his American counterpart, the Provençal cowboy wears a distinctive wide-brimmed hat that makes him easy to spot.

Gardianne, on the other hand, is not a cowgirl as you might think, but rather a traditional dish of beef in red wine that is served at local festivals. It is a kind of stew reminiscent of the well-known beef bourguignon (see page 24), except that the meat is not just cooked in wine, but also marinated in wine beforehand, and they do not bother with fancy little onions and mushrooms and other vegetables. No, this cowboy stew is all about meat, meat and more meat. (With lots of wine and a little cognac for good measure.)

We should probably not call it a stew at all, because a stew – according to the South African poet-cook Louis Leipoldt – is born from the flavourful interplay between meat and vegetables. But English simply does not have nearly the culinary vocabulary that French does. For something as basic as stew, French has a number of words: *ragoût, daube, carbonnade, estouffade*, to mention just a few referring specifically to red meat. A fish stew has different names, such as *bourride*, and one made from poultry or game birds can be called a *fricassée* or *salmis*. So many names, so many stews, so much pleasure for a confused cook who is still getting to grips with the language.

One major difference between the *manade* of the Camargue and the American ranch, is that the best bulls from the *manade* are destined for the bull fights, which remain very popular in this region. For tender hearts like me who do not share Hemingway's admiration for the bull fight, there is the consolation that the *course camarguaise* is a less bloody affair. The bulls do not have spears thrown at them; in fact they are not intentionally hurt at all, and they are definitely not killed. Ribbons and bows and tassels are tied to and between their horns, and these decorations have to be removed by teams of agile young men.

The purpose is to honour the bull rather than the bull fighter, as becomes clear the moment you see a poster advertising the *course camarguaise*. The bull's name is often printed bigger than those of his human opponents. There is no doubt who is the star of this show.

And yet there is one thing that confuses me. All the bulls from the *manade* that are destined for bull fights, are castrated at a young age. For some macho types this may seem a crueller lot than suffering a bloody death in adulthood, but be that as it may. My question is simply whether bulls without balls can still be called bulls?

I ask this not for sexist or linguistic reasons, but purely in the interests of cooking.

As I explained last time, the French make rather a fuss about the sex of the dead animal that ends up in the pot. Just like a proper *coq au vin* requires a cock and not a hen, according to residents of the Camargue a *gardianne* demands not just any kind of beef, but meat from a bull. As I understand it, the cowboy stew must therefore be made from the meat of the breeding stock on the farm, not the testicle-free fighting bulls.

If you want to eat cowboy food, but do not live near a farm where you can go and slaughter a bull yourself, you may of course buy ordinary gender-neutral beef. And if you think a *gardianne* sounds a little too much like a dish for drunk carnivores, there is a faster, easier and in my view tastier way in which our family regularly enjoy our (gender-neutral) beef.

Lick-your-plate-clean léche
4 SERVINGS

Lécher means "to lick" – and that is exactly what you'll want to do to your plate after eating these ultra-thin strips of marinated beef, flash-fried in cream.

5 T olive oil | 1 T tomato paste concentrate | 1 T fresh lemon juice 1 T chopped parsley | 1 stalk thyme 1 stalk rosemary | a pinch of freshly grated nutmeg | salt and pepper | 600 g beef, cut into very thin strips | 2-3 T crème fraîche

Combine all the ingredients except for the meat and the crème fraîche in a bowl to make a smooth marinade. Add the meat, make sure it is completely covered with marinade, and marinate for at least an hour.

Heat a heavy-based pan over high heat. When the pan is very hot, pour the meat and the marinade into the pan and stir-fry for a few minutes until the meat is just cooked. Remove from the heat, stir in the crème fraîche and serve immediately with fresh pasta or polenta.

Right: Gardianne – Provençal cowboy food

Gardianne – Provençal cowboy food

This cowboy dish requires an enormous amount of wine – and almost as much patience. The day before you plan on eating it, cut 1,5 kg stewing steak into cubes and place in a large dish with 2 glasses red wine mixed with 1 glass red-wine vinegar, 2 peeled garlic cloves, 2 onions, sliced into rings, 1 bay leaf, 1 stalk thyme, 2-3 cloves and a handful of parsley leaves. Season with salt and pepper, ensure that the meat is well covered with the marinade, and leave to marinate for 24 hours.

Next day, fry 100 g chopped smoked bacon and a finely chopped garlic clove in a large saucepan over low heat. Add 2 T olive oil and the marinated meat. Increase the heat and brown the meat quickly all over. Heat a glass of cognac or brandy in a small saucepan, pour it over the meat and immediately light it. Once the alcohol has burnt off, stir in 3 T flour. Pour over the marinade, vegetables and all, plus another 2 glasses of wine. (I told you this dish contained a lot of alcohol!) Season with salt and pepper, reduce the heat, put the lid on and simmer for about 3 hours. Check on it every now and then, and add a little water if there is not enough liquid.

Taste and season with salt and pepper if necessary. You can sprinkle some parsley over the top if you like, but cowboys are unlikely to worry about presentation so you can take the pan straight to the table. Serve with rice, preferably from the Camargue, or potatoes. And more red wine, of course.

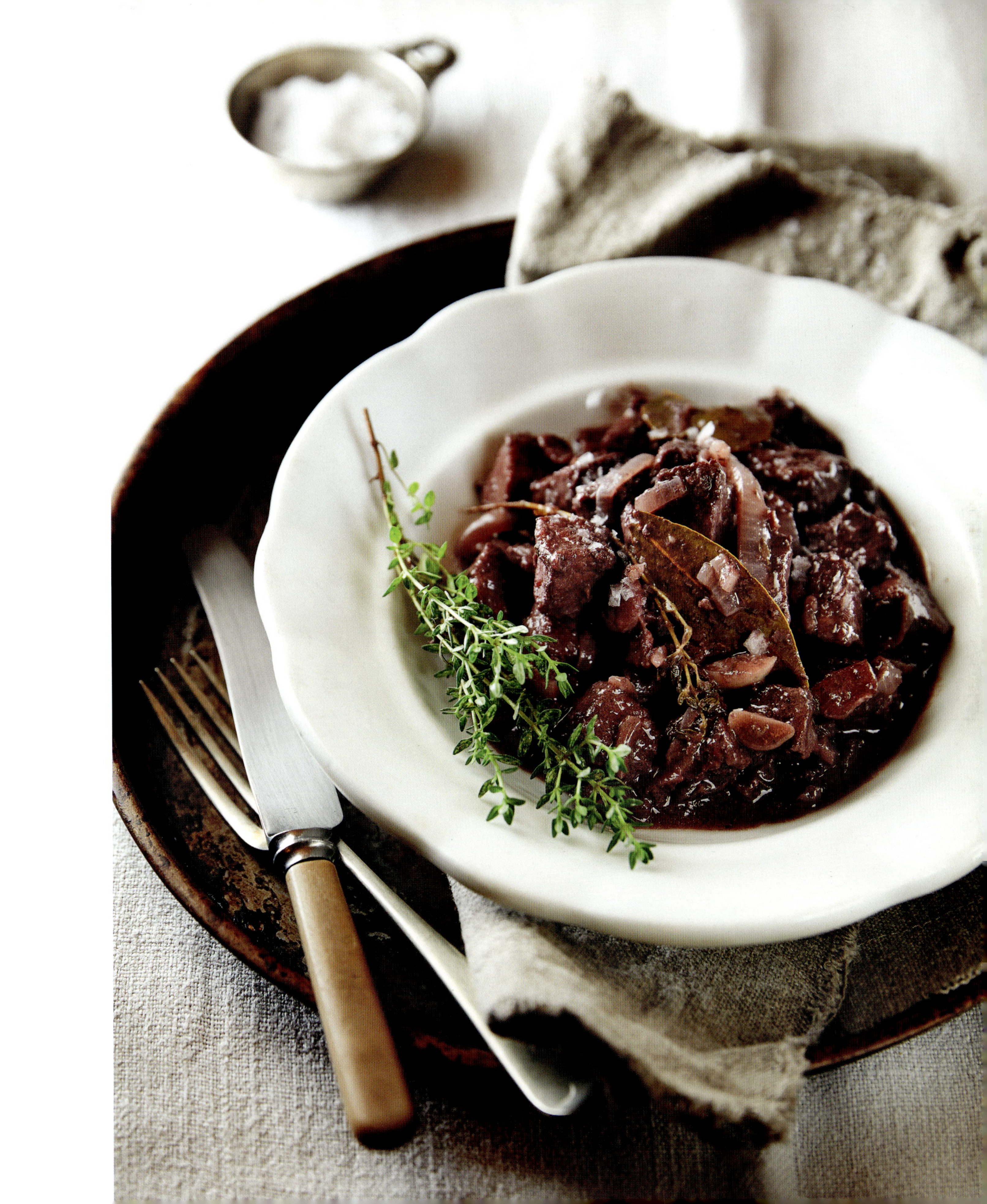

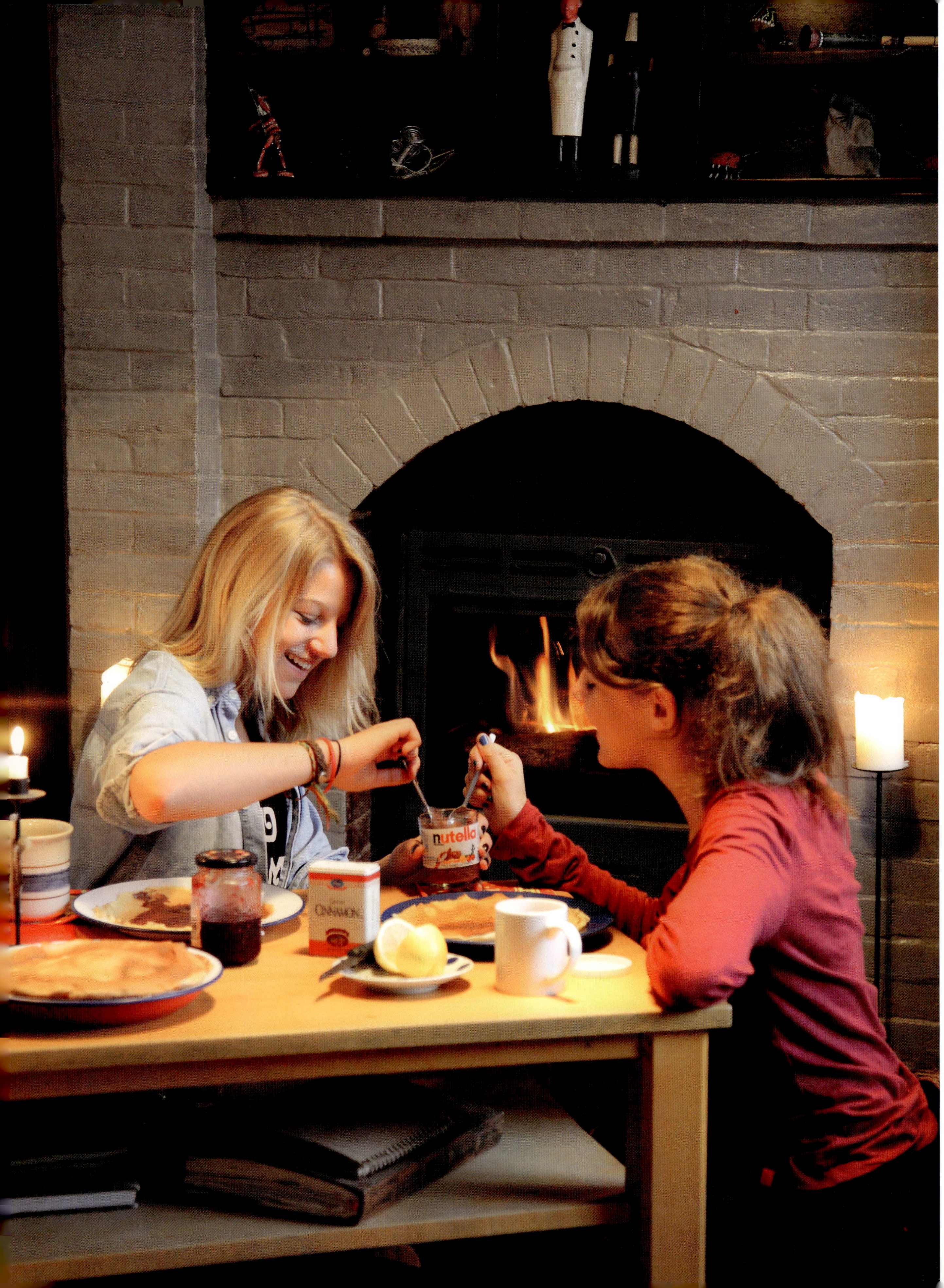
nutella
CINNAMON

PLENTY OF PANCAKES

"ONE TASTE OF CRÊPES SUZETTE, I REALLY BELIEVE, WOULD REFORM A CANNIBAL INTO A CIVILISED GENTLEMAN."

HENRI CHARPENTIER, FRENCH CHEF (1880-1961)

You are still wiping the crumbs from the last slice of kings tart from your mouth, when the next delicious galette feast comes along. This time it is the turn of *galettes crêpes* or "flat cakes", which originated in the north-western region of Brittany and are simply called *crêpes* these days. In English we know them as pancakes – although the French version is supposed to be thinner and more delicate than her sturdy Anglo-Saxon cousin.

In February, the French make pancakes like it is going out of style, for another important Catholic festival. *Chandeleur* can be translated literally as the festival of candles, or Candlemas, and celebrates the purification of the Virgin Mary. Up to now no-one has been able to explain to me the connection between candles and pancakes, but February is pancake month. Tradition is tradition.

Although this pancake tradition does cause a few identity crises in our multicultural family. Hugo insists on eating them in the French way, in a neat little chocolate-filled triangle, while Daniel likes to sprinkle them with cinnamon sugar and roll them up, like they do in the land of his birth. And Mia, true to her mixed genes, wants chocolate spread *and* cinnamon sugar on hers. A rather strange taste sensation that I would not recommend to everyone. You can push the envelope of multicultural food just so far before it tears.

And yet, pancakes are far more international – and much older – than most of us would expect. Archaeological research shows that "flat cakes" were among the oldest and most widespread form of cereal food in prehistoric communities. Although the shape, thickness and ingredients differ around the world, traditional versions with different names can be found on every continent.

In Anglo-Saxon countries like Britain, America and Australia (and for some South Africans too), Shrove Tuesday is commonly known as Pancake Day. The tradition of eating pancakes on this feast day probably arose because people wanted to get rid of the milk, sugar and eggs in the house before the period of strict Lenten fasting began the next day (Ash Wednesday). Fat Tuesday is exactly 47 days before Easter Sunday (except when a leap year messes things up), so it is usually celebrated sometime in February. Another good excuse, if you really needed one, to eat pancakes the whole month long. Whether they are paper-thin French crêpes with Nutella, or substantial Dutch *pannenkoeken* with cheese fillings, or thick American flapjacks with maple syrup, or Polish *plenze* with a layer of sugar, pancakes are delicious.

The most famous pancake in the world is probably the one that is set alight in such flamboyant style. Throughout his life, French chef Henri Charpentier asserted that as a teenaged waiter in Monte Carlo in 1895, he had accidentally set pancake sauce alight in front of the Prince of Wales. The prince, who later became King Edward VII, was charmed by the faux pas and suggested that the dish be called *crêpes suzette* in honour of a young lady at his table.

However, Charpentier's story has been disputed by the authoritative *Larousse Gastronomique* and other experts who believe it highly unlikely that an inexperienced fourteen-year-old waiter would have served such an important royal guest. Some sources suggest that it was rather the French actress Suzanne Reichenbach, who went by the stage name of Suzette, who was honoured in this way. In 1897 she played a role for the Comédie-Française in which she had to serve crêpes on stage. The chef who was to supply the crêpes for each performance had the bright idea of flambéing them – to entertain the audience and at the same time keep the dish warm for the actors who had to eat it every night.

Wherever the truth lies, the mysterious Suzette's pancakes have been a classic French dessert for more than a century. These days it has an ever so slightly retro flavour, making it even more attractive to gourmands who have become bored with trendy culinary fads.

Crêpes Suzette
6-8 SERVINGS

125 g flour | a pinch of salt | 3 eggs 2 T sunflower oil | 200 g butter 150 g sugar | 1 t vanilla essence 350 ml milk | finely grated zest and juice of 1 orange | 6 T Cointreau or similar orange liqueur | 3 T cognac or brandy

Mix the flour and salt in a bowl. Make a well in the centre and add the eggs, oil, 50 g of the butter, 1 T sugar, the vanilla essence and the milk. Beat well to form a smooth batter.

Melt a knob of butter in a small pancake pan and use a soup ladle to scoop a little of the batter into the pan. Shake the pan to spread the batter over the surface, fry quickly until golden brown and then turn to cook the other side. Slide the crêpe out of the pan and onto a plate kept warm over a pot of boiling water. Make more crêpes until you have used up the batter.

Make the orange sauce: Mix the rest of the butter and sugar in a bowl until smooth and creamy. Stir in the orange zest and juice, along with 2 T of the orange liqueur and 1 T of the brandy. Pour the sauce into a large pan and bring to the boil. Boil for 2 minutes and then reduce the heat. Add the crêpes one by one to soak up the sauce. Fold each crêpe in half and then in half again to form a loose triangle. Remove from the pan and keep warm in a serving dish.

For the final step you probably need an open-plan kitchen – or a small gas burner next to the dining-room table – so that your guests can enjoy the flaming spectacle with you. Heat the remaining liqueur and brandy in a small pan, light it and pour over the crêpes before the flame goes out.

If you have never done this before and are scared of setting your hair or your guests alight, rather wait until the alcohol has burnt off before pouring the sauce over the crêpes.

The Pleasure of Plenze
4 SERVINGS

Alain has fond memories of the *plenze* that his mother made for their large family. These potato pancakes of Polish origin are still popular in the north of France – where most of our family lives – probably because so many Poles came to work in the coal mines there. The basic version is enjoyed as a sweet treat with sugar, but they can also be turned into a filling savoury dish with the addition of onion, garlic, bacon or cheese.

1 kg floury potatoes | 3 eggs | 5 T flour | a pinch of salt | cooking oil sugar, for sprinkling

Peel and grate the potatoes. Drain all excess moisture produced by the potatoes, using your hands to squeeze it out if necessary. (The quality of the potatoes will determine the amount of water.) Add the eggs, flour and salt, and mix well. If the mixture is too runny, add some more flour.

Heat a little oil in a frying pan. Spoon 2 soup ladles of the batter into the pan to form 2 small pancakes. Cook for about 3-5 minutes until the edges start turning golden. Turn the pancakes carefully with a large egg lifter and cook the other side until golden brown. Keep warm and spoon more batter into the pan to make more *plenze*.

Enjoy hot, sprinkled with sugar. Or turn the pancakes into a side dish with meat by adding a finely grated onion to the mixture. Or make a light meal of it by stirring a finely chopped clove of garlic, 100 g chopped bacon, 100 g grated cheese and a little chopped parsley into the mixture. Remember though, the more ingredients you add, the "heavier" the mixture will become – and the more difficult it will be to turn the pancakes in the pan. So first master the basic version and then you can experiment to your heart's content.

Right: Crêpes suzette

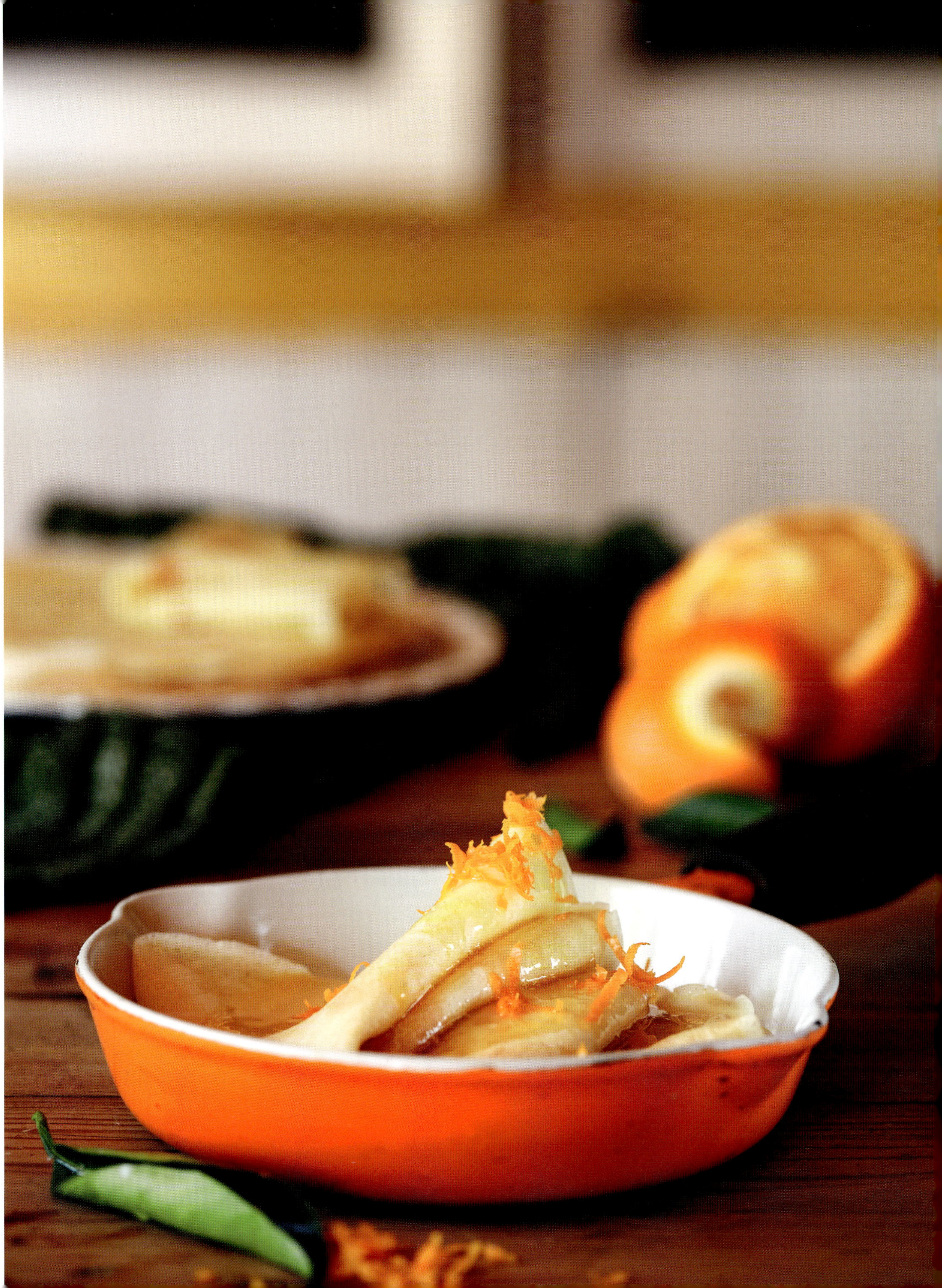

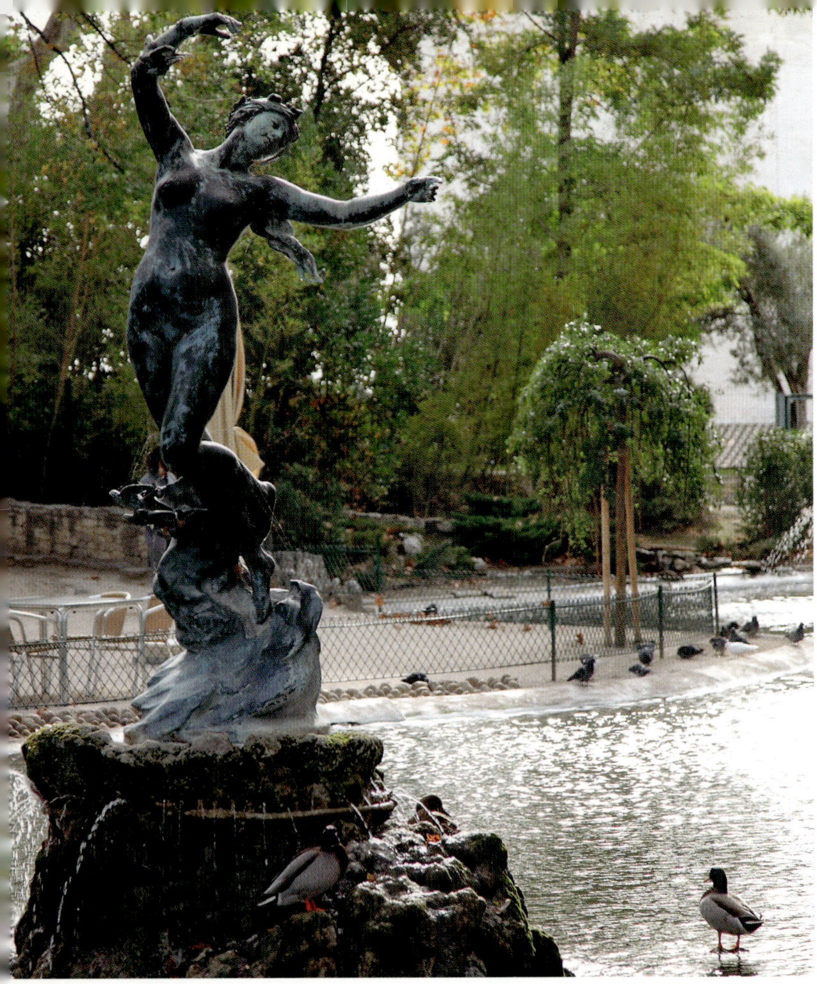
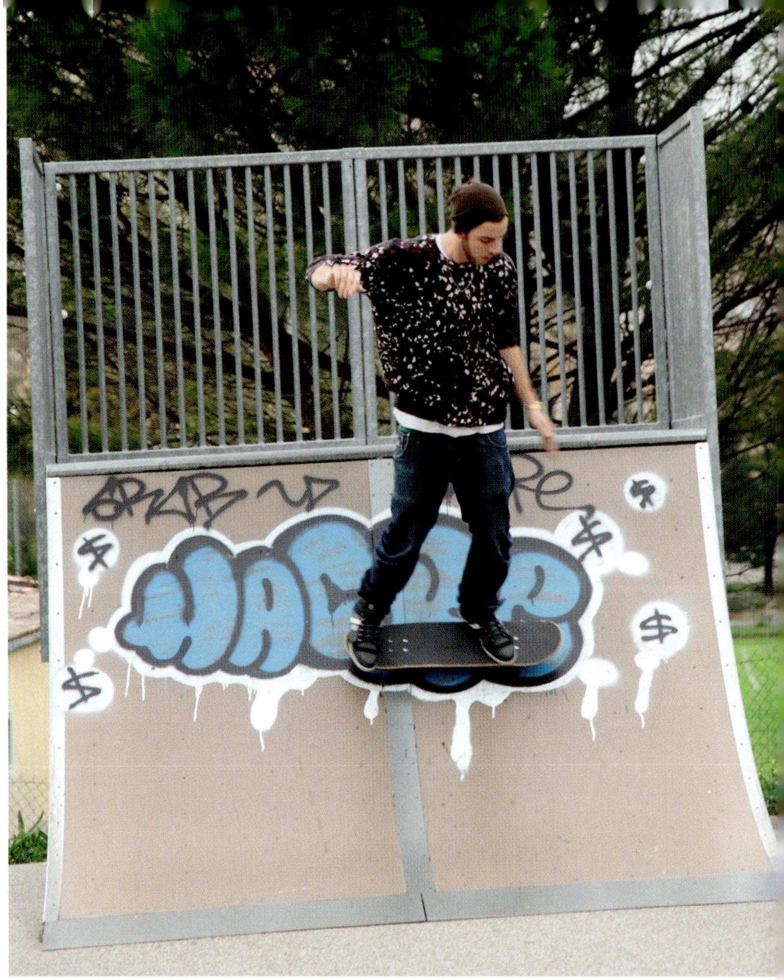
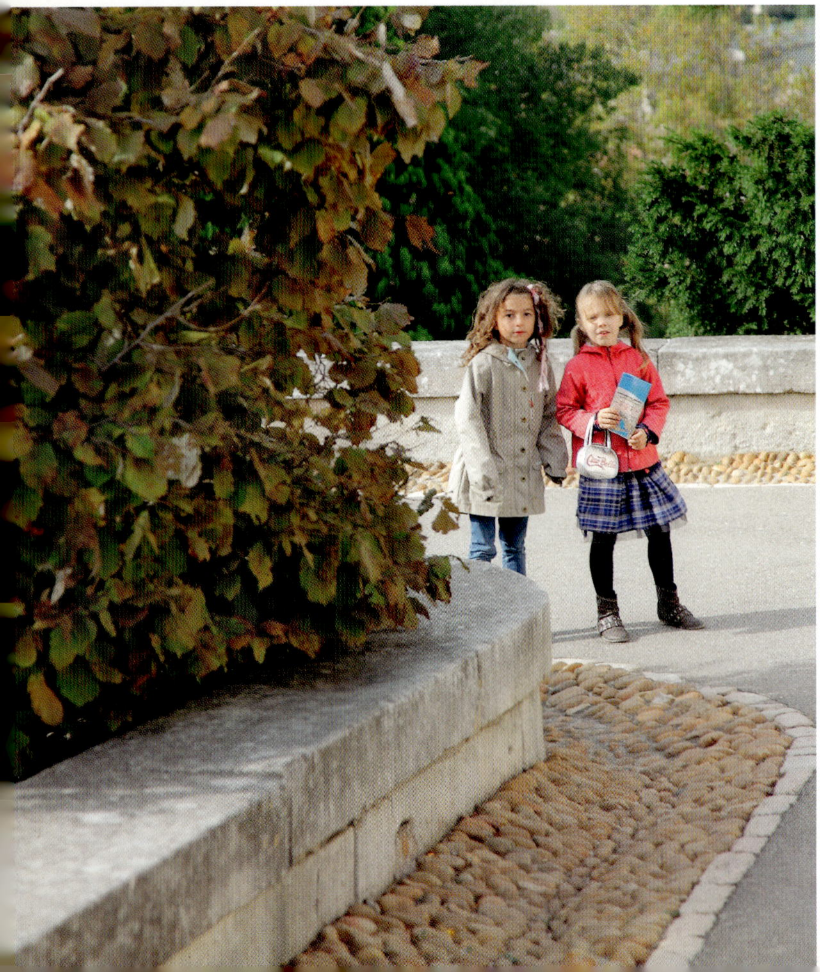
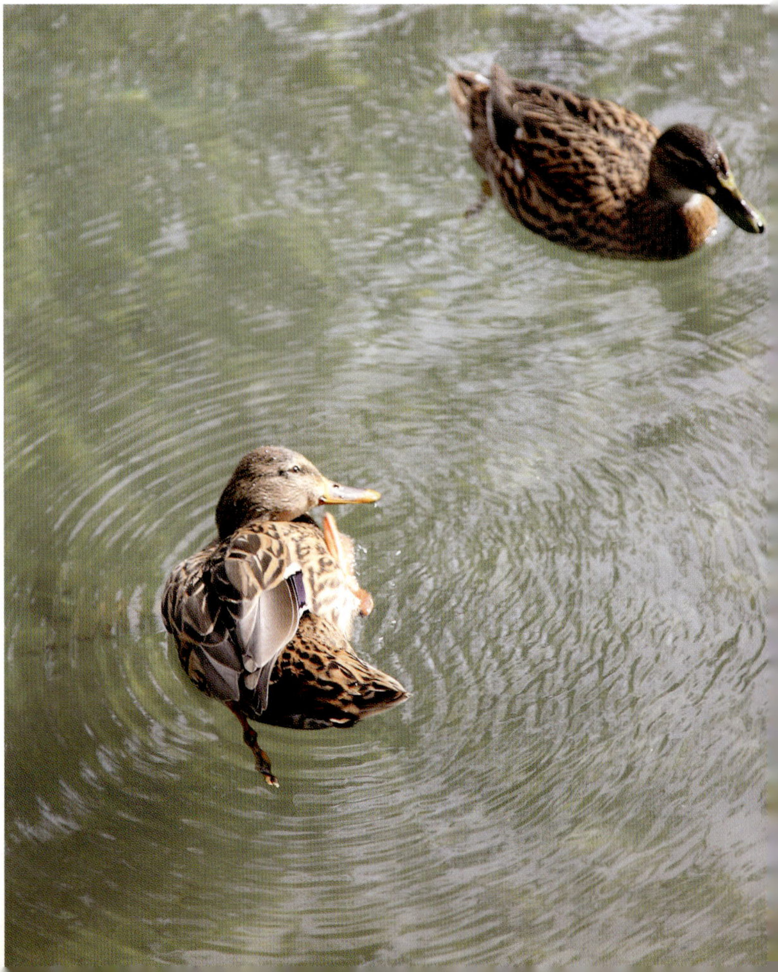

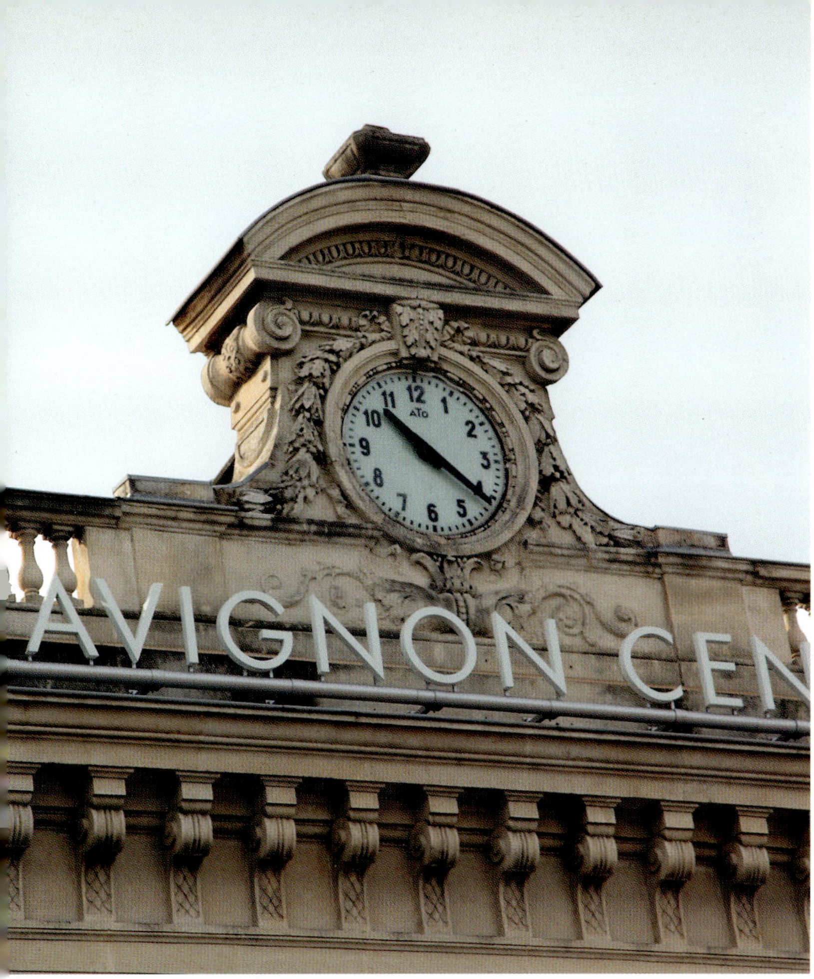

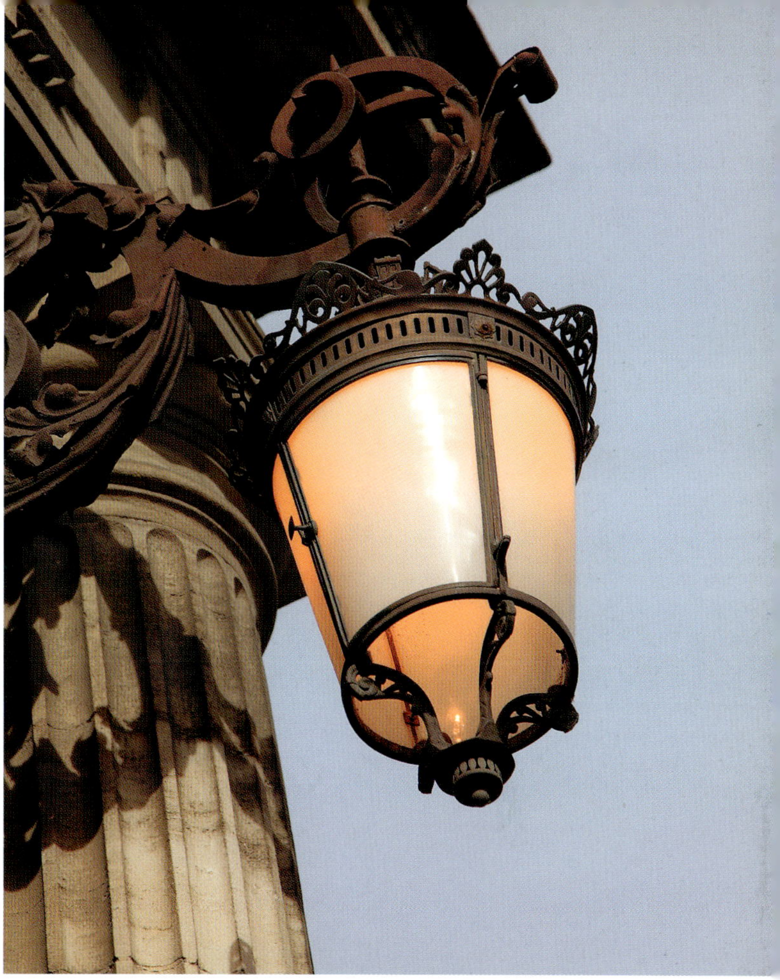

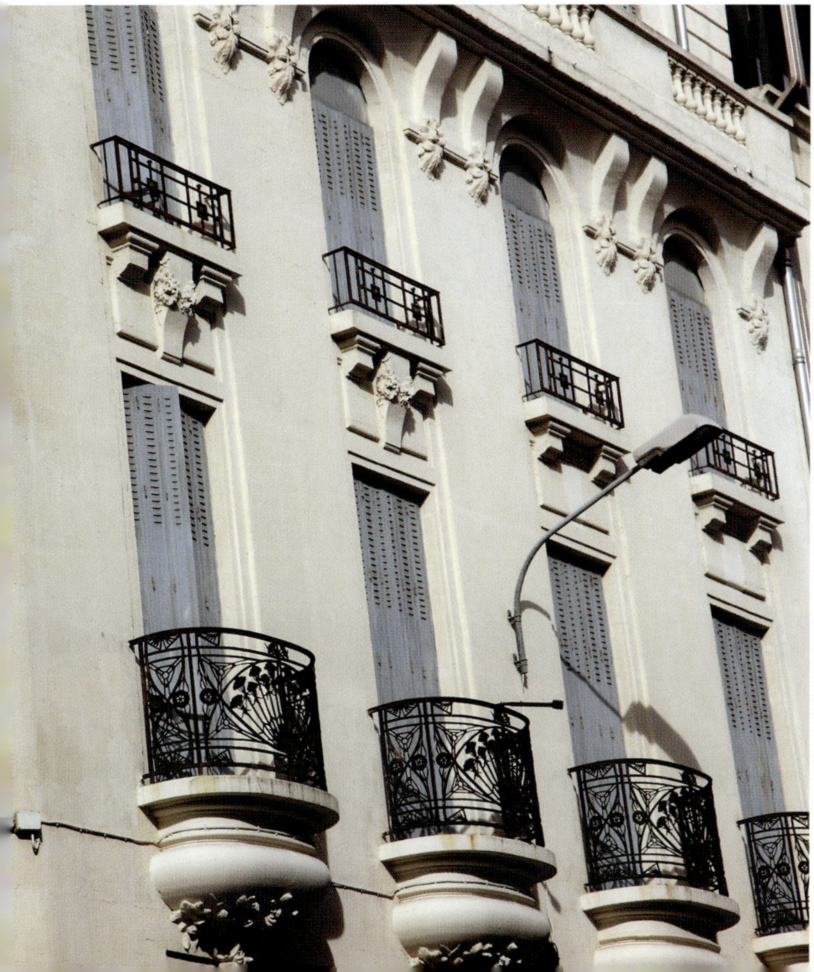

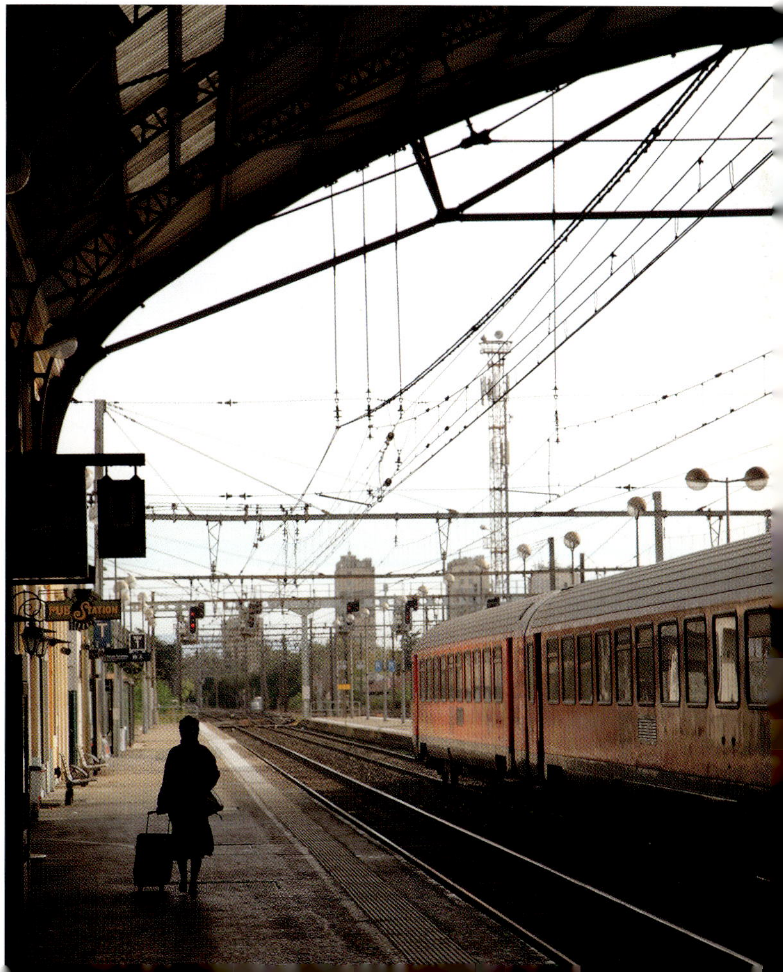

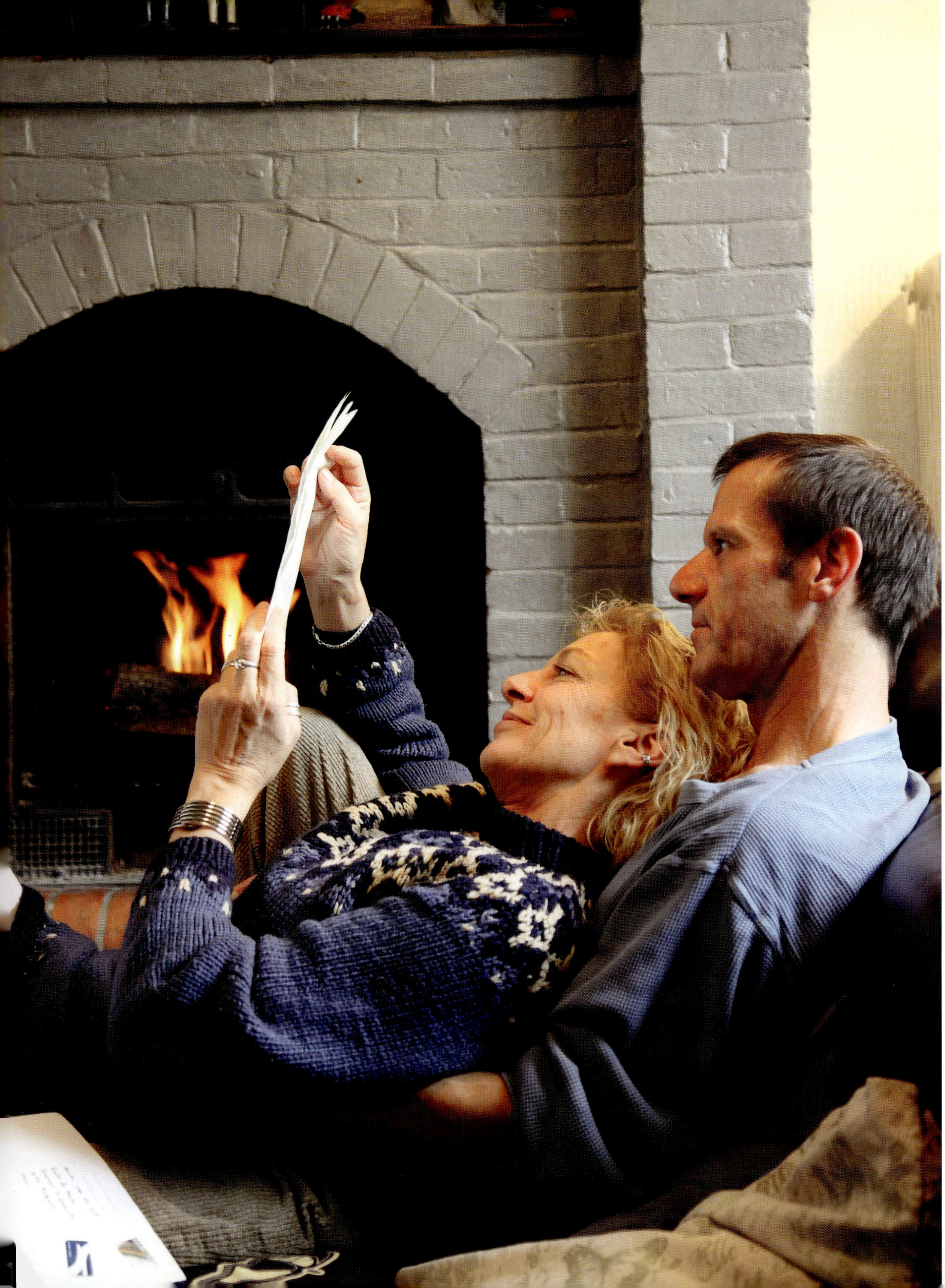

DUCK FOR COVER

"PAINTING IS SOMETIMES LIKE THOSE RECIPES WHERE YOU DO ALL MANNER OF ELABORATE THINGS TO A DUCK, AND THEN END UP PUTTING IT ON ONE SIDE AND ONLY USING THE SKIN."

LUCIAN FREUD, BRITISH ARTIST (1922-2011)

One of the most unforgettable food experiences of my life was the first time Alain and I ate together in a restaurant. We were young and in love and the food was divine. Well, we were actually not that young when we met, but we were very in love, and I thought the *magret de canard* we ordered at a modest little place in the Ardèche landed on our plates directly from paradise.

Months later, Alain confessed that the duck breasts were actually a bit fatty, and that the Côtes du Rhône rosé we drank with the meal, had not been served at the correct temperature. But I refused to be disillusioned. For me it remains a memorable meal enveloped in a cloud of romance, and probably the start of my passion for duck.

Still today I have a weakness for duck of any kind, from duck liver in the form of foie gras to the classic French dish *canard à l'orange*. And because French chefs can be amazingly innovative with duck, I am usually unerringly predictable when I come across duck on a restaurant menu. I was therefore not at all surprised to learn that the well-known Julia Child's passionate affair with French cuisine began with a meal that included duck. ("I had my first French meal and I never got over it … We had roast duck and I don't know what else.")

What more is there to say? Except perhaps that the unforgettable Billie Holiday was also mad about roast duck. "Singing songs like 'The Man I Love'," she once remarked, "is no more work than sitting down and eating Chinese roast duck, and I love roast duck."

I have never eaten in the famous Paris restaurant La Tour d'Argent, but when I win the French Lotto one day, I am planning on reserving a large table and inviting family and friends from various continents to join me in working our way through the extensive duck menu. *Caneton Marco Polo, caneton à l'orange, caneton rôti de saison…* The restaurant has been in existence since the sixteenth century and boasts an impressive variety of duck dishes, but it is the *caneton Tour d'Argent* in particular that has achieved legendary status. This dish, for which the duck's carcass is pressed to obtain the fresh blood for a rich and flavourful sauce, is an adaptation of a much older recipe called simply *canard au sang* or "blood duck".

Understandable, then, that the chef Frédéric Delair decided to change the macabre name when in 1890 he began numbering every blood duck ordered and recording the name of the person who ordered it. Over a million ducks have been served and many of the earlier names were famous ones, such as Emperor Hirohito of Japan and the Prince of Wales who later became Edward VII. These days the restaurant is viewed as a grand old lady of somewhat faded glory, patronised mainly by wealthy tourists looking for a classic French dining experience, although many numbered portions of *caneton* are still served every week.

By the way, *caneton* means "duckling", and these ducklings all come from Challans in the heart of Brittany, a region producing the world's most sought-after duck. Some gourmands say that the meat from the female duck (*canette*) is even tastier than that of the male – but it might just be the usual fuss about the sex of dead animals that I cannot for the life of me take as seriously as my French relatives. I tend to agree with Alice B. Toklas – another expat who on occasion laughed at the French and their eating habits – who had the following to say on the matter: "What is sauce for the goose may be sauce for the gander but is not necessarily sauce for the chicken, the duck, the turkey or the guinea hen." Amen.

140 | WINTER FOOD IN PROVENCE

Right: Canard à l'orange

CANARD À L'ORANGE
6 SERVINGS

The classic French way of preparing duck is still the most popular in our house.

50 g butter | 3 T olive oil | 1 duck weighing about 2 kg, cleaned and trussed | 4 cloves garlic, crushed 125 g good-quality uncooked ham (jambon cru), cut into thin strips 600 ml dry white wine | 200 ml chicken stock | 1 bouquet garni the peel and juice of 2 oranges | 1 T flour | 1 T wine vinegar | another 2 oranges, sliced as thinly as possible salt and pepper

Heat 25 g of the butter and the olive oil in a large, heavy-based saucepan. Add the duck and brown it evenly all over, over moderate heat until it is a lovely golden brown.

Add the garlic and ham and cook for 1-2 minutes. Add the wine and the chicken stock to the pot, bring to the boil and simmer for a few minutes until the liquid is slightly reduced. Add the bouquet garni and the orange juice. Season to taste with salt and pepper.

Put the lid on, reduce the heat and simmer gently for about 1½ hours. (Check on it every now and then and baste with the liquid if the skin on the top starts to look a bit dry.) Make a thin cut in the thigh right next to the leg to check if it is cooked through, and leave to cook a little longer if necessary.

In the meantime, cut the orange peel into the narrowest strips possible and add it to boiling water in a small saucepan. Blanch for 5 minutes, remove and drain well on kitchen paper. Set aside.

Now make the *beurre manié* (butter and flour mixture) by mixing the remaining butter with the flour in a small bowl.

Remove the cooked duck from the pot, cut it into portions and keep warm. Turn up the heat and cook the liquid remaining in the pot for a few minutes until it has reduced. Reduce the heat again and add the vinegar and orange peel. Add the butter and flour mixture a little at a time, stirring continuously until the sauce thickens.

Put each duck portion on a plate, pour a little orange sauce over it and garnish with the slices of orange. Serve with rice to soak up the remaining sauce. Delicious is simply not the word.

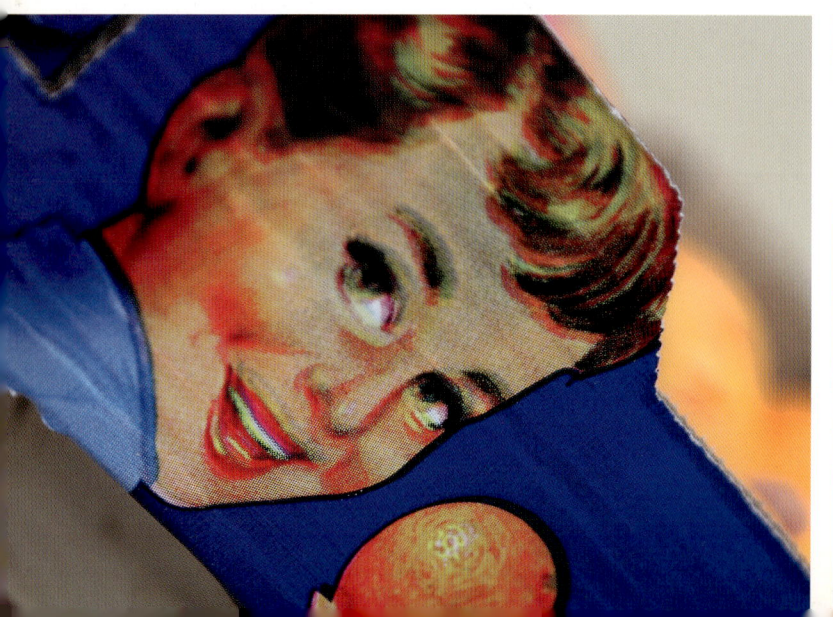

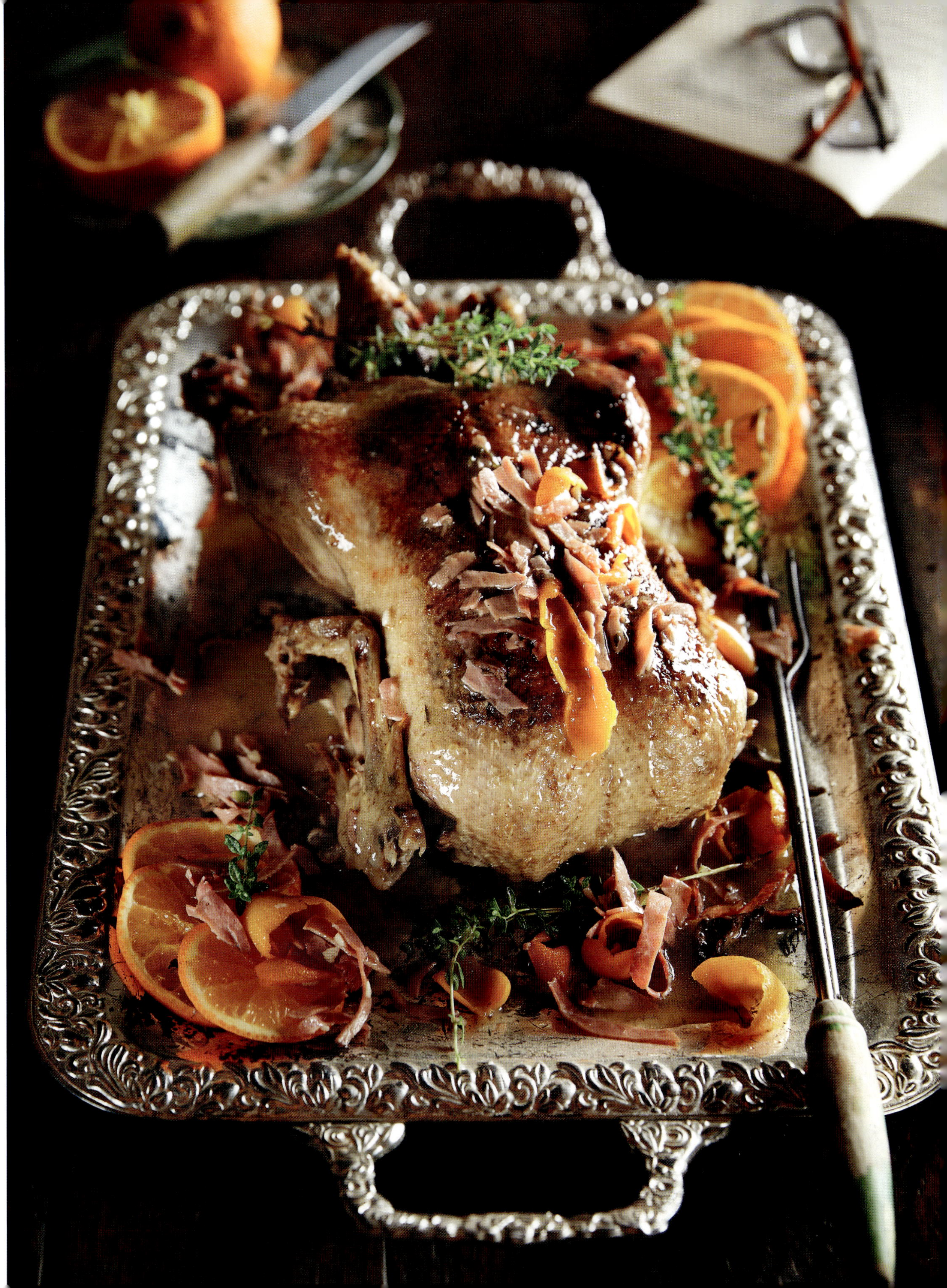

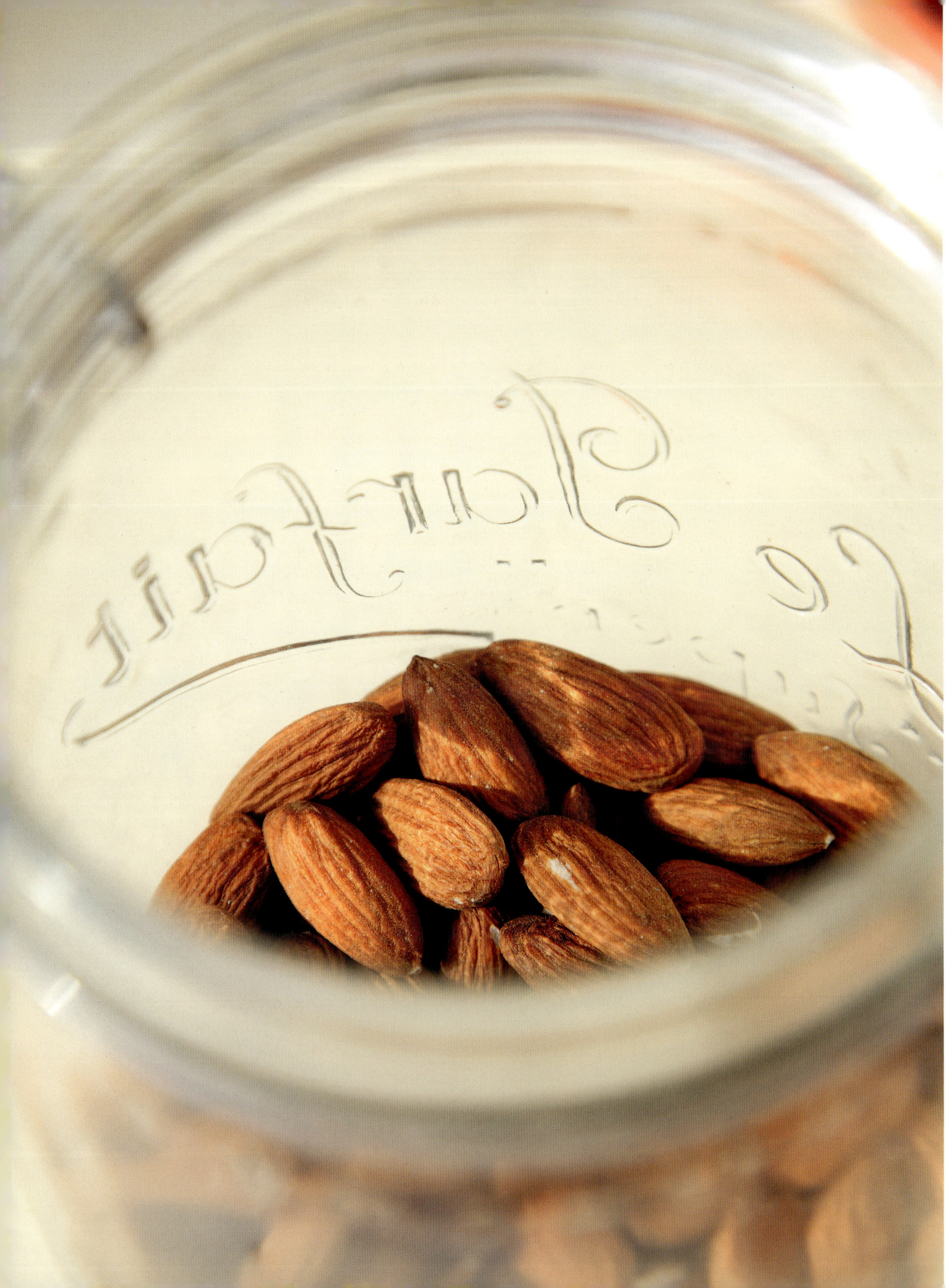

IN A NUTSHELL

"I SAID TO THE ALMOND TREE, 'FRIEND, SPEAK TO ME OF GOD,' AND THE ALMOND TREE BLOSSOMED."

NIKOS KAZANTZAKIS, GREEK WRITER (1883-1957)

When the days grow shorter and colder, and fresh fruit becomes scarcer, the French turn their attention to dried fruit and nuts. The south is particularly well known for almonds and almond products – like the world-famous nougat from Montélimar, for example – but any nuts are appreciated and used in food in all sorts of innovative ways.

One of the joys of early autumn is walnuts – and more specifically the AOC walnuts from Grenoble, a city in the foothills of the Alps, about two hours' drive from our home. (One of our sons is studying in Grenoble, which is why we know the distance almost down to the last metre.) The Romans, who introduced walnuts to the region many centuries ago, were convinced that the nut had miraculous properties because it looked like the human brain. These days the walnut is acknowledged as a so-called superfood with an especially high nutritional value – but it is the taste and texture of Grenoble's "supernuts" that set them apart from less worthy competitors. The advantage of any nuts is obviously that they can be preserved throughout winter, but if you want to refresh the succulent, just-picked taste of Grenoble walnuts after a few months, simply remove the shells and soak the insides in milk overnight.

Chestnut trees, which have also been growing near the Mediterranean for centuries, are amazing in that the blossoms, the fruit and even the leaves are used in the food industry. In spring the blossoms help bees produce the most delicious honey; in early winter the chestnuts are roasted over glowing coals at town festivals and sold piping hot in hand-folded paper cones; and in autumn the leaves are harvested for another famous product of Provence. The small, round goat's milk cheeses of Banon, which are wrapped in golden brown chestnut leaves and tied with raffia like precious gifts, are something really special. Initially the leaves were apparently just a way to pack the cheese to make it last longer, until the cheese-makers realised that the tannic acid in the leaves actually improved the taste of the cheese – and *voilà*, another AOC product was born.

Our South African ancestors, the Huguenots, regarded chestnuts almost as a staple food before they were driven out of France, using it to make flour for bread and other baked goods. Even today, chestnut flour is a seasonal speciality used in cakes, pasta and dough for doughnuts and other fried treats. Among the French, however, chestnuts are best known and loved in the form of *marrons glacés* (sugared sweets) and sweet chestnut paste.

By the end of winter, when the ground around the vineyards is frozen solid in the morning and Mont Ventoux wears a snow cap day and night, the almond trees are suddenly covered in snow-white blossoms, the only flowers in a bare landscape. "Almond blossom sent to teach us / That the spring days soon will reach us." This is how Sir Edwin Arnold praised the blessed almond blossoms, which always bring the first signs of mercy after an apparently endless winter. This is also why it was one of the first trees I planted at our new house among the vineyards. Believe me, one needs mercy after a cruel European winter.

Provence has been home to almond trees for centuries, as is proven by the many local almond products of renown: Aix-en-Provence's elegant sweets known as *calissons*, Vinsobres's little crunchy biscuits and, perhaps best of all, Montélimar's nougat, made from the best almonds, the sweetest honey and plenty of frothy egg whites. As you would expect, there are a number of stories about the origins of nougat, but my favourite is the one about the childless old woman who liked making sweets for her young relatives. Every time they would feign to protest that she was spoiling them (*Tu nous gâtes!*), and at her death sometime in the seventeenth century, a niece inherited the recipe for (*tu*) *nousgâtes* (pronounced "noo-gha") … The story is as improbably delicious as the sweet it celebrates.

Right: French nut "cake"

Nougatine

This is incredibly easy to make. For crunchy black nougat or nougatine you need nothing more than sugar water and almonds, some butter and a pinch of salt – and an eagle eye to prevent that little lot sticking to the pan. The number of servings will depend on the size of the shards you break it into.

270 g sugar | 120 g toasted almonds
20 g butter | a pinch of salt

Add the sugar to 6 T water in a small saucepan and bring to the boil. Leave the syrup to cook over moderate heat without stirring.

Remove from the heat as soon as the syrup turns golden brown. If you leave it even a few moments too long, it will darken and start to stick and burn. Immediately stir in the toasted almonds, butter and salt.

Scrape the mixture onto a sheet of baking paper using a wooden spoon. Grease a rolling pin with a little butter and roll out the nougatine into a thin layer. (If it gets too hard before it is thin enough, place the baking paper with the nougatine on a baking tray in a 150 °C oven. Remove as soon as the nougatine starts to melt again and roll out.)

Leave to cool and break into shards. Serve with ice cream (see our recipe for *còssa de Nadau* on page 100) or dip in melted chocolate. Once the chocolate has hardened on the nougatine, you will have a stylish treat to serve with coffee.

French nut "cake"

When the French talk about a *cake*, they do not mean what we mean by it. A French *cake* is something that is baked in a loaf tin and may be sweet or savoury. This nut loaf is sweetish, but tastes best hot out of the oven, spread thickly with salted butter.

100 g walnuts | 100 g hazelnuts
3 eggs | 200 g sugar | 30 g flour
30 g ground almonds | 100 g soft butter | 2 T orange blossom water

Process the walnuts and hazelnuts in a food processor, taking care not to turn them into powder. The mixture must still contain coarse pieces.

Beat the eggs and sugar together. Add the flour and ground almonds and mix well. Stir in the butter, processed nuts and flavouring.

Grease a loaf tin with butter and spoon the batter into it. Bake for about 30 minutes in a preheated 170 °C oven. It is done if the blade of a sharp knife comes out clean. Slice and spread with butter while the loaf is still warm enough to melt the butter. Irresistible.

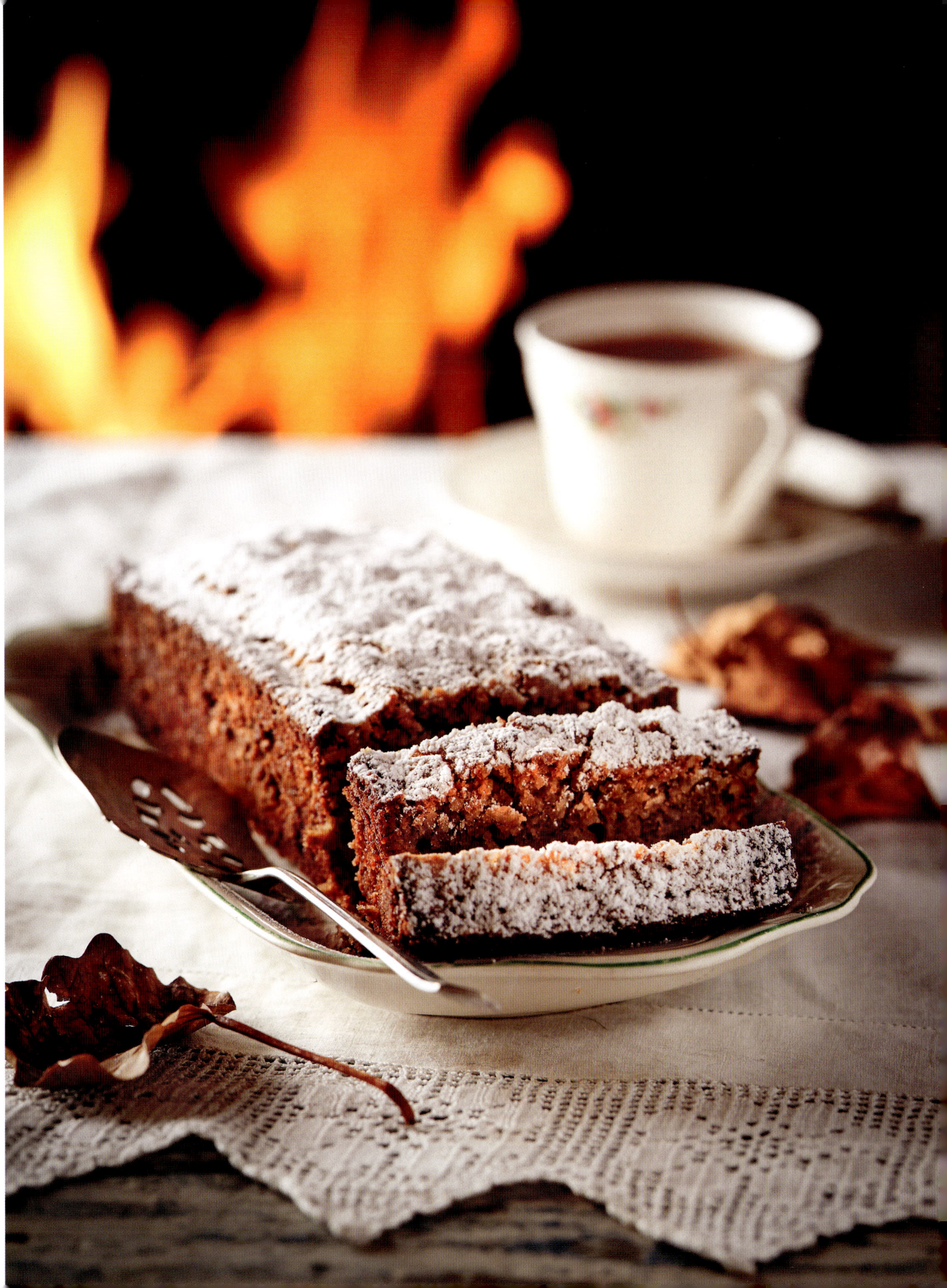

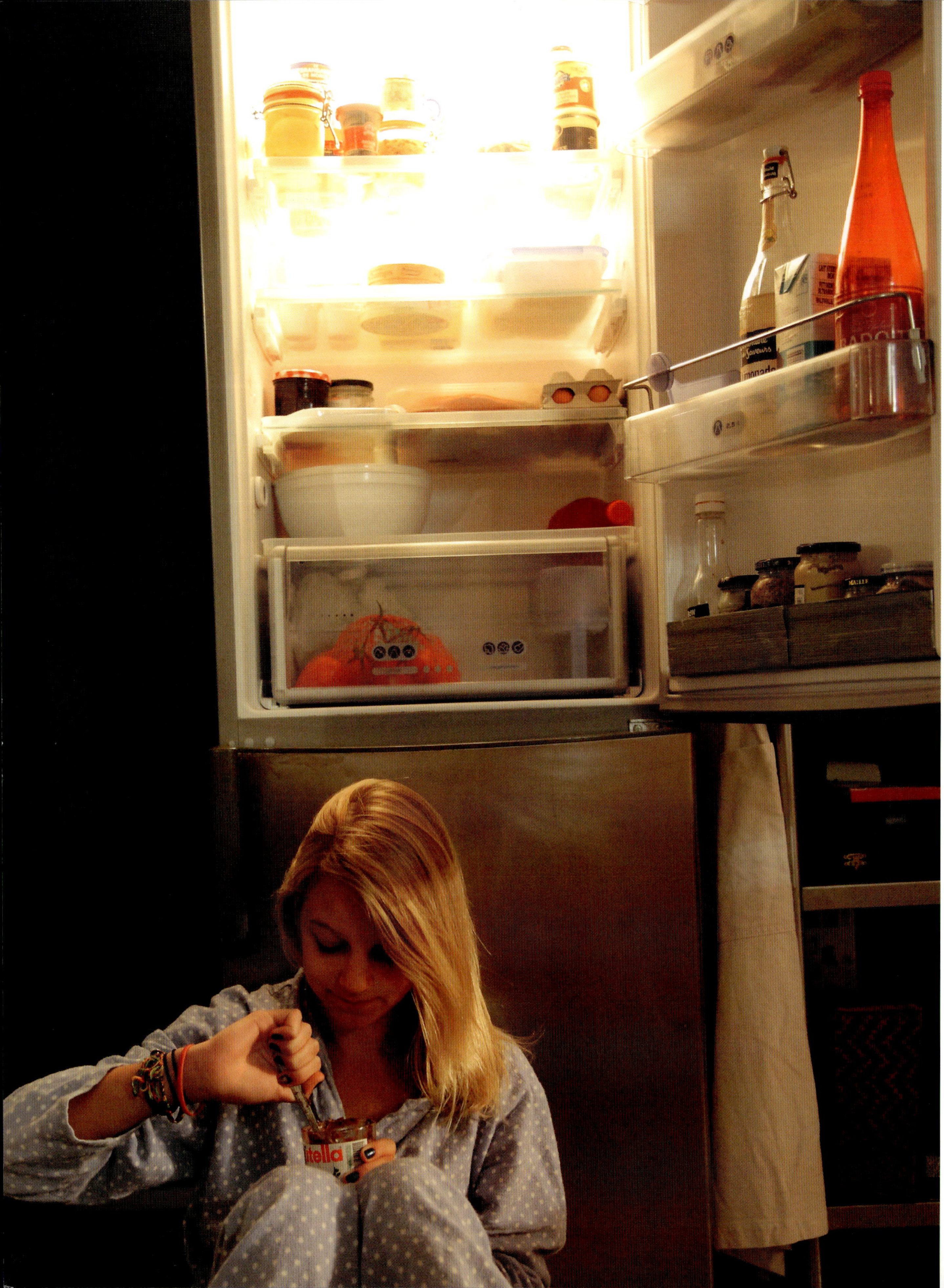

HERE'S LOOKING AT YOU, KIDNEY

"I HEARD A SOUND AS OF SCRAPING TRIPE, / AND PUTTING APPLES WONDROUS RIPE, / INTO A CIDER-PRESS'S GRIPE."

ROBERT BROWNING, ENGLISH POET (1812-1889)

Offal is one of those foods very few people are neutral about. You either love it or loathe it. I always thought I was one of the middle-ground minority. It is not something I would have chosen off a menu, but if someone put a plate of offal in front of me with a proud smile on his face, I would feel it was my duty as a guest to clean my plate.

For years my friend Hannes Myburgh held a fun, informal offal competition on the Stellenbosch wine estate Meerlust, with half a dozen cooks conjuring up different versions of offal, and all the lucky guests had to do was to eat until they were stuffed and then choose the winner.

Every year there were of course those offal loathers who would not touch the stuff and turned up purely for the social aspect, but I was a well-behaved guest who ate what was put in front of me. I even recall with some nostalgia a Natal offal curry, English tripe and trotters, an elegant Italian offal stew and a potent Polish dish consumed with a slug of vodka. I must concede that the vodka helped sway my vote in favour of the Polish cook that day. I wonder if that could be regarded as old-style Communist corruption?

For my French love, who would sell his soul for a plate of *tripes* like his mother used to make, this offal festival was one of the highlights of his introduction to the land of my birth. Because I am not exactly a fan of the stuff, and our children won't touch it, poor Alain sometimes gets such severe withdrawal symptoms that he smuggles a container of bought *tripes* into the house to be eaten furtively late at night once everyone else is asleep.

Like most true blue offal lovers, that day at Meerlust Alain voted for the simplest traditional "pale offal", the one without curry or alcohol or any other camouflage, the version that won the competition year after year. Offal in its full grisly grey glory. This is the litmus test that lukewarm fence-sitters like me just cannot pass.

While working on a cooking series for television a year or two back I realised that my husband's passion for offal is a feature of many French food lovers. Our TV crew travelled the length and breadth of France, and wherever we went, we had to taste tripe or entrails because it was regarded as the *crème de la crème* of the local cuisine. And I do not mean "ordinary" offal like liver or kidneys. No, what we were confronted with were truly exotic dishes. Bull testicles and rooster balls (the same as the bull's testicles, just considerably smaller) and sheep's brain and pig's trotters and duck heart …

And guess what? That was where I made my gastronomic discovery of the decade. In Nîmes, where we were filming an episode in an indoor market, as usual we were presented with all kinds of entrails. And because, as usual, the cameramen turned green around the gills at the mere thought of having to eat this, I felt obliged to eat on their behalf as well – as usual. This is not gluttony, you understand, it is an overdeveloped sense of politeness. But when I took the first tentative nibble of a crisply fried duck heart, salty and juicy and firm of texture, I knew that this was something special. Finally I had found an offal product that I really, really liked!

Offal was originally poor man's food, but like so many other modest foods, it has gained a hip edge. In France, famous chefs such as Alain Ducasse turn offal products like *ris de veau* (calves' sweetbread) into dishes that have blasé guests in the best restaurants swooning with delight. And let them swoon, I say. I don't need fancy, expensive offal dishes, just a morsel of meltingly soft liver or a couple of kidneys in cream every now and then. Though I wouldn't say no if you offered me a few juicy duck hearts.

Kidney crazy

We don't often eat liver, except for turning it into the delicious pâté for which the French are famous, and because we have already talked about liver elsewhere in this book, let's stick to kidneys. In my opinion, kidneys are the most "civilised" way of eating offal if you are not quite brave enough for tripe, brains and other scary bits and pieces. And wine is still the best way to soften the taste, texture and aroma of kidneys, which is why we usually stick to this classic Burgundy recipe. If you want to prepare them without alcohol, however, you can soak the kidney halves in salted water (1 t salt to 2 cups water) after removing the outer membranes, the inner white tubes and the fat. Then fry them quickly in butter, remove from the pan before they become tough, stir a little lemon juice into the butter in the pan, and pour this tasty sauce over the hot kidneys. Simple and delicious, or simply delicious.

Burgundy kidneys
4 SERVINGS

8 kidneys (preferably lamb's or sheep) | 2 T butter | 1 T olive oil 1 onion, finely chopped | 125 g mushrooms, chopped | 125 g chopped bacon | 300 ml Burgundy red wine (or local equivalent) 1 clove garlic, crushed | 1 bouquet garni | 1 T flour | 1 small bunch parsley, chopped | salt and pepper

Remove the membranes from around the kidneys. Cut the kidneys in half and remove the white tubes and the fat using a sharp knife.

Heat 1 T of the butter with the oil in a heavy-based pan. Add the onion, mushrooms and bacon, and sauté for a few minutes over moderate heat until soft. Remove from the pan with a slotted spoon and keep warm.

Increase the heat and fry the kidneys over high heat for a few seconds. Then reduce the heat and fry them gently for about 3 minutes. Transfer to a serving dish using a slotted spoon and keep warm.

Pour the red wine into the pan and return the onion, mushrooms and bacon to the pan. Season with salt and pepper. Add the garlic and bouquet garni. Bring to the boil, reduce the heat and simmer for 10 minutes.

Mix the remaining 1 T butter with the flour in a small bowl to make a *beurre manié*. Drop small lumps of this into the pan and stir continuously until the sauce thickens. Pour the sauce over the kidneys, sprinkle with parsley and serve immediately with baguettes or pasta or mashed potatoes.

Tripes à la mode de Caen

Tripes, or tripe to give it its English name, is a collective noun for the four different stomach sections of a ruminant animal such as a cow or a sheep, namely the rumen, the reticulum with its honeycomb texture, the omasum or manyplies, and the abomasum. Each has its own unique texture and flavour, and if all four are cooked slowly for hours with onions, carrots and a calf's foot, you get the famous dish from Normandy called *tripes à la mode de Caen*. This favourite of my Frenchman – which we never try to make ourselves because no-one else in the house would tolerate the smell of tripe cooking for hours – is apparently at its unforgettable best when the *tripes* of a calf is used.

Right: Burgundy kidneys

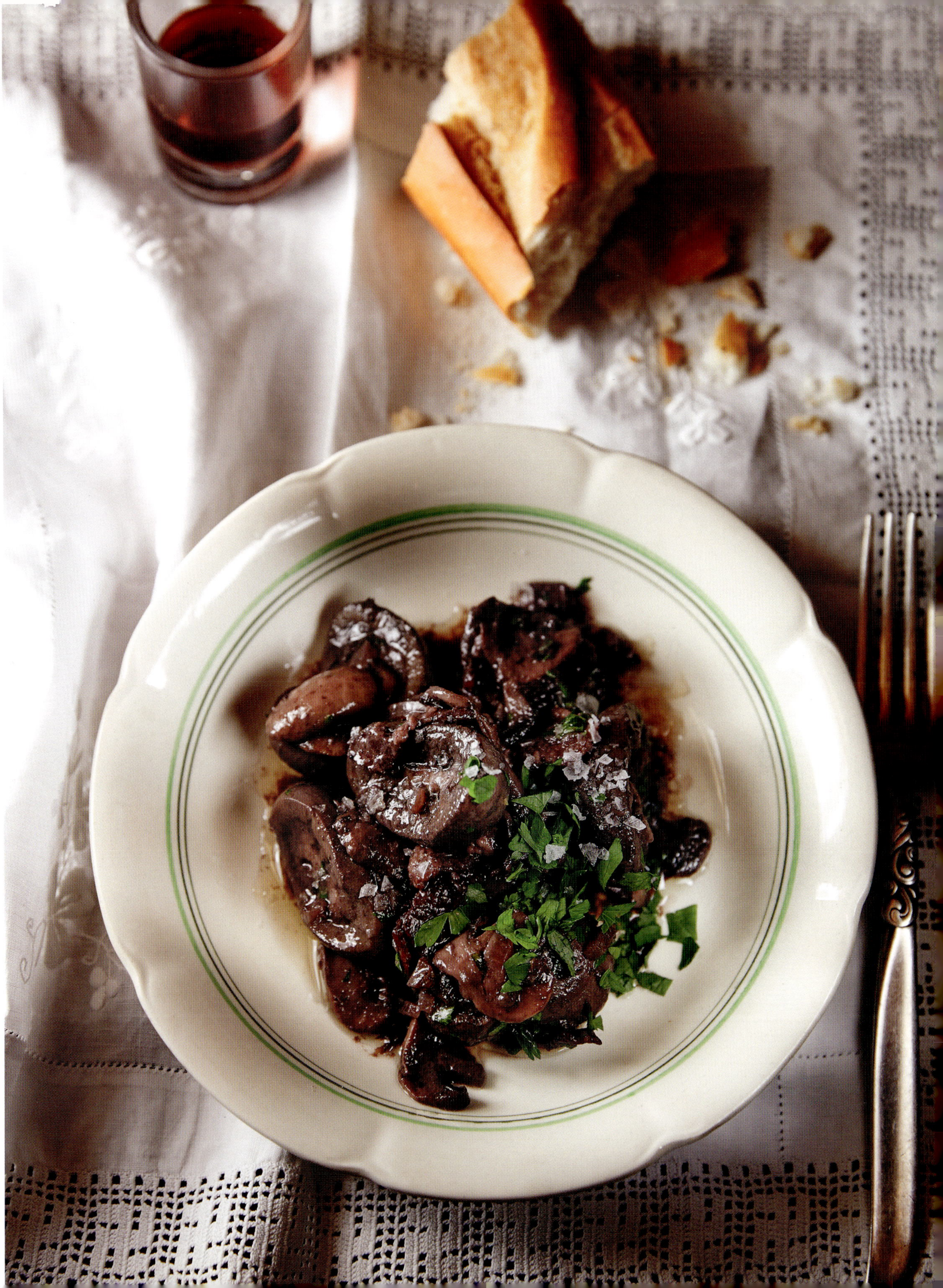

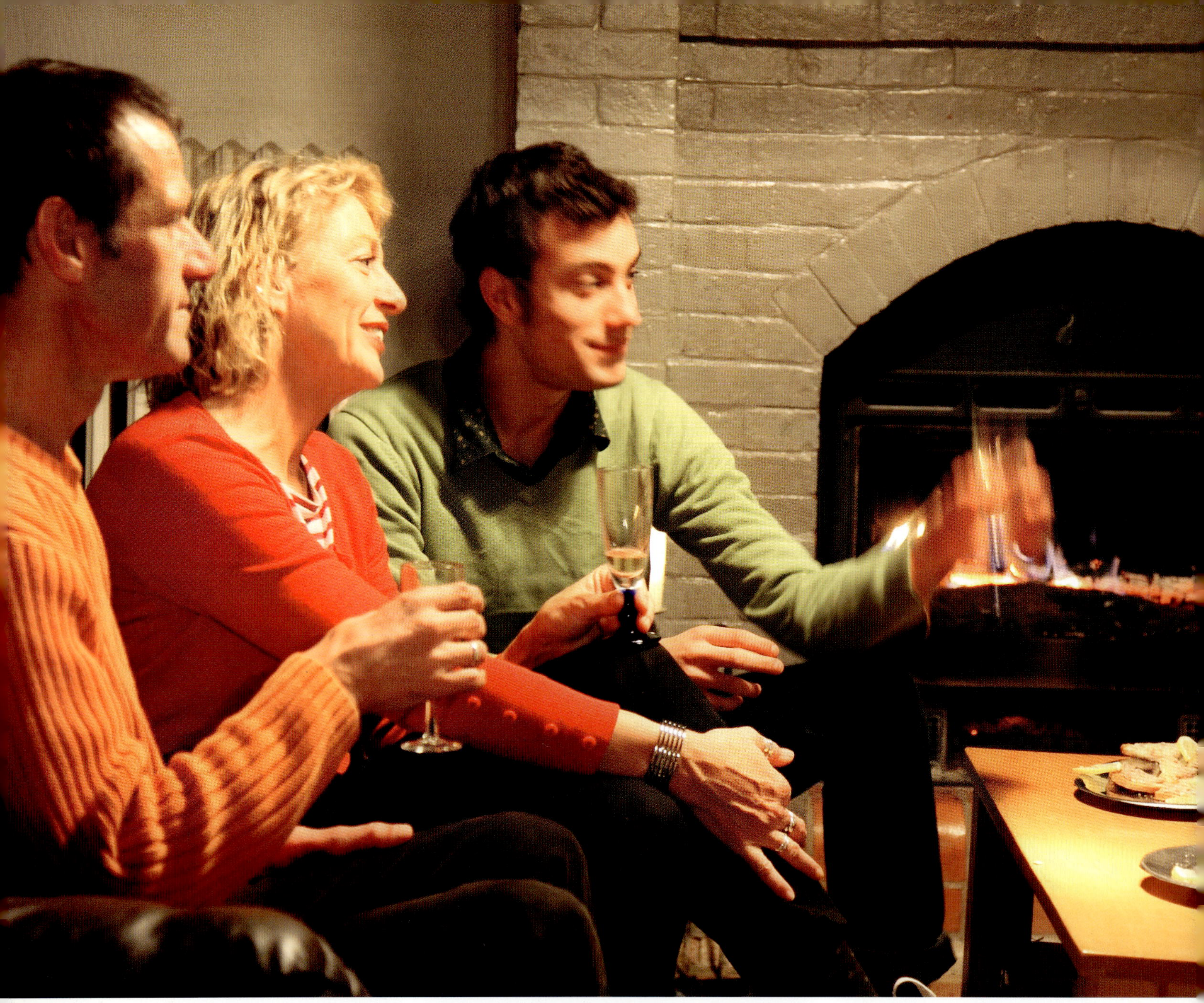
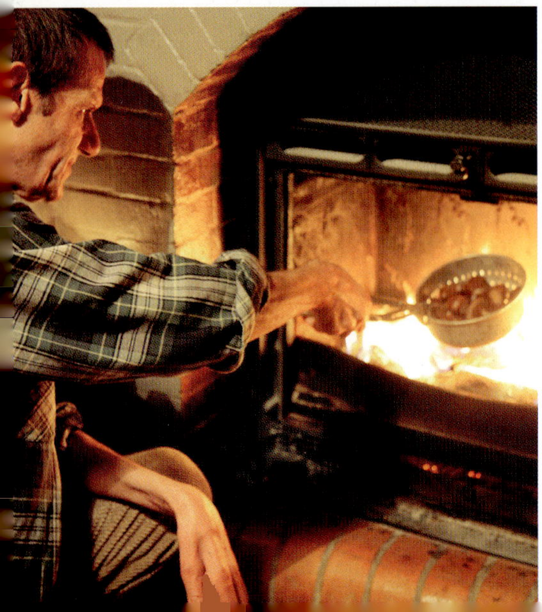
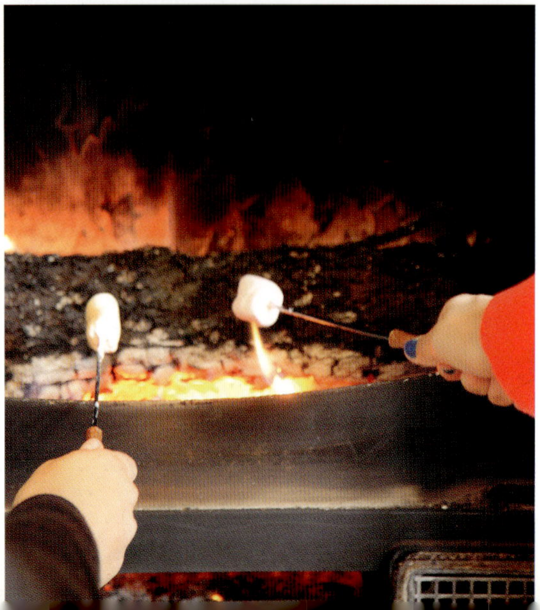
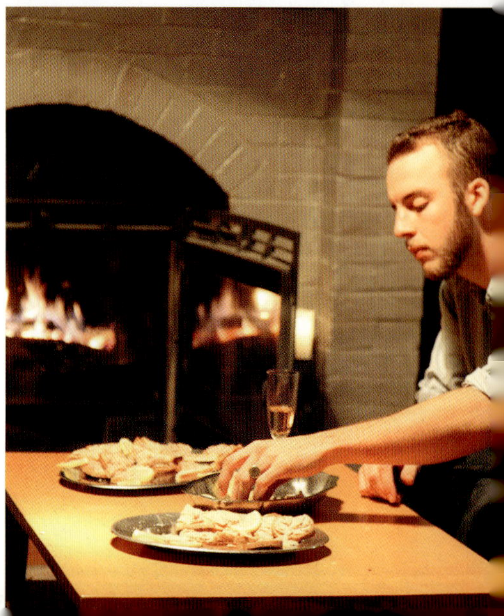

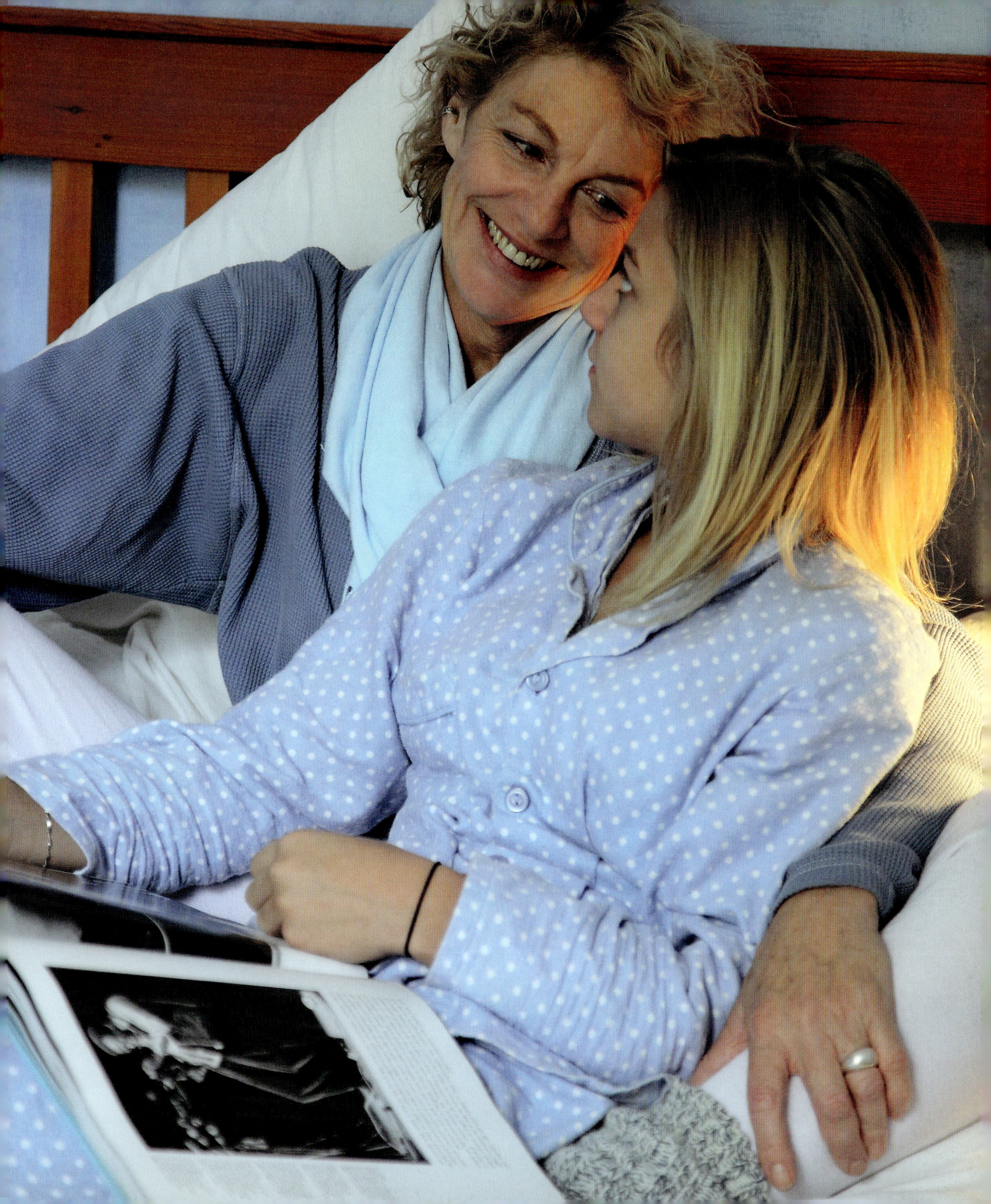

DIADUMÈNE

WHEN LIFE HANDS YOU LEMONS …

"LEMON TREE VERY PRETTY AND THE LEMON FLOWER IS SWEET / BUT THE FRUIT OF THE POOR LEMON IS IMPOSSIBLE TO EAT."

WILL HOLT, AMERICAN SONGWRITER (1929-)

This song, which Will Holt wrote about the poor lemon in the sixties, has been recorded by artists as varied as Peter, Paul and Mary and Bob Marley and the Wailers, but it was Trini Lopez's version in particular that became well known. Excellent advertising for the trees, but not totally fair to the fruit. Or so I thought as a child every time I heard the tune played on my dad's record player.

Because I have been enthralled by lemons since childhood. Not only by the vibrant colour and smell, but also by the unique taste that makes you suck in your cheeks in pure pleasure. Ice-cold lemonade on a hot day, a wedge of lemon with any seafood, a grating of lemon zest in icing for a cake, not to mention the infinite pleasure of my mother's lemon meringue pie!

As an adult I learned that a bowl of yellow lemons can lift the mood of the entire kitchen on a bleak winter's day. Lemons remind us of sunflowers and sunshine, of the light and joys of summer, of the fact that even the longest winter cannot last forever. Along with olive oil and coarse salt, lemons are to me the most essential ingredients in my Provençal kitchen. For Alain, on the other hand, they are thyme and garlic. Each to his or her own, I say – and my own tastes like lemon.

A century ago, most lemons in Europe came from the Provençal coastal town of Menton. Since 1934 the town has held an annual lemon festival which has evolved into a spectacular affair with firework displays and parades, and floats decorated with tons and tons of lemons.

According to legend, Eve took a golden fruit with her when she and Adam were driven from the Garden of Eden, but because Adam, the old coward, was afraid of the wrath of God, he commanded her to get rid of it. The model woman that she was, she obeyed and buried the fruit beside a beautiful Mediterranean bay that reminded her of paradise lost … Yes, you guessed it, today that bay is called Menton.

The less poetic version is that the ancient Romans brought lemons to Menton from the Middle East and started cultivating them on the hills around the town. It was soon clear that citrus fruit did extremely well in this mild microclimate, and before long Menton was synonymous with *citron*. By the way, the French word *citron* for lemon is what linguists call a false friend, easily confused with the English citron, which refers to a larger type of citrus fruit with a thicker skin and considerably less juice.

Lemons are an important part of classic French dishes like *tarte citron*. This is a more sophisticated affair than the ultra-sweet meringue pie of my childhood, thanks mainly to another Provençal winter "fruit", the almond, which plays a strong supporting role. But when it comes to making the best use of lemons, French cooks still have a thing or two to learn from their Moroccan counterparts. In this resourceful North African cuisine, lemons are treated with coarse salt, packed into clean jars and stored until the skin is soft and malleable. The unexpected salty-sour flavour of these preserved lemons is a feature of the best tagines and most delicious Moroccan dishes.

What's more, preserved lemons combine two of my three essential Provençal ingredients: lemons and coarse salt. In view of all this, I suppose I should be preserving my own lemons so that I always have a jar to hand. But, hey, no-one's perfect. Fortunately I have an industrious and generous Moroccan friend who sometimes takes pity on me.

Classic French lemon tart
6-8 SERVINGS

Right: Classic French lemon tart

You could make this tart using a shop-bought crust, but the home-made pastry contains more butter and less water, making it deliciously soft.

Pastry: *250 g flour | a pinch of salt | 125 g butter | 1 egg yolk*
Filling: *75 g sugar | finely grated zest and juice of 3 lemons | 2 eggs and 1 egg white (the rest of the egg you used for the pastry) | 75 ml crème fraîche | 125 g ground almonds | a pinch of cinnamon*
Syrup: *2 more lemons, cut into very thin slices | 125 g sugar*

Start with the pastry by combining the flour and salt in a bowl. Rub the butter into the flour with your fingertips until the mixture looks like fine breadcrumbs. Stir in the egg yolk, along with 2-3 T iced water (just enough to form a soft, non-sticky dough). Chill the dough for half an hour in the fridge.

In the meantime, make the filling. Mix the sugar, lemon zest and juice in another bowl. Add the eggs and egg white and beat well. Add the crème fraîche, ground almonds and cinnamon, and stir to form a thick, smooth mixture.

Roll out the dough on a surface sprinkled with flour and place it in a tart pan that has been lined with baking paper. Prick a few holes in the dough with a fork and spoon in the filling. Bake for 20-30 minutes in a preheated 190 °C oven, until the filling is set and golden. Remove from the oven and leave to cool.

For the syrup, place the lemon slices in a saucepan, add enough water to cover and simmer over low heat for about 10 minutes until the skins are soft. Remove and drain well. Reserve about 75 ml of the water in the saucepan, add the sugar and cook over low heat until all the sugar has dissolved. Increase the heat to bring the syrup to the boil. Add the lemon and cook rapidly until all the slices are covered with the thick syrup. Remove the lemon and arrange in a pattern on the tart.

Moroccan preserved lemons

In Morocco, small whole lemons are used, with only the tops cut off, to make the traditional *l'hamd marakad*. In France it is called *citron confit* and is also made with larger lemons, which are scored a number of times before being preserved. This is easy to make yourself: all you need is 8-10 scrubbed lemons, ½ cup salt, and perhaps a little more fresh lemon juice.

Cut off the top of each lemon. Score the lemons from top to bottom as if you wanted to quarter them, but make sure that the quarters are still attached to each other at the bottom. Roll the lemons in the salt, prise open the quarters with your fingers and sprinkle the flesh generously with the salt. Sprinkle 2 T salt in a sterilised glass jar and pack the lemons snugly into the jar. Squeeze each lemon so that its juice is released. The jar should be tightly packed and there should be enough juice to cover all the lemons. If not, add more lemon juice. Sprinkle more salt in the jar, close the lid tightly and store in a cool, dark place.

During the first couple of days, you can open the jars a few times to push the lemons further down into the jars to release more juice, and even add another lemon if there is room. After about a month the skins should be soft enough to start using the lemons. Once opened, you can keep a jar in the fridge for months until you have used up all the lemons. Before using the preserved lemons, rinse to remove the excess salt as well as the harmless white film that sometimes forms in the liquid.

Add the finely chopped peel to salads, or remove the flesh and use only the empty "shells" in tagines or sauces, or remove the pips and use the whole lemon for a stronger flavour.

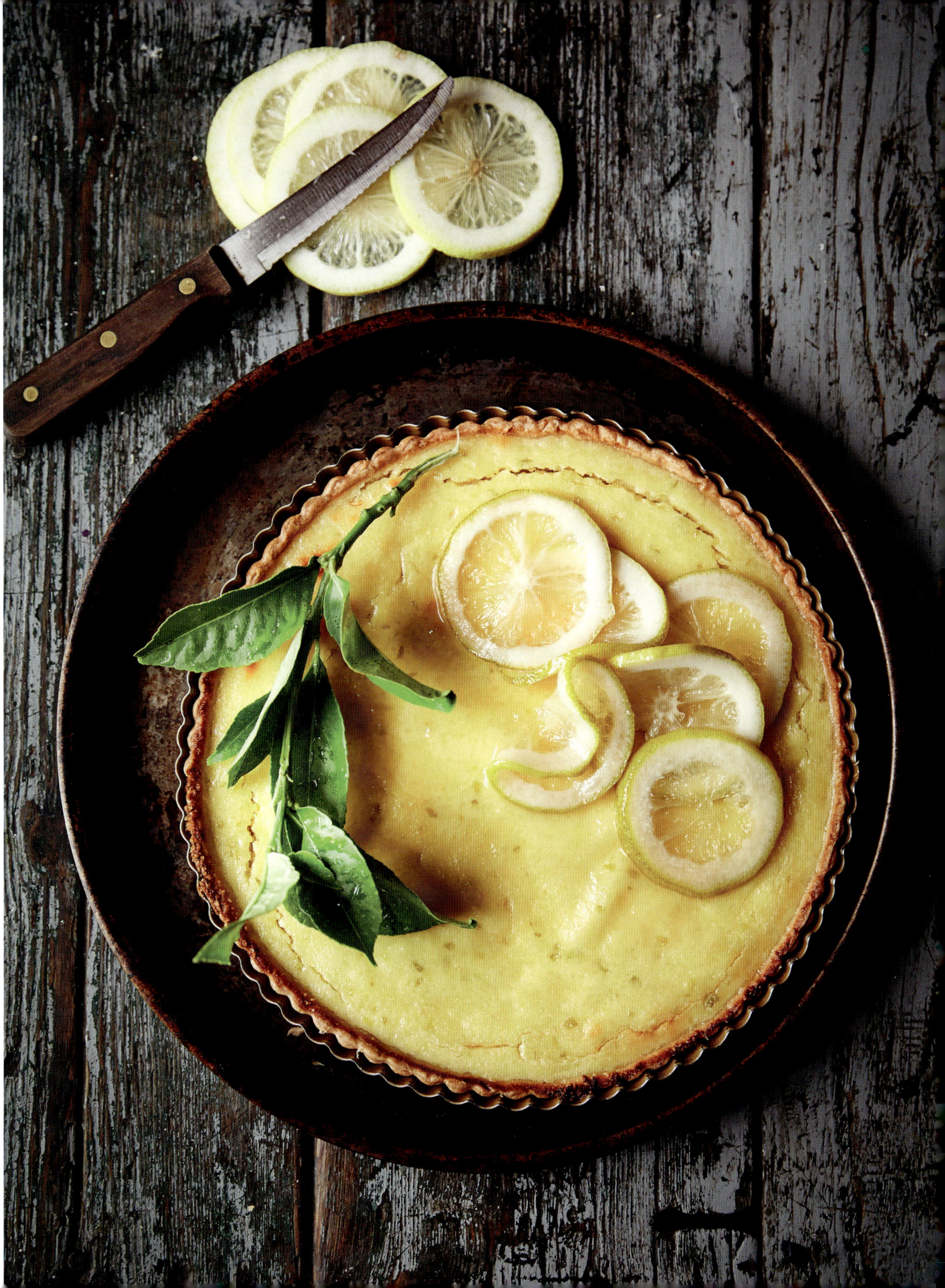

LIGHT HOUSE
FISHING
Sardine
ocean blue ocean blue ocean blue
TEAS & COFFEE
SEASIDE
Sardine
ocean blue ocean blue ocean blue ocean

OUR DAILY BREAD

"THE SMELL OF GOOD BREAD BAKING, LIKE THE SOUND OF LIGHTLY FLOWING WATER, IS INDESCRIBABLE IN ITS EVOCATION OF INNOCENCE AND DELIGHT."

M.F.K. FISHER, AMERICAN FOOD WRITER (1908-1992)

Our family are not great bakers, perhaps because baking is a more precise science than cooking, in which you can improvise all you like. We enjoy improvising in the kitchen, otherwise the process of preparing food becomes too boring. Mia, though, is showing promising signs of becoming a decent baker. She is already following baking recipes in French, English *and* Afrikaans – while her father, despite his considerably more advanced age, is still unable to follow a recipe in any language without making his own adaptations.

They say that one of the differences between South African and French eating habits is that South Africans (and the Americans and British too, I suppose) buy bread twice a week, while the French do so twice a day. And I have been living here long enough to know that "they" are not exaggerating, as is usually the case. It is not just that the French want bread at every meal; it must also be the freshest and the best bread – anything else simply would not do.

In one of the villages where we lived previously, for example, many of the locals refused to eat the local baker's bread. They would rather drive to one of the neighbouring villages twice a day to buy their bread there. The local baker sold fairly decent croissants, pastries and cakes, but his bread did not meet the locals' high standards. The baguettes were too dry and holey, the larger *pains* (plumper forms of the traditional baguette) were too soft and soggy, and the thin *ficelles* (the thinnest type of baguette) were generally regarded as a fiasco.

To add insult to injury, our local baker did not offer a wide enough variety, as the *boulangers* in the neighbouring villages did. His bakery never stocked enough round and oval loaves, enough bread made from whole-grain, maize or mixed-seed flours, and loaves dotted with pieces of olives or nuts. In short, general opinion in the village was that this *boulanger* did not take his very important occupation seriously enough.

Initially we supported him because we felt sorry for him and I was stupid enough to believe that bread was bread. Now that I've been here some time and gained in experience, I know that French bread is never just something to fill an empty tummy. No, bread is a serious aesthetic and gastronomic object of desire that can satisfy far more than just a physical hunger. "Give us this day our daily bread", indeed. While my French neighbours might still mumble this prayer, they would add: "And please make sure it is oven fresh and flavoursome, Lord, with a heavenly taste and perfect texture, not too soft inside nor too hard outside, with a crust that is not too pale but definitely not too brown either, otherwise we won't eat it anyway. Amen."

This obsession with perfect bread is contagious too. If you live here long enough, you are sure to pick it up, as I can testify. It has been years since I bought my bread from just any old baker. I drive to a neighbouring town – and not the closest one either – that offers me a choice of three bakeries. And I support the bakery at the furthest end of the town.

Sometimes I have to defend this baker's reputation in heated arguments with neighbours, who hold the view that the closest of the three bakers is the best. (Everyone agrees that the middle one should rather be avoided.) The closest baker was indeed the best a few years ago, but my husband and I and most of our local friends agree that the furthest one has deposed him. One bite of the latter's special baguette, called quite appropriately *festive*, is usually enough to convince the doubters. And now I must step away from my desk for a while to go and buy bread for the second time today. From the furthest baker, of course.

Alain's cheese loaf
6-8 SERVINGS

The French have such passionate opinions about traditional French bread that as an outsider I have never even tried to bake a baguette. What we do bake regularly at home is a ridiculously easy cheese loaf into which you can mix pieces of ham or olives or other titbits of your choice. It is not "real" bread because there is no yeast involved, but it is *our* kind of bread because it never flops!

1 cup self-raising flour | a pinch of salt | 1 cup milk | 2 eggs | 100 g grated cheese (we usually use Gruyère, but Cheddar will also do) butter

Mix the flour, salt and milk in a bowl. Add the eggs and mix well to form a smooth batter. Stir in the grated cheese.

Grease a loaf tin with butter and pour the mixture into it. Bake for about 20 minutes in a preheated 180 °C oven. It is done when a thin knife blade inserted into the middle comes out clean. Serve as *apéro* or an appetizer with olives and other Provençal snacks.

Flop-proof fougasse
6-8 SERVINGS

Fougasse, the French version of Italian focaccia, is the simplest kind of bread to make for those of us who are wary of baking. Believe me, if I can do it, anyone can. Unlike most bread recipes, you are encouraged to use your imagination. We like this version with pieces of chorizo, but you could replace the chorizo with leftovers or herbs of your choice: bacon, ham, anchovies, onion, garlic, olives, rosemary, sage …

1 packet instant yeast (enough for 250 g flour) | a pinch of sugar 250 g flour | a pinch of salt 12 slices chorizo, cut into smaller pieces | the leaves of 1 stalk of thyme 2-3 T olive oil

Combine the yeast and sugar with a little warm water in a small bowl and leave to rise for about 10 minutes.

Mix the flour and salt in a large bowl. Make a well in the middle, pour the yeast mixture into it and mix. Add a glass of lukewarm water gradually while kneading the dough until you can form a firm, non-sticky ball. Cover with a clean tea towel and leave to rise in a warm spot for at least 2 hours.

Fry the chorizo pieces in a non-stick pan until crisp and drain on kitchen paper. (Do the same if you are using bacon or ham to fry out the fat before mixing it with the dough. If you are using onion or garlic, also fry it first, but other pieces of vegetable can be added raw.)

Once the dough has at least doubled in size, preheat the oven to 200 °C. Roll out the dough into an oval shape on a large sheet of baking paper that has been sprinkled with flour. Sprinkle the thyme and half the chorizo in the middle of the dough. Fold in the sides of the dough to cover the chorizo and seal the "seam" in the middle.

Use a sharp knife to score the dough in the shape of a fern. Rub your hands with flour and open the cuts with your fingers. Push the remaining chorizo into the dough. Brush the dough with olive oil, slide it into the preheated oven with the help of the baking paper and bake for 30-35 minutes, until the fougasse is well risen and golden. There is no need to slice it – serve as is and everyone can pull off pieces.

Right: Flop-proof fougasse

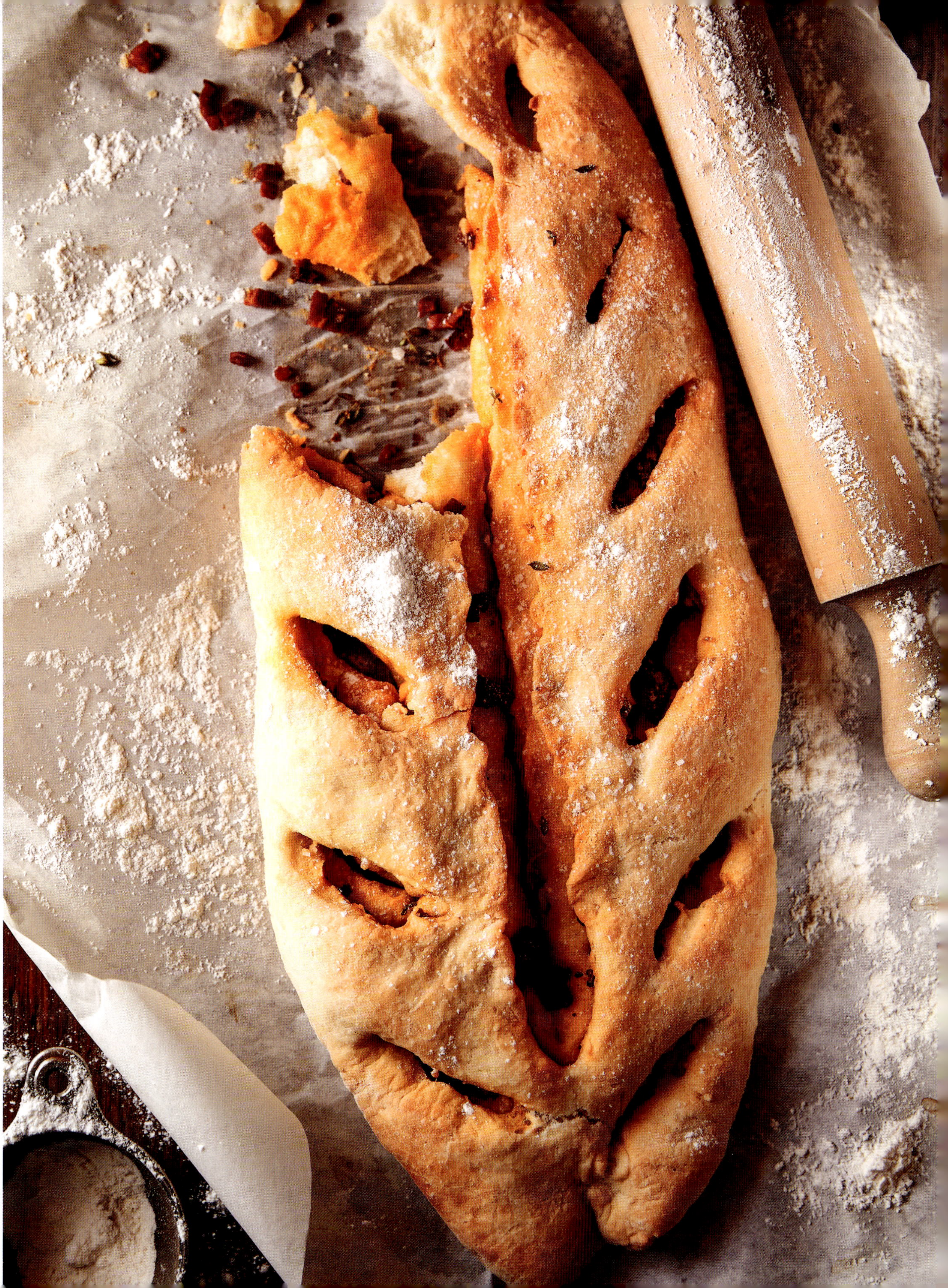

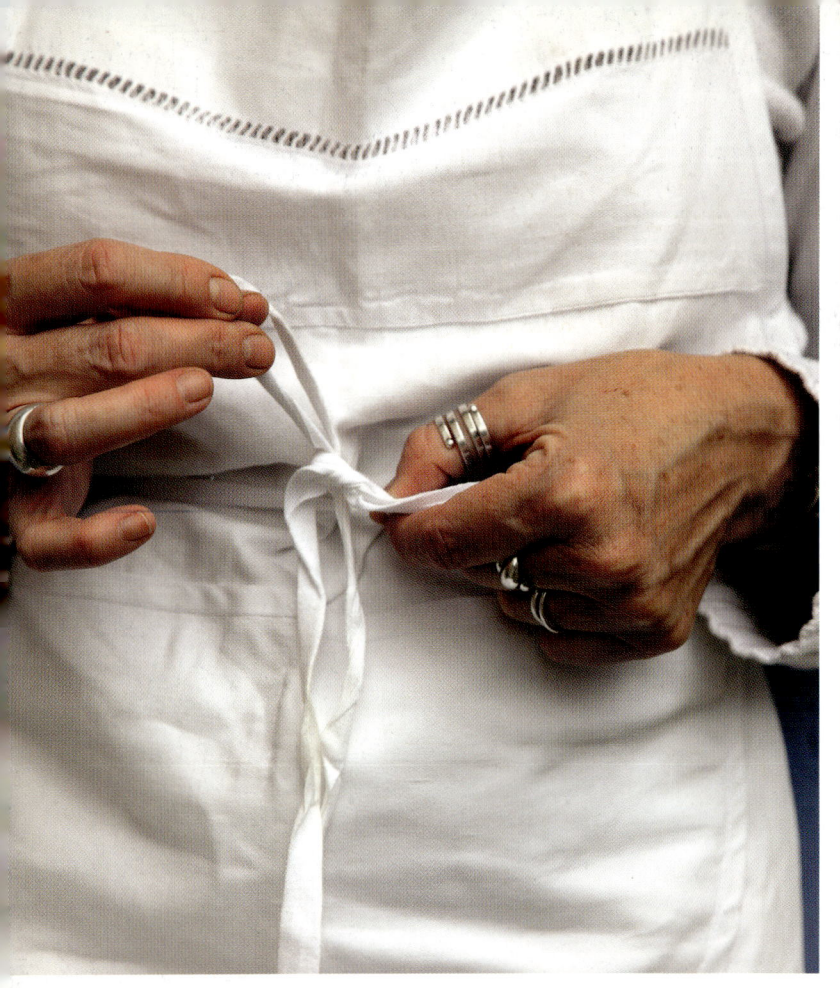

CRÈME FRAÎCHE
CAFÉ
RAISINS
CHAMPIGNONS
PAIN
CAMEMBERT

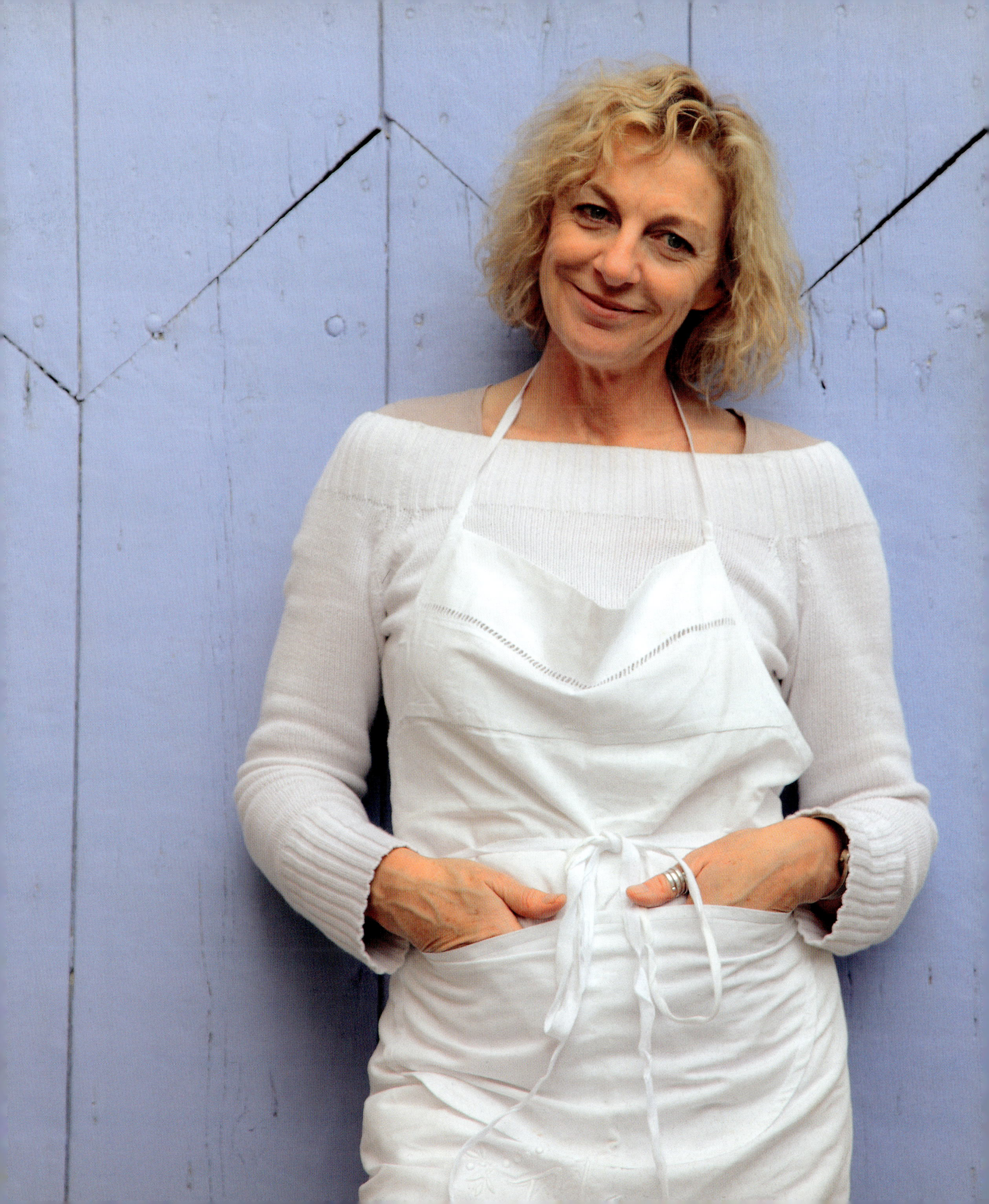

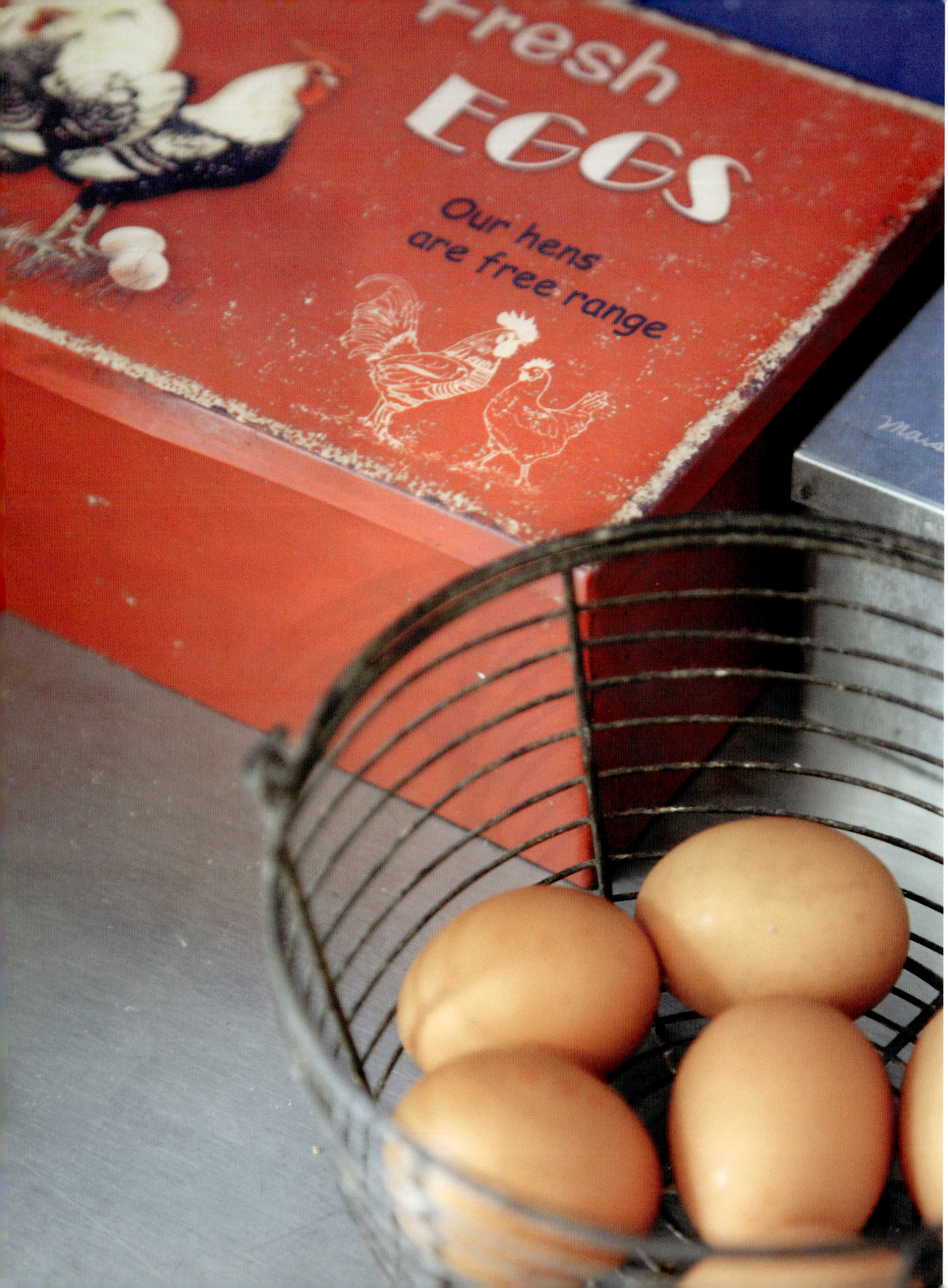
Fresh
EGGS
Our hens
are free range

YOU CAN'T MAKE AN OMELETTE WITHOUT BREAKING EGGS

"AN EGG IS ALWAYS AN ADVENTURE; THE NEXT ONE MAY BE DIFFERENT."

OSCAR WILDE, IRISH WRITER (1854-1900)

Making a soufflé is not something I would embark upon lightly. In a home economics class in high school many years ago, I was psychologically damaged by a soufflé that collapsed before my very eyes – and to this day I am nervous of them. Silly, I know, but you know how it is.

Fortunately I can do lots of other things with eggs – and here in France I have expanded my repertoire considerably, because the French know all about eggs. Besides the notorious soufflé, there are all the well-known desserts featuring egg whites, such as *île flottante* ("floating island", another beautifully poetic name for a pudding) and meringue and chocolate mousse, and the legendary sauces of French haute cuisine such as hollandaise and velouté, made using egg yolks.

It was Auguste Escoffier who around a century ago divided the hundreds of French sauces into five major "mother sauces" and numerous "daughter sauces". Of the Big Five (hollandaise, béchamel, espagnole, velouté and tomate), the last-mentioned is often produced in our kitchen. Not just because tomato-based sauces are more traditionally Provençal than the rest, but also because they are easier to make than hollandaise, in which the egg yolk and hot butter must "bind" – which they usually flatly refuse to do when I ask. And because they are lighter and healthier than three of the other mother sauces, which are all based on a roux of flour and butter.

I am not a fan of pretentious French sauces, but I have had my arm twisted to produce a hollandaise sauce for eggs Benedict, for instance (poached eggs and ham on two halves of a toasted English muffin with a generous topping of hollandaise sauce, and a really comforting breakfast on a freezing winter's morning). And I use the word "produce" for good reason, because it feels more like a concert than cooking. The problem is that you need some heat to prevent the egg yolks "separating" from the rest of the sauce, but too much heat can cause the whole lot to curdle because the recipe also calls for lemon juice and/or wine vinegar. Traditionally this is done using a bain-marie or double boiler, but even with a modern electric beater in an ordinary saucepan on a low heat, it is nerve-jangling stuff.

And what to do with the leftover egg whites when, contrary to all expectations, you do succeed in getting your hollandaise sauce to come together? Well, in our kitchen no part of an egg ever gets thrown away, besides the shell. If we need a single egg yolk to brush over the dough when making pastry, it is the perfect excuse to crack another few eggs for an Italian carbonara sauce, perhaps. (Or something simpler than a hollandaise sauce in any case.) Which then gives us the opportunity to use all the leftover egg whites for something like a pavlova … Waste not, want not is the motto in this house.

But if we want to use the white and yolk of an egg together for a quick, easy, tasty dish that everyone in the family enjoys, an omelette always hits the spot. The French word *omelette* has been around since the sixteenth century, although the dish it refers to was known by other names long before then. From *alumelle* and *alumete* in the fourteenth century, the word gradually became *aumelette*, which had officially taken on its modern spelling by the eighteenth century. Today, relatives of the original French *alumelle* are loved the world over. In Italy they are called *frittatas* and eaten open like pizzas, with vegetables, cheese, meat and even yesterday's leftover pasta on top. And in Spain you meet the *tortilla*, mixed with potato, onion, peppers and so on, a thicker and more homely fellow than his refined French *grandmaman*.

And yet, a traditional French *omelette aux fines herbes* remains the epitome of unsurpassed simplicity and taste. You only have to think of the title of one of Elizabeth David's best known books on French cooking: *An Omelette and a Glass of Wine*. Sometimes you really need nothing more to satisfy body and soul.

Piperade
6 SERVINGS

It is the chilli that gives this Basque dish its bite, but when we make it for children and sensitive souls, we use only a small piece of chilli. You do need to be generous with the peppers though, or the dish loses its lovely red colour. If you want to do it properly, you could roast the peppers in the oven and then peel them, but we usually take a short cut and cook the peppers with their skins on.

6 T olive oil | 4 red peppers, cut into strips | 4 onions, cut into strips 1 small red chilli, seeded and finely chopped | 2 cloves garlic, crushed a pinch of sugar | 1 kg tomatoes, peeled and chopped | 1 bouquet garni | 6 eggs | a knob of butter salt and pepper

Heat the olive oil in a large pan, add the peppers and fry for a few minutes over moderate heat until soft – stir every so often. Add the onions, chilli and garlic, and fry for 10 minutes, stirring regularly. Add the sugar, tomatoes, bouquet garni, salt and pepper and cook for a further 10 minutes – again, stir every so often.

Beat the eggs in a small bowl. Heat the butter in another large pan and add the eggs. Cook for 1-2 minutes over low heat without stirring. Remove the bouquet garni and add the vegetable mixture to the eggs. Stir everything together for 1-2 minutes over low heat. Season with more salt and pepper to taste. Serve immediately straight from the pan, along with slices of the best ham.

Vegetarian omelette stack
4-6 SERVINGS

This is a delicious vegetarian dish that is ideal for entertaining, a picnic or a quick lunch out the fridge, because it can be made ahead of time. Best of all, you can vary the vegetables and herbs according to the season. In spring you can replace the broccoli and onions with asparagus and spring onions, in summer with marrows and shallots, and in autumn with mushrooms and red onions – or whatever you like – just to keep things interesting.

10 eggs | 4-6 T olive oil | 3-4 broccoli florets, finely chopped | 1 onion, finely chopped | 1 red pepper, finely chopped | 1 clove garlic, crushed 300 g St Môret cream cheese (or cottage cheese) | a handful of thyme leaves | Parmesan shavings and rocket leaves (optional, to garnish) salt and pepper

Crack the eggs into two bowls, five in each bowl. Beat and season with salt and pepper.

Heat a little oil in a small pan (20-25 cm) and cook the broccoli and onion for a few minutes over low heat until soft. Remove with a slotted spoon, leave to cool and add to the eggs in one of the bowls.

In the meantime, fry the pepper and garlic for a few minutes in the same pan (add a little more oil if necessary) until soft. Remove with a slotted spoon, leave to cool and add to the eggs in the second bowl.

Heat a small amount of oil in the same pan and pour a third of the broccoli-egg mixture into it. Cook until the bottom of the omelette is golden. Slide the omelette out of the pan and onto a plate and place it under a hot grill for a few moments, until the top also turns golden brown. Remove and set aside. Make another two omelettes with the broccoli-egg mixture. Repeat the process to make three omelettes using the pepper-egg mixture.

Stir the cheese to make it as soft and spreadable as possible. Add the thyme and, if you are using plain cottage cheese, season with salt and pepper to taste. Place a large sheet of clingwrap on a plate and put one of the red pepper omelettes on the plastic, with the best-looking side facing down. Spread some cheese on the omelette and cover it with one of the broccoli omelettes. Repeat with the rest of the omelettes. Alternate the red pepper and broccoli omelettes, stacking them one on top of the other and sandwiching them with cheese. Wrap the clingwrap securely around the stack of omelettes and put it into the fridge for a few hours.

Just before serving, invert the omelette stack onto a clean serving plate. Sprinkle with a few drops of olive oil, season with a little pepper, and garnish with Parmesan shavings and rocket leaves. Cut into wedges like a cake, and tuck in.

Right: Piperade

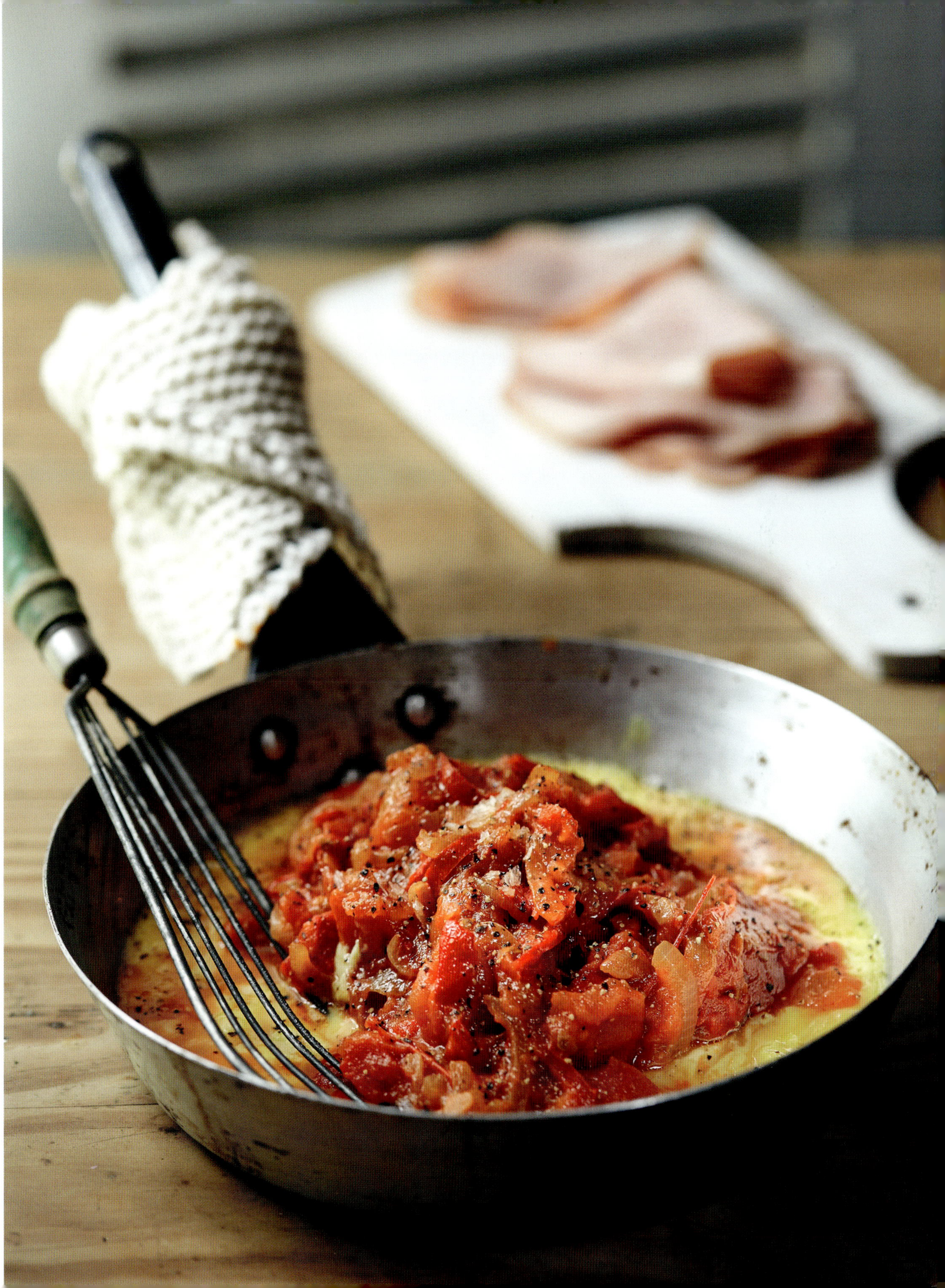

MERCI
St ANTOINE
DE PADOUE

MERCI A
St ANTOINE DE PADOUE

SUCCULENT SPRING LAMB

"ALWAYS REMEMBER: IF YOU'RE ALONE IN THE KITCHEN AND YOU DROP THE LAMB, YOU CAN ALWAYS JUST PICK IT UP. WHO'S GOING TO KNOW?"

JULIA CHILD, AMERICAN FOOD WRITER (1912-2004)

In France, Easter heralds the end of the long winter and the start of new life, symbolised by eggs and chicks and bunnies, especially of the chocolate variety for children of all ages. But in a Catholic country like this, Easter also signifies the end of a period of fasting during which eggs and cream, red meat and other rich foods are traditionally avoided. That is why egg dishes like omelettes and red meat are enjoyed with such relish during the Easter weekend.

Lamb is especially popular – because lambs symbolise spring and new life, and also form part of the Christian symbolism of Easter – and the most traditional meal for Easter Sunday is still *gigot d'agneau* or leg of lamb, served with fresh spring vegetables or, as an even bigger treat, creamy flageolet beans. In our previous recipe book I described this light green legume as the Rolls-Royce of the bean kingdom, and the combination of roast lamb and flageolet as a culinary match made in heaven. This is the view held by generations of food lovers – and I still agree.

If your family budget does not allow for a leg of lamb at Easter (and I speak from experience), you can still serve the most delicious meal of shoulder of lamb or even lamb cutlets. And in those years when Easter is celebrated at the very end of the month, when your bank account aquires the colour of the Red Sea (once again, I speak from bitter experience), you can buy cheaper cuts of lamb or even some mutton and stew it slowly in a wonderful Easter casserole that goes by the name of *navarin*.

As usual when it comes to the names of dishes, there are a number of explanations for this one. Some sources allege that the stew gets its name from the Battle of Navarino in 1827, when the French navy aided the Greeks in their struggle for independence, but it is more likely to be a variation of the French word for turnips (*navets*), which were originally added to the dish. The fact that it is made from cheaper stewing meat definitely does not mean this is an inferior dish – as any stew lover will tell you. Famous French chefs like Raymond Blanc are renowned for *navarins* that would have you swooning with pleasure.

Speaking of famous chefs, when it comes to lamb, for the best cooks in the land there is only one kind of meat, and that is the lamb from Aveyron. This region lies more or less in the middle of the country, in the Massif Central, and for two months the lambs born there are fed on milk alone to produce a pale, sweet and succulent meat that may be compared with the best veal. These special lambs are bred from the Lacaune breed of sheep, which are also famous because another major French food product is made from their milk: Roquefort, probably the best known blue cheese in the world, although many people still do not know that "real" Roquefort is made from sheep's milk rather than cow's milk.

You could even say that the lambs taste so good because their mothers' milk is so good.

And if you cannot afford Aveyron lamb for your Easter table, then you cannot afford it. Do not despair, because you can still tuck into an "ordinary" shoulder of lamb prepared the Provençal way with olives, tomatoes and herbs. And you don't *have* to wait for Easter either. Your guests will appreciate it any day of the year and in all four seasons. Just make sure you cook plenty because they will ask for seconds. Don't say I didn't warn you.

Right: Provençal stuffed shoulder of lamb

Provençal stuffed shoulder of lamb
6 SERVINGS

The Provençal mainstays of olives, tomatoes, garlic and rosemary combine to create a brilliant stuffing for a festive meat dish – a firm favourite in our house.

8-10 cherry tomatoes, halved | 200 ml thin cream (or full-cream milk) | 1 thick slice dry bread | 2 shallots, finely chopped | 2 cloves garlic, finely chopped | a bunch of flat-leaf parsley, finely chopped | 125 g black tapenade (recipe on page 177) | 50 g pine nuts | 2-3 T olive oil | 1 deboned shoulder of lamb (ask your butcher) | 1 stalk rosemary (or thyme) | 1 T butter | 200 ml dry white wine | 1 T beef stock | salt and pepper

Spread the cherry tomatoes on a flat baking sheet and place under a hot grill. Roast for a few minutes until the skins start to wrinkle.

Prepare the stuffing: Pour the cream into a large bowl and soak the bread in it for a few minutes. Add the roasted tomatoes, shallots, garlic, parsley, tapenade, pine nuts and 1 T olive oil. Mix well to combine and season with salt and pepper.

Place a little more than half of the stuffing in the middle of the deboned lamb shoulder. (Reserve the rest of the stuffing for the gravy.) Sprinkle the rosemary over the meat. Roll up the lamb shoulder and secure with string.

Heat the butter and the remaining olive oil in an ovenproof casserole dish that can also be used on the stovetop. Brown the meat quickly over high heat.

Place the dish with the meat in a preheated 200 °C oven and roast for about 40 minutes, until the meat is cooked through but still pink inside. (We prefer our lamb pink, but leave it in the oven for a bit longer if you like yours browner.) Remove the meat from the dish, wrap it in heavy-duty tinfoil and leave to rest for about 15 minutes. (This is to allow the meat to plump up a little after shrinking in the oven.)

Place the dish with the juices that have cooked out of the meat, back on the stovetop over moderate heat. Stir in the wine to lift off all those tasty bits that have stuck to the pan. Stir in the beef stock then add the remaining stuffing to make the gravy nice and thick.

Place the hot meat on a serving platter, pour the gravy into a gravy boat or jug and serve with baby marrows or flageolet beans, or any other spring vegetables with a light green colour. The aim is to please the eye along with the mouth and the stomach.

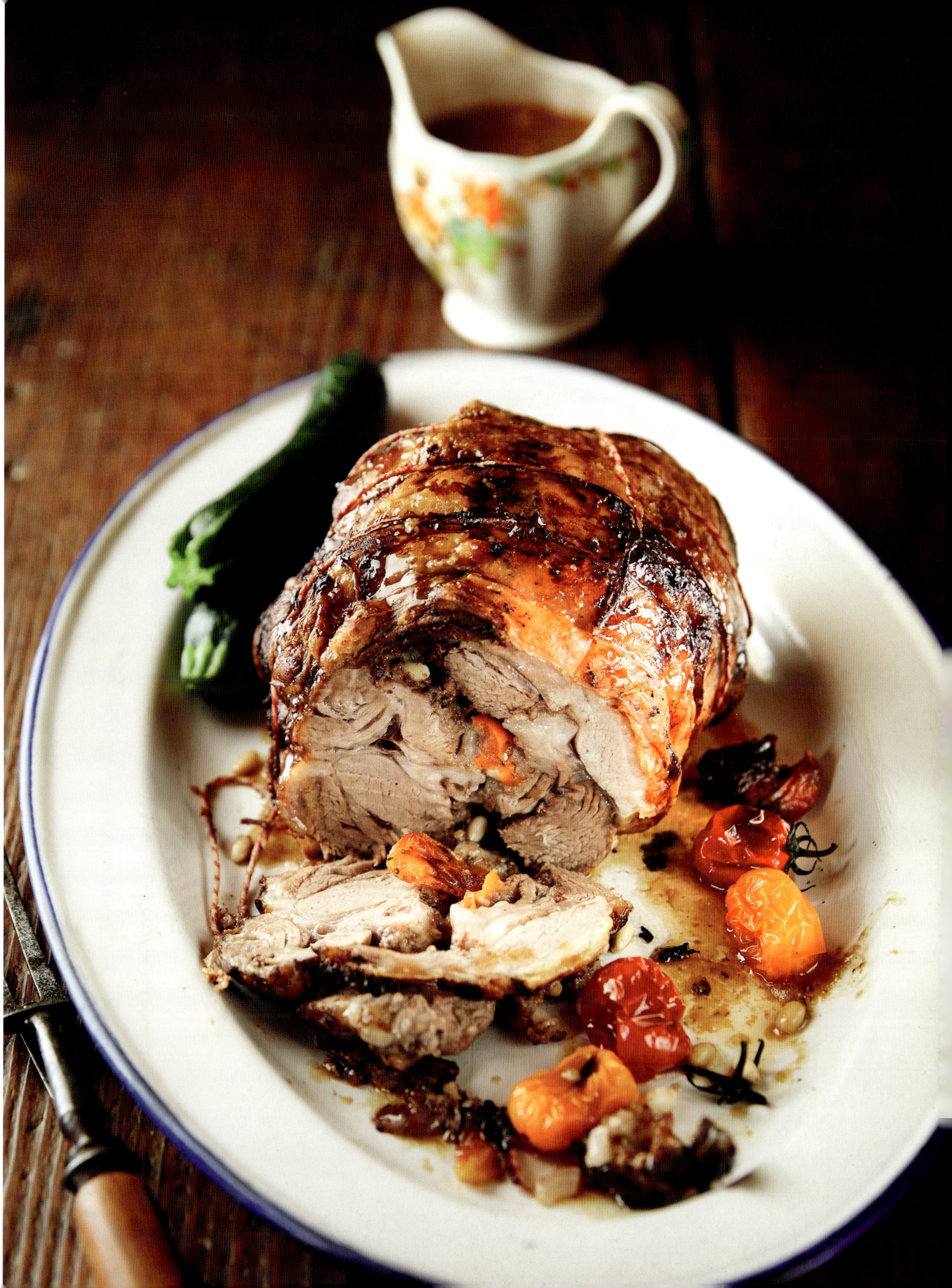

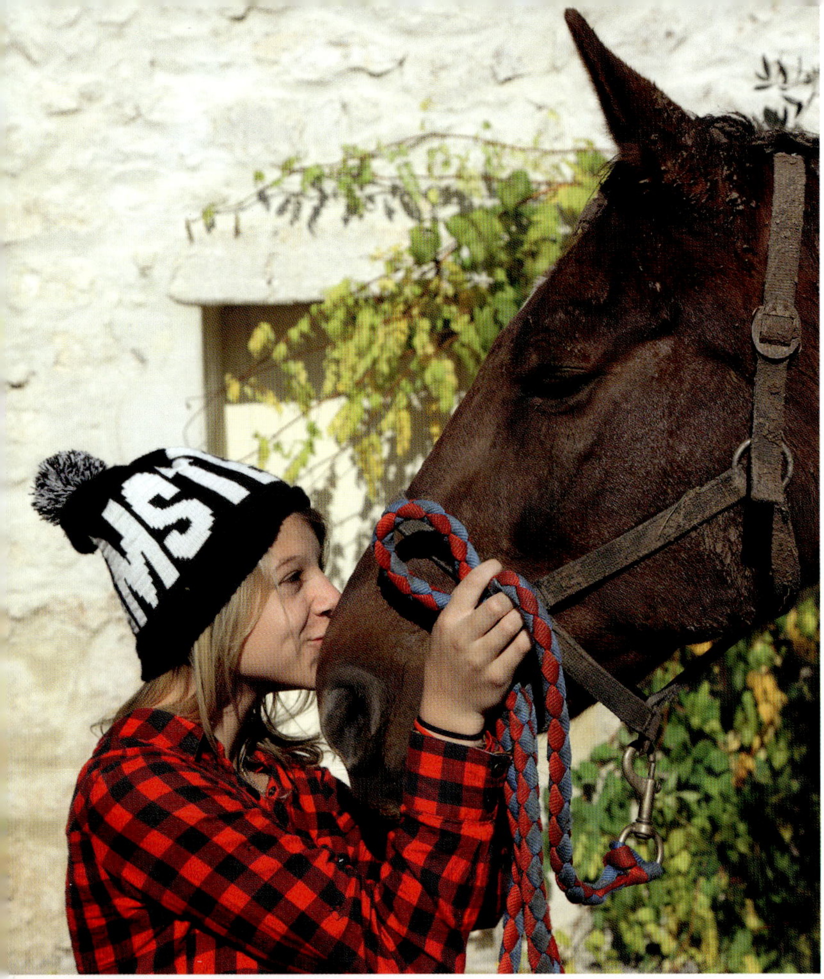

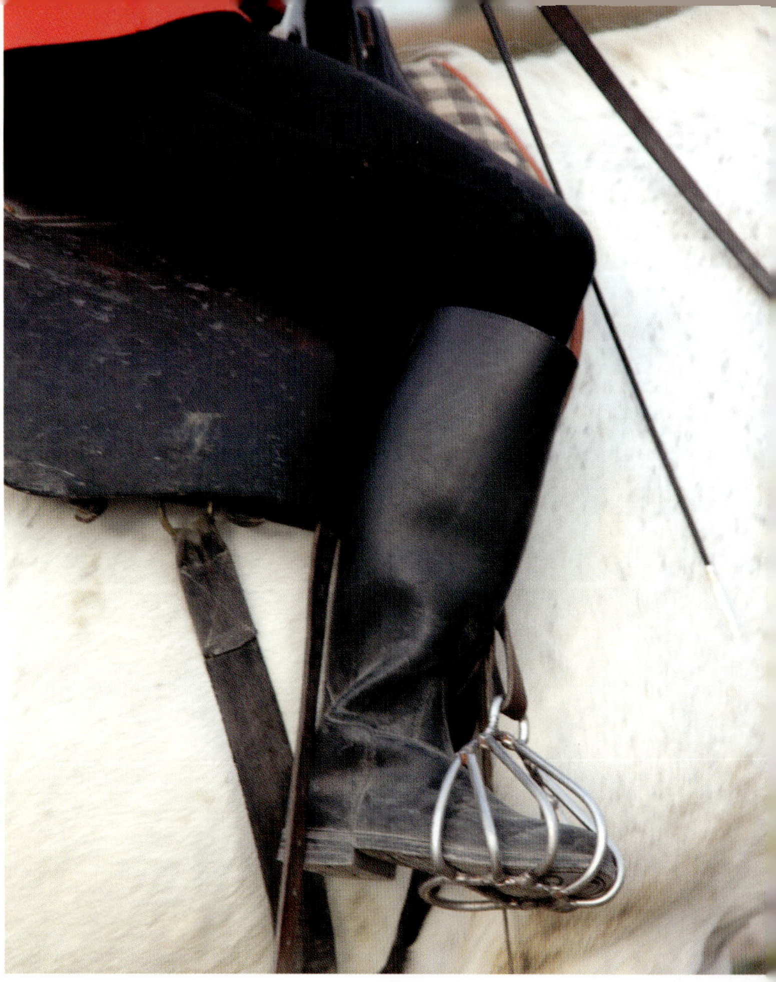

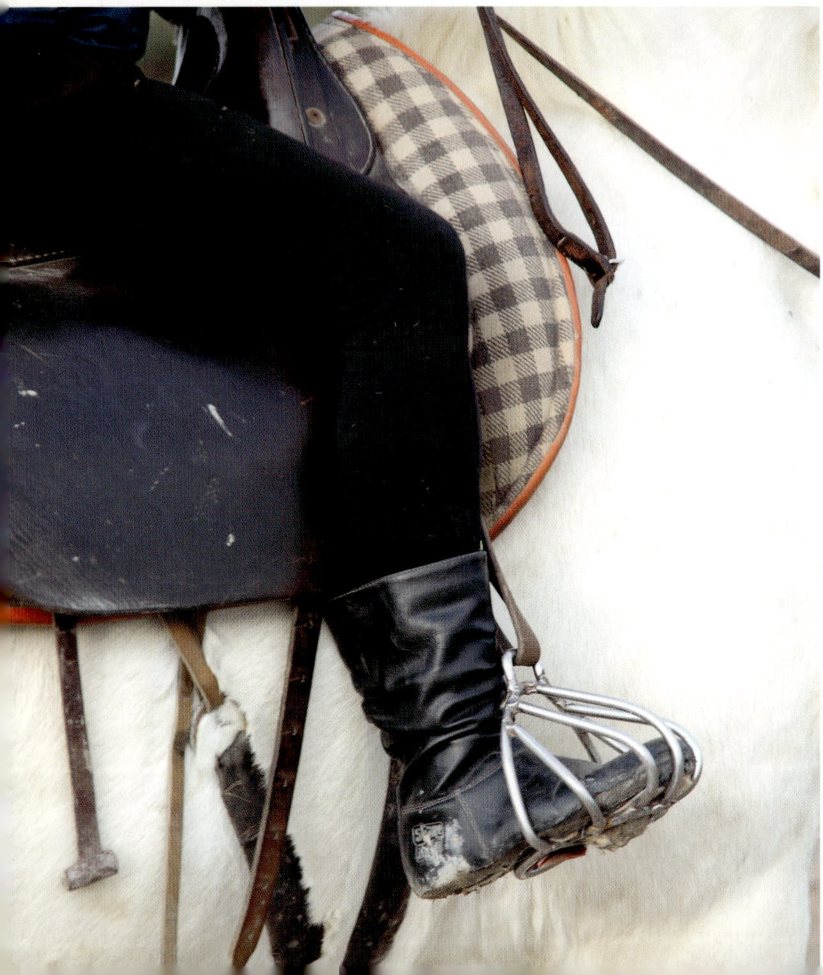

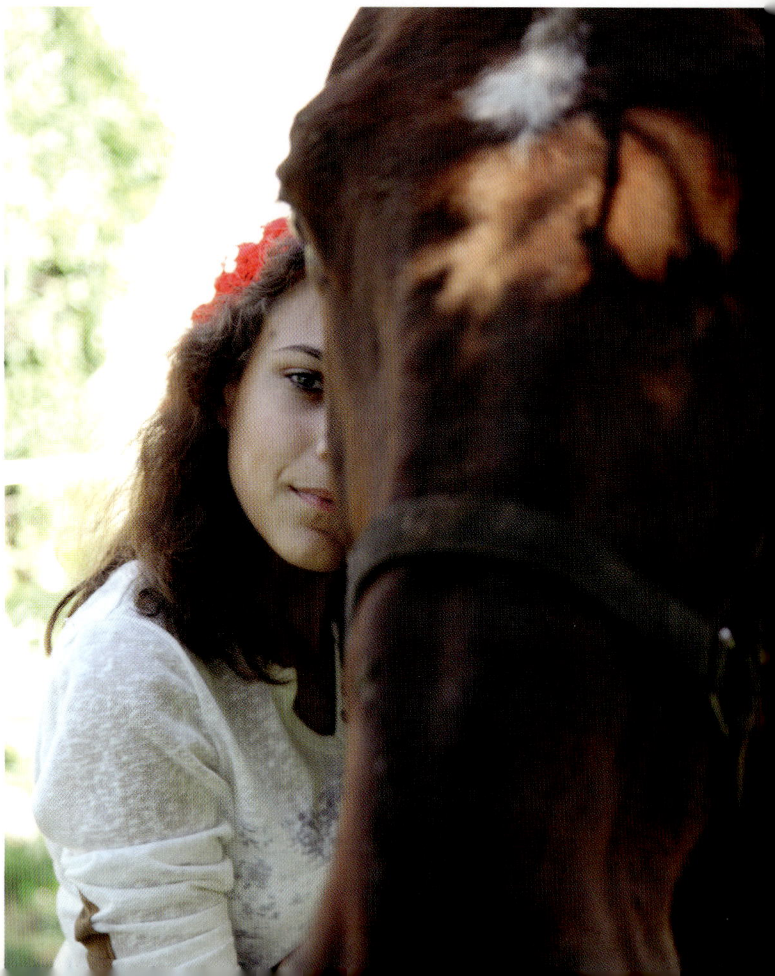

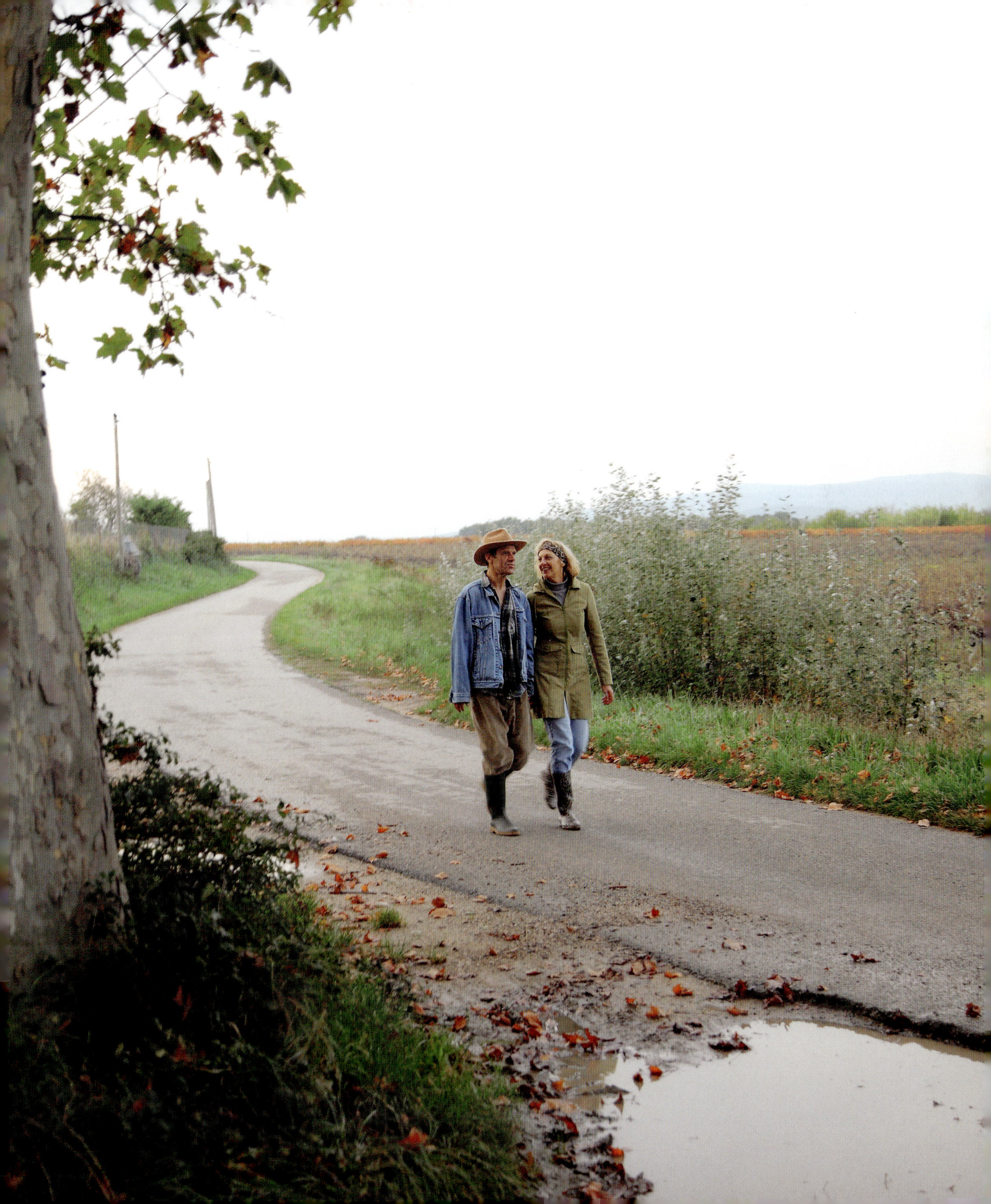

THÉS ET CAFÉS   CHOCOLATERIE

CHOCOLATE SEASON

"LOOK, THERE'S NO METAPHYSICS ON EARTH LIKE CHOCOLATES."

FERNANDO PESSOA, PORTUGUESE POET AND WRITER (1888-1935)

In the French countryside you cannot just pop into the supermarket on the way to someone's house to pick up a box of chocolates for your host. You can go and select handmade chocolate works of art individually from a pâtisserie or chocolaterie and have them packed before your very eyes, but large quantities of chocolate in boxes and other containers are only really available in the shops just before Christmas.

There are two major chocolate seasons in France: around Christmas at the start of winter, and at Eastertime in early spring, when the weather often feels more like winter. You could therefore say that chocolate was made for winter – or winter was made for chocolate. A steaming mug of hot chocolate (*chocolat chaud*) is one of the few things that can really warm you up from the inside when you are chilled to the bone.

It is not that chocolate becomes scarce at other times of the year though. You can buy a chocolate croissant (*pain au chocolat*) from your baker every morning to enjoy with your coffee. When I first moved here that is exactly what I did every morning, until I learned some self-control. However, at Christmas self-control is very, very difficult if you have a weakness for chocolate. Wherever you go, in friends' living rooms, in your child's headmaster's office, even at the bank manager's, there are bowls of chocolates you are continually invited to sample. Mostly in the form of *papillotes*, a word derived from *papillon* or butterfly, because the chocolates are wrapped in brightly coloured shiny paper. Once you have removed the outer wrapper, you will usually find another piece of paper around the chocolate with a silly riddle or joke printed on it – similar to the crackers we like to pull at Christmas in South Africa. (A tradition that is unknown in France and which I still miss every year.)

But Easter is when the art of the chocolatier reaches a pinnacle of perfection. Like the *papillotes* and other mass-produced chocolate found everywhere at Christmas, Eastertime also has its mass-produced Easter eggs, but it is the handmade chocolate eggs and other creations that capture my imagination every year. For our children, like most children, Easter eggs were always just something to consume in the largest possible quantities in the shortest possible time, so we usually bought them the cheaper, factory-made eggs.

In France, however, Easter eggs are not hidden in the garden by the mythical Easter Bunny, but rather by the even more fantastical *cloches de Pâques* or Easter bells. How on earth can a *bell* carry an Easter egg, I asked my French husband when I was still new to the country. Which Alain countered with: How do you think a *rabbit* manages it?

It took me a couple of years to get to the bottom of the bell story. I discovered that many years ago the Catholic church had banned the ringing of bells from White Thursday (the day before Good Friday) until Easter Sunday, giving rise to the popular belief in France that all church bells flew to Rome that Thursday to be blessed by the Pope. The Easter eggs would then be brought back all the way from Rome and given to good children, and when the bells rang out joyfully on the Sunday morning to proclaim the resurrection of Christ, it was a sign for children throughout the land that they could go outside and look for the eggs.

There is a small technical detail for sceptics like me who struggle to swallow the bell story. The bells are often represented with a pair of wings – presumably to help make the long flight to Rome and back possible. For our children it never really mattered who or what delivered the eggs, as long as there were enough of them. And deep in my heart I tend to agree. As long as there is enough chocolate throughout the cold months, from before Christmas until Easter, even the worst winter weather can be bravely endured. As long as there is enough chocolate!

CHOCOLATE PAVLOVA
8 SERVINGS

While a pavlova with cream and fresh red fruit is the perfect summer dessert, this chocolate version is ideal for cooler weather. And symbolically also perfect for Easter because it requires so many eggs. You use only the egg whites, keeping the yolks for another dish of course.

100 g dark chocolate (at least 50% cocoa butter, preferably more)
6 egg whites | 300 g sugar | 3 T cocoa powder | 1 t balsamic vinegar
500 ml chocolate ice cream

Finely chop half the chocolate. (This is easier in a food processor.)

Beat the egg whites in a glass or metal bowl (at a high speed if you are using an electric beater) until soft peaks form. Add the sugar gradually while continuing to beat the mixture until it becomes shiny and stiff peaks form.

Sprinkle over the cocoa powder and the vinegar. Carefully fold the finely chopped chocolate into the mixture, until everything is combined.

Spoon the mixture onto a flat baking sheet lined with baking paper. Shape it into a circle measuring about 23 cm and smooth the sides and top using the back of a spoon.

Bake for about 50-60 minutes in a preheated 150 °C oven, until the outside is crisp but still gives a little when you test it gently with your fingers. Switch off the oven and open the oven door a crack to allow the meringue to cool slowly before you take it out. (You don't want it to collapse like a soufflé!)

Just before serving, remove the ice cream from the freezer so that it can soften. Place the meringue base on a large, flat serving plate. Spoon the ice cream onto the meringue and carefully spread it over the top. Work carefully – remember, the base is supposed to be as fragile as a ballerina's tutu. Use a vegetable peeler to shave chocolate curls over the ice cream and on the serving plate around the meringue. Serve and wait for the compliments.

CRISP ON THE OUTSIDE, SOFT ON THE INSIDE

Pavlova was named after a Russian ballerina, of course, but unlike *crêpes suzette* and *poires belle Hélène* and *tarte Tatin* and so many other desserts that honour famous or unknown women, this one was not created in France. The pavlova comes from New Zealand, of all places. Or is that Australia? For decades these two nations have been arguing about rugby, sheep-shearing and the precise origin of pavlova. All that we ordinary cooks need to know is that the meringue base is supposed to remind you of a ballerina's tutu. In other words, it should be delicate and as light as a feather. The difference between a pavlova and an ordinary French meringue can be found in the middle. Both are crisp on the outside, but a pavlova has a meltingly soft heart under that brittle exterior.

Right: Chocolate pavlova

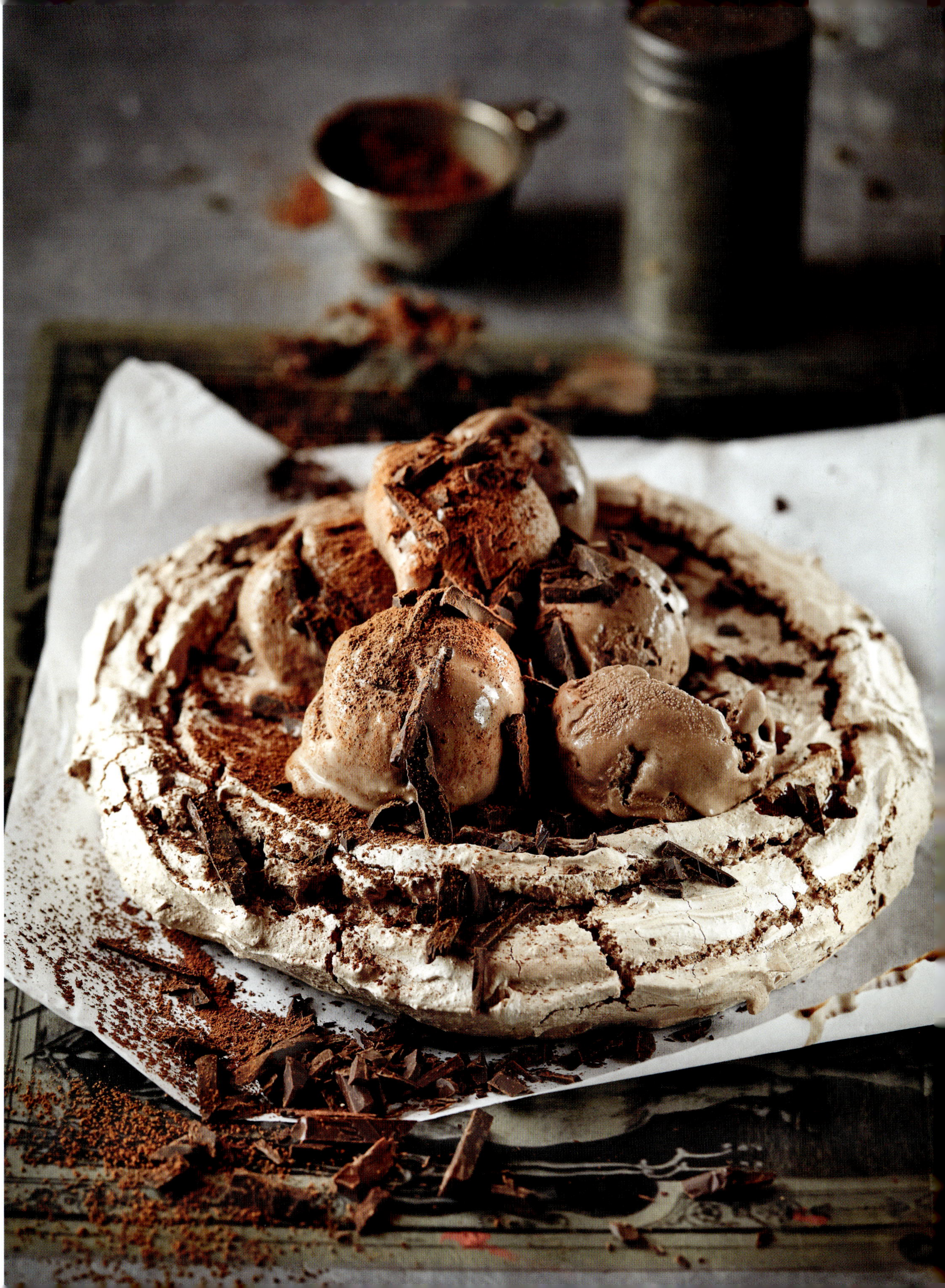

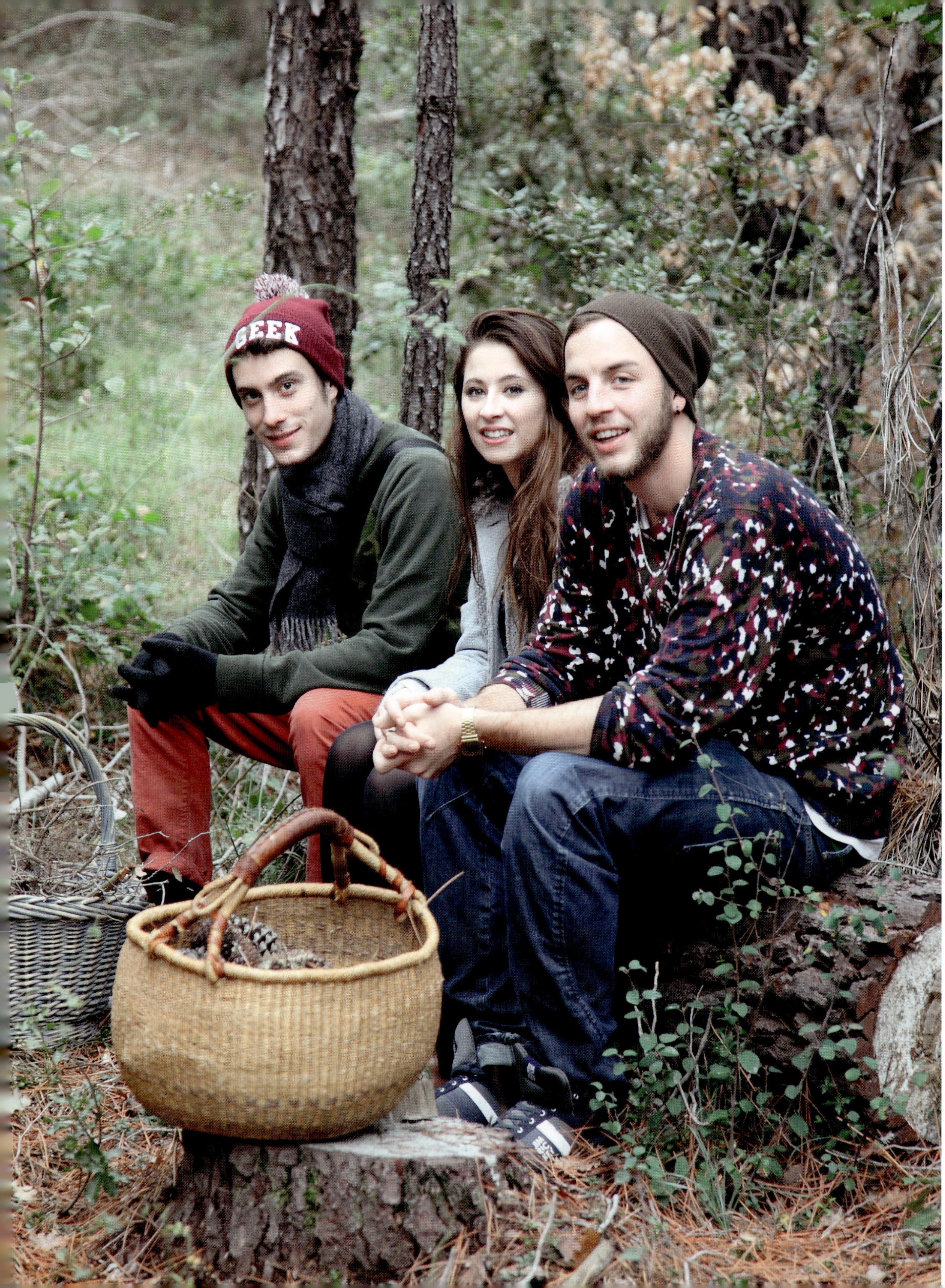
GEEK

INDISPENSABLE

"BY ECONOMY AND GOOD MANAGEMENT, BY A SPARING USE OF
READY MONEY, AND BY PAYING SCARCELY ANYBODY, PEOPLE CAN
MANAGE, FOR A TIME AT LEAST, TO MAKE A GREAT SHOW WITH VERY LITTLE MEANS."
WILLIAM MAKEPEACE THACKERAY (1811-1863)

TAPENADE (OLIVE PASTE)

You will need olives, garlic, anchovies and capers. Some recipes contain considerably more anchovy than others, some leave out the capers and others add basil leaves. The quantities are therefore not cast in stone, but this is what works for us. Feel free to use more or less of any ingredient until it tastes just right.

Pit about 500 g green or black olives (or buy them pitted if you cannot be bothered to do it yourself) and process along with 2 anchovy fillets, 2 T capers, 2 basil leaves (optional) and 1 clove garlic. You can do it the old-fashioned way with a pestle and mortar if you are feeling virtuous, but there is nothing preventing you using a food processor. Add a thin trickle of olive oil a little at a time until you have a soft, spreadable paste. Season with salt and pepper.

If you are not going to spread it on bread immediately, spoon the tapenade into a bowl, cover with a thin layer of oil and store in the fridge for a few days. Mix it with fresh pasta, or add a splash of vinegar to form the basis of salad dressing, or use as part of a deliciously moist stuffing for meat (see our recipe for stuffed lamb on page 168).

AÏOLI (GARLIC MAYONNAISE)

Of course, you could simply stir loads of crushed garlic into good-quality mayonnaise, but we strongly recommend that you go to a little more trouble. The traditional method is to crush 8 garlic cloves with a pinch of salt in a mortar, and then to beat the garlic with 2 egg yolks in a bowl. Add about 300 ml olive oil while you beat the mixture – drop by drop initially until the mixture is creamy, then in a thin stream. Season with freshly ground black pepper and a few drops of lemon juice if you prefer. It keeps well in a sealed jar in the fridge for a few days.

ANCHOÏADE (ANCHOVY SPREAD)

This is tasty as an appetizer on slices of baguette, or spread as a base on the dough when making a savoury tart, and can be kept for a few days in the fridge. Desalt about 100 g anchovy fillets and then chop them as finely as possible. Mix with 2-4 crushed garlic cloves and 1 T capers. Add 1 T vinegar and about 150 ml olive oil very slowly until you have a soft, luscious, spreadable pâté.

BÉCHAMEL SAUCE (WHITE SAUCE)

Anyone can throw together a quick white sauce with or without lumps – but here is the proper way to do it. Pour about 500 ml milk into a saucepan. Push 2 cloves into a peeled onion, cut a carrot into quarters, and add the onion and the carrot to the milk along with a bouquet garni. Bring to the boil and reduce the heat immediately. Simmer for about half an hour over very low heat.

In another saucepan, melt 50 g butter and stir in 50 g flour to form a smooth paste. This should take scarcely a minute; remember, if the sauce browns you will be left with a brown sauce and that is not what you are looking for. Remove the saucepan from the heat. Remove the vegetables and herbs from the milk and very gradually stir the milk into the sauce, until it is smooth and free of lumps. Return to the heat and bring to the boil, stirring continuously. Reduce the heat and simmer for 5 minutes so the sauce can thicken. Season with freshly ground salt and pepper and freshly grated nutmeg. *Voilà*, your very own *sauce béchamel*.

BRANDADE (COD PÂTÉ)

If ever you are fortunate enough to get hold of a piece of salted cod (*morue*), you can make your own creamy brandade to spread on bread or use as a filling for a savoury tart (see our recipe on page 80). Or why not

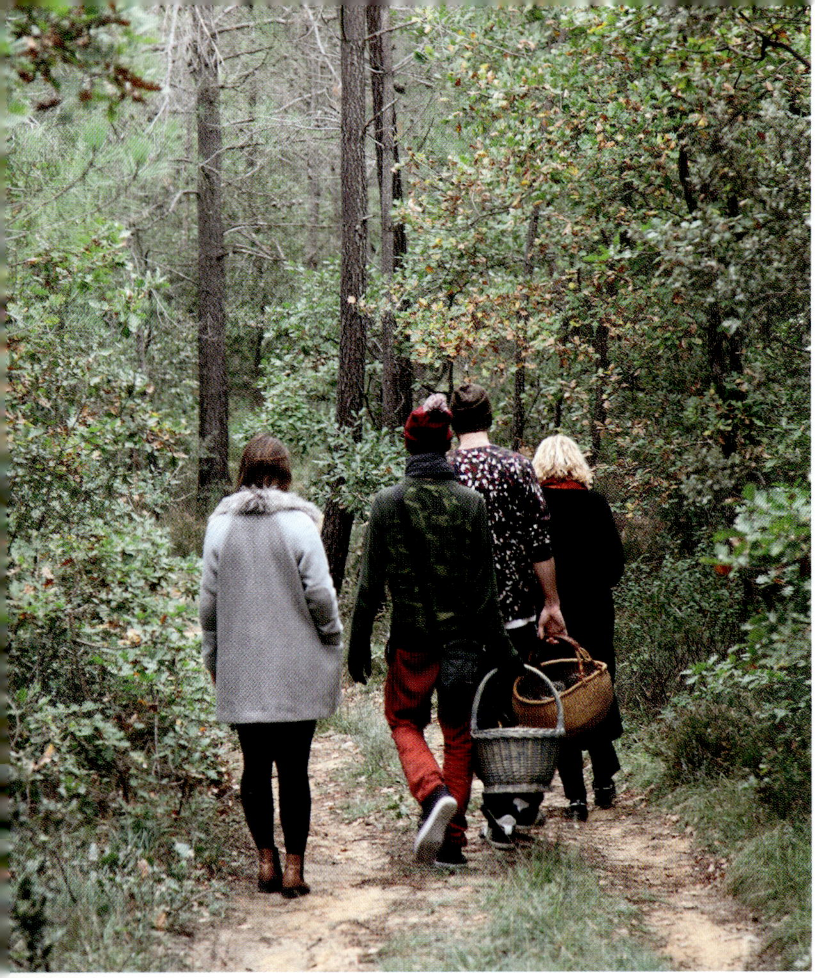
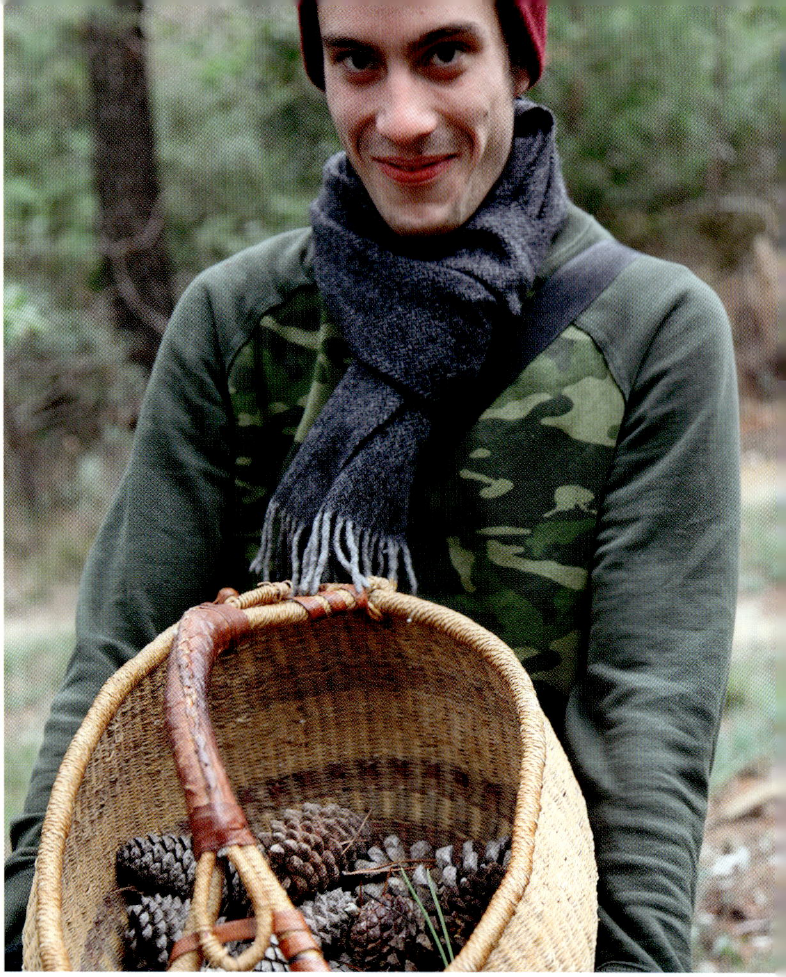
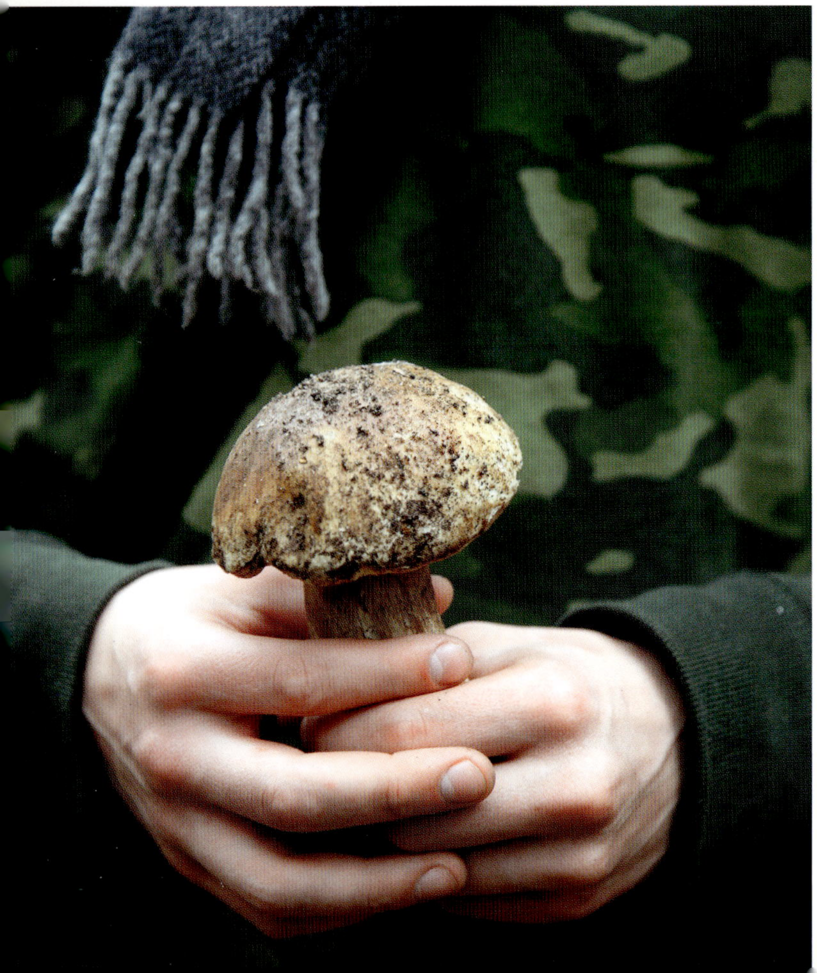
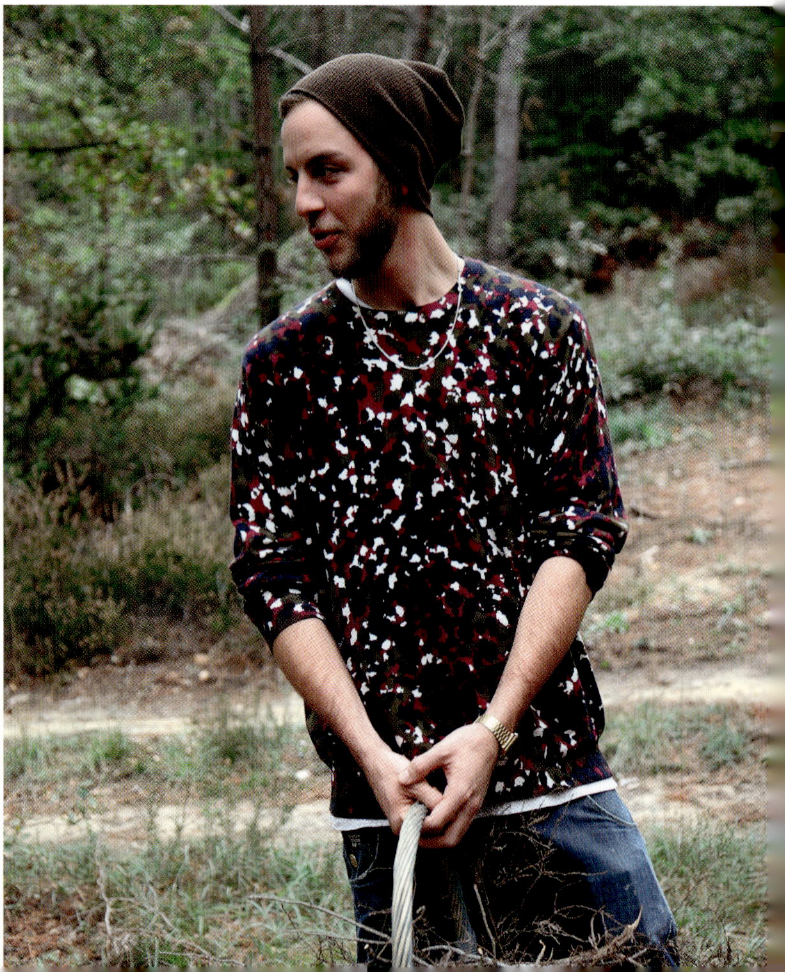

try it using dried and salted snoek? Soak 250 g of the salted fish for a day in water that you change regularly. (Don't be like me and ask why; just do it.) Drain the fish and cut it into pieces. Place in a saucepan with a stalk of thyme and a bay leaf, and cover with water. Bring to the boil and simmer for 5-8 minutes. Drain the fish well and mash with a fork. Set aside to cool.

In the meantime, crush 2 cloves of garlic and very slowly stir in a few drops of olive oil to form a creamy mixture. Heat in a small saucepan over very low heat and slowly stir in the fish, a little at a time, along with about 5 T crème fraîche or plain yoghurt. Keep stirring until it forms a smooth paste. Season with salt and pepper and a little lemon juice if you prefer.

ACKNOWLEDGEMENTS

I said it the last time and I have to say it again: For a writer like me, who usually sits all alone inventing stories out of thin air, a food book like this has been a wonderfully socially collaborative effort and a welcome change from the silence and solitude in which I normally work. With *Summer Food in Provence* we were not able to get the whole family involved in the photo shoots because two of our sons were working during the French summer holidays. This time we planned things so that all our children and their friends, partners and other attachments could be part of the project – making the entire experience that much more fun.

So thank you to our children, Thomas, Hugo, Daniel and Mia, and to Géraldine Lo and Julie Sauvage, Lou Spath and Cassandre Callebert, for all your patience and the early mornings and for smiling so nicely for the camera. I know it wasn't always easy for you, but you did make it look effortless.

Without Lien Botha and her camera, her enthusiasm and her eye for "the detail that kills," as the French say, this book probably would never have happened. One day she began sinking into the black marshy mud of the Carmargue and, imagining that her final moments had arrived, she shouted desperately: "Marita, come and save my *camera*!" Now that is sacrifice above and beyond the call of duty. Thank you too to Raymond Smith, our enthusiastic photographic assistant, who had to stand in the rain holding an umbrella to protect Lien and her camera when the rain became too much of a nuisance – and together with Alain had to "make" rain when the real thing failed to deliver on a day we needed it.

Thank you to Olivier Laboulais and his family from Domaine Rainvert near Rochegude, with whom Lien and Raymond could get their well-deserved rest after each hard day's work.

My thanks too to friends and acquaintances for their help during the photo shoots: the Franco-Afrikaans winemaker couple Naretha and Nicolas and the entire hospitable Ricome family from the Château de Valcombe near Nîmes; Laurent Lenaerts and Guy Boulanger-Kanter for allowing us to photograph their horses, dogs and beautiful home near La Garde-Adhémar; Loes Schillermans and Roline and Abraham van Zyl, who were commandeered at short notice to join us for dinner; the remarkable Hervé Jouve from the butchery and delicatessen Chez Georges, the chocolatiers Le Comptoir de Mathilde, the *brocante* shop Broc 'n Brock, and other businesses in Tulette; as well as the many smiling strangers who agreed to be photographed at markets and on the street.

In addition to the team in France, there was a highly professional Cape Town team involved in the project, and to each of them we owe a big thank-you. Our publisher, Ansie Kamffer, who was up to the challenge of embarking on another recipe book with us, with the same enthusiasm and commitment as before; designer Anton Sassenberg, editor Natasja Lochner, translator Vanessa Vineall, food photographer Myburgh du Plessis, food stylist Sonja Jordt, food assistant Gabi Veale, typographer Jean van der Meulen, production manager Ilse Volschenk, project manager Lindy Samery, media liaison Surita Jordaan, and the entire NB sales team.

But the most important member of this project is still my partner in life, Alain. For months on end he diligently tested recipes while I was chained to my computer writing food stories, and he did so without ever losing his calm demeanour and sense of humour. *Merci, mon amour.* Without you *Winter Food in Provence* would never have seen the light of day.

INDEX

A

aïoli (garlic mayonnaise) 9, 79, 80, 177
   winter 80
almond(s) 50, 99, 100, 116, 143, 144, 153, 154
   filling (frangipane) 115
   products of Provence 143
anchoïade (anchovy spread) 119, 177
anchovy 9, 74, 119, 158
   fillets 120, 177
   spread (anchoïade) 119, 177
   with olives 119
AOC label (Appellation d'Origine Contrôlée) 23
   walnuts from Grenoble 143
apples 43, 99
   tarte Tatin 115, 116
apricots, dried 70
asparagus 19, 164
Auvergne 85, 125

B

bacon 24, 34, 70, 86, 93, 126, 130, 134, 148, 158
Banon goat's milk cheese 59, 143
Beaufort 59
Beaumes-de-Venise 23
béchamel sauce (white sauce) 177
beef 24, 30, 85, 86, 94, 110, 126, 129, 130, 168
beetroot 34, 39, 40, 79
   roasted, with wild rice 40
   salad with broccoli and goat's milk cheese 40
   soup with orange and thyme 40
Bernhardt, Sarah 23
berry sauce 70
beurre manié (butter and flour mixture) 140, 148
Blanc, Raymond 167
boeuf à la Bourguignonne 24
Bordeaux 20, 23, 53
borscht 39, 40
boulangers 157
bourride 129
brandade (cod pâté) 79, 80, 177
brandy 24, 60, 130, 134
bread 24, 60, 73, 89, 104, 109, 110, 120, 143, 157, 158, 168, 177
Bresse chicken 73
Brie 60, 64
Brillat-Savarin cheese 89
broccoli 11, 40, 79, 80, 85, 164
bûche de Noël 99
   Mia's 100
Burgundy kidneys 148
butter and flour mixture (beurre manié) 140, 148
butternut 50
button mushrooms 19, 24, 30, 54

C

cabbage 80, 85, 86
   and mashed potatoes 86
   odour 85
   Savoy 85, 86
   stuffed 86
   varieties 85
cabillaud 79
Cairanne 23
calamari 30
calissons 143
Camargue 29, 30, 33, 63, 129, 130
   bullfighting (course camarguaise) 129
Camembert cheese 60
canard à l'orange 140
caneton 139
Cantal cheese 86
caramel sauce 116
carbonnade 129
cardoon 94
Catalan chickpeas 126
cauliflower 11, 39, 64, 80, 85
celeriac 93, 94
celery 90, 94
cellars 23
cèpes 19, 20
   à la Bordelaise 20
Challans 139
chanterelle 19
Charpentier, Henri 133
Châteauneuf-du-Pape, 23
Cheddar 86, 158
cheese
   croquettes, baked, with red jam 60
   varieties 59
   wheel, baked, with olives 60
"cheesecake" with nuts, quick 60
chestnuts 143
chicken 34, 40, 44, 50, 73, 86
   baked in a salt crust 34
   with quince and honey 44
   with sage in a salt crust 34
chickpeas 125, 126
   Catalan 126
Child, Julia 139
chilli 164
chocolate 23, 99, 100, 133, 144, 163, 167, 173
   pavlova 174
chorizo 30, 126, 158
chou farci au saumon 85, 86
citron confit 154
citrouilles 49
clafoutis 53
   with prunes 54
coarse salt 33, 34, 50, 80
cod 9, 79, 80, 93
   pâté (brandade) 79, 177
   salt 9, 80
Cointreau 134
Collioure 119
Comté 59
Conran, Superwoman Shirley 19
coq au vin 129
coquilles Saint-Jacques 89
còssa de Nadau 99
   our ice-cream 100
cottage cheese 164
course camarguaise 129
couscous 29, 44, 50, 70
cranberries 70
crêpes 133, 134
   galettes 133
crêpes suzette 133, 134
croquettes 60
croutons 120

D

dates 60
daube 24, 129
Daudet, Alphonse 23
Delair, Frédéric 139
Diat, Louis 109
Dickens, Charles 53
dough (make your own pastry) 154
Ducasse, Alain 147
duck 9, 103, 139, 140, 147
Dumas, Alexandre 109

E

eggs
   Benedict 163
   deluxe scrambled 64
   soufflé 163
   the secret of truffle 64
   vegetarian omelette stack 164

en papillote with herbs and garlic
    (game birds) 70
Escoffier, Auguste 79, 163
estouffade 129

F

fève 115
figs, dried 60, 99
flaugnarde 53
focaccia 158
foie gras 9, 11, 23, 103, 104, 139
    cooked 104
    history 103
    in a sauce 104
    raw 104
    raw, semi-cooked and cooked 104
food philosophy 9
fougasse 93, 158
    flop-proof 158
frangipane
    (almond filling) 115
French delicacies 11
French nut "cake" 144
French sauces (Big Five) 163
fricassée 129
frites 74
    fabulous 90
    moules 90
fruit, dried 70

G

galette des Rois 115, 116
galettes crêpes 133
game birds 69, 70
gardianne –
    Provençal cowboy
    food 129, 130
garlic
    mayonnaise (aïoli) 9, 79, 80, 177
    soup 103, 109, 110
gigot d'agneau 167
girolles 19
grape harvest 9, 23
gratin
    dauphinois 74
    de carde 94
    de chou 86
Grenoble's "supernuts" 143
grey salt 11, 29, 33
gros sel 33
Gruyère 158

H

hachis Parmentier 73
hake 79, 80
hazelnuts 40, 99, 144
hedgehog mushroom 19
honey 39, 43, 44, 60, 64, 143
    truffle 64
house hunting 13

I

ice-cream còssa de Nadau, our 100

J

jambon cru 140

K

kidneys - classic Burgundy recipe 148
King's Cake 9
klipvis 79

L

lamb, Provençal stuffed shoulder of 168
Larousse Gastronomique 133
léche, lick-your-plate-clean 130
legumes 125
Leipoldt, Louis 129
lemon(s)
    Moroccan preserved 154
    syrup 154
    tart, classic French 154
lentille verte du Puy 125
lentil(s) 125, 126
    green puy 126
    salad, warm 126
lettuce soup 110
l'hamd marakad 154
liver 103. See fois gras
loaf, Alain's cheese 158
lou fassum 85
Louis XIV 23

M

marinade 24, 130
marrons glacés 143
marrows 164, 168
mayonnaise
    garlic 80, 177
Mediterranean salad with spinach,
    bread and anchovies 120
Meerlust 19, 147
Mistral, Frédéric 93
Mont d'Or 59
morille 19
Moroccan cuisine 44
Moroccan preserved lemons 154
morue 9, 79, 80, 93, 177
moules
    frites 89, 90
    velouté de 90
mushroom(s) 11, 20, 24, 30, 54, 80,
    99, 100, 129, 148, 164
    Superwoman's stuffed 20
    varieties 19
    wild 19
mussel(s) 30, 89, 90
    braderie 89
    soup 90
Myburgh, Hannes 147

N

nougat 99, 100, 143, 144
nougatine 144
nut loaf 144
Nyons 13

O

offal 147, 148.
    See also kidneys; tripes
olive(s)
    baked cheese wheel with 60
    paste (tapenade) 177
    pickle your own 14
    turning a jar into something special 14
    with anchovies 119
omelette stack, vegetarian 164
orange sauce 134, 140
Ossau-Iraty 59
oyster mushrooms 19
oysters 9, 89

P

paella 29, 30
papillote, en 70
Parmentier, Antoine-Augustin 73
Parmesan 30, 164
partridge 70
pastry 154
pâté
    brandade 177
    cod 177
    liver 103, 104
pâtés, French 104
PDO (Produce of Designated Origin)
    119
peppers 30, 163, 164
petit salé 125
pheasant 69, 70
Picasso 119
pie compared
    to a tart 115
pied-de-mouton 19
pilchards 119
piperade 164
pissaladière 119
plenze 133, 134
    the pleasure of 134
pleurote 19
pommes
    Parmentier 73
pompe à l'huile 99
porc au pruneaux de Tours 54
porcini 19, 30
pork 11, 54, 85, 104
    fillet (filet mignon) 54
portobello
    mushrooms 19, 20
potage
    Parmentier 73

potato(es) 34, 39, 53, 59, 73, 79, 80, 86, 89, 90, 110
  floury 74
  "in dressing gowns" with coarse salt 34
  pancakes 134
  salad 34
  salad, Provençal 74
  selecting 74
  varieties 73
  waxy 74
potirons 49
poutine 119
Provençal 11, 33, 49, 50, 79, 85, 100, 115, 129, 153, 158, 163, 167
  almond products 143
  Christmas 99
  Christmas meal 9, 43, 93, 94
  daube 24
  flavours 24
  gardianne – cowboy food 130
  grand aïoli 9
  landscape 9, 13
  markets 119
  paella, easy 30
  potato salad 74
  quince paste 44
  stuffed shoulder of lamb 168
pruneaux d'Agen 53
prunes 53, 54
  clafoutis with 54
pumpkin 39, 49, 50, 64, 80
  pie, sweet 50
  roast 50
  varieties 49
puttanesca sauce 120

Q
quails 69, 70
  with dried fruit, Lynn's 70
quince 43, 44
  cheese (pâte de coings) 44
  jelly 54
  paste 43, 44

R
rabasse 63
Raclette 59
ragoût 129
raisins 50, 60, 70, 99, 100
Rasteau 23
ratte 73
redcurrant jelly 54
red-rice risotto with mushrooms 30
rémoulade 93, 94
  creamy 94
rice
  festival 29
  red-rice risotto with mushrooms 30
  varieties 29
  wild 29, 30, 40

rillettes, creamy 104
risotto, red-rice, with mixed mushrooms 30
riz rouge 29, 30
roast pumpkin couscous 50
Robbins, Tom 39
Roquefort 59, 167
rosé 23, 139

S
salad
  beetroot with broccoli and goat's milk cheese 40
  dressing (truffle oil) 64
  Mediterranean, with spinach, bread and anchovies 120
  Provençal potato 74
  warm lentil 126
salad dressing 177
salmis 129
salmon 85, 86
salt
  crusts 34
  fleur de sel de Camargue 33
  flowers 33
  mixture 34
Santiago de Compostela 89
sardinade 119
sardines 119
  baby 119
sauce 20, 24, 39, 54, 59, 60, 70, 90, 94
  béchamel 177
  berry 70
  caramel 116
  creamy cheese 86
  French (Big Five) 163
  orange 134
  puttanesca 120
  white 94, 177
  wine 90
saumure (brine) 14
scrambled eggs, deluxe 64
sheep's milk cheese 59
shellfish 11, 89
shiitake 19, 30
snoek, dried 79
snoek pâté 80
soufflé 163
soup
  beetroot with orange and thyme 40
  garlic 110
  lettuce 110
  mussel 90
spéciale Gillardeau 89
spinach 94, 120
steak 20, 24, 59, 104, 130
stew 49, 125, 129, 167
  fish 129
St Môret cream cheese 164
stuffed cabbage 85

sultanas 50, 60, 70
Swiss chard 93, 94
Swiss fondue 59

T
tapenade (olive paste) 177
tart
  Alain's tarte à la brandade 80
  classic French lemon 154
  compared to a pie 115
  tarte Tatin 115, 116
Thirteen Desserts 9, 43, 93, 99
Toussaint 49
Treize Desserts 9, 43, 93, 99
tripes 147, 148
  à la mode de Caen 148
truffle(s) 9, 11, 19, 63, 64, 93
  black 19, 63, 103
  eggs, the secret of 64
  fresh 64
  honey 64
  oil, make your own 64
  peels 64
  Périgord 63
  varieties 63
trumpet of death (mushroom) 19

V
Vacqueyras 23
vegetables
  baked in a salt crust 34
  winter 59, 80, 94
vegetarian
  meal 50, 164
  omelette stack 164
velouté de moules 90
vendange (grape harvest) 9, 23
vinaigrette 40, 74

W
walnuts 20, 40, 99, 100, 143, 144
wines, Provence's Côtes du Rhône 23